CONTEMPORARY

NATIVE AMERICAN

ARCHITECTURE

CONTEMPORARY NATIVE

CAROL HERSELLE KRINSKY

AMERICAN ARCHITECTURE

Cultural Regeneration and Creativity

New York   Oxford
Oxford University Press
1996

Oxford University Press

Oxford   New York
Athens   Auckland   Bangkok   Bogotá   Bombay
Buenos Aires   Calcutta   Cape Town   Dar es Salaam   Delhi
Florence   Hong Kong   Istanbul   Karachi
Kuala Lumpur   Madras   Madrid   Melbourne
Mexico City   Nairobi   Paris   Singapore
Taipei   Tokyo   Toronto

and associated companies in
Berlin   Ibadan

Copyright © 1996 by Oxford University Press, Inc.

Published by Oxford University Press, Inc.,
198 Madison Avenue, New York, New York 10016

Oxford is a registered trademark of Oxford University Press

Book design by Nicola Ferguson

Library of Congress Cataloging-in-Publication Data
Krinsky, Carol Herselle.
Contemporary Native American architecture: cultural regeneration
and creativity / Carol Herselle Krinsky.
p. cm.   Includes bibliographical references and index.
ISBN 0-19-509739-4 (cloth). - ISBN 0-19-509740-8 (paper)
1. Indian architecture—North America.   2. Vernacular, architecture—North America.
3. Architecture, Domestic—North America.   I. Title. E98.A63K75   1996
720' .89' 97—dc20   95-34918

135798642

Printed in the United States of America
on acid-free paper

PREFACE AND ACKNOWLEDGMENTS

In preparing a book about a new phenomenon—the culturally sensitive but modern Native American building—I have had to seek help from many people, as there is little written on the subject. Useful writings address matters that bear on my topic, such as history and law, the political activity of Native Americans, cultural development, and recourse to the past to cure ills of the present. But much of the information in this book has come from approximately 13,000 miles of automobile travel to many of the sites, and from interviews in person or by telephone with people closely connected to the work. Unattributed quotes come from those named in the same text passages; it seemed superfluous to add footnotes attesting to the obvious.

The projects are all within the contiguous forty-eight states because they have a coherent history and are affected by the same federal laws. The histories of Hawaii and Alaska are distinctive, as is that of Canada, where different laws apply; had buildings in these regions been included, the book would have been far longer, unnecessarily complicated, and prohibitively expensive for me, but the points made would not have been significantly different.

"Native American" and "Indian" refer to a person descended from those who inhabited the Americas before Columbus arrived. The first is a modern expression, devised to correct Columbus's misidentification of the people he found. It is often regarded as courteous, although some scorn it as "politically correct." The second is the customary word, a misnomer, but one used so widely by the people themselves and one so common in learned and legal texts that it is artificial to discard it. The word "Indian" leads to confusion with Asians; "Native American," to confusion with all people born in the Western Hemisphere. Neither is perfect, but both terms are used respectfully in this book.

I use the terms "Native American," "Indian," "Amerindian", "indigenous person," and "Native American Indian" interchangeably, in part for verbal variety in writing. There is no universally preferred term, although most of my contacts have referred to themselves by their tribal/national names or, in the aggregate, as Indians. In this book, "Euro-American" describes those of that ancestry alone, and "Anglo," a slang term common in the Southwest, describes an aggregate of people of any descent other than Native American.

No term implies uniformity among the people named, as indigenous cultures were as varied as those of other continents and have become even more so with intermarriage and with cultural and technological transfers. Nevertheless, there are both legal and customary definitions of Native Americans. Many thousands of people have exclusively indigenous ancestors. Law aside, identity is partly self-given, partly given by the group. Each tribe establishes its own membership criteria, enabling some people of minimally indigenous ancestry to enroll while occasionally excluding others of wholly indigenous ancestry. If the federal government rationalized the rules, it would violate tenets of the self-determination that has been official Indian policy for the past two decades.

It is common in social-scientific works to add a person's Native American nation after his or her name. As this book deals primarily with architecture, I have used an asterisk in the text and notes to indicate Native American ancestry and have given the affiliation—when I knew it—in the index. For people who may call themselves Chippewa, Anishinabe, or Ojibwa, I have used Ojibwe unless the tribe or band's official name includes one of the other words; this choice was made after an unscientific survey of usage in tribal and regional publications and after hearing culturally sensitive individuals describe themselves. The word "Sioux" is used only when referring collectively to the Lakota and Dakota, or when someone said he was a Sioux. As of the time of writing, Navajo was still the official name of that nation, although a proposal to use Dine'e awaits a vote. Where people have voted to change a name, I use the new name (for example, Tohono O'odham instead of Papago).

"Native nation" and "tribe" are used here interchangeably. "Tribe" may reflect historical reality, but in some cases is a government construct because some peoples were organized in independent bands and did not see themselves as parts of larger polities. Seventeenth-century writers used "nation," "kingdom," or "confederation"—terms familiar in Europe but not necessarily among indigenous North Americans. When treaties were signed, British-American legal thinking admitted treaty-signing only between nations, so aggregates of Indians were accorded this status. For administrative purposes, the United States at other times created "tribes" when there had been none. These political entities have held the status of "domestic dependent nations" since the nineteenth century, and in recent years they have been able to practice increased self-determination. Accordingly, when their officials have asked to see the relevant parts of my text in exchange for information, I have acceded to their demands, but no one has wished to or been able to censor the text.

Other expressions are also controversial. The common term "pan-Indian" may yield to "supratribal," for which serious arguments have recently been made. "Medicine man" or "medicine woman," a title often used by the individuals concerned, is well understood by social scientists, but "spiritual healer" expresses the point of their work more clearly to others for whom "medicine man" may evoke the crude caricatures seen in comic books.

Multiple opinions about words match the varied opinions about the works of architecture described in this book. Some of the buildings and most of the projects are not fully formed, because the sponsors and architects are unfamiliar with the problem of contemporary Native American design or because unprecedented building programs can rarely guide an architect perfectly. Trial and error are needed to achieve perfection, but if only one cultural center is to be built for a tribe, the client and architect will never have the luxury of trying a second time to achieve a better result.

There is often uncertainty about the values or degree of Indianness to be expressed. When architects cannot translate aboriginal structures into modern form, they must find alternative ways to show tribal sponsorship. One group may want to develop contemporary buildings from precontact types in order to bypass the culture of oppressors; another group will want buildings that show Native ability to adopt Western technology and to adapt to new situations. In a city or on a reservation with multitribal residents, whose traditions will dominate in a referential building? What can be done for tribes that have lost most of their ancestral traditions? How is consensus secured, and will people who live off-reservation be consulted? Who integrates acceptable suggestions—tribal representatives? architects? The answers vary from one group to another, but however generally satisfactory the solutions may be, they may seem inauthentic to some individuals. The idea of authenticity itself is debated.

* * *

In trying to work through these problems, I have had the help of everyone named in the text and notes. Among those not named there are, for Arizona and New Mexico, Mary Camejo (Jemez), Solomon Katz, Mario Nick Klimiades, Larry Linford, Susan McGreevy, Steve Rogers, Ranger Steve Sandrell, Beverly Singer*, Karen Swisher*, Nancy Bellin Waldman, Henry Walt, and Richard Winchell. In California, I owe particular thanks to Nelson H. H. Graburn, Robert Easton, and Zena Pearlstone, as well as to Betty Thomas*, Virginia Jansen, Daves Rossell, Lynn Fox, and Richard Steward*. For help in Connecticut, I am grateful to Jack Campisi. Helpful for the Dakotas were Sherry Salway Black* and the late Lyle LaFramboise*. Terry Heide*, Kathy Tate, and Andrew Gokee* led me to information in the upper Midwest. In New York State, Elizabeth and John Fadden (Mohawk), Perry Ground (Oneida), and Michael Rubin deserve mention, and George H. J. Abrams* merits special thanks for reviewing the text wisely. Karen Blu, a colleague at New York University, provided insight about North Carolina. In Washington, D.C., I have benefited especially from help given by W. Richard West (Cheyenne-Arapaho), Cynthia Field, Dominic Nessi, Amy Ballard, and Alison K. Hoagland. Other generous people around the country were Carol Betts, Jane Booher, William R. Butler, Kathryn Gettles, Arlene Hirschfelder, Jerome and Isabelle Hyman, Alice Krinsky (our daughter), Cheri Soliday*, Mary Lee Baranger, Fred Myers, Irving Sandler, Sheila ffolliott, and Shepard Krech; and in Geneva, Switzerland, Fabrizio Frigerio and Stella Frigerio-Zeniou.

I owe special thanks to those who spent at least one day with me or in scouting sites on my behalf, even if their names are mentioned below: my parents-in-law, Josephine B. and Milton Krinsky, Barbara and Sherman Sass, David and Marilyn Chelimer, Leon Satkowski, Katherine Solomonson, Mary Ellen Sigmond, Minnesota State Representative Phyllis L. Kahn, Ellen Amsterdam Walker, Tom Martinson, Robert Levin, and several people who had previously been strangers—Richard Thern, David Smotrich, Thomas H. Hodne, Jr., John Cuningham, Robert Zakaras, Dennis Sun Rhodes*, Surrounded-by-Enemy* (Denby Deegan), Jim Hahn, Joe Cushman, and Nancy Fuller. For expert and exceptionally careful photographic printing, I must praise Ilse Friesem York. Leslie Yudell and Irene Pavitt at Oxford University Press gave the text meticulous attention.

Research for this book, investigation of new projects, and writing ended in October 1994. I had the chance to add a few words until May 1995. This will explain the omission of some conspicuous projects that may be constructed before publication date. Because the identification of relevant projects depended to some degree on luck as well as on research, and because much of the information comes from people's inevitably fallible memories, some building dates and architects' names could not be given here. Pictures and plans were those that could be obtained; most of the projects have not been professionally photographed. All photographs without other credits were taken by the author between November 1990 and August 1993.

Indispensable financial assistance and moral support came from the Arnold W. Brunner Award of the New York City chapter of the American Institute of Architects, and from a Design Arts Award given by the National Endowment for the Arts. I am grateful for this help and for the confidence expressed in the project by those who recommended it.

My deepest gratitude for extraordinary support and wise counsel belongs to my husband, Robert D. Krinsky, to whom I dedicate this book. While it is a commonplace to thank one's spouse, it is no cliché to say that this book could not have been written without him. It was he who did the driving along those 13,000 miles.

New York C. H. K.
September 1995

CONTENTS

Part III   Specific Building Types

CONTEMPORARY NATIVE AMERICAN ARCHITECTURE

Introduction

This book is about a new kind of architecture, reflecting culture in formation. Of course, cultures are always being formed or modified, but there are moments when people feel driven to accelerate the usual pace of change. When this happens, we open new chapters in our history books. We write about the art of Augustan Rome as different from that of Republican Rome, although the former clearly descended from the latter. A new personality taking charge after a time of uncertainty, new governmental forms, added conquests, new buildings—all were instrumental in defining the early Roman Empire. We open another chapter for early Christianity because, almost overnight, Christians had to invent a public architecture under the auspices of the Emperor Constantine; and we begin another for early Islamic buildings because of that momentous religious change. Historians today wish that more people had recorded the changes as they were occurring, and this book attempts to provide a record of contemporary Native American architecture.

Since the mid-1960s, Native Americans have taken part in a widespread movement of cultural regeneration, a term that embraces continuity, reinforcement, and invention. This rebirth or revival or creative movement is evi-dent in many parts of the country where indigenous people live. As a significant part of it, tribal governments and supratribal urban groups have commissioned dozens of culturally appropriate buildings, creating something new—a modern Amerindian architecture. The buildings are schools, tribal offices, tribally sponsored colleges, casinos, houses, clinics, cultural centers and museums, religious and community facilities. They may be made of traditional adobe or wood, or of reinforced concrete, steel, and glass, depending on function, climate, cost, building codes, available expertise, and personal taste; after all, the sponsors live in the twentieth century and build for our own time, not in response to atavistic fantasies. Some buildings serve traditional purposes, while others are as bound up with contemporary life as the computers and dialysis machines that they contain.

I first noticed this new American architectural phe-nomenon in June 1975, while looking at recent buildings in Minneapolis. A noteworthy one was the Minneapolis American Indian Center (115, 116), finished in 1975 to the design of Hodne–Stageberg Partners assisted by Dennis Sun Rhodes*, an Arapaho with a degree in architecture from Montana State University. The building fit well into the modern Midwest, but aspects of it had been sensitively conceived to reveal its connection to the Native American population. I wondered how much more there was of this kind of design, and spent much of my time from 1990 to 1994 in finding out.

There is little written about these buildings. Most of them are small, located on reservations that are often far from paths normally trodden by those interested in architecture. Few are published in the architectural press. Some of the architects lack the money for the handsome photography demanded by prestigious magazines; others lack the time to devote to self-promotion; still others have no interest in publicity. In one case, the architects believe that their building was neglected by architecture journals because writers found it imaginative but bizarre and did not want to insult the minority-group clients by offering adverse criticism. Many of the buildings are too modest in size or budget or too closely tied to the culture of a tiny tribe to warrant nationwide attention, however ingenious their cultural solutions may be.

It was necessary, then, to find the buildings by reading Indian newspapers, by writing and telephoning to tribal offices, and by traveling in the contiguous forty-eight states. It soon became clear that the American Indian urban center in Minneapolis was one manifestation of a major change in Amerindian cultural orientation, evidence of the movement toward self-determination found throughout Native American society in recent years. That is why there are chapters here about the pertinent aspects of past and present; they are essential if the architecture is to be understood properly as more than a group of unusual designs.

What perspective did I bring to this investigation? (One reads increasing numbers of demands for writers on minority-group topics to make their positions known at the start.) The answer, at first, was "None at all," as I had not previously studied Native American culture and history. The termination and relocation policies were, for instance, entirely unknown to me, although I was well able to read when they were implemented. I knew the white men's Indians—Tonto, who was clever at finding villains on whom to spy, and Longfellow's Hiawatha, not the real one. We were taught that Native Americans were able to track animals and people when no one else could and were ingenious at making waterproof canoes from bark. I saw conditions of stunning deprivation among the Navajo during a family tour of the West in 1948, but was introduced to their weaving skills and to Pueblo pottery during the same summer. Informal discussion suggests that this minimal "knowledge" is typical of people my age raised in eastern urban households.

There is, however, more than just a first answer to the question. I am a member of a minority group, although a religious one, and object to a unitary treatment of my group just as Native Americans do, given the diversity of their origins and cultures. "There simply is no *the* Indian viewpoint in the writing of history," said Alfonso Ortiz*, a Tewa,[1] nor is there a single standard for Amerindian architecture. I understand Native Americans' resentment at being defined only by outsiders, especially as the definition has so often been injurious. For that reason, my text reports on what I have learned and leaves final judgments about suitability and authenticity to the people who commission and use the buildings.

It is difficult to assess the reception of each building. I had neither the time nor the opportunity to do a scientific sample of opinion. It is possible that a building promoted by one political group will be resented by opponents, irrespective of functional or architectural merits. Some respondents may band together against outsiders to conceal negative opinion on the reservation. There are also people largely indifferent to aesthetic matters, while others are uncomfortable with either revivals or innovations. Nevertheless, I include such evaluations as were offered by users and sponsors, and have taken heart from Henry Louis Gates, Jr., who wrote that while our social identities matter, "No human culture is inaccessible to someone who makes the effort to understand, to learn, to inhabit another world."[2]

Personal understanding of minority status, however different the specifics may be, is not all there is to the answer. In 1985, I published a book called *Synagogues of Europe: Architecture, History, Meaning.*[3] What I learned from investigating that topic has informed this one. Because of the Jewish population increase in the nineteenth century, when this minority group was accorded more legal rights and a better place within the majority society, many synagogues were erected. The most interesting design issues concerned the ways in which the buildings expressed the special position of Jews in an age when architecture was meant to reveal the national and historic character of building sponsors. Were the Jews really French, entitled to use the "best" Gothic style of medieval France? Were they to share the architecture of Christian Germans or Swedes? Would they be allowed to make their own choices, and if they did so, how safe was it to look different from the majority?

Those familiar with recent American Indian history will already have noticed some parallels. Since the end of a policy to terminate the status of tribes—that is, since the mid-1960s—Native Americans have become more numerous and more conspicuous in the United States. Laws and court decisions have, with some exceptions, generally helped to improve the position of Native Americans in terms of rights, resources, and opportunities. This has also occurred in an age of nationalism and historicism, although now we speak of postmodernism and "roots." The nation proclaims—but doesn't always practice—adherence to social unity and integration. Will Indians who preserve their traditions be accepted as "regular" Americans? Will they want this acceptance? Will they have full liberty to express or even emphasize their differences, while suffering no social consequences?

It surely made no difference to anti-Semites in Europe that some synagogues were designed in styles that sought to integrate their congregations with the majority population. It was noticeable, however, that some were designed in foreign, supposedly unpatriotic styles, principally the "Moorish" mode, which connected Jews with the exotic Islamic Middle East rather than with Europe. Will there be negative consequences for Indians who gather in buildings of highly unusual design? Will they be seen as eccentric, as still primitive, as ridiculous, or as extravagant? Will it be politically safer to design integrative buildings, whether or not the sponsors want to integrate? Or are group identity and pride in one's heritage too valuable to conceal, and impossible to conceal even if one wishes to do so?

The book about synagogues was written naively in that I thought of it simply as a package of information. I had no idea that architects and congregational leaders would want to mine it for ideas about designing postmodern—that is, historicist and specifically ethnic—synagogues in the United States. This time, I am writing to let tribal members and their architects know what solutions have been devised already, so as to save time and facilitate contact.

This, then, represents the perspective from which the present study was undertaken, and accounts for the impact made on me by the American Indian urban center in Minneapolis: It was conceptually familiar. There are many differences between European synagogues and recent buildings by and for Native Americans. But an approach based on parts of my own history has supplied the emotional intensity that supported hours of poring over previously unfamiliar journals in anthropology, ethnography, sociology, demography, and law.

It hasn't been drudgery, either. Dealing with largely unpublished work offers the delights of discovery. I saw parts of the country previously unknown to me, where help was given by dozens of creative, intelligent, and generous people of all racial and ethnic backgrounds. And I saw architectural culture being created. Because of that, perhaps I know a bit about the reactions of emperors Augustus and Constantine, and of the early Muslim authorities, all of whom understood the importance of connecting architecture to politics and culture. In return, I hope that the information offered here will be of use and interest to scholars and students of contemporary Native American life, to tribal officials contemplating new construction, and to architects charged with executing the commissions appropriately.

PART I

The Background

1

Essential History

This land is your land.
It once was my land. . . .
And you pushed our nations
To the reservations.
This land was stole by you from me.
**Pete Seeger, after Woody
Guthrie, "This Land Is Your Land"**

Rancherias are small Indian reservations in California, usually occupying a few acres of remote countryside. We drove to one of them, the Sulphur Bank El-em Pomo Rancheria near Clearlake Oaks, where on one side of the road stands the tribal office building (1), a small structure with a band of ornament under its distinctively curved roof. On the other side is a wooden polygon one story high (2). Finding no one in the office but hoping to get permission to photograph the buildings, I was glad to be accosted by Betty Thomas*, who wanted to know what an intruder was doing on Pomo premises with two cameras over her shoulder. Was I not aware that it is discourteous to enter someone's property and to take away pictures of it? Did I not know that this wasn't public land but sovereign territory, and that I had no right to be there?

Betty Thomas was patient enough to listen to an explanation. I had tried to get permission to photograph, but had been told that the rancheria chairman, whose name was listed in my directory, had recently left office and canceled his telephone service. She found my excuse truthful, asked more questions, and for thirty minutes summarized several aspects of contemporary Amerindian life and culture described in this book.

She asserted tribal sovereignty first. This has to with

the fact that about one-third of the approximately 1.9 million Americans identifying themselves as Indians in the 1990 census live on land that has a special status because the tribes are "domestic dependent nations." This status is derived from treaties signed by the United States government and various tribes to establish ownership of land under American law, and from Supreme Court decisions since 1828. Land owned by tribal governments or held in trust for Native Americans by the federal government is not subject to all the laws of the surrounding state. Many tribes insist on their limited sovereignty and maintain a goal of self-determination.

Betty Thomas was concerned about my photographs. On many reservations, most residents are poor, inhabiting deteriorating homes. Intruders who cannot help to remedy the problems are understandably unwelcome when taking pictures to satisfy their own sensationalist or sentimental urges. Most new houses not built by the occupants are manufactured, often trailers, as several were at this rancheria. Others are supplied by the United States Department of Housing and Urban Development (HUD) or are improved by the Bureau of Indian Affairs (BIA) in the Department of the Interior. There is very little market-rate housing on Indian land.

Health care, road paving, water supply, and utilities

1. Tribal office, Sulphur Bank El-em Pomo Rancheria, Lake County, California. A. C. Morse (contractor), 1983.

are made possible by HUD, the BIA, and the Indian Health Service (IHS); the potential for uncoordinated activity leaps to mind. At various times, other departments of the federal government have made their presence known—in this case, by providing funds for the tribal office, roofed and ornamented to suggest Pomo artistic and architectural forms.

The idea of a modern Indian architecture has developed only in the past quarter century, in tandem with a widespread movement to renew and enhance other aspects of Native American culture, as a later chapter will explain. The polygonal building known as a roundhouse or dancehouse is a ceremonial structure built by local residents for Pomo religious rituals that strengthen the community. In these buildings, those invited to take part can reach back to ancestral ways different from the traditions of Christianity professed by some or all of the participants.

One of my informant's children who lives on the rancheria has been active in rebuilding the roundhouse since its predecessor burned down in the 1980s. Wooden boards form the sides, and shingles crown the roof. Language preservation and renewal are related to ceremonial continuity; Betty Thomas's husband, Delbert, Sr.*, who knows the Pomo language, conducts classes in it that are attended by eager students. Some of the young men in the study group work in Oakland, a drive of about two hours away, but they return for weekly lessons.

In short, in a very small space several buildings and forces convened that are typical of activities on reservations and rancherias today—a modern building intended to "look Indian" on a small budget; a traditional one erected as late as 1990 embodying the recent renewal of culture and language; and evidence of problems with Indian housing and environmental services.

There are additional types of buildings elsewhere meant to express aspects of the Native American experience, but the aspirations and problems can be seen even on a remote site and on a few acres little known to outsiders.

* * *

Aspects of Native American history must be summarized to help explain these recent developments in Indian architecture. Reasons why Indian settlements are usually found in harsh climates and far from cities, why the economy requires outside funds for most architectural work, why certain forms prevail, and why there is a cultural revival—all these are parts of the story.

Native American cultures had for centuries been developing buildings as a response to climate, means of subsistence, available materials and resources, belief systems, and other elements common to all of humanity. The number of Indians in 1492 within the present contiguous forty-eight states is a matter of scholarly debate, but there was enough space available to permit migration, separation, and interaction.[1] The Navajo, for instance, Athapaskan people who moved to the Southwest, seem to have learned about four-pole hogans and depressions in the earth from pueblo residents.[2] This productive prehistoric contact is the positive side of interaction; current territorial disputes with the Hopi represent the negative side.

The arrival of Euro-Americans and the increasing frequency of their contacts with Native peoples caused changes in Native life that loom larger in history than earlier ones do because they were recorded. Each colonial-era culture had a different relationship to the Native population, with different consequences for architecture.

In Spanish settlements of the Southeast, Southwest, and Far West, the conquerors used indigenous labor for mining, agriculture, and construction, taking advantage of local expertise in building. In the western areas, adobe workers modified their techniques, with bricks replacing clumps of material. New building types such as colonial governors' palaces and churches were introduced. The interlocked cubic character of terraced pueblos endured, however, modified as required. Those who could escape the full force of Spanish evangelizing and exploitation retained their buildings throughout much of the nineteenth century, and to some extent, into the twentieth. Whether in Mexico or in the United States, the Indian

population was generally kept poor and powerless, but no one could prevent people from preserving surreptitiously certain beliefs and practices that still impart a special character to life in most of the nineteen pueblos.

Native expertise in hunting and trapping attracted the Russians in California and the Northwest, and the French in the East and Midwest. In areas of French activity, the mobile fur trade did not foster permanent settlements, so the impact on Native architecture was indirect. This was the case for the Dutch and British fur trade as well: When the animal supply was reduced in the East where Europeans concentrated, tribal participants moved west to new hunting and trapping grounds. As they did so, they created friction with preexisting residents, leading to wars and to population movement that tended to impoverish those involved. In addition, if woodland people moved to the Great Plains, they had to alter their traditional building types because different construction resources were available. They adopted, syncretized, or invented forms according to the possibilities at a given place and moment.

The English were primarily interested in agriculture, on small northern farms and on southern plantations. Unable to force Native people to perform suitable farm labor, they imported slaves for that purpose and tried to

2. Roundhouse, Sulphur Bank El-em Pomo Rancheria. Rancheria resident builders, ca. 1990–1993.

shunt the Indians to less desirable land or to the West. To do this, the colonial powers used force and dishonest business practices, or gave gifts as part of more ethical negotiations.

Following the Revolutionary War, Americans debated federal versus state jurisdiction over Native people, and whether and how to remove Native Americans from lands that whites desired. The Articles of Confederation (1781) had reserved the handling of Indian affairs for the federal government, and the Northwest Ordinance (1787) embodied the will of the federal legislature in regard to Native peoples; the Constitution reserved to Congress the plenary power to regulate Indian commerce and the right to make treaties.[3] Indian affairs were administered from 1788 by the Secretary of War.

The new country resented the many Indian alliances with the British, and the victors were not always inclined to respect the Indians' postwar rights. After the Treaty of Paris, which ended the Revolutionary War (1783), the Ohio Territory, ceded to the United States, opened for settlement. Native people at times reacted violently when the recent arrivals ignored the Indian Intercourse Acts of the 1790s and 1802, which attempted to regulate Euro-American actions in trade and land occupancy. The tendency of most Indians to favor the British in ongoing anti-American action gave the new nation an excuse for indifference or even hostility to Native needs and claims after the War of 1812. Andrew Jackson's defeat of the Creeks, leading to their cession in 1814 of about 23 million acres, was a prelude to his policies as president, when most eastern Indians not previously displaced were pushed west of the Mississippi under the Indian Removal Act of 1830. Those Native people who were able to resist and to evade capture included ancestors of the present Seminoles of Florida, Cherokees and Lumbees of North Carolina, and other smaller groups.

State governments, beholden to geographically circumscribed white voters, were particularly eager to move Indians elsewhere, and it was in response to states' intent to encroach on federal prerogatives that Supreme Court opinions were issued in 1831 (*Cherokee Nation* v. *Georgia*) and 1832 (*Worcester* v. *Georgia*). The Northwest Ordinance required Indians' consent for the taking of their land or property, stated that their territory was not to be invaded or disturbed except in wars authorized by Congress, and said that laws might be made affecting Indians if the laws were meant to prevent wrongs against them or if they promoted peace and friendship. These virtuous pronouncements were often vitiated by cynical legislators and by white lead-

ers who painted the thinnest possible veneer of legality over corrupt practices, but they remained law and provided some basis for later federal responsibility on lands held in trust for certain tribes and individuals. The provision for consent led to the writing of treaties with Indians. As treaties can be written only between sovereign nations—albeit here unequally powerful ones—the Supreme Court judgments stated that Native aggregates constituted sovereign nations, although within the United States and dependent to some degree on the same federal government with which the treaties were written. This conclusion forms the basis for today's emphasis on Indian nationhood and self-determination.[4]

As Native religions were tied to specific holy sites and rooted in particular lands, removal damaged severely the spiritual basis of Indian life, ruined the Native economy, and wrenched families from customary ways. Some could not recover from these traumatic events, and maintained a dispirited existence under a gradually assimilated surface. Others managed to make their way materially in the new circumstances. Underlying many of the altered lives were ancestral memories that needed expression when doing so became possible, as it is today when our country is willing to hear alternative ideas if not always to endorse them.

One vitally important consequence of treaty-writing was the creation of the idea of organized tribes, although there is no official definition of the word. American representatives of cities, states, counties, and the nation thought it natural to have unified governmental forms embracing the whole population of a given territory. Few Native people had the same idea. Many were affiliated with small bands, some of them sharing a culture but not always sharing allegiance to a single leader or oligarchy. They found it mystifying that their rights to ancestral territory could be abrogated by people from other bands who had no more authority than they did. But the white men needed people with whom to sign treaties and designated willing Indian counterparts, who then became the official "representatives" of people whom they had never represented before. The authority came from the BIA in Washington, embodied in agents responsible to area superintendents. At times, the agents designated chiefs even where no such office had been recognized earlier.[5] Ongoing perception of illegitimate authority has been one factor underlying intratribal political problems since the creation of the superintendencies in 1786.

For a century after *Worcester* v. *Georgia*, the history of relations between Indians and the rest of society was doleful from the Native viewpoint. Lands west of the Mississippi were supposedly guaranteed to the tribes that had settled there, but many guarantees proved worthless. The Indian Territory was designated through the Indian Trade and Intercourse Act of 1834, first in a broad area west of the river and later, only in what is now Oklahoma. The Cherokees were expelled to the Territory from the Southeast in 1838 and 1839, along the "Trail of Tears." One's delight in the statehood (1907) celebrated by the famous Rodgers and Hammerstein musical must be tempered by the knowledge that it established substantial governmental control over most of the Native Americans of the area and abrogated rights formerly proclaimed as permanent. The new status of the former Indian Territory only made official the de facto white dominance there, officials, missionaries, and teachers having tried since the 1840s to make Indians become Christians and literate farmers. These agents of assimilation were active throughout the West, and still are. While some Native people welcomed their ideas, others preserved traditional ways in private while "acting white" in public, and still others responded barely, if at all. Differing degrees of assimilation still cause conflict even within small reservations and tribal groups.

Equally tragic events occurred throughout the Plains, mountain states, and West Coast. Settlers continued to encroach on Indian land and continued to receive protection from the territorial, state, and federal authorities. Travelers over the trails to the West disturbed Native hunting patterns and lifeways. Anglos displaced buffalo from their herding areas and competed with Indians as hunters, thereby bringing economic ruin and starvation to the Native population. The Fort Laramie Treaty of 1851 tried to bring some order into a volatile scene, but did so primarily for the benefit of settlers. It established boundaries between tribes, sometimes to their detriment. It guaranteed annuity payments for varying periods of time to Indians forced to yield land and to accept Anglo policing of settlers' trails through their territory—toward other Native areas. The annuities, however, represented only a small fraction of the value of the lands.

Violent attacks made on whites by desperate Indians were met by even more violent retaliation, and defeated tribes consequently lost territory throughout the West. Tribal members still commemorate such egregious acts as the deathly Navajo "Long March" to confinement with Apaches at Bosque Redondo, New Mexico (1864–1868) and massacres of Cheyennes and Arapahos at Sand Creek (1864), and of Lakota at Wounded Knee, South Dakota (1890). These, following on the expulsion of Cherokees and wrongs committed against many others, are events that

must still be dealt with by public atonement, restitution, and commemoration. Some of the conflicts may be partly exorcised through works of literature, dance, music, art, and possibly even architecture.

The Civil War made matters worse because some tribes favored the North; neighboring tribes, the South. Individuals within each no doubt disagreed with their fellows. There was some danger of Indians being sold into slavery; other Indians owned slaves. With their own economy disrupted, Euro-Americans were not eager to provide materially for the Native population even though the latter had to depend on the federal government once their own means of self-support had been taken away. Resentment at the costs and enduring provisions of treaties made Congress unwilling to continue to approve them, and it must have seemed possible unilaterally to cease treaty-making with people too weakened to protest effectively. From the Native American viewpoint, the treaties had often proved worthless anyway.

The last treaty was written in 1868, and in a rider to an appropriations act in 1871, Congress put an end to further treaty-making. After that, unilateral acts of Congress replaced the bilateral negotiations, although some agreements were signed between the federal government and tribal officials who may or may not have been legitimate representatives of their people. Native Americans had also to contend with corrupt individuals. Some superintendents and Indian agents profited personally from funds, goods, and rations intended for the Native population. In the 1880s, civil service tests and public awareness of reservation officials' corruption led to more honest administration of Indian affairs, but disrespect for Anglo government had been fostered. This attitude extends at times to tribal chairmen, considered by some Native people to lack legitimacy and to be mere agents of the powers in Washington.[6] These problems make as much self-determination as possible seem desirable, although conflicts may occur between rights guaranteed by the United States Constitution and those specified by individual tribal governments.

* * *

Ironically, the areas where self-determination—or at least self-administration—can be practiced are reservations, frequent causes of criticism for other reasons. As the name implies, these are lands set aside for occupancy by Native Americans after the Anglo takeover of other places where Indians had lived according to their own ways.[7] The Iroquois, among others, occupy lands reserved from their ancient territory, but when tribes could not occupy aboriginal lands, the reservations reinforced a bitter sense of loss.

Areas too infertile or remote for whites to desire were usually left for the Natives. That is why tribes with little in common sometimes inhabit a single reservation, as at Fort Belknap, while groups with almost everything in common, such as the Lakota and Dakota ("Sioux"), are separated into several. Whites established few businesses on reservations and fewer still that employed Indians; even today, it is difficult to attract business and industry to these remote areas. Medical help equal to that for small-town whites was unavailable.

The neglect of education led to the provision of boarding schools for Native youth. Children had to be wrenched from home to attend them, and instruction was offered in settings that enforced assimilation to Euro-American norms. Education on reservations also suffered from insensitive attempts to "Anglicize" the children. Students stayed away for many reasons, including difficulties in reaching distant schools, inability to speak English, lack of money for adequate clothing or for school supplies, and no convincing rewards at the end of the process. The goal of the majority population, however, was clearly to acculturate the Indians, and schooling had therefore to be provided, although teachers, normally single women, were reluctant to live on reservations. The federal government solved the problem after 1870 by letting religious missionaries teach, as they tolerated personal privation in exchange for a monopoly over souls on the reservation. As a result, an extended family might have Catholic relatives in one part of the north central and Plains states, Episcopalian cousins in another, creating additional splits within an ever-diminishing population.

By the late nineteenth century, the United States had long experience with reservations, as the first one was established for the Quinnipiac in Connecticut in 1638, but little had been learned except how to dissolve or limit them. Their purpose changed subtly from that of separating Native Americans from newcomers to that of confining Indians while some of their land was alienated. There has never been a simple definition of a reservation or a single way of creating one. Their boundaries have been established by treaty, by law, by order of the president or courts, or by purchase. In most cases, if the tribe holds federal recognition, its land is recognized as a place where the tribe has jurisdiction. The land itself may be owned by the tribal government or as fee-patent land by individuals who may be tribal members or outsiders; other land is held in trust by the federal government for the tribe or for members of it.[8] No real-estate or income taxes are paid to state and federal governments by those who live or maintain businesses on tribal or trust land. This fact explains both the reluctance of states to see more land attain that status and the presence of tax-free roadside cigarette shops on lots owned by Native Americans.

The difficulties of policing, serving, and regulating the often remote reservations were evident to everyone by the late nineteenth century. Acculturating and assimilating the Indians seemed elusive goals. The plight of Native Americans touched the hearts of humane people to whom it seemed only decent to abolish the reservation system and the associated confinement, paternalism, and corruption. It could be replaced by grants of land so that the hapless dependent people could become self-supporting individual farmers. Guardians of the public good also knew that most Indians were not citizens but, by then, generally passive wards of the government. They might, however, begin what Anglos called productive activity if they had a material stake in the United States.

In 1887, therefore, the General Allotment Act, known from its sponsor as the Dawes Act, gave 160 acres to each Indian head of family, with 80 acres designated for single people over age eighteen and all orphans.[9] Training, tools, and equipment were to be provided—but weren't always—to tribal members newly "liberated" to compete with the rest of the population for the material goods and psychological satisfactions of the American way. Native Americans obtained citizenship if they took their lands in severalty, free from reservation status.[10] It appears not to have occurred to the well-meaning legislators that their view of the good life might not be shared by the supposed beneficiaries or that the Indians might be correct in their attitudes.

Some who voted for the Dawes Act may have done so from cynical motives, knowing that unsuccessful farmers sell their lands eventually. The law gave the federal government trusteeship over allotments for twenty-five years so that allottees could not immediately be swindled out of their land; they would also be free of taxation during the trusteeship period. Thereafter, Indian lands could be released; in fact, laws passed as early as 1902 and 1906 let the Bureau of Indian Affairs sell certain allotted lands.[11] In addition, some reservation lands not allotted were declared surplus, available for sale to Anglos. The Dawes Act and its successors were passed at a period when great numbers of immigrants were arriving in America, and the needs of these potential farmers and of existing ones must have seemed more pressing to members of Congress than the traditions of a dwindling number of Indians, who had become inconvenient dependents of the government.

The transfer of ownership occurred because many Native people were neither inclined to farm, having been hunters or gatherers, nor prepared adequately to do so. The ongoing strength of cultural patterns might have overwhelmed even sensible and generous governmental action. Moreover, no farmer could make a living if the 160 acres were infertile. Some new Native landowners had to forfeit their lands when they became unable to pay taxes on them. Some allotments were sold as soon as possible; others, later. By 1934, when the allotment policy was abandoned, about 90 million acres—two-thirds of the total—had passed from Indian to Anglo possession. This left about half the Indians landless, and of the 47 million acres remaining, about half were semiarid or desert.[12] A good many reservations were and are checkerboarded with some parts in tribal hands, others in individual ownership, and some held by Anglos. This has consequences for the perception of group and cultural unity, and it affects the ability to build certain facilities where they would best be located.

In response to the misery of reservation life, ongoing persecution, disease, and the confusion engendered by the Dawes Act, the Native American population sank to its lowest point at the turn of the century. But signs of change appeared. Some, like the Ghost Dance revitalization movement, which began in 1890, spread widely around the West but eventually declined.[13] Others were long-lasting—for instance, the Supreme Court decision in Winters v. United States (1908) that the creation of a reservation meant that enough water had to be made available to make life sustainable there. Native Americans also developed their own agencies of change. Among these were the Society of American Indians (1911) founded by acculturated individuals; Wassaja, an independent journal established in 1912; and the Native American Church, incorporated in 1918 but of older origin. The Native population also began to increase.

It is possible that the crisis caused by the Dawes Act catalyzed cultural innovation: In connection with the uprooting of immigrants, sociologist Herbert Gans has recognized a social-bonding process to re-create Italian village life in America's cities, and sees widespread urban renewal giving impetus to the historic-preservation movement.[14] It is possible, too, that the crisis precipitated by federal policies after 1945 contributed to the present cultural efflorescence.

Nevertheless, conditions of Native life were so generally wretched that the Institute for Government Research (later part of the Brookings Institution) was asked to prepare a definitive report about them to guide future policy.

Known as the Meriam Report, named for Lewis Meriam, who directed the research, Problem of Indian Administration (1928) confirmed the need to alter the allotment policy and to end various financial and social abuses.[15] Major change awaited Franklin D. Roosevelt's New Deal, when in 1934 Congress passed the Indian Reorganization Act (IRA).[16]

* * *

The Indian Reorganization Act, also known as the Wheeler-Howard Act, forms the basis for much reservation life today.[17] It was passed along with other societal reform laws, and one of its aims was to stimulate the Indian economy, just as the general economy was being addressed. It was essential for any government professing an interest in progress to do something about Indians' decreasing land and increasing poverty, but the debate then and ever since has been about just what needed to be done, how to do it, and how much it should cost.

The most important point in the IRA was that no more land was to be allotted. The act encouraged the consolidation of land fractionated by its descent to many heirs. "Surplus" land was to be restored to Indians. Any Indian land to be sold or transferred could change hands only after approval by the Secretary of the Interior, who was authorized to purchase or obtain more land for tribes and add it to existing reservations; he was allowed also to create new reservations. Trust status over Indian land was to be extended indefinitely, but Indians who held title to land could keep it. These parts of the law received widespread approval from Native people.

Another major point was that each tribe was allowed—and encouraged—to adopt a written constitution and bylaws, and could ask the Secretary of the Interior to provide a charter of incorporation. This enhanced the power of any tribal government created under the IRA. Unfortunately, the traditional and often internally dynamic methods of selecting leaders, the autonomy of small bands, decisions made by consensus, and time-tested negotiating procedures were downgraded or even eliminated by the Anglo-inspired written constitutions. Elections held to decide whether a tribe would accept the new way of organizing led to discord that sometimes endures today. A majority of Native Americans rejected the IRA by vote or by abstention, but about ninety tribes wrote constitutions or had them written in Washington and about seventy drafted business incorporation charters. Sometimes the officials produced identical documents, and some of those were inevitably unsuited to particular tribal circumstances. Despite their flaws, the constitutions made it possible to conduct government in ways compatible with those of the rest of the United States. Defenders of the IRA point out that traditional systems had been changing; some were even dissolving. Indeed, many tribes that rejected the IRA's provisions later devised similar forms of government or voted to accept the act. No matter what the tribal decision was, the tribes retained their government-to-government relationship with the United States, a matter of great importance today.

The act also helped to establish Indian preference in obtaining work with the Bureau of Indian Affairs, superseding existing civil service requirements. This has increased Native American employment and has made it possible for Indians to work on, and occasionally manage, programs affecting their people. At the same time, however, it has created substantial resistance to change within the BIA lest jobs be lost, although there is widespread criticism of the agency by other Native Americans.[18]

Overall, the IRA, other New Deal legislation, and the policies of John Collier, Commissioner of Indian Affairs from 1933 to 1944, were meant to strengthen tribal government and Indian identity. The Johnson-O'Malley Act of 1934[19] contributed funds for supplementing children's education, and Collier promoted day schools on the reservations to avoid separating children from their families and cultures in assimilationist boarding schools. Religious freedom and curtailment of missionary activities at schools also helped to promote Native concerns. Bilingual education became an option for tribes that wanted it. Health care on reservations improved somewhat, and small hospitals were constructed on some of them. The Indian Arts and Crafts Board, established in 1935 under the Department of the Interior, helps Native people market their work and supports organizations and businesses that train artists; some aid goes to cooperative enterprises. In the three museums that it administers in Oklahoma, South Dakota, and Montana, sales outlets provide income for Native craft workers. Felix S. Cohen compiled the *Handbook of Federal Indian Law*, which remains the authoritative source on the subject a half century later.[20]

Support for tribal life and culture was embodied in a few new government-sponsored buildings, and in Historic American Building Survey work at Acoma Pueblo. Collier's earnest hopes are expressed in an article he wrote for *Indians at Work*, a periodical about activities of the BIA.[21] He announced plans for reservation buildings that would be "an additional step toward Indian control of Indian activity." With money supplied by the Public Works Fund, schools, hospitals, and houses were to be built "to fit the local landscape . . . use the local building materials, and . . . employ the Indians and such other workers, preferably local, as may be needed." Architects—there were then no Native American ones—would "strive to embody the spirit of the Indians in these Indian buildings." He believed that "there ought to flower into expression a new architecture," an expectation realized only a generation later. W. Carson Ryan, Jr., Director of Indian Education in the BIA, expected adults and children to help landscape their new schools and make interior furnishings as part of vocational training.[22]

Mayers, Murray & Phillip of New York City were the architects employed to design a school for Navajo children at Cove in the northern part of the reservation.[23] They based the design of small domical pavilions (for classrooms, staff housing, offices, and toilets) on the traditional hogan, but rejected the smokehole and single doorway as impractical for the new purpose. They refused to create "a tricked-up hogan constructed with imported materials" and, instead, built octagonal forms in stone and wood with cedar and pinon bark between the logs, and packed adobe on the curved roofs under waterproofing concealed by earth. Collier described other building procedures using natural, local materials in an article addressed to architects in 1937, in which he described a similar school complex with octagonal buildings at Shonto and other hogan-like schools in Arizona and New Mexico—some using adobe blocks, stone, and vigas (projecting log beams). In the upper Midwest, at Grand Portage, Minnesota, the school was made of dark painted whole logs on a heavy stone foundation, the sort of construction known in late Ojibwe drum dance halls.[24] All had been erected with local materials, some with all-Indian builders, the rest with almost all Native workers. In the Southwest, such features as vigas, rounded corners, porches, patios, and chimneys were meant to integrate the new buildings with existing ones nearby.[25] If, as at Zuni Pueblo, adobe was judged inadequate for a high school and hospital, red sandstone was used, quarried by the Zuni on their own land. At San Carlos, the school of local stone, however well intentioned, could not be considered traditional: "This was a wickiup culture, so how could tufa [volcanic stone] buildings be appropriate to that?"[26]

These, some buildings put up by the National Park Service at historic Native sites, and the Tonawanda Seneca office building in New York State are the ancestors of the buildings with which this book is concerned. The methods used today to fit the building to the land and people are sometimes the same, but there is a significant difference:

3. Navajo Council House, Window Rock, Arizona.
Mayers, Murray & Phillip, 1935.

In Collier's time, decisions were made for the Native peoples, even though he was aware that paternalism caused problems. He hoped to inculcate a sense of responsibility among the indigenous population for the upkeep of buildings on which they had worked, to prepare them "for the building trades, and at the same time inspire them to utilize the materials that they have at hand for more permanent homes for themselves."[27] Today, Native Americans themselves are seen capable of determining their own levels of responsibility and inspiration.

The most conspicuous of the Collier-era buildings was the Navajo Council House at Window Rock, Arizona (3), designed by Mayers, Murray & Phillip but built by Navajo laborers with funds from the Public Works Administration. This is an octagon meant to suggest a hogan, although hogans never had two stories, as this building has. It is 72 feet across, with two small octagonal committee rooms extending about 25 feet beyond two of its faces. In the main room, seats run along the octagon's faces and stand in rows before a platform. Given the absence of any encompassing Native government on the Navajo Reservation before the advent of the Business Committee in 1922, and given the Navajo majority that initially rejected the IRA, this arrangement can hardly be regarded as traditional. The architects did, however, place the main door at the east, and had no windows on the north, to conform with Navajo building tenets. The council house was built of local rubble stone finished inside with adobe plaster, which was also used to cover the roofs. The upper roof rests on rough logs that reach into the stone piers at the octagon's corners.[28] These attractive inventions created a problem, however, and one that collaboration with the Navajo would have avoided: Traditional hogans did not have these conspicuous features, and reservation residents do not consider the council house to be suitably indigenous in feeling. What's more, some residents believed that the site was cursed by a rattlesnake.[29] It is possible, however, that if the Navajo had had a better relationship with the IRA and federal agencies, they would have regarded the government-funded council house with greater sympathy and found a way to avoid unwelcome design elements. Certainly Collier found them suitable, for in an article in *Indians at Work*, he said that the building would be a "tangible symbol of tribal self-government" and the "first of many such adaptations by the Indians in their efforts to renew and govern themselves under their recently granted Magna Charta."[30]

Apart from these governmental efforts to formulate a modern architecture for Indians, there were rare private attempts to do so. Mary Cabot Wheelwright, who was inspired to learn about the Navajo religion by the spiritual leader Hastiin Klah*, feared that Navajo culture was soon to disappear. She persuaded Klah to explain Navajo tenets so as to preserve them at least on paper, on replicated sandpaintings, and in a museum at first called House of Prayer,

which she established on a 10-acre site in Santa Fe, New Mexico (4). The information and paintings were intended for a new endowed wing at the Laboratory of Anthropology there, but the laboratory directors felt that a hogan shape would not suit their pueblo-style building. As the design seemed essential, Wheelwright employed William Penhallow Henderson to design a separate building as "an interpretation in modern form of... a synthesis of the two types of ceremonial hogans now in use.... Its projecting entrance and skylight above are from the older type, and the octagonal shape from the modern type. It faces East, as all Navajo dwellings do."[31] The principal room on the upper floor has a cribbed-log roof and a skylight. Wheelwright wanted the building to "give the feeling of the aloofness and quiet of a ceremonial hogan, and to create the sense of surprise and wonder... face to face with the strange world of Navajo religion." The museum's form is

4. Wheelwright Museum (interior, ca. 1940), Santa Fe, New Mexico. William Penhallow Henderson, 1937. (Courtesy Wheelwright Museum of the American Indian, Ernest Knee, no. 60/549)

too vertical to suggest genuine hogans, which in any case lacked plumbing and electricity, but the donor, architect, and Klah understood the practicalities of the situation. The museum has endured, albeit with some modifications.[32] When comparable buildings are erected today, they are put up by the Navajo and not for them.

Many whites, too, disagreed with the Roosevelt-era measures. Some were driven by greed and were frustrated by the IRA's safeguards on land. Some expected to cut assistance as the economy improved. Others believed that the best way to end reservation poverty and isolation was to get Indians off the reservations and free them from traditions that some whites regarded as backward and stultifying. During the Second World War, they were glad to see young Indians enroll in the military service, considered a great equalizer.[33] When John Collier resigned from the BIA in 1945, opponents of the "Indian New Deal" gave a new direction to Native American life. This new direction, involving the practices of relocation and termination, was so disruptive to Native Americans that it provoked a major political reaction and restorative creativity during the 1960s.

* * *

By war's end, there were enough educated Indians, often the products of boarding schools, enough people of mixed ancestry, and enough acculturated war veterans exposed to an intense alternative experience, to create a new supratribal organization for the postwar era.[34] In November 1944, they formed the National Congress of American Indians (NCAI). It provided a forum for the expression of Native concerns, although younger critics later saw it as a creature of the Department of the Interior.[35] This organization and other groups had a great deal to do during the following quarter century, because as early as 1946 plans were laid to end the special status of tribes.

These schemes were not visible immediately. In fact, the federal government seemed to be supporting Native interests when Congress passed the Indian Claims Commission Act in 1946[36] to settle claims about illegal trespass on or alienation of Indian land and other grievances. Not surprisingly, the commission was prohibited from restoring the land to its rightful owners; the Anglos on it would have protested, and members of Congress who supported the Native Americans would probably have lost in the next elections. Instead, the commission offered money or unoccupied land that was often of no interest to the petitioners, especially when the alienated land had been sacred. Although eventually the deadline for filing claims was extended beyond the original narrow limit and although

some compensation is usually preferable to none, the purpose of the procedure was to extinguish Indian claims that might delay the termination of tribal status. There were to be no more nations within the nation, no more dependency, and as little left of the supposedly backward and superstitious (that is, not always Christian) cultures as possible.

Termination was announced as government policy before the National Council of Social Work at its San Francisco meeting in April 1947, although it took until 1950 to implement. An ominous sign was the appointment of Dillon S. Myer as Commissioner of Indian Affairs in 1950. His sympathy for minority groups was not evident when he directed the infamous relocation of Japanese-Americans to concentration camps during the Second World War.

At this period, the general level of respect for Native American tradition may be gauged from the popularity of cowboy-and-Indian films, which usually showed Indians as savage. The architectural situation is suggested by the abundance of tipi-shaped snack bars and motels along America's roads; the Wigwam Motel at Grants, Arizona, is a famous example, apparently made of concrete, and others survive in Palm Springs, California, and Nambe, New Mexico, to name just a few.

In the summer of 1953, the House of Representatives passed unanimously its Concurrent Resolution 103 to "Free Certain Tribes of Indians from Federal Supervision".[37] This document informed tribes judged capable of supporting themselves through sawmills, fishing, and other activities that their status as tribes would end after a payment in compensation for government services promised in treaties and agreements. Tribes that wished to be free of federal supervision were also allowed termination. Some took up the offer, being eager to liberate themselves from the largest visible oppressor, but they seem not to have realized the consequences of being placed under state jurisdiction with legislators elected by non-Indians eager to obtain more Indian land, forests, and water. The unctuous language of the document said that termination would make Indians "subject to the same laws and entitled to the same privileges and responsibilities as are applicable to other citizens...and...end their status as wards." They would be granted "all the rights and prerogatives pertaining to citizenship," although Indians presumably had them anyway, having been citizens since 1924. The real point was that tribes would lose the privileges of their special status—tax exemptions on their lands, federal health and educational services, their own governments—and they would perforce be assimilated into the larger society. Paternalistic laws prohibiting the sale of liquor to Indians were repealed, as if to affirm the maturity of the soon-to-be-liberated people, although states were allowed to introduce their own rules. In an attempt to dismantle the BIA, its supervision of medical care was shifted to the Public Health Service in 1954, beginning a process of spreading the number of agencies concerned with Indian affairs to a number that now causes overlapping and bureaucratic delays.[38] Congress passed PL 83-280 two weeks after the termination resolution, empowering state legislatures to take over civil and criminal jurisdiction on Indian reservations.[39] The proponents did not discuss the inevitable result of termination and state jurisdiction: Even more Anglos would take over Indian property and resources.

At the same time, an increase in the Indian population made reservations on remote and barren lands unable to support all their residents. No one knew how to create enough jobs on reservations to allow the residents to stay. The history of attempts to do so is lamentable in virtually every respect.[40] Federal policy therefore promoted the relocation of working-age Indians to cities, at first far from their own areas, where they would presumably become acculturated to the Anglo population. The policy had few positive results, owing to the migrants' inadequate preparation for unfamiliar forms of work and insufficient training for jobs and urban living, and the inadequate rewards offered. The combination of termination and relocation was disastrous in leading many young Native Americans to unemployment in settings unfamiliar to them, and then to rootlessness, frustration, and alcoholism. The architectural consequence of the relocation policy was the development of urban Indian centers. Many of the first were church-funded, as some still are, while support came later from secular sources. This is a new building type in which Native Americans and others provide social service and a place for fellowship meant to be congenial but not specific to any single indigenous culture.

Those who remained at home included some who adhered to their old culture, seeing it as potential support in a changing society. They revived the Sun Dance, for example, and practiced other traditional rituals and arts, some of them intended as reformative actions meant to change the existing cultural situation.[41]

The best result was "ironic...that the BIA and the urban experience have done more to foster the pan-Indian movement than all the great chiefs of the past."[42] Native Americans from many tribes began to organize for political action, creating a new solidarity in the 1960s. It was seen clearly at the American Indian Chicago Conference, a week-long event held in 1961 at the University of Chicago, paid for by the Fund for the Republic, arranged primarily by Sol Tax (a white anthropologist but endorsed by the NCAI), and attended by at least 400 Native people from at least 67 tribes and nations.[43] Their deliberations were embodied in *The Voice of the American Indian: Declaration of Indian Purpose*, published by the university's press in that year. Readers could learn what Native people themselves had to say about problems and potential remedies. And there, at the beginning of a turbulent decade in which youth came to play an increasingly important role, young people founded the National Indian Youth Council, led by those who found their elders' responses too passive. Deeply concerned with the threat of assimilation, staunchly defending Indians' treaty rights and ownership of land, the council members were leaders in many subsequent attempts to protect what could still be protected and to support Native cultural revival.[44]

This was the first year of John F. Kennedy's presidency. His associates were more sympathetic to Indian rights than were their predecessors in the Truman and Eisenhower administrations. The Secretary of the Interior appointed the Task Force on Indian Affairs, whose mimeographed but authoritative *Report* in 1961 rejected the termination policy, promoted self-sufficiency through vocational training and educational assistance, and protected rights of Native people who lived off the reservation. The Commission on the Rights, Liberties, and Responsibilities of the American Indian, established in 1961, reported critically about termination.[45] The Kennedy administration regarded Native American problems as part of the general problems of poverty in the United States and therefore tended not to introduce laws specifically for this group of citizens, but it did set up "Indian desks" in its various antipoverty offices, and in 1962 opened the Division of Economic Development within the BIA. The pace of change quickened during this decade, with laws being introduced each year to benefit Native Americans and to give tribal governments more authority, and 1962 saw the last of the termination acts.

The Economic Opportunity Act of 1964[46]—most famous for initiating Head Start, Upward Bound, and VISTA programs—had as its Title II measures to increase "Urban and Rural Community Action Programs," including "maximum feasible participation" of the recipients of government help. Native Americans began to manage some of the programs, and tribes developed enough management skill to redirect various grants when they needed to. The idea of local management even stretched to include experiments in Native-run education, with the first example being the school at Rough Rock (1966) on the Navajo Reservation.[47] It is true that some participants gave up their previous food-growing activities to participate in the wage economy. Some bureaucracies formed. Industrial parks, resorts, and arts facilities developed under the Economic Development Administration (EDA) employed insufficient numbers of Indians to justify the expenditures on them, and several inadequately planned facilities closed. Despite the many problems, the programs were significant in giving the opportunity for fostering Indian administration; for developing community facilities, including buildings; for creating at least a few jobs, even if many were temporary; and for providing college scholarships for thousands of Native Americans. Initial results were bound to be variable in terms of their effectiveness, but in its early phases, "the therapeutic value of tribal self-government…[reduced] existing causes of psychological stress," which had earlier hindered group and individual development.[48] By 1970, it was clear that Native Americans were doing anything but vanishing.[49]

* * *

On July 8, 1970, President Richard M. Nixon sent a message to Congress with his recommendations for Indian policy.[50] He proposed economic development legislation, additional funds for Indian health, as well as funds for urban Indians and for legal representation and protection of natural-resource rights. He envisioned greater Indian control of education and promoted the restoration of certain sacred tribal lands. In this message, he directed federal policy in a way that has governed the years in which most of the culturally relevant buildings were designed: He began clearly to promote respect for the interrelated matters of tribal sovereignty, economic self-sufficiency, and cultural self-determination.[51]

Despite certain tragic episodes, such as a lethal confrontation of Lakotas and government agents at Wounded Knee, South Dakota, in 1973, the next few years were marked by effective protests and legal decisions over abrogated rights, as well as by Indian efforts for self-development. They were also marked by less effective laws and reports concerning education and economic development through 90 percent government-guaranteed loans to reservation businesses. More dynamic was the Indian Self-Determination and Education Assistance Act, signed in 1975.[52] An observer in 1991 asserted that "during the past twenty-five years, Native Americans have moved further towards the goals of self-determination than at any time since European colonization. Tribal rights are being

aggressively asserted on a growing number of reservations. Traditional cultures are being rebuilt and the strength of traditional values are [sic] increasingly respected. Economic development is being promoted and political savvy is no longer rare."[53] Changes in tribal administrative and business activities, such as those concerned with building, now allow tribes to contract for services formerly provided by the BIA.

Contracting is no panacea. For reservation school operations, money must still come from the federal government. The Office of Indian Education Programs within the BIA, for example, had a "backlog of over $550,000,000 in 1993, largely because of [building] code and functional deficiencies. Funding has been below the annual deterioration rate and…new requirements have been imposed…such as handicap codes [and] fire sprinkler regulations".[54] Most of the budget in most tribes is derived from eighteen federal assistance programs, but 53 percent of federal money "budgeted for Indians is taken up with administrative costs before it reaches" reservations, and the funds are monitored "despite supposed Indian control".[55] The bureau has not diminished in size even though some of its functions were taken over by the tribes, so that there is duplicated activity more than a replacement of the BIA by tribal administrators.

The tribes have, however, exercised more control over services provided to them. The aim of the act as enunciated in its title has strengthened the self-perception of tribes as sovereign nations, increasingly able to determine their own future.[56] The new cultural awareness, of which we shall have more to say later, contributed to this optimistic situation.

Federal and state legislation in 1976 and 1977 provided funds for libraries and for health-care facilities. The Tribally Controlled Community College Assistance Act of 1978[57] encouraged the formation of these institutions, some of which have been able to commission distinctive buildings with the help of federal funds. The American Indian Religious Freedom Act[58] protected certain sites and practices, although weakly.[59]

Particularly during the 1970s, Native Americans came to be regarded as model ecologists. Indigenous religions emphasize specific land forms, the cardinal directions, astronomical features, and other aspects of the world and cosmos, although this is not the same as refusal to alter or even damage certain lands. The late Abbott Sekaquaptewa*, former Hopi tribal chairman, separated Indian religious thinking from that of ecologists and "new-agers" when he said, "I just don't think that many older people can get interested in the problem of ecology.... Why should we be concerned with it, when the very basis of our existence, the land, is slowly being taken away ...?".[60] All the same, the public perception of Indians was enhanced by the ecological connections and by attribution of modern thoughts to Chief Seattle and to fictional characters.[61]

Land-restitution claims and sovereignty issues became particularly prominent during the 1980s, when courts determined that the northern two-thirds of Maine had been taken from the Passamaquoddy and Penobscot people illegally, prompting a monetary settlement, and when the Mashantucket Pequots of Connecticut, among others, also succeeded in gaining federal recognition. The research and the courts' judgments have strengthened Native historical knowledge and ethnic pride—ironic benefits of burdensome rules.[62] On reservations and restored and purchased land, the Oneida and Pequot tribes have been active builders, planning and constructing casinos, housing, and museums (112, 125, 146). Their ability to operate gambling halls was secured by the Supreme Court's decision in *California* v. *Cabazon Band of Mission Indians* (1987), which prevents states from regulating or prohibiting bingo on reservations, since "tribes retain attributes of sovereignty over both their members and their territory."

As sovereign to a limited extent, tribes were confirmed in their ability to define their own members, regulate the use of their property, levy taxes, establish business corporations, and administer their own governments—all matters with potential consequences for building construction or selection of architects. By 1991, several tribes and bands were participating in a demonstration project in which their governments took over BIA programs, and as of 1993, twenty-nine tribes had self-governance agreements, with fourteen more applicants and a possible twenty others.[63] Secretary of Energy James D. Watkins formalized a policy of "government-to-government" relations, including prior consultation when Indian interests or treaty rights might be affected.[64]

An important measure affecting architecture was the Native American Graves Protection and Repatriation Act of 1990, signed after three years of deliberation. It set forth procedures for federally funded institutions to settle claims to human remains and Native objects in their possession.[65] The settlement might and often did involve repatriation, and repatriation might lead to plans for buildings designed to receive these treasures.

States and gambling interests had created so much pressure on Congress over the issue of Indian-sponsored casinos that PL 100-497, the Indian Gaming Regulatory Act (IGRA), was passed in 1988. It requires that tribes and states draw up compacts and that a commission supervise gambling operations. The process of negotiating compacts gives states the opportunity to stall, as a number have done. Tribes find it unwise to erect ambitious casinos or to commit gambling revenue to other building projects before the compacts have been negotiated, so that the act has had some impact on architecture built for gambling. Indirectly, it affects buildings for which gambling revenues pay. In 1994, forty-nine governors, competitive Anglo gambling interests, and others allied to increase regulation of tribal gambling establishments.

The limits on sovereignty embodied in the act suggest that all problems are far from having been solved in "Indian country." Robert Grey Eagle* suggests that traditional laws should be written, despite "the so-called taboos on writing.... There are tribal members who would be happy to live by them if they were written.... Sovereignty will take on true meaning."[66] Laws have little effect if they are not enforced, and those that provide helpful programs need to be supported with adequate funding.[67] Congress has been reluctant to safeguard sacred Indian sites; some are in the way of strategic and scientific installations, and legislators may find it hard to think of mountains and lakes in the same way that they might think of Mount Calvary or the Pool of Siloam.[68] The Native American Church's use of peyote during worship arouses fervent opposition from people who want a drug-free America, although not all propose to prohibit alcohol or tobacco.

Social-welfare programs, job-creation and -training efforts, and even the best of the current educational programs have limited effect because of inadequate funding, difficulties of attracting expert personnel to reservations and retaining them, and other reasons. It is not usually cost-effective to offer adequate incentives for businesses to locate on reservations, as adequate infrastructure often does not exist; besides, Indian lands are usually far from cities, with their business resources, and are often subject to harsh climates. Shipments in or out require long hauls by truck. Businessmen complain of tribal bureaucratic obstacles to obtaining permits, and some claim to fear entanglement in tribal courts where rules and procedures may differ from those of state and federal government. Reservations with low educational and skills levels lure few businesses that pay good wages from areas with larger labor pools.

That helps to explain reservation social conditions.

Among Plains tribes, "9.8 per 1,000 live births experience defects resulting from Fetal Alcohol syndrome—the highest rate recorded in the country".[69] "The education dropout rate between kindergarten and the 12th grade is over 75%."[70] The county in which these statistics are found is the poorest one in the United States: Shannon County, South Dakota, site of the Pine Ridge Reservation, where the average annual per capita income is $3,417.[71] The unemployment—80 percent in 1992—and underemployment figures there help to explain the social problems that left 63.1 percent of all residents living below the poverty line.[72] The unemployment rate is 86 percent among Cheyenne River Sioux in Eagle Butte, and 87 percent on the Rosebud Reservation. The average rate of unemployment on all reservations is 35 percent, and of those holding jobs, 60 percent work for the federal or tribal governments. This adds to the appeal of multiple layers of government despite the disadvantages of bureaucratic obstruction. The percentage of households headed by unmarried mothers in Todd County, site of the Rosebud Reservation in South Dakota, increased by 51.2 percent between 1980 and 1990.[73] Other horrifying statistics can be assembled for rates of diabetes, alcohol-related deaths, tuberculosis, academic failure, suicide, and numerous other problems.[74] The political climate since 1980 has not helped much, since bringing reservation infrastructure, health, and education to acceptable levels requires the kind of expenditure that officials were elected to reduce, and even in the compara-tively sympathetic 1970s, some of the apparent gains were illusory.[75] Even something as fundamental as clean drinking water is difficult to obtain in many parts of the Navajo Reservation and in parts of South Dakota; 20 percent of the Pine Ridge residents lack running water or electricity[76] but some positive change is expected from the new Mni Wiconi water project.

Among the other problems has been federal opposition to the American Indian Movement in the 1970s and the Mohawks at Oka in 1990—groups seen in certain quarters as patriots. It took until May 1994 for the ban on religious use of eagle feathers to be lifted. Whites eager to practice native religions crowd sacred indigenous sites and pollute them with abandoned refuse. Sports fans refuse to change demeaning names and mascots, and individual prejudice exists.

There is always hope for improved legislation, increased expertise and effort, self-help and ingenuity, and perhaps the infusion of funds. There is at least temporary hope attached to gambling revenue, which has already eliminated involuntary unemployment on reservations where casinos are well managed. And at a higher level, there is hope invested in the idea that the Indian way—or Native American culture—can help to alter depression and, indirectly, destitution, giving youth a better material and spiritual future than their recent ancestors have had. The architecture described in this book bears witness to this progress and to the anticipation of a better future.

2

Culture

There was a time when it wasn't easy to be Indian in this country. . . . I could have been absorbed by mainstream America. But I'm glad I didn't do it. . . . There is a re-awakening, a movement to resurrect our language and culture. . . . Some still exist, however, who do not understand why Indians still want to be Indians. Including some Indians. . . . There is a re-education process going on. Many are now beginning to look outside of Christianity to the concept of the sacred ceremonies. Many are not taught these things at home or school. So they are searching. It's a slow process. We are restructuring a whole nation.

Elgin Bad Wound, in *Lakota Times*

For a long time, few people would have disputed the opinion of T. J. Morgan, Commissioner of Indian Affairs, when he wrote in 1889 about the future of the indigenous people of his country: "This civilization," he explained to the Secretary of the Interior, "may not be the best possible, but it is the best the Indian can get. They can not escape it, and must either conform to it or be crushed by it."[15]

Native Americans had for several decades been pushed onto reservations or gathered in Oklahoma, then known as Indian Territory. The General Allotment (Dawes) Act had recently been passed, and Commissioner Morgan could have anticipated the eventual end of wars, displacements, and starvation. He realized that Native people were, however reluctantly, about to begin a process of integration.

Indeed, some were. They retained their lands, farming and doing what was expected of them within the larger society, forming part of the American mainstream. Buildings to facilitate assimilation rose on reservations and in towns—boarding schools, clinics and small hospitals, or offices for the Bureau of Indian Affairs administrators who controlled much of life on tribal lands. By directing movement and social activity, by framing acculturating activity,

by confusing habitual spatial patterns, and by enforcing dependence on commercial rather than homemade materials and technology, whites turned the buildings into subtle suppressors of Native culture.

Other Native people could not become successful farmers or assimilate, either because the obstacles to success were too great or because their own values made absorption into American life exceedingly difficult. People who had made decisions by consensus found decision by majority rule to be unfair and illegitimate. People accustomed to modesty and submission to group norms felt that aggressive competition implied a kind of personal corruption that was unthinkable to a moral adult, although ritualization of competition in sports was acceptable. For male hunters to become farmers meant, in some groups, a feminization of men that destroyed a sense of self-esteem and damaged family values. People accustomed to living from season to season found alien the idea of storing goods and food. It was even wicked to save rather than to share, when societies had survived because of mutual help. A number of Native cultures still cannot internalize Euro-American habits, such as the insistence on consulting clocks and being prompt at the same time each workday morning, or creating hierarchies even in children's classrooms. Indian children may not be trained to count and quantify or to acknowledge certain kinds of leadership considered natural by the Euro-American school system.[2] Little wonder that despite some pockets of prosperity, many reservations could not quickly become centers of American-style prosperity, even if sufficient—let alone treaty-designated—resources had been provided to them.

A considerable part of the Native American population doubted that the choice lay only between assimilation and extinction. For a long time, until Roosevelt's New Deal, there was little opportunity to exercise other options in public. But on their own lands, and even off the reservations on private holdings, in towns and in cities, some Native Americans maintained older ways and altered them to suit new needs. They managed to pass along values that could be held in defiance of superficial changes. Their hold on tradition could be tenuous. In places, it could cease to exist, so that now even some Indians are impatient with their fellows who refuse to assimilate completely and who emphasize their Native heritage. But in many parts of the contiguous United States, enough distinctive beliefs and lifeways survived to make their invigoration possible. The compression of formerly dispersed bands into reservation communities often fostered the idea of a tribal identity, even when none had existed earlier; this new unity could be used as a means of maintaining difference from the majority culture.

Some of the indigenous groups' traditions have been preserved by simple resistance to unwelcome innovation. Red Jacket*, a Seneca, informed missionaries near Buffalo, New York, in 1805 that "we will wait a little while and see what effect your preaching has upon them [whites]. If we find it does them good, makes them honest and less disposed to cheat Indians, we will then consider again what you have said." One may guess that any profession of Christianity by Red Jacket's followers was made under duress or for the sake of avoiding further interference by whites.

A telling example of resistance occurred at Pisinemo in Arizona, where a priest persuaded the Tohono O'odham villagers to paint Indian designs on the Catholic church, while he or a colleague threw out Native religious figures and images. The villagers, however, rescued and then buried the sacred objects. When the priest moved elsewhere, the Indians covered over the images on the church facade, removing the signs of enforced subservience to domineering, insensitive outsiders.[3] The often-expressed notion that southwestern Indians were passive, even childlike followers of the clergy is denied by this and many other instances of resistance that lay dormant until a time for action arrived. More recently, the political activism and organization of the 1960s had cultural consequences.

Victories in land claims, fishing rights, control of mineral resources—all of these empowered groups who sought cultural support for changes in their self-perception. As Vine Deloria, Jr.*, an activist himself, put it, "No one had dreamed that the offshoot of activism had been to revive the inherent strengths of basic tribal beliefs."[4] "For Indians in the 1960s," said Henry Gobin*, a Tulalip tribal administrator, "change was on the horizon," as he could see while studying at the Institute of American Indian Arts in Santa Fe.

"Cognitive tension increases the realization that the 'natives' will never be accepted as Western, or equal to them," writes Christine Plimpton, speaking of colonialized people, among whom Native Americans can be considered. "The result is a complex reaction involving the reassertion of certain traditional cultural elements while rejecting and retaining elements of the foreign colonial power. The repudiation of adopted colonial traits and the reacceptance of native cultural manifestations are often accelerated and intensified when the colonial domination has been weakened or eliminated," as the Euro-American version began to be in the 1960s.[5] Edward Saïd, discussing today's "politics of national identity" as reflected in literature, writes of much "early cultural resistance to imperialism" as having been "salutary…[helping people] to reclaim their identity" and "enlarging, widening, refining the scope of a narrative form in the center of which has heretofore always been an exclusively European observer." One may see this as well in Amerindian cultural practice since the 1960s, including architecture.[6]

During the next decade, the pace of cultural revival accelerated. Federal funds helped to create museums and cultural centers, colleges and tourist facilities. When the Upper Skagit Tribe of Washington State achieved federal recognition, the residents promptly reinstituted canoe races, giveaways, naming ceremonies, the First Salmon Ceremony, and burnings (annual feasts for the spirits of the dead). Some of these activities were borrowed from neighboring tribes to foster community life among people previously dispersed and culturally deprived.[7]

* * *

In the past, tradition was reinvigorated at the urging of religious leaders whose visions convinced others to follow them, even though few of their systems of belief were long-lived. The present reinforcement or regeneration of culture is less abrupt and impassioned than those, perhaps because the nature of the cultural crises to which they respond is different; despite the importance of religion today among Native Americans, the primary forces behind the cultural activity seem to be those of personal identity and political standing.[8] Round- or dance- or smoke- or longhouses and sweathouses known in earlier religious belief continue to be built, especially in isolated locations. The relocated and virtually duplicated Coldspring Long-house, replacing one on land taken for the Kinzua Dam in New York State in the 1960s, and the Hupa sweathouse of 1965 in California, exemplify the quiet persistence of older ways. The distinctions created between Christian, assimilated, literate Indians and those who preferred oral communication, reliance on memory, and adherence to ancestral beliefs and existing lifeways underlie the current interest in continuing or renewing indigenous religions. Old forms may be modified, and there may be mutual influence between Indian and Christian beliefs.

One enduring movement is that of the Native American Church. Now practiced with local and personal modifications,[9] widely known as the "peyote cult," this blends Christian belief with old and new elements of indigenous and possibly Mexican origin. Adherents enter a temporary, peyote-induced state conducive to spiritual meditation, witness-bearing, confession, and a sense of fellowship. Worship is conducted in temporary structures, even including tipis erected on the Navajo Reservation; in buildings used for other functions if necessary; and in small churches, usually on reservations, protected from disturbance by outsiders. Elsewhere, traditional religion survives, in forms that reflect the evolving ideas of the culture in question; Christianity today is not what it was in 1492, either. Betonie, the spiritual healer in Leslie Marmon Silko's* novel *Ceremony*, points out that "at one time, the ceremonies as they had been performed were enough for the way the world was then. But after the white people came, elements in this world began to shift; and it became necessary to create new ceremonies.... Things which don't grow and shift are dead things."[10]

Americans are growing accustomed to having people follow religions other than Judaism and Christianity; the recent alteration in immigration laws, bringing more Hindus, Muslims, Buddhists, animists, and others to the United States, has been one factor in making public statements about "our Judeo-Christian culture" appear less immutable and inevitable than they used to. It seems increasingly reasonable for Native people to agree with Don Talayesva* when he said, "I could see that the old people were right when they insisted that Jesus Christ might do for modern whites in a good climate, but that the Hopi gods had brought success to us in the desert ever since the world began." It has also been said that "Indian religions are good ones for living. Christianity is a good religion for dying."[11]

In a country where various religious choices are increasingly viewed as legitimate, Christian churches attempt to reconcile Native religions and their own by incorporating and interpreting compatible aspects of indigenous belief. Books by Jesuits, such as William Stolzman's *The Pipe and Christ: A Christian–Sioux Dialogue* and Patrick J. Twohy's *Finding a Way Home: Indian and Catholic Spiritual Paths of the Plateau Tribes*, treat Native American religious beliefs with respect and assist their survival, albeit subordinate to Christianity.[12] Several Protestant denominations ordain Indian ministers for Native congregations. Occasionally, Christian groups build churches that express the interrelationships; this is also done now by missionaries abroad. Christian Indians may use Native musical patterns when singing hymns in churches.[13]

The Mazakute Memorial (Episcopal) Mission Church of 1975 in Saint Paul, Minnesota, was enlarged by John Cuningham to reflect the 150 Native American worshippers' preference for a central communal focus rather than for a hierarchical long view toward a distant altar. The plan and lighting emphasize centrality. Subsequently, even some local Episcopal churches serving Euro-American congregations adopted central plans, which Roman Catholics had been using since shortly after the Second Vatican Council's endorsement of them in 1962.

The aim of the Christian churches remains that of persuading the unconvinced to accept Christ, but a greater respect for Native belief is maintained en route to the goal. A noteworthy product of this tendency is Our Lady of Fatima Church on the Navajo Reservation in Chinle, Arizona, designed primarily by Father Blane Grein, a Franciscan priest, and six Navajo parishioners (5).[14] Navajo contractors provided heating, plumbing, upholstery, roofing, and cement-finishing. This is an octagon, 70 feet wide, of rough-hewn full logs, as close to the genuine hogan in structure as possible, evoking a form indigenous to the Native population who constitute about 60 percent of the parish—although few people inhabit hogans now, and most of those who do live far to the west.

Inside, the juniper-log altar is covered with deerskin, and the log and branch tabernacle cover suggests a Navajo summer home. It rests on a pedestal meant to recall a Navajo travel shrine or prayer pile. The most remarkable feature is the 6-foot-wide depression in the center (6); this

5. Our Lady of Fatima Church, Chinle, Arizona. Edward Preston and Father Blane Grein, 1990.

circle of compacted sand is exposed at the center of the concrete floor. The depression is the lower part of the cosmic axis known in various Native cultures, an axis that ties the earth and the underworld to the sky; it is the hole from which new life emerges, and it is here that the baptismal font stands, where new life enters the church. Staves and other appurtenances of southwestern indigenous religions are placed in the depression. Three- by 6-foot paintings by Navajo artists, showing the four sacred mountains, will be mounted on the walls to remind the Navajos that they live within their boundaries.[15] In the vestibule, etched glass ye'i figures adorn the doors. A spiritual healer conducted blessing rituals between the first Mass at Christmas 1989 and the dedication by the diocesan bishop in June 1990.[16]

Other hogan churches on and near the reservation include the first of them, Wheatfields Mission, erected in 1962 under Franciscan Blase Brickweg. John O'Gorman, a contractor from Texas, volunteered his services here and at two other churches; he also paid most of the costs. A room on either side of the octagonal hogan is used for classes or meetings. The altar occupies the center of the octagon, and through a large window behind it one sees a sacred conical volcanic mountain. Constructed of wood-

slat siding, strengthened by a stone base and sloping angle buttresses, the church was recently covered with wire under stucco.

Believing that "every culture has seeds of Christianity" and that "the seeds of the Gospel present in ancient Navajo ways should be allowed to grow and ripen,"[17] the Franciscans have an intellectual and evangelizing commitment to the validity of Navajo culture. They began to read the Gospels in Navajo as early as 1955, having published a catechism in that language in 1932, but met some opposition from those whom whites had persuaded to think of their culture as backward; Navajo is now used in parts of the Mass. Building on a tradition of scholarship in Navajo matters practiced especially by Fathers Berard Haile and Anselm Weber, the Roman Catholics led other churches in bringing together elements from various faiths and cultures.[18]

Jimalee Chitwood Burton*, a Cherokee artist, donated the nondenominational Ho-chee-nee Trail of Tears Memorial Chapel to Tahlequah, principal town of the Oklahoma Cherokees. Charles Chief Boyd*, a tribal member, designed it before 1977. The artist died in that year and left money in her will for Chenoweth Constructors of Tulsa to

6. Our Lady of Fatima Church.

erect this memorial to the Cherokees who died along the trail, to be used for other memorial and funeral services as well as weddings. Massive sandstone walls are similar to those that Boyd designed for the Cherokee museum nearby. Three poles recall the Trinity, the longest one representing Jesus. They also relate to poles in the council house. The donor and architect included as much number symbolism as they could.[19]

As the federal government no longer places churches in charge of education on reservations, it is less possible to enforce religious uniformity. Society at large has become more tolerant, and religious programs on radio and television offer unprecedented choices. Indians are now more likely to follow only Native spiritual beliefs than they would have been earlier, when it was prudent to adhere to the Christianity still professed by most Native Americans. The emphasis on Native American pride and the acceptance of alternative lifeways may also have contributed to the revival or reinstitution of Native religion.[20]

Discussions with Native Americans and articles and books about them focus also on spirituality, which is often spoken of as being different from specific religion. Native Americans refer to spirituality as being something distinctive that they share but that is less common among full participants in Western, industrialized society. It may be personal, "a pattern for living that goes on from birth to death"[21] or political empowerment associated with self-determination. Lorraine Canoe*, despite being a professor in Manhattan, likes to wash clothes on a washboard because it has to do with political aspects of spirituality—apparently, resistance to Western technological dominance.[22] To some degree, this reflects frustration with the political and social system, and if one cannot affect politics, one can at least lay claim to aspects of culture.[23] William Powers, an anthropologist with long experience and appreciation of Lakota life, observes that spirituality is applied to Native Americans who "like the idea and apply it to themselves," although neither they nor others attribute spirituality to residents of "Harlem or New Brunswick, New Jersey."

Spirituality can be connected to architecture. Camp Courage, a summer program for 120 children in South Dakota, aims to teach spirituality and Lakota cultural values; it is not for economy's sake alone that the campers live in tipis.[24] In new buildings, spirituality is a characteristic that many Indian clients want to see expressed somehow.

* * *

Another private aspect of the cultural revival is the teaching and recording of Native languages, described in peda-gogical literature, newspapers, and Smithsonian Institution publications. The offices of Bilingual Education and of Indian Education in the United States Department of Education in the early 1970s funded programs directed especially at children. The Native American Language Act of 1990 (PL 101-477) endorsed language protection and promotion as United States policy, and SB 2044, signed in 1992, authorized the Administration for Native Americans to make grants for developing community-based language programs. They are needed despite the persistence of culture because large numbers of Native Americans had lost contact with the old lifeways, beliefs, and practices. "If someday...nationalities all lose their language as they jump in the melting pot of America, if someday their grandchildren want to learn it...the Swedes can go back to Sweden, the Italians can go back to Italy...and they can regain their language that way. But where does the Mohawk go?" asked Sakokwenionkwas*, a Mohawk chief.[25] "A lot of times, linguistic survival is considered the same as cultural or tribal survival,"because "without your language, you can't sing sacred songs or ceremonies, and then you lose your religion."[26] William J. C'Hair*, founder of an Arapaho language camp in 1986, said that the practice of tribal religion "is meaningless without language. It would be like using Japanese metric tools on an American car. The basic tools are there, but they just don't fit." One risks losing one's identity as well: "If we don't speak our languages, we'll just be brown-skinned white people".[27]

Language is also important as an ethnic boundary, because those who lack appropriate powers of speech can be excluded from group activities, especially Native religious rituals. Native Americans may wish to keep some would-be participants away for the sake of religious purity, in order to separate the indigenous population from others in social terms, or even to hold some terrain that potential conquerors cannot invade. Tim Giago*, editor of *Indian Country Today*, and Wilmer Mesteth*, spiritual leader at Pine Ridge, report that some Lakota healing ceremonies may be restricted to tribal members and that some tribal governments are considering sanctions to prevent the revealing of too much to outsiders, although offers of money for religious knowledge are impossible for some people to resist. Regis Pecos* said that Pueblo people had adopted secrecy to protect their religion during periods of oppression and against those who sought to convert them.[28] As self-determination reinforces Indian ideas of nationhood, monuments project a national image and are languages' companions in the formation of national identity.[29]

The effort to teach children their ancestral tongues became a factor in developing tribally operated schools and school systems, an idea initiated in the 1960s among the Navajo that spread to other reservations. The Ojibwe, Pueblo, Lakota and Dakota, Oneida, Navajo, Menominee, and Mohawk schools (20–22, 63–64, 75–77, 92, 97–98, 114, 128–130) are among those that have responded to the cultural revival manifested in the drive to preserve and transmit tribal language. Insofar as such schools cut the dropout rate, they may assist tribal and personal economic survival as well.[30]

* * *

Religious survival and revival, and language renewal, are visible to outsiders only by invitation of the participants. A more public manifestation of cultural renewal is the powwow. Originally a dance associated with Plains peoples, it has become widespread. Now sometimes held in urban arenas as well as on reservation grounds, the powwow is an occasion for confirming identity. It is also a place for testing innovations in dance, music, costume design, oratory, ceremony, and entrepreneurial skill. "The Gathering of Nations" powwow held in 1990 attracted 30,000 people, and while some found the standards untraditional in various ways, truth to the past was not the reason why they came. A Cree woman explained that "we are finding some pride in our culture and our religion. Now our songs and our dances are being taught to our children with respect, unlike 30 or 40 years ago."[31] Others, although trained in the arts of American success, nevertheless dance at powwows to find renewal and cultural fellowship.

Bill Franklin*, a well-known Miwuk dancer, said recently that "within the last few years, our Indians have come alive to their senses. They say that they are Indians and they want to keep their traditional things going and keep their culture alive.... I see this a lot. I go to big times [festive gatherings] and see the younger generation picking it up and taking charge of it."[32]

Franklin himself began to practice Indian dance about a half century ago, and the ritual Sun Dance was revived at Pine Ridge in South Dakota during the 1950s,[33] but the widespread movement came later. In the late 1960s, tribally controlled colleges and Native American Studies programs began. Just then, the Hupa of California became vividly aware of their status as Indians by facing the threat of termination, by reading about land claims, and by organizing against a dam. Local observers discerned increased youthful participation in dance, a gradual rise in craft work, the writing of tribal history and autobiography, and the cooking of traditional acorn soup. In the 1960s, the fed-eral government realized that sending Anglo instructors to teach Indian arts was an outmoded idea and began to emphasize partnership and joint planning.[34] By February 9, 1970, Time had noticed enough of this kind of activity to devote its cover story ("Tonto Is Dead") to Native feelings of Indianness, including the quest for ecological balance, and political activism.

From that time to the present, Native American culture has flourished in most parts of the country. While fewer than twenty Indian artists of the Northwest Coast produced work for sale in the early 1960s, now about a hundred do so.[35] Architect Rina Naranjo Swentzell* finds more study and explication of culture occurring among the Tewa, to which several prominent Indian intellectuals belong. The Harry V. Johnston Cultural Center in Eagle Butte, South Dakota (53), held a workshop to show techniques of butchering and tanning buffalo.[36] The Nez Perce formed a Cultural Resources Program in 1988, having for some time revived beadwork, corn-husk-basketmaking, and buckskin tanning.[37] Tribal arts, powwows, the Sun Dance, healing rituals, and religious activities experienced a remarkable expansion in the 1970s.[38] The 1960s and 1970s also saw a resurgence of interest in traditional dress.[39] In the early 1990s, the White Mountain Apache "used the Persian Gulf conflict as an occasion to rejuvenate the prayer and communal responses embodied in their War Dance."[40]

Several hundred Osage attend cultural education events, forming a "very active group" inspired by a "relatively recent idea. Survival mechanisms that have lasted thousands of years are being reactivated....There's a Renaissance going on in Osage culture," according to Carl Ponca*, former director of the Osage Museum and teacher of the language. Although an Osage museum opened first in 1938, it was renovated in 1967 and reopened in its present form, displaying some of the beadwork, finger-weaving, embroidery, metalwork, and other arts that are also practiced by Ponca (Pun-kah-wah-ti-an-kah) and his wife, Billie*. In the East, the past generation has seen "a moment of change: from cultural decline" into a period of reconstruction (71).[41] Farther west, important changes in Navajo rugs have been made by the weavers since the 1980s; they move away from "regional styles developed primarily at the insistence of the area trading posts".[42] Cultural references are employed in teaching unlikely subjects; Vi Colombe*, a teacher in South Dakota, shows children how to make dreamcatchers, originally Canadian Cree artifacts that the Wisconsin Oneida believe they created and that members of many tribes have adopted.[43] She relates dreamcatchers to the Lakota legend of the weaver Ikotomi, E. B. White's *Charlotte's Web*, Native American history, and mathematics.[44] Finally, in 1990, the Indian Arts and Crafts Board Act (PL 101-644) prohibited people who are not members of state or federally recognized tribes, or not certified as artisans by such tribes, from selling their art as Indian-made. While this has caused hardship to people whose ancestors did not exert themselves to join the tribal rolls, it offers support for the greatly expanded activity of officially recognized Native Americans in the arts.[45]

Courses in pottery, beadwork, quillwork, basketry, canoe-carving, and numerous other traditional activities are offered at tribal schools and colleges, at reservation museums, and by Native American artisans. They are intended primarily for people of indigenous descent for whom these arts constitute a source of income as well as personal satisfaction, but other participants may be welcomed. The University of California at Berkeley is duplicating photographs, recordings, and anthropological notes to help tribes learn about lost aspects of culture.

Cultural invention and adoption have occurred before. Bessie Dog* introduced the still popular jingle dance dress in 1931, and tribes in South Dakota adopted fancy-dancing from Oklahoma Native performers in the 1950s. Elmer Schuster*, Yakima member of the Sagebrush dance group, points out that "most of the war dances they do did not originate from the Yakimas. Not until the late 1800s and early 1900s did the Yakimas even perform war dances." He and his group were trying to develop dances corresponding to Yakima legends—that is, they were modifying tradition and inventing parts of an innovative and continuing culture. Nampeyo*, a Tewa woman whom the Hopi instructed, was the key figure in the Hopi pottery revival around 1900. San Ildefonso Pueblo's famous polished black ware was a conscious revival of a ceramic style found in excavations, with potters encouraged by the School of American Research in Santa Fe. Fostering of craft work was intrinsic to New Deal Indian policy. These efforts were, however, more sporadic than current ones are.[46] James Clifford believes that identity, "considered ethnographically, must always be mixed, relational, and inventive," just as its physical manifestations must be, whether in literature or in architecture. He writes of every culture as "an impure present-becoming-future."[47]

A sixfold increase in membership in a craft cooperative occurred at San Juan Pueblo between 1968 and 1977, and there was noticeable improvement in the production of ritual objects and the authenticity of ceremonial dances during the 1970s.[48] At this time, the Oke Owe'enge Arts and Crafts Cooperative building (1973) was built by Bradbury & Stamm, working with architect Andy Acoya*. Emphatically horizontal, the pale-surfaced building recalls the solid geometry of pueblo architecture, despite the considerable amount of untraditional glass on the facade, which is well shaded by a deep overhang. Not demonstrative, but suited to its purpose of offering work and display space, the building combines aspects of old and new architecture, just as the cooperative understands both ancient techniques and modern marketing. It reinstates pueblo tradition among the buildings near it, which are larger in scale, more sculptural, and colored differently.

* * *

The cultural manifestation closest to architecture is contemporary Native American literature. Like architecture and the other arts, literary activity has been newly vigorous since the 1960s. The writers compose in English and use forms such as the novel, essay, and poem, which have their basis in Europe; the architects build schools, office buildings, and museums of European origin. There is no single literary direction, nor is there a single Amerindian dance or religion or modern building form.

Nevertheless, themes common to many works of recent Native American prose and poetry are found in architecture. Among them are the definition of identity; the hope for connection to sites and a culture that may be mixed or unitary; conflict and compromise with the majority's lifeways and demands; the presence of wise older people or of individuals with mystical powers, who may be modern shaman figures and who sometimes determine building programs; and frequent reference to alcoholism and family instability—for which cures may be assisted by the appropriate built environment.

Like books and poems, but unlike some of the more private events such as religious rituals and language classes, the new buildings are directed both at the creators' own people and at others: "Inwardly-directed arts help to maintain ethnic identity, while externally-directed arts project to an outside world an ethnic image that is part of a boundary-defining system."[49] Ray Halbritter*, the business representative of the Oneida in New York State, implies that individual development and group self-confidence precede successful external projection of culture. He emphasizes continuing "strength in ourselves. Vietnam POWs kept their belief in being American. . . . Indians—if you have that belief, and that's why we emphasize the culture—if you were moved to Asia, you'd still be an Indian. . . . You have to start with the substance," the group traditions still meaningful today. It may be that Indians "continue to identify with a way of life that in reality is once removed in time or space and is largely ceremonial, symbolic, and emotional in its manifestations,"[50] but while the revivals "may not be the traditions of 100 or even 1,000 years ago,...they do reflect that the people and their traditions are as dynamic as the environment that shaped them."[51] Coast Salish people "are trying to piece back together those teachings. The teachings come from all of the tribes, and all of them have a valuable role in our future."[52]

Approaches to the past vary widely. Some Native Americans disagree that being Indian means resurrecting precontact or nineteenth-century practices, while others strive to adapt historical phenomena to modern needs.[53] Comparable issues affect the arts of other minority groups.[54]

Halbritter stresses that economic independence enables the culture to flourish: "Maximum freedom and money is the most fungible resource, in my opinion. I want our people to be hard-working again. A lot of our leaders don't say that. They say, 'White people took it from us and now they have to pay.' That's true, but what do we do now?" He proposes not complaint, but education: "Some people just want to drink, so we have to aim at the children. Three years ago, there were just four [Oneida] people in higher education. Now there are sixty-six, including vocational education. We work person by person. We employ someone to go and find them. Be a welder—anything!"—although he finds a four-year college better than a two-year school, vocational education more practical than art school.

Charles Wheelock* of the Oneida Nation's planning department in Wisconsin hopes to create buildings that express the culture and the place in which it is found, to contribute to the well-being of the tribe. Like many other tribal planners and architects, he is aware of working within a "larger context of cultural revival...throughout the country...connected to the revitalization of our heritage and pride." The Oneida used not to address these issues, but the improved economy, based on casino revenues and other income sources, allows them to do so.

They study and incorporate their culture in both houses and community buildings by responding "to natural materials and to the environment," although Wheelock is quick to point out that an exemplar of those interests in Wisconsin was the Euro-American Frank Lloyd Wright. Nature and historical building practices are also emphasized in new buildings for the New York Oneida.

Conceiving even newer and freer designs will mark what Wheelock calls a "new phase" of integrating ideas "artistically and functionally." The artistry is a relatively new concept, because the Oneida have begun to think of exteriors, the public communicators, as well as of plans and function. "We're rediscovering some of the dynamics of Native American architecture," he says, and doing the research to accomplish this "takes more than building just a tipi." They have become "resensitized" to the tribe's origins in New York and to issues of nationalism, which have "led us back to the Oneida world view, or...defining exactly what that is."

Another result of this new approach is a plan to remodel the exterior of Tesuque Pueblo to its condition in the 1930s, a period for which accurate records exist. Arctic Slope Consulting Group will adapt the interior spaces for current use, especially at ceremonial periods, and this may involve modernization. It is unnecessary to do all the proposed work merely to attract tourists, so Pueblo members must regard this as a desirable effort from a cultural viewpoint. They hope to recapture a modern period within living memory, but one that antedates television and the pickup truck.

Inventing a new tradition based on historical models is an additional type of response. Pojoaque Pueblo plans the Poeh Cultural Center, for which several designs have been made (65, 66).[55] A document produced in connection with the first plans by McHugh Lloyd Tryk of Santa Fe quotes Pojoaque sources indicating that "between the late 17th and the early 20th century, all of our traditions were lost because our people were scattered....Today we have a very real and active interest in reviving our arts and crafts and have asked for the help of our Pueblo neighbors in this effort. In 1973, for the first time in many years, we performed the Comanche, the Buffalo...[and other] dances." The neighbors may have been glad to help, having in some cases revived other traditional forms themselves: Acoma had at least six times as many potters in 1992 as in 1972; San Felipe revived beadwork; Santa Ana revived pottery and weaving in the 1970s.[56]

Even more invention is important for the Fort McDowell Reservation in Arizona, where the proposed Beeline Highway has stimulated the tribe to ask what the roadside architecture will suggest about the Yavapai Apache. Developers want to build commercial and industrial facilities along 4.5 miles that touch tribal lands. At the tribe's request, Don W. Ryden and Wyatt*/Rhodes, architects in Phoenix, prepared development guidelines in April 1993.

The architects were asked, among other things, to "create a style" responsive to landscape and climate, the desert setting being the "unifying theme." Innovation is needed because aboriginal cave and wickiup dwellings cannot be transformed to serve today's needs. Such elements are specified as moderate height, battered parapets, stone veneer or sand-finished stucco, separate rather than ribbon windows, colors that blend well but with darker tones preferred, Yavapai symbols and Yavapai basket patterns for ornament, rustic materials that harmonize with more modern ones, and landscaping with desert plants. Elements of regional architectural tradition can be chosen after consideration and debate; they can then inaugurate a new phase of Yavapai architecture. The architects and their clients find that Yavapai interaction with other Native peoples and with Anglos is as important a part of their history as the pre-Columbian stage, so that elements taken from the land and the earliest known traditions can be blended with those introduced during the building of the army fort, and with elements from later times. All of them now belong to the group.[57]

Tradition has been invented elsewhere. Essays edited by Eric Hobsbawm and Terence Ranger describe the development of the Scottish tartan, British royal ritual, Welsh lore, and other matters often regarded as dating to a period obscured by Celtic mists.[58] The process of inventing a godlike image of the homely Emperor Augustus was displayed in sculptures at the British Museum about a decade ago. When Emperor Constantine issued an edict of religious toleration, the process of inventing tradition was quickly revealed: Church leaders had to find ways to house Christian ritual in ways that reflected imperial patronage; formerly, house churches and small conventicles had been scarcely visible from the street. The great five-aisled pilgrimage basilicas of Rome and Jerusalem, the frequently used three-aisled plans, the symbolic associations of centrally planned churches all developed by the end of the fourth century, initiating traditions that we now take for granted. On a smaller scale, but with equally wide geographic distribution, we now see the invention of modern Amerindian architecture, and many participants hope that it will establish new traditions.

* * *

There is another and vitally important reason for emphasizing the Native component in much recent Amerindian architecture. Even the least aesthetically successful of these new buildings has to do with what their sponsors call medicine. In customary English usage, the word means a tangible substance taken internally or applied to restore

health. Among Native Americans, it may also be intangible yet effective, as good psychotherapy is. There are times when the Indian Health Service's pharmaceutical products are no substitutes for rituals, actions, relationships—or today, the renewal of culture. Architecture has become an aid to restoring communal health.

The diseases to be cured are those described by poets and novelists, social workers and teachers, tribal leaders and statisticians. Following destruction by Euro-Americans of the customary lifeways, poverty and purposelessness developed on many reservations. Poor and inappropriate educational services, lack of employment, and unwelcome pressures toward assimilation were coupled with ongoing discrimination against even those who tried to do what the majority society demanded. Joseph Cushman, planner for the Nisqually in Washington, summarized the situation: "Anyplace you poke, it hurts."

Beautiful or merely appropriate architecture cannot solve all these and other problems. They are caused by national policy, by social tendencies, by personal factors. They can be cured only by comprehensive treatment, aided by the majority society's good will, money, and legal help. But architecture can provide a supportive enclosure facilitating individual and group activity. Its siting, whether secretive or prominent, expresses community values and the desire to communicate only with tribal members or with others. Its materials and colors, its external form and interior spaces may reinforce tradition or revise tradition to suit modern needs and expectations. The process of building may unify fragmented groups, or it may reinforce a sense of communal solidarity through decision-making and construction practice. A building that abstracts elements of the damaged culture, refreshing it and preparing it for use in a more optimistic future, can be an important symbolic adjunct to other healing processes.

The connection is so frequently made between healing and cultural reinforcement that it has become almost commonplace. When there is the possibility of building something to enclose a healing activity, the connection between architecture and "medicine" is made as well. A headline in the Lakota Times about fitting the Rosebud IHS Hospital into its setting announced, "Art is a powerful medicine for new Rosebud hospital."[59]

"Music," says Pura Fe*, a performer, "is not just an art form, it is medicine, a very important tool used for rehabilitation. The revolving door syndrome that many Native people with addictive personalities find themselves in seems to stop turning when you reinforce their treatment with traditional art." Maggie Hodgson*, organizer of the

"Healing our Spirit" conference of indigenous people, sponsored by the National Association for Native American Children of Alcoholics, echoed Pura Fe's sentiments. Parris Butler* said flatly that "the high degree of alcoholism is a result of the cultural vacuum that we have." The Association on American Indian Affairs appealed for funds in 1994 to support the "Healing Circle" program of alcoholism treatment supplemented by Native therapeutic "practices such as sweatlodges, pipe ceremonies, and the customs of elders," citing success with such programs as the Standing Rock Sioux's Good Red Road in Iowa, and the Pueblos' Turquoise Lodge in New Mexico. The Native American Rehabilitation Center of the Northwest in Portland, Oregon, offers an outpatient clinic, two residential treatment centers, and a cultural-awareness program, which would be endorsed at the other end of the United States. In New York City, Nancy Stremmel wrote to members of the American Indian Community House that "we are seeing now, in substance abuse programs, a generation of Native Americans who were raised without a sense of their traditions or culture. . . . The results of the Narcotics and Drug Research Institute study prove that cultural connections are important to mental health." John Luke Flyinghorse*, owner of a tipi-making and crafts business in South Dakota, "did not realize he could use his artistic talents to open a business until he quit drinking." Matt Vera* said that "in our communities, where alcoholism and drug addiction is rampant, I believe that the revival of our language would restore balance to our world." Eagle Butte, South Dakota, resident Randolph G. Runs After* believes that "with the return of the language, our youth will feel the pride and resulting self-esteem that comes with realizing you can have the best of both worlds without sacrificing who you are. A war on alcohol is unwinnable if the takojas [grandchildren] can't understand the wisdom of their elders." In Minneapolis, the Indian Women's Resource Center is a drug-treatment facility centered around Indian religion, and Porky White*, who has a sweatlodge at Long Lake and who leads ceremonies and instructs others, was honored at a New Year's Eve Sobriety Powwow. In the same state, The City, Inc., offers culturally appropriate counseling to youths and families in trouble with the law, and makes available an Indian Education Curriculum, a Drum and Dance Group, a maple-sugar-bush camp, and trips to the sacred catlinite quarry at Pipestone.[60]

Young people are special targets of attention. The Denver Indian Health and Family Services has for four years sponsored a Sobriety Run "to recognize those who have lost their lives directly or indirectly to the use of alcohol and other drugs and to promote healthy alternatives and lifestyles for all people." Proceeds will be used, among other things, to "defray costs of a traditional camp for American Indian Youth" living in the area.[61] The American Indian Community House in New York City lists the concerns of the National Youth Agenda: spirituality, unity, environment, heritage, sovereignty, family, individual, education, health, economy, sobriety, and service. Sinte Gleska University's Lakol Wicon Project is a "culturally-based drug and alcohol treatment program." In Lame Deer, Montana, the Buffalo Visions Camp helps "youths break away from use of drugs and alcohol through traditional native teachings. The national Indian youth group, UNITY, co-sponsors advertisements with the National Institute on Drug Abuse cautioning that 'Drinking and Powwows Don't Mix. Choose Tradition, Not Addiction.'[62] Social scientists have not yet been able to assemble convincing evidence of the healthful effects of Native American culture or religion,[63] but many American Indians are convinced that they exist and that they may even help in the prevention of AIDS. A traditional medicine wheel is used in Vancouver to symbolize the infection's path,[64] and the Declaration of the International Indigenous AIDS Network resolves "that effective prevention of, and care for HIV/AIDS in our communities will require a return to traditional cultural values."[65] George H. J. Abrams*, former Seneca museum director, warns, however, that "charlatans have entered the shaman/healing/teaching field, to the detriment of legitimate Indian practitioners. Some Indian people have created new 'ceremonies'. . . for the benefit of marginal Indians, New Agers, and others seeking enlightenment."

For serious believers, Lori Cupp*, a Navajo doctor, "has encouraged the Indian Health Service Hospital [at Gallup, New Mexico] to add a medicine man to perform healing ceremonies. She has also recommended that when a new medical center is built, it include a traditional Navajo round room [sing room] for such ceremonies. . . . Dr. Cupp strongly believes that such steps not only show respect for the Navajo as a people but may also help in healing."[66] Her hospital pays spiritual healers to bless new additions. The pioneer healing room in privately owned hospitals may be the one at the Lander, Wyoming, Valley Medical Center.[67]

The hogan-shaped healing room for Navajo at Chinle, Arizona (1983), has a central fireplace and a square foot of sand before it, implying a connection to the earth under the building. Therapeutic sandpaintings are executed in this room, which has a fire pit in the center.[68] A steering committee of spiritual healers and community members gave continual advice and made successful demands, such as requesting the flat roof.[69] Bennie Gonzales, who designed the hospital in collaboration with Stone, Maracini, and Patterson, "did hogans for the entry area" and added a pattern to the exterior that was "almost like a [Navajo] rug." Since modern medicine requires facilities larger than the New Deal's small clinics, it is impossible to have the entire building suggest a hogan; one part suffices.

The Acoma-Cañoncito-Laguna Hospital (1978) for Pueblo peoples reflects that architectural tradition as much as was possible within the modern building, and includes a healing room used for Native American ceremonies (7).

George Clayton Pearl of Stevens, Mallory, Pearl & Campbell designed the exterior form to express the virtues of solar heating and cooling, and tried to soften institutional elements foreign to the people served.[70]

Robert Kallstrom of BLGY in Austin, who has done master plans for hospitals and worked on the Chinle building, says that even at master-plan level, his firm strives to address the culture. A Navajo building must face east and the morgue must be in a separate building, as one does not enter or use a hogan in which a person has died; cleaning staff may hesitate to enter the morgue. Because modern life requires people to work far from their families, elders, formerly cared for at home, need sympathetic housing and health care. Only recently has the Indian Health

7. Acoma-Cañoncito-Laguna Indian Health Service Hospital (spiritual healing room), San Fidel, New Mexico. Stevens, Mallory, Pearl & Campbell, 1978. (Courtesy George Clayton Pearl)

8. Hopi Guidance Center, Second Mesa, Arizona.
David Smith, ca. 1986.

Service paid for substance-abuse facilities, although those that employ culturally appropriate therapies have been urgently needed for a long time.

Prevention of illness is an active concern, so that instruction is given in traditional parenting by the Benefits of Sobriety Children's Curriculum Project for the Lakota, and a social powwow sponsored by the Healthy Start program officials in Sioux Falls is part of an "initiative to reduce infant mortality by 50% at 15 demonstration sites nationwide over the next five years."[71] Judy Roy*, chairwoman of the Red Lake School Board, said that one reason for educating Ojibwe children in their culture is to help give them a sense of self-worth, so as to fortify them against abuse of controlled substances. Arthur Zimiga* at Oglala Lakota College connected such revived traditions as the Sun Dance to a reduction of suicides among youth, and emphasized culture as an antidote to the discrimination experienced by his people. Swinomish tribal chairman Robert Joe, Sr.*, says that "we have come to a stage where our people are beginning to recognize the value of our culture and beginning to turn to it. They have wanted to turn from alcohol and drugs and are wanting a new life."[72]

Ironically, "traumatic experiences can also be considered responsible for efflorescence in the arts. For example, construction of the Kinzua Dam caused the Senecas at Allegany to band together during the 1970s. People began to express a concern for Iroquois traditions by doing beadwork and other crafts."[73]

A portion of the 1 percent for art allocated to federal building projects has paid Native American artists for work in Indian Health Service hospitals (15, 118). Cultural artifacts are installed in patients' lounges, visitors' waiting rooms, and other conspicuous locations. Tribal symbols, colors, and images provide exterior ornament. Indoors, murals include clan symbols, the medicine wheel—a particularly suitable form seen in ornament and posters—landscapes, animals, and people engaged in ritual, healing, or productive traditional activity. The hospital alone is important to physical health and to people's future; one designed in a culturally sensitive way may help to cure the whole person, not simply one disease.

Buildings are therefore significant in this process. Some of them accommodate ritual. The buildings embody tribal values and traditions, or they proclaim supratribal affiliations to promote communal pride that may enhance psychological well-being. Gary Beck*, former tribal chairman at Happy Camp, California, insisted on an attractive office building that suited its wooded surroundings rather than on one that demonstrated modular efficiency; it is hardly coincidental that above the reception desk hang T-shirts bearing messages that contrast traditional wholesome culture with the evils of substance abuse. Bright yellow T-shirts commemorated the completion of the Stanley Red Bird Lakota Studies Building at Sinte Gleska University on the Rosebud Reservation (110, 111); the workmen included tribal members who studied construction skills after years of trouble with alcohol, and the construction supervisor, Jim Stands-and-Looks-Back*, is a recovering alcoholic proud of his ability to work for his Lakota people since achieving sobriety. The Hopi Guidance Center, where personal and social prob-

lems are treated, incorporates walls of an older stone (and in that sense, traditional) building because concerned tribal members insisted on it (8).[74]

Murals with Native American themes, one of them by a Navajo, Little River Simpson*, adorn the Intertribal Indian Organization social-service center in Farmington, New Mexico, because the artist was sentenced to execute it as a penalty for public intoxication.[75] Dennis Sun Rhodes*, the Arapaho president of the AmerINDIAN Architecture firm, believes that "Indian spirituality is a powerful way to get people off alcohol." He hopes that in a rehabilitation facility that his firm is planning for the Omaha in Nebraska he "can meet the challenge of enabling the program to work more effectively." The architects are thinking of "a meditation court as one element in the plan."

Lawrence "Okie" Joe* and his son-in-law, Izadore Thom*, direct healing activities at a longhouse (smokehouse) erected in 1986 behind Joe's house on the Upper Skagit Reservation in Washington (9). People who are ready to free themselves from abuse of alcohol or drugs apply for treatment—minors must obtain their parents' permission—and then live in the building for ten to eighty days, undergoing rehabilitation based largely on cultural

9. Ceremonial lodge (smokehouse), Upper Skagit Reservation, Washington. Lawrence Joe*, 1986.

10. Ceremonial lodge (smokehouse).

Inside the main area, beds line all sides (10). Curtains afford privacy to each patient, or "baby", who is there "to start a new, cleaner life. He is taught how to walk as a new person…from that first day. A babysitter follows him around all the time"; the supervisor is also known as a "dad," and he may look after the "baby" even after the patient leaves the building.

In California, Bill Franklin*, when learning about Miwuk dance,

> began to learn about drugs and alcoholism. So I built this house out here in back, 36 feet by 24 feet, and we had our meetings here Saturday and Sunday. Saturday night, we'd practice singin' and dancin'. This keeps the kids…from going down and drinkin' or carousin' around….That was one of the things I was thinkin' about when I built this building here, to keep the young people out of trouble…and you're learning something about our culture and keeping it alive.[76]

practices originated by the tribe or absorbed by it. "We're trying to make Indians out of Indians in this place," said Lawrence Joe. Nooksack and Swinomish people initiated those from the Upper Skagit Reservation, and the initiation ritual was borrowed from the Lummi. It could not be generated from spiritual centers on the reservation, as "no place is left where we can send them [patients] now…. Nothing sacred is out there anymore," said Joe, in apparent reference to the injured sacrality of the natural surroundings.

The modest structure may not appear to be a religious setting, but it is purified, just as other spiritual settings are. Someone cleans it before any course of healing is begun. A ritual swim in cold water, at an isolated site suggested by experienced hunters, is taken at an intermediate point in the cure. The building was originally a shed for drying nets, but Lawrence Joe's family moved and completed it. "I drug it here, practically put it up by myself," he said. "My granddaughter nailed the shingles," and others assisted. He was familiar with this type of building because his great-grandfather, Jimmy, "owned a smokehouse at Sauk," and he "also used Charlie Moses's large one in Marble Mount, Washington." The usual building of this type is 80-feet long; this is a "mini-one." Usually, a small kitchen building stands beside the longhouse, but here, a kitchen was added at the left end, as space was limited. Smokehouses are usually made of wood; this one is constructed of any available materials. It is nonetheless recognizable because of its function and overall rectilinear form.

Other examples exist elsewhere. For Oklahoma's Indians who need treatment for alcoholism, the Kullihoma residential treatment center on Chickasaw land near Ada, not originally intended to be culturally referential, is a particularly suitable place, since it is built within a berm and from the approach side resembles an aboriginal earth lodge.[77] A sweatlodge has been built on the grounds. Children with problems are counseled in the tipi at the center of the Four Winds School at the Fort Totten Reservation in North Dakota, as the medicine-wheel plan of the building allowed for a circular heritage and ceremonial area where four axes cross (77).

For youths in serious trouble, two new hogan-inspired juvenile detention centers at Chinle and Tuba City on the Navajo Reservation are designed to reinforce the lessons to be learned there (49). The word "jail" is not used, as rehabilitation and not just punishment is intended. Even a detention center "goes against the Navajo tradition," as a BIA administrator points out, but since something of the kind is needed in today's mixed society, these are meant to be improved versions.

For the first time, community members have been consulted about design. Just as there are different areas of occupation in a hogan, determined by the cardinal points, there are functional and religious distinctions in these plans. The entrance is at the east, and separate areas are designated on the other sides for men, women, and the overseers. Both have central courtyards for gathering the inmates and for performing Navajo ceremonies. Robert

Webb, the architect in charge of these projects, has worked with the BIA to develop national standards for detention facilities in which the "intent is to take them back to their roots" to increase the "strength they get from their culture and beliefs."[78] Both Navajo facilities are made of concrete block, but the exterior patterns are different in response to the wishes of tribal consultants. The group at Chinle wanted a design with a central smokehole, but at Tuba City concern about water leakage suggested a sloping roof.

To enhance historical knowledge, to increase group pride, and as preventive medicine, Lakota heritage is taught at the Little Wound School in Kyle, South Dakota, in a significant place: the head of the modified buffalo-shaped plan (92). No longer must Native children attend schools where the intent is to "kill the Indian, save the man"—that is, to suppress Native culture and religion in favor of those imposed by Euro-Americans. Children who have not absorbed Native lessons about wholesome living need other accommodation; conversion to a young people's alcohol-rehabilitation center is anticipated for the former Chief Gall Inn near Mobridge, South Dakota, originally built as a tribally owned resort that evokes an encampment of tipis (70). George Barta, director of the Native American Alcohol Treatment Center in Sioux City, Iowa, said that "a cultural approach would most likely be used to help teens recover from alcohol and [substance] abuse."[79] People of all ages will receive counseling in a special room within the proposed Northern Cheyenne Cultural Center. Architect Dennis Sun Rhodes* makes the connection, too: "We have to keep telling ourselves that we're a viable people, that we come from a culture that has a lot of symbolic beauty and philosophical truth. We must continue to tell and show by good examples these things to our young people so that we can help give them a positive identity—give them the positive sense that they're good Indian people. We should strive to maintain life as free as possible from negative addictions."[80]

* * *

Not all tribes commission culturally sensitive buildings. Some believe that their traditions have been irretrievably lost, and they have no desire to borrow ideas from their neighbors. It costs less to erect a prefabricated shed than something more thoughtful, requiring more hours of an architect's time. Many tribes lack the resources to erect anything more than the cheapest building. Some Native Americans hope to wean other Indians from what remains of their ancient ways "for their own good," for the sake of their immortal souls, or for the sake of an American "melting-pot" homogeneity that others find has melted away. It is remarkable nevertheless that there have been many attempts to erect appropriate buildings, that many of them satisfy their users, and that Native people feel increasingly empowered to express their needs and opinions, thereby contributing to a more satisfactory and healthier built environment.

3

Authenticity

"That white girl," Mama went on, "she's built like a truck driver. She won't keep King long. Lucky you're slim, Albertine."

"Jeez, Zelda!" Aurelia came in from the next room. "Why can't you just leave it be? So she's white. What about the Swede? How do you think Albertine feels hearing you talk like this when her Dad was white?"...

"My girl's an Indian," Zelda emphasized. "I raised her an Indian and that's what she is."

Louise Erdrich, *Love Medicine*

How "Indian" is the architecture discussed here? The question of authenticity arises with any innovation for peoples widely perceived as more traditional than those in the majority culture. Answers to the question may be found, or at least approximated, by reflecting on the historical and cultural situation of Native Americans in the past generation, and by applying insights from disciplines other than architectural history.

Before doing so, we must remember that there is no single definition of the people involved. Some are recognized by the United States government because they are enrolled in tribes, but there is no standard method for attaining federal recognition as a tribe; there are rules, but also several ways of becoming recognized outside them. What's more, each tribe determines its own criteria for membership. Some people are Native American because of their fully indigenous ancestry. Others are officially Indian because their sole Native ancestor was named on a tribal roll at a particular moment.

A problem in certifying that something is authentically Native American is that there are no universally recognized spokesmen, even within one tribe, and no single American Indian opinion. More than 500 recognized tribes and

bands represent great geographic and cultural differences. Membership ranges from a few families to tens of thousands. Tribal leaders are created by election, designation, and inheritance. In view of this, it is hard to find one person or even a few who can speak for all. Even supratribal organizations have had their authority challenged by young and old, by traditionalists and assimilators.

Contemporary changes in Native America that have led to architectural innovation are due to laws and court decisions, to altered expectations of the entire American society, to increased education and the enhanced self-image found in many Native groups, and to a sense of urgency in the face of threats to both culture and health.

Courts have restored alienated territory, including sacred sites, to many tribes that had to produce voluminous research to make the claims successful. For these tribes, and even for those that lost their claims, the research has strengthened community historical knowledge and ethnic pride. Native peoples have obtained federal recognition of their tribal status after documenting aspects of common history and bonds that the recognition process itself can strengthen—an ironic benefit of burdensome rules. Laws have empowered tribes seeking to solidify their populations by preventing members of other races from adopting Native children and by returning some adoptees to tribes of origin. Laws have established the legality and limits of gambling enterprises, which currently enrich several tribal governments, and other laws have supported Native businesses by adding Indian preference to contract evaluations. They have helped Native artists by making it illegal to sell art- and craft work as Indian-made when it is not.

Changes in society include the impact of the civil rights movement, which gave dignity and increased power to African-Americans and by extension to other minority groups. The idea of "Black Power" was taken up by "Red Power" advocates. They occupied various sites, including Alcatraz[1]—since property taken by the government was to be returned to Indians when it was no longer used—set up "fish-ins" developed from African-American "sit-ins," and demonstrated elsewhere. They founded tribally controlled colleges and staffed Native American Studies programs, probably inspired by Black Studies programs and the aims of historically black colleges (Hampton Institute had originally educated Indians as well). They initiated Native-oriented and Native-directed publications, enhanced cultural activity from powwows to poetry, performed on television and on the Mall in Washington, and eventually saw Ben Nighthorse Campbell, an enrolled Northern Cheyenne of mixed ancestry, elected to the United States Senate in 1992. Many of these activities followed from the gradually increasing numbers of formally educated Native Americans who write books and direct lawsuits and establish curricula and lobby legislators. These developments led to an enhanced self-image and public image for Native Americans. Indians also came to be associated with ecologically sensitive approaches to the environment, a societal interest that coincided in time with their enhanced public position and with their widespread desire to affirm their Native affiliation.

The news since the 1960s has not been all good, however. The high rates of unemployment, especially on isolated reservations, are related to substance abuse and family dysfunction, limited educational attainment, and high dropout rates. The pull of alien values characteristic of the majority culture has been a constant problem. Job-training and mental-health programs directed and staffed by Indians, tribally centered self-help recovery groups, and business development are among the many ways to fight the battles. One weapon of uncertain effectiveness is an enhanced sense of group culture, tribal or supratribal. Architecture has been given a role to play in this movement.

Most of the cultural activities are traditional ones (although, as in every culture, the practices and content are always being transformed), and they attract more public notice than architecture has done so far. Tribal office buildings, museums and cultural centers, health facilities, schools, and houses with indoor plumbing are not traditional buildings, and they have received little attention outside their places of construction. Although these buildings are produced once in a generation—not continually, as pottery and baskets are—they become the focal points for personal and community activity. They deserve consideration as conveyors of aspiration or of the stance of Native Americans between their own and the majority cultures. Although some Indians in remote locations may ignore the rest of the United States as much as possible, tribal government, federal rules and money and commodities, income from land and mineral-rights leases, television, pickup trucks, and countless other factors have brought everyone into the majority system to some degree, demonstrating that all cultures are permeable. Coercive government policy used to bring Indians and others together, but today Native Americans insist on determining just how much acculturation is acceptable, when and how to assimilate, if ever, and what messages their buildings will convey.

* * *

Then how "Indian" are these buildings? People ask this question about the products of societies seen as altered by previous colonial domination; they do not ask this question about the culture of the dominators. People ask it about smaller societies that have grown too large or complicated to allow personal communication; they do not ask it about societies that have had this character for centuries.[2] There is also a certain tendency to confuse the ancient with the authentic, as though only traditional culture—at an arbitrarily chosen moment—could represent the folk. The folk must then be seen as different from members of technologically oriented societies. Janet Abu-Lughod provides a useful summary:

> In our idea of the traditional are the following assumptions: that it is collectively built (that is, it derives from some shared sense of how its pieces connect to one another, how each dwelling is related to the space of others); that it is collectively interpreted (that is, that common meanings are attributed to its forms); and that it is collectively consumed (that is, that the use to which any single part is put is somehow related to the uses of the whole ensemble).[3]

Contemporary buildings by and for Native Americans do not always meet the first of these criteria, but they may satisfy the other two. When they do, they are at least partly traditional. They may take on some of the associated characteristics of authenticity, even in the eyes of those who imagine Native Americans as fixed in the 1890s, ignoring changes to which everyone else is expected to respond. Countering this misconception, George Horse Capture*, a well-known art curator, connects innovation to cultural strengthening when he says that "we are now engaged in the long struggle to regain some of our former glory and traditions. To do so, we must adapt some of the white man's ways and methods, but do this in such a way that we reserve and preserve our 'Indianness'."[4]

Chauncey H.* knows how to do that. He lives in a wooden house, painted white, on a standard lot on a straight street in a town in eastern North Dakota. Despite the Anglo exterior, any visitor recognizes immediately after stepping inside that this is an Indian home affected by the taste and interests of a person of Chauncey H.'s social class in America. The owner is a carver of catlinite pipes, used in Native American religious ceremonies, and is a landscape painter; his wife creates modern crafts such as lampshades in tipi form. These cultural preoccupations do not preclude having on the mantelpiece an image of the Good Shepherd flanked by Indian dolls dressed in fringed clothing and beads. A Native "God's Eye" hangs on a wall near the Christian motto "God Bless Our Home." A prominent photograph shows a granddaughter, now a lawyer, in uniform during her military service; the prestige associated with warriors and leadership is associated with a young woman today. An Indian home consists of more than direct responses to climate, materials, and ritual orientation; cultural and individual needs, available options, and symbolic function play their part here, as in all buildings.[5]

It is easier at first to understand the home of Selena Hill* on the Hopi Reservation as an Indian one because it is traditionally rectangular, with the stone-faced exterior

11. HUD house, Second Mesa, Arizona. David Sloan* & Associates, 1991.

and the log and cross-pole ceiling that are known from the Hopi past (11, 12). But the house was financed by a federal program and administered by a tribal housing authority established to administer the federal money. The house is made of concrete block under the stone, not of purely local and natural materials, and was designed by David Sloan*, a Navajo. Nevertheless, Selena Hill looked forward to moving into the house and leaving the Anglo-style residence of similar size in which she had been living, and several tribal officials expressed their pleasure in having, at last, housing that was appropriately Hopi in form.[6]

A project of a much larger scale poses the questions more obviously. Fond du Lac Community College in Cloquet, Minnesota, is affiliated with the state-college system and with the network of tribally controlled colleges (99–101) . More students are Anglo than Native American. The design architect was Thomas Hodne, of Norwegian descent. But much of the conceptual planning was done by Native people; the school was conceived particularly with the needs of American Indian students in mind; it incorporates tribal archives, ceremonial space, and traditional references; Hodne has had more experience than most architects in working for tribal clients to whose cultures he is sincerely devoted; and the local Native American population regards the college as theirs.

Most architects of contemporary Indian buildings are white, with a few Asian-Americans, and at least one of partly African ancestry. Increasingly, however, Native Americans are executing the work, although some who are legally Indian have only 25 percent Native ancestry, and some may have less than that. Native American architects executing culturally directed commissions are most numerous in Oklahoma, Arizona, New Mexico, Minnesota, and the Dakotas, with others located particularly in the Pacific Northwest; this reflects population concentrations.

Since architects of all backgrounds receive training based on European and Euro-American models, even Native American architects deeply attached to traditional culture have been trained under Anglo models of learning and exposed to the white culture that dominates their profession. All this has not diminished their desire to build in a culturally appropriate way; schooling gives them tools with which to realize that desire.

Architects today appear to take seriously the charge to learn about Native culture when the clients show interest in it; Edward Norris, who directs a community assistance program at the University of New Mexico School of Architecture, thinks that "more consideration should be given to

12. HUD house. (Courtesy David N. Sloan*)

maintaining or reviving traditional values, rather than abandoning them for the modern design that was requested by the current tribal council" at Santo Domingo Pueblo.[7] Several architects have become so absorbed by the culture that they spend years working on Indian projects and are proud of honorary adoption by the tribes. Others assert that by the end of their preparations, they knew more about tribal history and culture than their clients did, although they may not have met the tribal members who retained the most cultural knowledge. Nevertheless, when a Native American architect designs a building for his (rarely her) own people, he brings to the process an intimate familiarity normally denied even to the most studious outsider.

Building codes, licensing rules, and other legal matters are determined by the majority society, but tribal governments may adopt them willingly in the interests of safety and health. Apart from funds recently obtained from gambling profits, most of the building money comes from federal sources, although some of it is the tribes' own, held in trust in Washington. Other money comes from special acts of Congress and from appropriations for generally applicable programs in education and health and—since 1964—housing.

The buildings should be considered Indian all the same. One reason is that the tribal clients say they are theirs—one might call this the Zelda's daughter principle, following the epigraph for this chapter. Another reason becomes clear by analogy: Trade blankets and silver jewelry were not aboriginal, but have become acculturated in certain tribes and are identified as Indian by everyone. Moreover, since the passage of the Indian Self-Determination and Education Assistance Act of 1975, more Native Americans have managed architectural and other projects, as well as federal programs. The character of the buildings is established by the tribal clients within budgetary limits. A tribal museum, for instance, may incorporate or combine features absent from local historical museums, such as chambers for sacred ceremonies, craft-work studios, language-teaching laboratories, or religious symbols either overt or concealed in the plan. Native Americans now insist on determining just how much acculturation is acceptable, when and how to assimilate, if ever, and what messages their buildings will convey.[8] The buildings emphasized in this book seem to have been adopted by the tribes for which they are intended. Tribes in the past engaged in technological and religious adoptions because enriching a society is different from making its components inauthentic. Perhaps questions about the buildings should be phrased as "Is this building accepted?" rather than "Is this building authentic, or legitimate?"

There are, of course, dissenters. George Horse Capture* is among them. "I've never seen a building that is Indian architecture except the 'Turtle' [95, 96], and maybe not that," he said, although he discussed the culturally sympathetic aspects of the Plains Indian Museum, where he was curator, without denigrating them. In trying to define a distinctive Native American design, he proposed that "European buildings are ornate and excessive. Ours are simple and functional." He dislikes architects who add "diamond shapes and step pyramids to earn their megabucks." Perhaps there cannot be such a thing as an Amerindian architecture entirely separate from that of the mainstream, or perhaps it is hard for any culture to devise its own complete expression after not quite three decades of trying.

"At one time," said Horse Capture, "we wanted to be like you [whites]. Now we want to keep our differences." In

his circles at the University of California at Berkeley, it was generally agreed that those entitled to maintain those differences were "a quarter or more Indian; raised in a cultural context that shaped your thought which has to come from your heart and not from a book you read in Anthropology 101; recognized by the tribe; and ready to give something back to their communities."

He is not the only authority who finds that people unable to meet these criteria cannot contribute—at least not ideally—to Native American communities. Henry Gobin*, a Tulalip tribal administrator, quotes Dave Warren*, a cultural consultant and administrator, who some years ago found reservation buildings designed by outsiders to be not "valid." Warren said they were not "an appropriate survival mechanism....If a building is designed, you and I [Native people] have to be there." Apparently reluctant to give up Indian control when that control still was new, he declared that "we [Indians] have to pull ourselves [up] by our own bootstraps." By now, other Native American cultural leaders can assure him that they *have* been there, participating in the increasingly collegial processes of decision-making.

* * *

Only rarely before have architects attempted to join modernity and Indian specificity. The possibility of doing so today is an aspect of the cultural relativism that is increasing in American intellectual and artistic life, generated partly by literary and political theory and partly by disillusionment with the universalist approaches of early-twentieth-century modernism. We question the idea of a single American way or a "typical American" person. Our old notions of cultural purity may have been based on politicians' or on ethnographers' perceptions rather than on the universal belief of the people being observed. Now "we are in a period of heteroglossia...in a world where syncretism and parodic invention are becoming the rule, not the exception."[9] Architectural publications today more often focus on buildings in regions, or those used by specific cultural groups.[10] In this context, contemporary Native American buildings are expected to generate ideas, not about pure architecture or spatial potential alone, but also about nationhood and culture—culture surviving, and culture being regenerated.[11]

Aspects of Native American arts are being discussed with the same open approaches. Mark St. Pierre*, when writing about recent Lakota arts, says that "we must examine the notion of cultural purity. Contact with the non-Indian is seen as a deadly influence. This extremely ethnocentric view denies the reality of precontact intertribal wars, migrations, etc. There is and never was any such thing as a pure culture." Trade alone, in objects and ideas, fosters intercultural exchange. Asian Indians find their work similarly misunderstood. Vishaka Desai, director of galleries at Asia House in New York City, faced the "attitude that if it's Asian art, it's always traditional, and if it is contemporary, it has to be western."[12]

Criticizing the "morbid attachment to the date 1890 as the end of any valid Sioux art," St. Pierre[13] makes a point applicable also to current architecture that need not be aboriginal in order to be expressive within tribal culture. According to S. R. Dixon, "What a Native person calls traditional may not be what an outsider would call traditional. The reverse is also true.... Many artists working in 'non-traditional' forms speak of their work using much the same language as those" whose work more obviously continues older art forms.[14] Thomas F. Johnson, a musicologist, sees danger in establishing a standard of authenticity in Native American music, from which an analogy may be made to architecture; he wonders whether the live, evolving musical tradition will ossify through transmission by records and tapes, and pleads for process rather than fixed tradition.[15] It is also possible for traditional living patterns to be maintained in buildings that do not look traditional. And untraditional buildings may also embody certain new aspirations of those who commission or inhabit them.

The years around 1890, with the last Indian physical resistance to domination, marked an important stage in power relationships. But using 1890 to define the limit of genuine Amerindian culture ignores the variation in mutual influence between Native people and others before that date. Cultural descriptions of that time should be evaluated carefully before being taken as binding on the present and future because it was a particularly traumatic period in Native American history, when we might find special emphases given in descriptions of religion and in historical narrative. Even before that date, there were probably few immutable ways to record tradition, as human memory is fallible and not everything requires equal precision in the recording. While sandpainting may demand the perfect repetition of healing formulas, Shonto Begay*, a Navajo artist, acknowledges that origin stories and other religious lore may be transmitted in different ways on different parts of his reservation:[16] "A new understanding of other cultures would insist that any study, no matter how exhaustive, remains rooted in a particular time, just as particular ceremonies, on a particular night may be true for that moment and perhaps different the next time or in a different longhouse."[17]

Many creative people engaged with the arts of this moment resent being measured against late-nineteenth-century standards. Robert Houle* says that "Native artistic expression must find...and manifest itself through twentieth century medium, technique, and content. This does not mean...abandonment of one's cultural identity." Carl Beam*, an Ojibwe artist, states that "new rituals should be fabricated in order to bring along the species. The idea that the old ones have to remain the same, unchanging for thousands of years, is ridiculous." Oren Lyons* wants a "living and continuing society" that includes a traditional, rather than a BIA-approved, government, run by Onondaga who know the native language but who can also speak fluent English. Jim Enote*, project leader for the Zuni Conservation Project, says that "there's a history to each day. My elders told me, 'Don't try to make it stay the same. Since time immemorial, we have always changed and adapted.'"[18]

Even Native American religions have experienced strong outside influences. The famous explicator of Lakota belief, Black Elk*, spent years as a Christian catechetist. The All-Pueblo Indian Center's exhibit texts assert that "most Pueblo practice both religions and continue to believe there is one Creator," leaving room for as much syncretism as the individual desires. Anthropologist Murray L. Wax discerns in the text of Ed McGaa's* widely read *Mother Earth Spirituality: Native American Paths to Healing Ourselves and Our World*[19] a synthesis of "Oglala tradition with pertinent items from Euro-American tradition"—such as Empedocles' division of matter into earth, air, fire, and water—and sees McGaa's "casual incorporation of concepts stemming from Western history."[20] If the incorporation is not casual, it may be a purposeful redirection of Native belief. Living cultures adapt, and they also adopt and reject.

T. H. Lewis, when studying the changing practices of Oglala healers, found a "resurgence of half-remembered...pre-conquest mythology, beliefs, and rituals" modified for modern life by "political considerations, contaminated by exploitive factions, and diluted by invented or borrowed material."[21] At Pine Ridge, Sun Dances held between 1968 and 1972 abbreviated certain older preparatory procedures. Were these modifications made unconsciously, vitiating the strength of tradition? Or are they not as likely to have been made in response to altered conditions, just as all faiths have cast off some ideas while adopting others in response to new social and religious circumstances? Lakota spiritual leader Pete Catches* performs weddings—a non-Indian concept encouraged by nineteenth-century missionaries. He includes mixed rings and a wedding certificate, but also gestures made with a sacred pipe of blessing, and a ritual of drinking water from a bucket with a dipper. These ceremonies can be regarded as enriched by both traditions important to the participants rather than as corrupt versions of authentic Christian and Lakota activities.

There has also been a "reconstruction of legal traditions, as modern legal systems can call for a good deal of inventiveness, which raises a question of whether there is a point at which traditions become more 'invented' than 'real.'"[22] If the novelties are important enough to the culture, they are likely to endure, becoming incorporated within existing tradition. Perhaps kin-based sharing is a response to poverty rather than to ancient Native practice, but no matter: It is an idea now embedded in the lifeways of modern Native Americans.

Visitors to pueblos, which are popular symbols of cultural difference, are sometimes unaware of the extent to which ancient indigenous tradition has been altered. Spanish colonial powers introduced the framed adobe brick, the wheel used for transportation and pulleys, hallways and winding stairs, swinging doors and locks, windows, and metal tools. The areas that antedate the twentieth century, however, retain a distinctive appearance, and even areas laid out recently may include kivas. Indians have long known how to incorporate aspects of other cultures for their benefit, while retaining essentials of their culture.

If we are tempted at the pueblos "to mark out as 'authentic' some vestige of 'authenticity' beneath layers of Euro-American influence, [that] is to engage in a practice reminiscent of 19th-century romanticism.... We must firmly insist that our own experience is no less authentic than that of our ancestors, even if our existence has changed considerably from theirs. No one, after all, would say that *Beowulf* is more authentically English than *Oliver Twist*."[23]

Some alterations to tradition earn widespread disapproval, including the adoption of other tribes' ceremonial garments for purely commercial purposes, or the desecration of cultural symbols by using them to trim taco stands. Equally unpalatable are the Honest Injun and Ten Little Indians Native-owned tax-free cigarette shops in North Carolina and Oklahoma, although the owners may plead that the names are necessary for financial survival. Some tribes even hesitate to add any traditional ornament to bingo halls and casinos lest the forms be vitiated by association with purely mercenary goals, but other tribes, proud of their ability to generate income, use robust wit to make

obvious their ownership of gambling facilities (149, 150). Architect Dennis Sun Rhodes* advises people to remember the long history of gambling in many Native cultures, including those of the Navajo and Plains nations. Money is being made in connection with religion, but even though this is new for Native Americans, it is a practice well known from other cultures and religions and should be judged similarly by outsiders. The Roman Catholic religion maintains its dignity despite the popularity of bingo in the parish hall and medals showing the fictitious Saint Christopher. Native religions also maintain their dignity despite occasional dubious activities.

There are times when practices that appear inauthentic at first have an underlying sincerity. Executants who imitate Navajo sandpaintings explain that they alter the format, material, and critical details so as to preserve the distinction between the sacred and the profane.[24] When presenting aspects of Shinnecock culture to visitors to her reservation on Long Island, New York, Elizabeth Hale*, who calls herself Princess Thunderbird for these occasions, wears a Seminole-style skirt and southwestern jewelry. The name and attire proclaim cultural difference immediately, and that, rather than any specific tribal tradition, is the point. Other reservation residents concerned with cultural regeneration and strength also know that much tradition has been lost so they must relearn it, borrow it, or invent it.

Similarly, the Mashantucket Pequots' powwow at the Hartford Civic Arena in 1993 imported models for regenerated dance and other cultural activity, as their own traditions had largely disappeared. At the Indian Cultural Center at Pembroke State College in North Carolina, Plains dances predominated and women wore clothing that looked Seminole, the choices having been made by the participants.[25] N. Scott Momaday* wrote that his mother, as a young woman, "began to see herself as an Indian.... She imagined who she was. This act of the imagination was, I believe, among the most important events of my mother's early life, as later the same essential act was to be among the most important of my own."[26] Why should Indians not do this, when other cultures constantly shift and alter their ways, incorporating useful new elements within a still-recognizable identity?

Virginia Dominguez is clear about the preconceptions involved in this discussion, finding it a nineteenth-century idea to distinguish between traditional and modern societies, the latter implicitly "more flexible, less invariant, more able to change and grow. 'Modern' became the self-perception of those in northwestern Europe.... 'Traditional' societies are assumed to be rooted in the past but to undergo little historical change."[27] The modern people did their own inventing during periods of rapid transformation of societal and therefore cultural change. Reflecting a comparable situation today, Native Americans decide when to change and how to do it.

Native people may call on the expertise of outsiders—architects, linguists, or others. The Winnebago asked James Howard to teach them their history.[28] Tribes welcome their architects' research, as the historical sources are rarely available on a reservation. Museum personnel and historians know that their presentations may have an unpredictable impact on Native American cultural change. Herman Viola, editor of a Smithsonian volume on Indian life, described his admiration of a Gros Ventre Sun Dance lodge. "Oh, yes," said a tribal member, "It's exactly the way it should be. We laid it out following a photograph we saw in a Smithsonian book."[29] George Horse Capture* might have predicted that when he said wryly, "In the old days, there were only a few real Indians. Now there's a boom. You run to a book to learn about Indians."

Michael Ames, director of the Anthropology Museum at the University of British Columbia, finds that "museum anthropologists have assisted in the creation, promotion, and distribution of acculturated artifacts on the Northwest Coast of North America, thus contributing to what is now being referred to as the 'renaissance' of Indian art in that area."[30] Anthropologists decipher meanings in works of art. Critics and historians promote and legitimize art and artists through exhibitions and other means.[31] There is potential distortion in having an anthropologist appear on tribal land at a particular moment to record current activities that, through the process of recording and writing, later become canonical accounts of the culture. Recorders work under limitations—the number and aptitude of informants, circumstances relating to the political situation, the time spent among respondents, and so forth.

Of course, museum displays do not convince everyone. At the Makah Cultural Research Center at Neah Bay, Washington, the man in charge said that the building was designed like the longhouse reconstructed from material excavated at Ozette, a site occupied by ancestors of the present Makah. That longhouse had a single-sloped roof, although the museum has a double-pitched section at one end (36). Photographs made around 1900 of longhouses demolished by government order in 1903 show a double pitch, but the museum representative said that they were "not authentic." Despite the evidence of cultural change, he maintained that only the oldest known architectural form could represent the true Makah architecture.

The Native Americans for whom culture is being regenerated or invented are distinctive, but the phenomenon of cultural invention for political and social purposes is not new. When Emperor Constantine's Edict of Milan legitimized Christianity, officials of the early church immediately had to commission new building forms—large, public churches—that suited the religion but were worthy of the emperor's patronage. They had to become authentic expressions of early Christianity. Constantine's architects faced the same challenge that confronts architects working for tribes today: how to design visually distinctive, spiritually or emotionally persuasive buildings that are culturally specific in a manner understandable to contemporary users. In both cases, the buildings had to be partly up-to-date so as to imply a progressive future, but in both cases, there was also recourse to the venerated past—in Rome, to the columnar halls of the first two Imperial centuries and to parts of disused pagan buildings, and in America, to evocations of indigenous Indian building types, spatial principles, myths, and ornament. In both cases, some experiments were abandoned. We know about the eventual development of standard church forms along with the exceptional ones, because church architecture has an almost 1700-year history. We can separate the great examples from the lesser ones, or at least each generation of historians can do so. The same holds true for mosques, also invented in response to changed religious practices.

We have had only one generation of contemporary Native American architecture. We cannot know whether this movement will also endure, or which examples will form a canon, although we can form our own critical opinions. At least a study of the recent Amerindian buildings meant to be culturally appropriate allows us to be in at the beginning, to see what the creators of something new have to say while they are dealing with the challenges. We do not often have that opportunity in architectural history.

PART II

Clients, Architects, and Design Strategies

4

Clients and Architects

We know we can never go back to teepees or lodges
but we can survive as a people by picking up the
good things the elders have left along the trail
for us.

Theodore Hoagland (Waasamo Mi Gabow),
in _Mino-Bimadiziwin_

A quarter century's experience with Native American directions in architecture may not suffice to let us predict the future. A new Bramante or Frank Lloyd Wright may appear and alter the course of Amerindian architecture. Legal and economic trends may change. There may be a shift from postmodern pluralism to a new orthodoxy in architecture.

Nevertheless, for today at least we can identify several tendencies in Native American architecture, and some may endure. Examples of each are functionally and socially successful, and they have appeared simultaneously in many parts of the continental United States. Even if the design strategies prove to be short-lived, the buildings show attempts to solve architectural and social problems. They embody Amerindian aspirations and exemplify decision-making processes of the past three decades. Paul Oliver, an anthropologist, has said it well: "The value of a built environment, therefore, is a conglomerate of its actual physical existence and the historical memories and myths people attach to it, bring to it, and project on it from other, often distant places."[1]

The direct clients are tribal officials. They may be the spokesmen for tribal councils, but some officials operate with considerable autonomy. The most important clients are all the tribal members or reservation residents — they may not be the same — but it is also necessary to satisfy the government agencies and foundations that fund many of the buildings.

Mark Speer of Architectural Resources in Hibbing, Minnesota, says that "Native Americans are our best clients from the design standpoint. They are open, it seems to me, to creativity almost more than anyone else." Other architects have found tribal members eager to offer suggestions and explanations, collaborating actively from a project's initial programming phases to the end of construction.

It is not always easy to elicit information or design ideas from inexperienced clients in any ethnic or social group, but architects who work with rather than just for Native Americans have found themselves gradually able to learn what they need to know. The process tends to take more time than it would with middle-class urban Anglo clients whose lifeways are familiar to most architects. A set of elementary guidelines for architect–Native-client inter-action was recently published in _Our Home: A Design Guide for Indian Housing_.[2] The suggestions were developed after Native American architects led regional meetings of people interested in improving Native American housing.

Who are the architects? Until the early 1970s, most Native American houses were built on reservations by indigenous craftsmen. Graduates of architecture schools were called in to design community buildings—schools, clinics, and tribal offices. Much reservation and urban work even now goes to people without Native ancestry. They usually own small firms that win commissions for nearby reservations after bidding successfully on projects announced in public notices. Some specialize in schools, health-care facilities, or housing and seek only those jobs. At several schools of architecture, studios have been held in recent years to expose Anglo students to intercultural design issues and to offer help to tribes. Among the ones not mentioned elsewhere in this book are those led by Carl Lewis at the University of Illinois, Mary McLeod at Columbia, the late Charles Moore at UCLA, and Patrick Cudmore at Harvard.

Some architects now are Native American, and for about a decade, preference points have been available for them on many reservation projects in order to enhance their competitive position. Some of the firms are only 51 percent Indian-owned, and others have mostly Anglo staff but a Native American principal. Several people properly enrolled as tribal members have European ancestors also.

Few Amerindian architects are over sixty years of age, and most are under fifty, because hardly any Indians older than that were encouraged to earn architecture degrees. The older men may not have been in practice longer because some had to defer their education until they finished preparatory schooling, military service, or the employment that financed their studies. For many years, reservation schools stressed vocational education, and the low level of many other schools serving Native Americans would have disqualified their graduates for architecture programs. Norman Suazo* at the Bureau of Indian Affairs in Albuquerque says that children were poorly prepared in mathematics and physics, and many lacked adequate skills in the English language.

Few Native American families could afford to have their sons living away at college, even if the young people were able to deal with the unfamiliar settings and assimilative pressures found there. Harrison Martin*, a young Navajo finishing his master of architecture degree, recalled that the only Native American architecture taught to him was that of the pueblos, and that few people were interested in vernacular or organic architecture. (He sees these as related to Native American work and admires the designs of Douglas Cardinal*, which impress him as organic.) Martin feels that American Indian architects need to go back to try to pick up threads dropped in pre-

contact times and leap from there to the present, although that is a difficult feat to accomplish.

Engineering is the profession suggested to most young Native American men—and now women—who are adept at mathematics and the physical sciences, as it seems to offer a more predictably secure future. There is even the American Indian Science and Engineering Society to encourage young people in those fields. Architects, by contrast, have fewer quantifiable skills. The perception of their design abilities is to some degree subjective. Moreover, notably successful architects often have personal contacts that help them gain commissions, but since Native American architects generally come from small towns,[3] and most, perhaps all, attended public universities, they have few contacts among private home owners or corporate patrons. Good sales technique is an important skill for architects, aided by a bit of bravado and an appropriate vocabulary, but it is contrary to many Amerindian social practices to push oneself forward, to compare oneself favorably with others, or to initiate conversations with strangers or older people. Charles Archambault*, a construction engineer, points out that "given the background we have had growing up on the reservation, we haven't a lot of self esteem or self-confidence.... [S]o till we get to the point of being able to create and assert ourselves, we're forty. We have to live with prejudice, especially in the private sector, so our market is more or less limited to Indian people."

Native American architects formed the American Indian Council of Architects and Engineers in the 1980s for mutual support and exchange of information. Some members have created a consortium large enough to participate in major projects like the study and storage facility of the National Museum of the American Indian in Suitland, Maryland. Not all eligible architects have elected to join, however, and the organization is little known to rich clients with jobs to offer. Small firms generally lack the resources to hire the excellent architectural photographers whose work impresses magazine publishers, and the firms also cannot hire public-relations specialists to promote their achievements. Some Native American architects live in states seldom represented in national design magazines, or they live on reservations where much of their work is located well away from Anglo notice. Two of the most interesting Native American designers do not own telephones, although they can be reached through intermediaries. Two highly intelligent and skilled architects, with markedly different design inclinations, execute few buildings today: Rina Naranjo Swentzell* accepts only selected house commissions, although she has been a consultant on other projects, and Dennis Numkena* has concentrated on stage design and painting since becoming exasperated by cumbersome federal rules for architecture. Under the circumstances, it is amazing that there are any Native American architects at all.

They exist because of growing public awareness that the United States cannot afford to lose the talents of minority-group youth. Colleges began to offer scholarships to Native Americans, among others, particularly from the late 1960s onward, and some studied architecture. The Navajo sponsored the training of David Sloan*, because they expected him to work for his own nation when he finished, as he has done. A few Native families may have been able to finance their children's education then or earlier. The more tolerant and optimistic climate of the 1960s and early 1970s may have encouraged Amerindians to enter professions formerly closed to them. Foundations also began to take more notice of Native needs, while state parks and education departments sometimes commissioned work on historic Amerindian sites from Native architects. At the same time, the Economic Development Administration and the Indian Health Service funded reservation projects on which they could be employed. Larry Edmondson*, an architect in Tulsa, says that "Oklahoma Indians did assimilate till around 1974. In 1974 or 1975, government money came in, so they began to reinvent the tribe."

Some opportunities lie in fields complementary to architecture, such as interior architecture, landscape architecture, and historic preservation. The first has lately attracted several Native Americans, including Bonnie Aaby* in Washington and Nancy Redeye* in New York. Ron Melchert* in Minnesota has participated as landscape architect on a number of tribal and urban Indian projects, as has James Smith* in New York; Johnpaul Jones* of Seattle is collaborating on the National Museum of the American Indian, having previously worked on Native American landscape projects in several states. Amendments added in 1992 to the National Historic Preservation Act of 1966 include provisions for support and administration of programs in tribal cultural settings.[4] One way to develop them will be to educate Indians so that they can bring Native perspective to the issues of what is worth saving in architecture, and proper ways of saving it.

Native American architects are concentrated in states with substantial Indian populations. Among those who have received degrees in architecture and related fields are Orrin Anquoe, Ron Begay, Jon M. Clark, Albert Damon, Hemsley Martin Lee, Loren Miller, Dennis Numkena, Tsosie Tsinhnahjinnie, and Burke B. Wyatt in Arizona; Vernon DeMars, Darrell A. deTienne, Jasper Vassalle, and Marlene Watson in California; Richard D. Drapeau, Steve Goldade, A. Calvin Hewitt, Surrounded-by-Enemy (Denby Deegan), and Doug Zacherle in the Dakotas; Pliny Draper in Hawaii; Leo M. Martell in Kansas; Mark Three Stars in Massachusetts; Tamara Eagle Bull, Joseph Flores, Ron Hernandez, and Dennis Sun Rhodes in Minnesota; Larry Olson, Roger Shourds, and Richard Wyman Smith in Montana; Andy Acoya, Delbert Billy, Roland Chico, Edmund Gonzales, Theodore Jojola, Fred Marionito, Harrison Martin, Robert Montoya, Dyron Murphy, David Riley, Leo Shirley, David N. Sloan, Norman Suazo, Rina Naranjo Swentzell, Michael Trujillo, and Louis L. Weller in New Mexico (a number of them employed by the BIA and several in the Sloan firm); Charles Chief Boyd, Larry Edmondson, Neal A. McCaleb, and Dean M. Wadley in Oklahoma; Fred C. Cooper and Mike Holleyman in Oregon; Gerald Eugene Stone in Texas; and Bonnie Aaby, Jeff Bartow, Gilbert Honanie, and John H. Meyer in Washington. Several are not independently licensed as registered architects, not all the registered architects execute designs for Native American clients, and some of them have withdrawn from active practice.

No matter what the background of the architects, the strategies used to make buildings specific for Native Americans are generally similar. The principal difference related to background culture is that Amerindian architects seem to feel freer to be boldly imaginative, as though their background gave them a freedom to experiment that is not available to outsiders. Ron Hernandez* suggests that the Native person's work is perceived as almost automatically supportive of tribal desires rather than of the architect's ego. The most visually striking zoomorphic and symbolic forms have been conceived by Native Americans or have been influenced by them. More Anglo architects appear to hold back slightly, as if fearing to create caricatures or buildings that might be misunderstood.

* * *

There are ways other than the ones given here to organize an account of recent architecture meant to be culturally sensitive. Sometimes the decision was made to place a project in one chapter when it might as easily have fit another, although the preponderant idea behind the design dictated the final placement. I trust that the arrangement will prove useful even though it is a first attempt, and I look forward to seeing someone else's description of the next quarter century's work.

5

Ornament

Applying ornament is the simplest way to suggest Native American possession of a building and pride in it. In Denver, a radio station catering to Native American listeners displays a stylized image of an eagle on the facade, as does a house at the Coyote Valley Rancheria in California. Farther south, the walls of the Morongo Reservation Clinic are adorned with waves and eagles in tan, brown, and turquoise. The Miami tribe of Oklahoma employs abstract shield designs on the outside of its government office, and at the Southern Ute Cultural Center in Ignacio, Colorado, symbols are painted onto the flat cinder-block structure. An ornamental band decorates the brick-faced Chickasaw Housing Authority building of 1975 by Ray James. Four seasonal images accompanied by sacred animals were the subjects chosen for the Assiniboine Community Center by Surrounded-by-Enemy* at Brockton, Montana, in the late 1970s. Geometric and linear designs on the Las Vegas Paiute Tribal Administration building of 1981 suggest that those in charge meant to advertise their distinctive identity. This was certainly the case when David Sloan* remodeled the Fort Defiance Navajo office building, which won a HUD award in 1995 for redesign. Self-proclamation is likely also for the earth-colored zigzags recalling basket designs on

the Owens Valley Paiute and Shoshone Indian Cultural Museum in Bishop, California, by Michael Black.[1] Ray Byron Frogge, Jr., added stepped designs taken from Mayan art to symbols of earth, sky, water, and moon; he included feather designs, too, on a multipurpose building for the Eastern Shawnee (13). There are many other examples of painted and inlaid ornament. It is even more common simply to display locally made artifacts and photographs on interior walls.

Health-care facilities now commonly include referential ornament. Turtle Mountain IHS Hospital in Belcourt, North Dakota (1991, Hewitt*–Drapeau*) has cornice designs recalling feathers, and lobby displays tie the practices of spiritual healers to those of today's medical personnel. On Neal McCaleb's* cast-in-place concrete tribal office and clinic for the Seneca–Cayuga in Miami, Oklahoma, the precast fascia, about 4.5 feet high, shows male and female figures holding hands in a healing prayer circle. This "made a statement about the synergism of the power of prayer of the community," although the adjacent tribal business building has the same images (14). At the Navajo Shopping Center, Church's Chicken store is decorated with a stepped-mountain motif common in the West and Southwest; its meaning of "auspicious life" is more pertinent at the Ardmore, Oklahoma, Indian Health Service Clinic, or at the Indian Island School of 1986 for the Penobscots in Old Town, Maine, by WBRC Architects & Engineers.[2] Other health-care facilities with Native American ornament are the IHS Hospital in Sacaton, Arizona, for the Gila River Pima–Maricopa primarily (1988, Wyatt*/Rhodes and DWL Architects), which opened with a traditional blessing, and the Puyallup Health Center of 1982 in Washington, with its own medicine wheel. At the Rosebud IHS Hospital in South Dakota of 1991, architect Fred C. Cooper* hoped "to interplay the structure's design to the natural landscape and heritage of the Rosebud Sioux." Diagonal beams cross above the lobby (15) to suggest lodgepoles on the exterior, geometric patterns on the white surface material suggest beadwork, and a medicine wheel hangs at the rear of a round "spiritual room."[3]

These are supratribal ornaments, employable by several tribes at least within a given geographic region. A quick listing of a few examples may give the impression that these are inconsequential, but they express the desire for distinctive identity. Not every organization can afford to do more. Not every Native American group can match its past experience—or what is left of its heritage—to today's architectural expression in nontraditional buildings.

The low budget for the prefabricated metal community building built in 1977 in the harsh climate of Oswego, Montana, allowed Surrounded-by-Enemy* to use only symbols of people in rust on gray insulated panels. The yellow, white, red, and black that are given symbolic meaning by many tribes, especially those of the Plains, appear on the facets of a geodesic dome that serves as the Indian Learning Center in Pierre, South Dakota. At the Dunseith Day School, the "windows in the library symbolize the Indian warriors facing all four directions,"[4] although the statement has the character of a later invention; literal allusions to Indianness appear in the entrance logo and in feather-like designs along the upper parts of the walls.[5] "The Indian features are mainly graphics and murals," at the Warwick, North Dakota, All-Indian School by A&E, where Ron Melchert* of ANA Landscape Architects suggested "circles and patterns like their lodges" as the basis for the design.[6]

Ornament based on tribal art is widely used. The

13. **Eastern Shawnee multipurpose building, West Seneca, Oklahoma. Ray Byron Frogge, Jr., Associates, ca. 1990. (Courtesy Ray Byron Frogge, Jr.)**

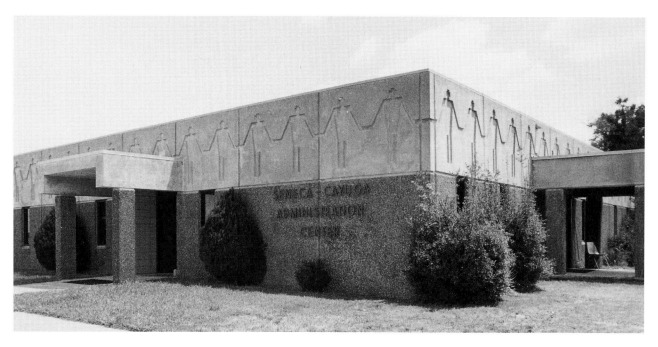

14. Seneca–Cayuga Administration Center, Miami, Oklahoma. Neal A. McCaleb*, Jack Nusbaum, and Robert L. Thomas, 1977.

Cabazon Bingo Palace in California has painted wood trim with step patterns and a metal grille with stick figures taken from its basketry, and basketry inspired the cornice patterns on the Sulphur Bank El-em Pomo Rancheria tribal office (1). At Indian Island School, split-faced and split-ribbed block basketweaving patterns on the exterior show air as clouds, earth as mountains, and a river as rippling water. Woven-fiber designs can be seen also in concrete block at the Wah-he-lut Tribal School in Olympia, Washington, where tribal members showed a picture of a basket to the architect, Winton Smith of Arctic Slope Consulting Group. Shopping centers on the Navajo reservation by David Sloan* display colors, patterns, and woven designs that he thinks are "pretty Navajo." Interweaving boards in triangular shapes recalling tipis can be seen along the base of the Brotherhood Community Health Center in Porcupine, South Dakota, on the Pine Ridge Reservation, built in 1987 to the design of Dennis Martin.

Ceramic patterns have also inspired architectural ornament. George Clayton Pearl of Stevens, Mallory, Pearl & Campbell in Albuquerque designed a frieze of red and white bird heads taken from the earliest Laguna pottery when that Pueblo commissioned a new tribal building. At the time, in the early 1950s, virtually no one imagined that

an entire building could be culturally referential in design, although tribal official Lee Marmon* supported the architect against Pueblo residents who "wanted [the building] to look up-to-date and functional." When the BIA demanded a precise final cost, Pearl had to employ an experienced white urban contractor who had figures available; today, Laguna Pueblo would surely see to it that Native residents were given the work to do.

Brightly colored 1-inch tiles in squares and diamonds are worked into patterns within 5- to 6-foot-square fields at the Cultural/Tourism Center for the Assiniboine at Poplar, Montana, built in about 1978 by Surrounded-by-Enemy*. The result is different from the floral ornament of the woodland peoples or the bold graphics of the Northwest Coast Indians. The designs represent the earth, with lines for four winds coming from each corner. The architect determined the subjects, colors, and size, and Douglas Runs Through* won a competition to do the work. Controversy arose when a spiritual healer said that the group could not depict religious rites, even though the tribal council had permitted it. The architect wondered how children could be taught their religion without the use of illustrative material. Nevertheless, the squares were emptied of their original contents and replaced by tiles in black on the west, white on the north, red and yellow on the other sides, with green on the floor, depicting earth.

Murals are more elaborate additions showing aspects of identity on Native American buildings. Some murals refer to more than one tribe, as at Keams Canyon shopping center on the Navajo Reservation, where murals show a Navajo hogan and Monument Valley, but also a pueblo. Most, however, have specific local references. Young Menominee artists designed murals for the interior of a new government building, and scenes from tribal history adorn the school cafeteria. The latter were planned by a committee of tribal members who had to insist forcefully on what they wanted in the face of opposition from the state and the contractors.[7] This may have made the murals all the more meaningful as symbols of self-determination. Ten murals depict Kiowa history at the Kiowa Nation Culture Museum in Carnegie, Oklahoma, executed around 1984 by Parker Boyiddle*, Mirac Creepingbear*, and Sherman Chaddleson*. The four seasons are represented at the Sanostee School, built around 1990 on the Navajo Reservation. At the Red Cliff Ojibwe recreation complex in Wisconsin, Rita Vandeventer*, whose father had painted murals around 1920 in the local Catholic church, continued her father's work as a muralist by depicting seasonal activities such as canoe-making, trapping, ricing, and building with logs.

Red Lake IHS Hospital in Minnesota has two cycles of murals by Johnson Loud, Jr.* The first, of 1980, shows animals and landscapes important to the seven clans of this Ojibwe band (113). The second, of 1991, shows a more fluid style for the cycle of life—from parents cradling an infant through carefree childhood, the learning of skills, and the ability of elders to offer instruction to children around a campfire. The same hospital has other paintings of Indian subjects done by Patrick DesJarlait* in 1971, a small totem pole, and written materials in display cabinets.

Ornament derived from wampum belts can be seen at the Indian Island School and in more fully developed form at the Seneca–Iroquois National Museum, built in 1977 in Salamanca, New York (16). Lloyd Barnwell*, a Seneca contractor, hired tribal workmen paid under the Comprehensive Employment and Training Act (CETA) with funds from the EDA. Only the brown color of this barnlike industrial shed relates to a "woodland theme," but Barnwell thought that Tudor-arched construction reminded him of a longhouse, and therefore placed an arched structure in the center of the building.

Artist Carson Waterman*, working at the suggestion of George H. J. Abrams*, then director of the museum,

15. Rosebud Indian Health Service Hospital (waiting room), Rosebud, South Dakota. Cooper* Consultants, 1991.

designed exterior images based on the stylized figures and symbols of ancient wampum. He had wanted bronze-tone bricks inlaid on black slate, but economic considerations forced him to settle for brown and pale bricks. Because the images change rather than repeat symmetrically, the reference to a message given in wampum is more persuasive than mechanically aligned designs would have been.

Waterman's work areas were brick walls, 10 by 80 feet on the east and west, with a wider south facade bisected at

16. Seneca–Iroquois National Museum, Salamanca, New York. Brick designs by Carson Waterman*. Lloyd Barnwell*, 1977.

the entrance. Barnwell asked him to design something that would show "Iroquois identity." At first, Waterman imagined "stylized floral designs to have a woodland identity," and some appear on ceramic tile in the museum's logo at the front door. He then realized that wampum belts were made of small cut quahog shells, like tiny bricks, and thought incorrectly that they were specifically Iroquois. He did some research and consulted Phil Tarbell*, a Mohawk then working with the New York State Museum's Education Department in Albany, who sent information on wampum belts that were "safe, with nothing sacred about them that might be offensive to traditional Iroquois people." Waterman "was basically after identity [but] it reached out further than just identity. It also made a statement about agreements and treaties."[8]

On the east side, one sees the George Washington Covenant Belt. In the center is a peaked house, like a longhouse, combined with a log cabin, symbolic of a living dwelling.

On either side...are the leaders of the United States, such as George Washington or the President, and the leader or spokesperson of the Grand Council of the Iroquois, the Tododaho. This is a title, like an overseer, though he doesn't necessarily direct the Grand Council. There are thirteen figures joining hands, representing the original thirteen colonies. This wampum belt documented peace between the Iroquois Confederacy and George Washington when the thirteen colonies were forming the United States.

In fact, the size of the wall and the size of facing bricks forced a reduction of the number of figures, but few people stop to count.

On the south, "on the right of the entrance, is the ever-growing Tree of Peace, which has a pine tree shape. The pine tree was a symbol of peace, with white roots going...north, south, east, and west. The leader of each nation of the Confederacy buried weapons under the tree…as a gesture of peace. These days, you usually see an eagle sitting on top of the tree. The eagle symbolizes oversight on account of his extraordinary vision. He sits on top, watching everyone." This image is also called a "dust fan—presented in Council to clear the dust from the air so that people can see clearly."

"On the left side is the Hiawatha [Belt]. The objects in the center represent the Tree of Peace and the Central Fire. The Central Fire is at a central location, at [the] Onondaga [Reservation] which was centrally located" between the Mohawk farthest east, the Oneida next, the Cayuga close on the west, and the Seneca at the west. The tribes are symbolized by squares on each side, while the open ends show that other nations could join the Confederacy, or Hodenosaunee—the People of the Longhouse. The artist emphasizes the importance of this image, which formed "the basis of the structure of a democracy among the Iroquois, who sent chiefs and clan mothers to the central fire, and made decisions together as a democracy." He believes the much- disputed idea that Thomas Jefferson and Benjamin Franklin heard of this governmental structure and visited the Iroquois to see how it worked; later, when they were framing the Constitution, they are supposed to have sent representatives to obtain further information.[9]

On the west wall, Waterman represented the "Seneca Women's Nomination Belt, which…belonged to the clan mothers. The figures join hands. The square in the center is the council fire. Before the council came up, there would be discussions of what was on the agenda. If they didn't agree with the chiefs, they [the clan mothers] would not present the belt. Then what was decided on wouldn't be legal. This showed the voting rights of the women and clan mothers."

The images are unusually comprehensive as an ensemble in recent Native American imagery. Waterman "didn't create the wampum, but…did bring it out so that the public could see it, and it could promote understanding." The images address outsiders by referring to the interaction of the Founding Fathers of the United States with members of the Iroquois Nation, and assert the Iroquois' political advances beyond those known by white men. The wampum belts show that the Iroquois could compose a symbolic language. The images address the Iroquois—the Seneca specifically—by indicating moments of their history and, remarkably for 1977, emphasizing the essential role of women within the Iroquois system of government.[10]

In the early 1990s, homeowners in the area feared being dispossessed by the Seneca, who own the land under the town of Salamanca, New York, and who had given long-term leases to settlers at ground rents that were astoundingly low.[11] The controversy was strong and bitter, but at the end of a peace march held in Salamanca in 1992, those who assembled to hear speeches sat near the museum.[12] The depiction of civil means of reaching agreement, recorded in the wampum belts and treaties, were symbols with current importance for more Americans than just the Native ones.

* * *

Does using ornament alone represent a failure of imagination among architects and clients? Sometimes it does. In many instances, however, budgetary constraints dictate this limited solution to "Indianness." Some tribal sponsors find it foolish or even detrimental to experiment by building something untested. Members of certain tribes insist on living outwardly as the American majority does, feeling that Native ways should be manifested comprehensively in private. Strictures against the public display of religious symbols at Poplar, Montana, suggest that some ornament is thought to have more power than mere decoration has. Respect for religion and tradition suggested the stone facing on the electric-meters building at Mishongnovi to make it less offensive to those Hopi who believe in living a traditional life without electricity. The choices of architectural solutions for affirming Native American culture vary with the individuals and nations or bands. There is no single "Indian way."

6

Individual Elements

Devising meaningful ornament is more difficult than merely trimming a building, but even more challenging is introducing a Native American architectural element into modern architecture. Designers who adopt this method of "making the buildings Indian" may use more than one such feature, but the introduced forms remain discrete and the architects do not try to make the entire building into an old or a new Native phenomenon. The disadvantage of this design method is that the Amerindian element may look like something casually stuck on to proclaim an Indianness that does not pervade the building. Some clients, however, want to show through architecture their participation in the American mainstream while they retain their Native heritage. The use of individual building elements can satisfy their wishes.

At other times, this is all that can be done—for instance, in Indian Health Service hospitals where having a "sing room" for traditional healing rituals helps certain patients without interrupting modern scientific care (7). The polygonal walls envisioned for Navajo housing in the tribe's "Navahomes" study[1] both allow for culturally specific activity without enlarging budgets unrealistically and accommodate the late-twentieth-century lifeways practiced by the occupants (136). Anna Mitchell*, a Cherokee ceramic artist, hopes to build a seven-sided structure adjacent to her house in Vinita, Oklahoma, to reflect the number of clans of her nation.[2] For their new high school, the Tohono O'odham requested a learning core in a central pit, an element of ancestral architecture.[3]

At the economically built Sierra Mono Museum, a cement-block structure owned and operated by the tribe in North Fork, California, sloping poles meet over the entrance, as they did in front of traditional buildings (17). A smaller, pyramidal cedar-bark house stands to the right of it. As a bark pyramid was ill suited to an untraditional tourist facility, it has been invoked at the entrance to emphasize the Indianness of the sponsors and to suggest the distinctive contents to be found inside. The rough stone on the exterior indicates that the Sierra Mono admire nature's own materials. Not a glass-walled rural museum built by chic urbanites on vacation, this is something down-to-earth—in this context, Indian. This impression is an accurate one: Clifford Bethel*, the late tribal president in office when the building was erected, promoted democratic decision-making in a spirit regarded as traditional. No federal or state money built this—the tribe lacks federal recognition, so government funds are hard to obtain—and the staff and directors are all tribal members.[4]

17. Sierra Mono Museum, North Fork, California. Lee Hatfield, 1971.

18. Red Cloud Administration Building, Pine Ridge, South Dakota. Hodne–Stageberg Partners, 1975.

Tribal offices are logical places to expect some cultural reference, but much of the business conducted in them was introduced into the local culture by the Indian Reorganization Act of 1934. One or a few features of plan, and some decoration, therefore suffice in many places to suggest a Native component. Hodne–Stageberg's Red Cloud Administration Building (18), in Pine Ridge, South Dakota, has a circular tribal council room at the southwest, and a circular outdoor community space at the southeast delimited by wooden walls, but the rest of the building is rectilinear to suit modern offices and to relate to the street grid of the town. The circular parts stand along a line that parallels the path of the summer solstice and follows an east–west orientation, thereby achieving somewhat greater cultural depth than they might have if placed elsewhere.[5]

For the Winnebago Business Council in Wisconsin, Bruce Knutson designed an office building that may actually be erected on the Nebraska Winnebago Reservation (19). Rectilinear blocks of office space delineate three sides of an elliptically vaulted glass-roofed atrium with curved longitudinal and U-shaped transverse struts based on those of a longhouse, a reference that the clients expected. The central feature is based on a ceremonial bark lodge, as Knutson understood it from a brief description in Paul Radin's *The Winnebago Tribe*. At 9000 square feet, the atrium is probably twice as large as the grandest aboriginal building, and at two and a half stories, twice as tall. The aim seems to have been an impressive contemporary design, functional for flexible office subdivision, with basement areas usable for a gymnasium, lounge, and food service, yet in some way identifiably Winnebago. Neither passersby nor tribal members would be disturbed about disparities of scale because no reasonable person could expect a bark-covered small tribal office. This thought mollified the few elders who found using a longhouse form for an office to be sacrilegious. The Winnebago offices would look as modern and technologically sophisticated as other such buildings in the area, with its stone and brick exterior walls, its steel columns, and its plank and open-web joists. And yet anyone who entered the atrium could quickly learn its historic reference, and might notice the Winnebago symbols cast in place on the terrazzo floor.[6]

The Oneida Tribal Services Building in Green Bay, Wisconsin, has a split-faced concrete-block facade adorned with images of three traditional clans—a bear, a turtle's body, and a wolf's head. They recall the entry to an Iroquoian longhouse that is reflected in the building's length, although it is U-shaped. The architect tried to avoid angles in the reception area and left unenclosed and cornerless spaces when possible. A wampum belt and a tree of peace

19. **Winnebago Nation Tribal Complex (project). Bruce Knutson, 1993. (Courtesy Bruce Knutson)**

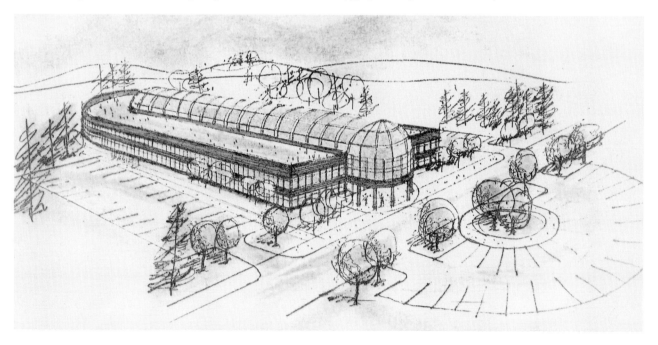

20. Nay-Ah-Shing Lower School, Onamia, Minnesota. Cuningham Hamilton Quiter, 1993. (Courtesy Cuningham Hamilton Quiter)

are seen in tile designs, and an Oneida artist, Scott Hill*, won a competition to design six murals. The Oneida elements are kept separate here, but recombined. This is more literal than the methods of Lakota artist Colleen Cutschall*, who invents "a way of representing Lakota cosmology that extracts elements—design conventions, the treatment of the figure, the disposition of elements on a field—from sources such as hide paintings and beaded garments and bags. She draws, that is, on existing historical forms and recombines them."[7]

A similar procedure governs Ron Hernandez's* design for the Lower Sioux Community Center Building in Morton, South Dakota, where one may enter at the four cardinal points. A tipi motif appears in rock-faced concrete block, and over a central room in a pyramidal form. Ornament appears underfoot, in a starburst design on the floor. Instead of a porte-cochère, there is a sweatlodge sculpture on the west, the main entry side. Here, says the architect, one cleanses one's mind before entering a community space.

Other architects in the upper Midwest assumed that Native clients would want virtual copies of older forms or would want inventive buildings that abstracted or para-

phrased traditional architecture. The firm of Cuningham Hamilton Quiter had to discard these preconceptions—if they ever had them—when the clients asked for modern, technically sophisticated reservation schools. The Nay-Ah-Shing Lower and Upper Schools comply, and are functional, modestly low but varied in outline, and bright and appealing in appearance. Modernity does not imply that the clients want full assimilation to Anglo ways, for the schools teach Ojibwe language and culture, include weekly pipe ceremonies to instill cultural pride and respect for elders, and teach about such historic and continuing activities as ricing, harvesting maple sugar, fishing, and hunting.

The Lower School incorporates a large round skylit activity room just beyond the entrance (20), and the Upper School has a circular entrance room lit by a large clerestory, in which pipe ceremonies are held at the start of each week (21). These spaces may have been inspired by central-plan ceremonial buildings or by the idea of the circle of life. The four sacred colors associated with the cardinal points refer to Native teachings, and wood is used widely for its connection to nature. The primary impression, however, is of buildings that project values of

Individual Elements   **63**

21. Nay-Ah-Shing Upper School, Onamia, Minnesota.
Cuningham Hamilton Quiter, 1993. (Courtesy Cuningham
Hamilton Quiter)

group cohesion and progressive thinking. These are values embraced by many band members, and they can be expressed in modern design.[8]

The Chief Bug-O-Nay-Ge-Shig School in Cass Lake, Minnesota, stands in a tall evergreen forest that separates it from the access road (22). Wings for the elementary school and the middle school flank the entrance. In skylit corridors are such displays as portraits of young tribal members serving in the armed forces, a poster honoring veterans, historic photographs, and wood cabinets containing trophies and a medicine wheel. Ojibwe language is taught here, and its words label several of the rooms. The architectural feature related to cultural identity is a polygonal "Ojibwe Room," with radiating glue-laminated wood beams. Tall glass walls allow views of the sylvan surroundings. A circular shallow pit in the center of the carpeted floor is used in ceremonies. At other times, tribal members who are teachers, aides, and cultural leaders meet here to plan their activities on behalf of preserving tribal ways among the youth. The culture is capable of development within a late-twentieth-century setting.[9]

The newly built Navajo Museum at Window Rock, Arizona, embodies comparable ideas that have been articulated only during the past quarter century (23). Displays will present tradition from the Creation to the present and show the meshing of Navajo perspectives with those of

22. Chief Bug-O-Nay-Ge-Shig School (Ojibwe Room), Cass Lake, Minnesota. Partners of
Architectural Concern, 1984.

23. Navajo Museum, Window Rock, Arizona. DCSW Architects, 1995. (Courtesy Dave Dekker)

the modern world. A building based purely on historic hogan forms would therefore have compromised the museum's mission. Dave Dekker of DCSW Architects in Albuquerque, winners of a design competition, "tried to achieve a contemporary expression of the traditional value system.... The hard thing was to incorporate tradition... but not a Hollywood interpretation or a blatant knockoff" of an older form.[10]

An existing museum, established in 1941 and occupying its present modest headquarters since 1981, has some permanent exhibits and offers contemporary crafts for sale. The new facility is based on what Navajo people want to preserve and know, not on an appeal to tourists. The Navajo plan library collections focused on their history, reservation, and culture. They want archives containing land claims research, treaties, and tape-recorded memoirs. Classes will counteract what some see as the baleful effects of BIA-sponsored education, public schools, and television. These facilities are seen as the "last bastions against total eradication of endangered spiritual and cultural systems."[11]

Because the Navajo emphasize the entire course of history, Loren Miller*, a Navajo architect with DCSW, points out that the main room, an octagon, reflects the form of a traditional hogan but not of the earliest, conical,

type. The size of the octagonal facets was suggested by railroad ties, used in nineteenth-century construction, although the exposed wood here is twentieth-century laminated framing inside an exterior shell of concrete block. Older ways are evident in a patch of earthen floor used for ceremonies, the natural lighting used when colors will not fade, and the colors used for the cardinal directions—shell white at the entrance and at the east for sunrise, turquoise at the south for learning, tan from abalone at the west (where administrative offices are) representing adulthood and work, and jet black on the north for thoughtful reflection and for the library. Tradition is present but less obvious in the clockwise circulation path. More fancifully, the walls around the core are meant to remind people of entering a canyon. Overall, the museum design keeps its historic values inside rather than displayed in an obvious way.[12]

George Horse Capture* emphasizes that Native Americans were "usually viewed in a past tense," so he was pleased when the Plains Indian Museum at the Buffalo Bill Historical Center in Cody, Wyoming, increased its mutual activity with Native people in the late 1970s. Earlier projects had been "structured and administrated by non-Indians" so that they were limited in "effect, range,

24. Wakpa Sica Historical Society Visitor Center and Rest Stop (model), near Fort Pierre, South Dakota. AmerINDIAN Architecture, 1994. (Courtesy Dennis Sun Rhodes*)

25. Akwe:kon dormitory, Cornell University, Ithaca, New York. Flynn Battaglia Architects, 1991.

accuracy, and potential."[13] Eight Native Americans on an advisory committee said that the museum could not be a square, so it has a central plan with an eastern entrance, and they said that a skylit atrium, where plants were originally placed, could not house such disrespectful activities as disco dancing and cocktail parties. Horse Capture says that "squares do not occur in nature" and that the circle refers to the world, the seasonal cycle, and the "ages of man from childhood to childhood."[14]

The 50-foot-high Great Hall contains several tipis; it must be closed to sunlight in order to avoid damage to the painted covers from ultraviolet rays. A "sacred room" is open only to Indians and scholars who enter it to study and pray. When speaking about the character of the design, within an institution governed by Euro-Americans, Horse Capture said that one could "call this an Indian-influenced building."

The smallest building with juxtaposed traditional references may be a highway rest stop for the Wakpa Sica Historical Society of Fort Pierre, South Dakota (24), designed in 1994 by Dennis Sun Rhodes* of AmerINDIAN Architecture. The building lies along a Euro-American road, but

will house exhibits about the area's Native heritage and the indigenous people's interactions with migrants to the region. The structure is a wooden-palisaded recollection of a fort, with a wooden tipi-like form serving as its entrance. The tipi marks the beginning, and the fort—a product of the settlers—recalls the postcontact history of the nineteenth century in the northern Plains.

Along with the Warm Springs Museum (40–42), the most elaborate assembly of individual building elements that refer to Native concerns is at the Akwe:kon dormitory, built in 1991 at Cornell University in Ithaca, New York (25). The school allows certain students of the same race or ethnicity to live together and has encouraged its Native American students to do so for mutual support. Their own dormitory was meant to reduce feelings of estrangement from the culture around them, and to mitigate problems associated with poverty, "alcoholism, lack of family support, and much more";[15] the university hoped to reduce the dropout risk. The building name means "all of us" in Mohawk, and Cornell now proudly claims a retention rate of 80 to 90 percent, although this is due to careful recruiting and to support from the American Indian Program, not to the dormitory alone or even to the auspicious tobacco-burning ceremony held shortly before the building opened.

The university solicited ideas in 1989 from Dennis Sun Rhodes*, who suggested that the building be designed in the shape of a snipe; from James Smith*, an Osage landscape architect from New Orleans who had studied at Cornell; and from others. The commission went to Flynn Battaglia Architects in Buffalo, New York, which worked with Darryl L. Jones, a landscape architect, and Nancy Redeye*, an interior designer. The fact that Peter T. Flynn was a Cornell graduate may have made him particularly attentive to the building's setting on former Cayuga land, and to the needs of an Ivy League institution with its own image.

A dormitory can be likened to a longhouse in that several families—in this case, members of separate families—live in one building. This one has 11,500 gross square feet (7500 net) in which thirty-five students can be housed along with guests, a resident adviser, seminar rooms, a library, a lounge, a kitchen, a laundry room, and offices. The plan is T-shaped, with the top formed by a community room. The three wings that extend from it have been likened to longhouses, and the barrel-vaulted ceiling and curved outer wall of the community room suggest the same traditional model.

The exterior is shingled in western red cedar to approximate the bark cladding of indigenous dwellings. Most of the shingles are gray but some are purple, such as those around the upper community room windows and in a circular medallion at the right end; purple refers to part of the quahog shell used in making wampum. Shingled lintels above the windows and ornamental designs on the walls relate to the circle, the Wing Belt, and Hiawatha wampum. A wall approaching the building from the west and then circling it in a counter-clockwise direction is made of bricks that substitute here for shingles in suggesting the Two Row Wampum Belt. The American Indian Program staff extends the interpretation to suggest parallel but separate paths taken by Iroquois and by other peoples throughout history. On the grounds, a circle and six boulders represent the Six Nations, which finally formed the Iroquois Confederacy. Native plants and a symbolic white pine were planted. Clusters of five needles emerging from one point remind the Cayuga, Onondaga, Seneca, Mohawk, and Oneida that they were the original confederates.

The interior and its decoration were developed in consultation with students. A round design inlaid in the hardwood floor of the principal gathering room represents the clockwise and counter-clockwise dance circles that express the counter-clockwise circle of life. Inlaid squares point to the four main directions. Windows in five sections refer to the five original nations of the Iroquois Confederacy.

Beyond these obvious references, people associated with the program discern many symbolic ones, such as the eagle-like shape of the plan and a semicircular sky dome or the domed back of the turtle central to the Iroquois world-origin concept. The architects are unaware of having incorporated these ideas. The American Indian Program publishes an interpretation of the building and its symbols, as many people will not recognize them, especially if they are not Iroquoian. This is not the only instance of ex post facto interpretation; medieval intellectuals persuaded Christians for centuries that virtually every form in a church was introduced for symbolic meaning. Cornell's interpretation is considered important for enhancing self-image and group pride. The interpretations have emotional and psychological value, then, even if the intellectual elaboration seems forced. In this case, the student-led addition of individual referential elements suggests that the young people, as well as Cornell–the official client—cared about the design and the supportive messages it could offer.[16]

* * *

While buildings that juxtapose individual referential elements may seem merely eclectic, there is usually something meaningful about the whole that transcends the limited significance of each part. In other cases, it may be impossible to invent a significant plan, elevation, cardinal-point orientation, or spatial setting for buildings as simple as highway rest stops or as complicated as Akwe:kon, which have functions and a context that make demands equal to or greater than that of cultural appropriateness. Our icons of modern architecture—that is, most of the beautiful buildings thought of as having deep meaning matched to significant form—have been designed for rich, well-educated individuals attracted to the avant-garde, or for corporations and governments. Few Native Americans have enjoyed the same privileges, and the interest in tradition makes most reservations relatively conservative places. Fewer still are tribes with resources at hand when there arises the occasional opportunity to commission architecture that embodies a distinctive, original, and profound world view. Under these circumstances—and given that some tribes want "Anglo" architecture with only some reference to Native identity—including individual referential elements in modern buildings is one reasonable way to design for today's Native Americans.

7

Modified Continuity

Despite the impact of Euro-American culture, Native Americans continue to build traditional structures for traditional purposes. Grass houses were built in the 1970s for Wichita tribal members in Oklahoma. Forms of the winter mat lodge are preserved by adherents of the Washat religion in the Northwest, although brick or plank floors have replaced earlier earthen ones.[1] The Yakima have built earth lodges. In the Southwest, pueblos have changed significantly since pre-Columbian times, but their general disposition survives at the community's core, and construction methods known since the arrival of the Spanish continue to be employed. These have inspired a good deal of twentieth-century architecture for all groups in the region, from luxurious hotels to such unobtrusive structures as artist Wo Peen's* house at San Ildefonso. A kiva may be found even among newly constructed, untraditional houses at or near the center of house clusters.[2]

Even today in the right climates or seasons, families can live satisfactorily in certain types of traditional dwellings—if they do not insist on indoor plumbing. The Tigertail family, Miccosukees of Florida, occupies raised, thatch-roof houses on an island visited along the tribal tourist circuit. These chickees are well ventilated and

shaded, suited to the climate. The occupants do not live wholly aboriginal lives, but they pursue hybrid lifeways in traditional structures.

Plains and Great Basin peoples erect or rent tipis while they spend several days at powwows and intertribal ceremonies during the summer, those at Crow Fair in Montana forming an exceptional assembly. Art curator George Horse Capture* admires the broad sweeping planes, the towering spires, and the variation brought about by the angles of the flaps, but refuses to romanticize. He remarks on the opening to the rising sun, acknowledging that prevailing west winds would blow smoke into a western entry. He finds ideal tipi poles to be about 30 or 35 feet long, but recognizes that they are hard to transport on the roof of a small car: "Long poles, they look pretty. That's why we do it, not to save the earth." And although he enjoys sleeping in a tipi, he rolls a carpet on the ground because, unlike some others, he prefers not to sleep over "anthills and cow pies." Nevertheless, for him, tipis signify Indian pride, and he says that one way to make a positive statement about identity is to revive older customs—tipis being the most visible of them—to be used whenever possible.[3]

Tipis are seen even among northwestern groups, as at the Yakima Nation summer encampment in Washington

State. Skokomish artist Bruce Miller* has built a tipi and a wigwam sweatlodge on his property.[4] Among the Navajo, tipis house Native American Church services because they are easy and cheap to build and are mobile; the religion may have reached the Navajo from the Plains.[5] Four tipis stood near an arts and crafts building on the Navajo reservation in 1991, apparently to advertise the Native craftsmanship of the merchandise. The frame alone can evoke strong cultural references for the Apache, among whom it represents White Painted Woman's sacred home during female puberty rites.[6] "As a traditional architectural form, the tipi symbolizes growing Native American awareness of self within the larger context of mass culture." Even ceremonies sponsored by the federal government "provide the background for expressions of Indian awareness."[7] The Festival of American Folklife, held on the Mall in Washington, D.C., in 1976 provided one such occasion. Hodne–Stageberg Partners, using the talents of Dennis Sun Rhodes* and Gerald Johnson, erected a pavilion inspired by tipi construction and silhouette; its dismantled parts now lie in a warehouse.

Sun Rhodes and several colleagues erected a genuine tipi in the early 1980s on the Wind River Reservation in order to videotape the construction procedure and associated lore. It was about 20 feet in diameter, with poles 34 to 40 feet high. Members of the Arapaho Women's Society instructed the team, as women were traditionally responsible for erecting and dismantling tipis. The structure was secured with a rope that was not tied until a prayer invoked the purpose of what was going to take place. Reservation residents still know the difference between a family's tipi with three poles, a ceremonial tipi with four, or special ones with as many as thirty-two poles. They know about decoration with beading or quillwork, and about the inner linings for religious leaders where prayer messages lift utterances to the Creator. They know how to strew willow inside for a pleasant aroma, and how to insulate the tipi with blankets.

Many tipis today are commercially manufactured and distributed by firms in California, Colorado, Wyoming, and elsewhere; Native Americans own at least one company. People of other races sometimes use them, too. New Yorkers drawn to indigenous spirituality erected one on top of a loft building in Manhattan.[8] At Kah-nee-tah resort, owned by the Confederated Tribes of Warm Springs in Oregon, tourists may choose to sleep in one of the tipis aligned in two bright white rows. Tribal sponsorship makes these different in spirit from early motels composed of concrete tipis.[9]

For Anglos, tipis are nearly universal signs of Native American identity. The Bicentennial tipi on the Mall was followed by one erected by Molly Kicking Woman* during the 1979 American Folklife Festival. Another was set up opposite the White House in 1991. A tipi is raised in front of the New Mexico State Fair Indian Market, even though tipi-dwelling peoples were in the minority there. Native Americans know the limits of this idea of universal Indianness; insisting on their cultural difference, Yurok in California refused to pose in front of a tipi erected by a non-Indian vendor who attended the dedication of their rebuilt village at Patrick's Point State Park. The park staff asked the vendor to remove the inappropriate construction.[10]

Recently, some Plains nations casino operators have exploited their tipis. Examples include the concrete and steel four-sided canopy over the wood-shingled casino on the Shakopee Mdewakanton Dakota Reservation near Minneapolis (69).[11] Close by is a large casino, its first section shaped like a truncated cone from which searchlights rise, to meet like lodge poles (149, 150). The proposed Sisseton Wahpeton Dakota gambling establishment features a gigantic tipi and several smaller ones in front of the casino—advertisements to attract patrons for the benefit of the tribe. By contrast, tipis erected during the protest encampment at Wounded Knee in 1973 had a deeply serious purpose, and others represented disputants in political controversies at the White Earth Reservation and at Porcupine Butte, South Dakota, in 1992.[12]

* * *

In the Southwest, Shonto Begay*, a Navajo, feels that "living without a hogan is like living with a vulnerable space in your life." He erected one for his family about 30 feet in diameter and about 14 feet high. He believes that materials need not be traditional if the shape is retained and the builder respects the orientation to the four directions; the hogan can be blessed and made fit for use by the spiritual leaders. For the Begay family, the four directions affect the use of the house. The west, for example, direction of holiness, accommodates the grandmother or a visiting spiritual healer, while the east, direction of innocence and youth, is the section appropriate for child-rearing. When he added a 10- by 30-foot greenhouse in 1989, Begay built a studio on the opposite side of his hogan and filled in the space between the additions, so as to keep the sense of a cycle embedded in the architecture.[13]

Hogans of traditional form appear widely on the Navajo Reservation. In remote districts, some are still used as housing, but even close to sizable settlements like Chinle, people observe taboos and traditional precautions

26. Pawnee roundhouse, Oklahoma, 1974.

in their domestic hogans.[14] Some are used for storage or as outbuildings on ranching or herding land. Families may also erect them for sleeping if their government-built houses are too hot in the summer; some find modern houses unsuitable in other ways, and eventually use them primarily for storage. Hogans are used also for religious observance, including some for the Native American Church.[15] Hogans can be seen on school grounds—for example, at Rock Point and Many Farms—where they are used to instruct pupils about Navajo culture. There are, in fact, two at Rock Point: one of logs and the other of masonry. With the increasing though wholly inadequate provision of government-funded modern housing, and because hogans cannot be federally funded without passing safety tests if electricity is installed, the hogan is gradually becoming identified as a religious building. A hogan may be called a "sanctuary for the spirit"[16] even though its traditional purposes included both holy and secular activity. The Yurok in California also maintain some plank houses "for cultural and religious reasons."[17]

* * *

The oldest surviving roundhouse or dancehouse is an early-twentieth-century structure at Hominy on the Osage Reservation in Oklahoma; the Nomlaki dancehouse at Grindstone Creek Rancheria in California is the oldest

one still in use in that state. More recent ones have been built for the Wichita, the Pawnee, and various California peoples, including the Pomo (2), Miwuk, and Chukchansi Yokuts. On the Stewart's Point Rancheria is a roundhouse of uncertain date behind a manufactured house. Its walls are of carefully matched wide planks, well constructed without chinks or cracks, and the roof is wood shingled. The interior is softly lit and spacious, impressive but intimate, warm brown in color. The low walls support a roof that slopes to about 10 feet at its peak, strengthened by umbrella-like ribs. In diameter, it is broader than a nearby trailer, and perhaps also broader than the manufactured house. Like tipis, roundhouses have passed into the regional vernacular where they may spring up as Christy's Donut Shop in Fresno or other centrally planned commercial buildings, but just as we can differentiate between an A-frame house and a peak-roofed church, we can ignore the superficial similarities and respect the tradition preserved in the genuine roundhouse.[18]

On the White Earth Ojibwe Reservation in Minnesota, tribal members lamented the loss of traditional buildings. In late 1992, people from Naytawaush and Roy Lake met to plan a roundhouse for drum ceremonies, small powwows, and education. Wes Mattson, an architect in Minneapolis, contributed plans that were ready in late

Modified Continuity   **71**

27. Pawnee roundhouse.

1993 for an octagon of logs, with pole rafters, forming a 60- to 70-foot diameter.[19]

Modifications of past practices are permissible. Some elderly Wichitas criticized their roundhouse's earthen floor as being warm enough for those who danced, but too chilly for those who could only sit and observe;[20] the essential thing is to dance on the earth, but the perimeter of the dance area can be covered with wood or cement. The materials do not alter the essentials of the building, which have to do with the polygonal windowless form, roof ventilation, and a connection to the earth. The ceremonial roundhouse for the Pawnee in Oklahoma could not have had its breadth of diameter without the hollow steel poles that support the roof (26, 27). Economy probably dictated using vertically aligned plasterboard on the walls, some wood and some acoustical tile above, and cement for the floor around a central earthen circle. All the same, it remains a roundhouse, used for funerals, dances, meetings, and children's instruction. There may have been some criticism of these and other modified traditional buildings, just as there was at Laguna Pueblo when a new kiva of the 1970s was constructed of concrete block,[21] but innovation and adaptability characterize all human groups.

A roundhouse erected by the Northern Sierra Miwuk at Chaw'Se Grinding Rocks State Park in California has had an unusual history, reflecting interaction of Native Americans and Anglos. In the late 1960s, tribal members conceived the idea of a cultural center near rocks formerly used for grinding acorns into flour. Clyde Newland, the superintendent of the California Department of Parks and Recreation, had been "raised amongst Indian peoples and he had an interest" in their culture, so he seemed an appropriate person for Bill Franklin*, a Miwuk cultural leader, to approach about a site where the Miwuk "might build our culture and keep it alive, to show it to the public." To the Chamber of Commerce and the county Board of Supervisors, Franklin stressed potential benefits from tourism. Newland, in turn, appealed for support to his contacts in Washington, D.C., and by 1969, a reconstructed Miwuk village, roundhouse, and ball field had been erected and blessed in the park. Franklin's understanding of the political backing needed for the project was useful eight years later when the Miwuk pressed the state for funds to build a cultural center near the village.

In time, however, the Miwuk came to resent the state's fees and regulations, and the presence of vendors selling inauthentic objects presented as Indian. For their new roundhouse not far away, they obtained framing poles

28. Coldspring Longhouse (rebuilt), Steamburg, New York, 1965.

from a man who was clearing trails at Grizzly Flats, and made the walls of logs and bark for lack of the rocks that would have been preferable.[22] This is just one of about a dozen roundhouses in California, most of them open only by special permission.

* * *

Longhouses, sometimes known as smokehouses or ceremonial lodges, have been built especially in the northeastern and northwestern states, where wood construction has an enduring history. In New York State, longhouses include those for the Tonawanda Seneca near Basom; one at Steamburg (28), to which the ceremonies were moved from Coldspring when that locality was taken for the Kinzua Dam; and for the Cattaraugus Seneca at Newtown. The Onondaga longhouse, built in 1991 with the financial help of Christian churches, is made of warm red-brown logs, and is centrally located at a fork in the village road. Here in the autumn, people sit for six days to thank the Creator for food, animals, and children, and at ceremonies, ask the Creator for protection.[23] Similar buildings exist just over the Canadian border on Mohawk lands and on other Iroquois Canadian reserves, while Seneca and Cayuga members who moved to Oklahoma took this architectural tradition to the former Indian Territory while the Oneida brought it to Wisconsin.

The Northwest boasts a number of longhouses—for instance, in Washington at the Lower Elwha, Sko-

29. Swinomish longhouse (interior under construction),
Swinomish Reservation, Washington. Cedar Tree Associates
and reservation resident builders, 1992.

komish, and Upper Skagit reservations. One has been built among other reconstructions on the Hoopa Reservation in California. Others are in the Makah and Toppenish museums. The Simnasho longhouse on Oregon's Warm Springs Reservation, a broad wooden hall with a pitched roof, is another example; tribal members erected an addition in 1985.[24] The Umatilla in the same state own another.

The Swinomish longhouse (29) is the most impressive and is one of the most remarkable of all recent Native American buildings. Like most longhouses, it consists of a major room surrounded by banks of seats. A smaller room is adjacent. The special character of this longhouse is due to its grand spaciousness and to the massive logs of which it is built. This is, with the Tulalip longhouse of 1968, one of two three-fire longhouses in Washington. For open fires, the Swinomish safety code of 1988 requires a building taller than the traditional one. The wood has to be dry, as smoke and cinders create a fire hazard with green wood.

The interior is finished in raw wood and plywood panels. Part of the floor is earthen for the proper performance of ceremonies.

The longhouse was initiated by the tribe and built largely by Swinomish workmen. The general contractor, Vernon Lane*, a Lummi, bid on the foundations and general structure, but the cedar shake roof, the shingle cutting, and other tasks were performed by the Swinomish. Folke Nyberg of the University of Washington School of Architecture, and his colleague Art Peterson, worked with the tribe. During construction of a previous longhouse, a worker was killed and his death was seen as a bad sign, the project having been commenced without permission from appropriate leaders. This one was begun under the correct auspices.

Funds came from a settlement with the Seattle City Light Company, which owed the tribe money in connection with a dam and power plant. The tribal council voted to put the entire $400,000 into this project. Water and sewer lines raised the final cost, but the Indian Health Service provides these because the IHS has some responsibility in case of fire.[25]

The Sauk–Suiattle longhouse is still under construction (30). It received tribal centennial project money and many contributions of funds and labor from tribal members and outsiders. Initiated by Norma Joseph* when J. Lawrence Joseph* was chairman, it has been coordinated by Marvin Kastning, a local Euro-American artist who is deeply interested in the harmony between Native and Roman Catholic religious beliefs. The contractor, Mariah Log Homes, employed Indian laborers.

Many tribal members belong to the Roman Catholic church, but the local traditional religious authority is Kenneth Moses*, a Snoqualmie raised with the Sauk–Suiattle and well known in the Pacific Northwest. Some of his teachings may come from coastal tribes, but they are inte-

grated into modern Sauk–Suiattle life, just as the traditional building includes some new features. The longhouse will be insulated at floor level, as people want elders to be comfortable and as children are now unused to interiors without insulation. A sprayed fire-protective substance was donated to treat the wood. Traditionalists wanted a large fire and low building, so elaborate measures were taken to vent the smoke properly without allowing metal to be visible. Elk hide, already prepared, will cover the entrance to keep out drafts so that heat will rise. Old and new ideas blend here and in the Swinomish longhouse, retaining tradition while providing for safety and modern comfort.[26]

Another traditional building form in the Pacific Northwest is the canoe shed (31). Canoes were used in fishing, travel, and war, and as status symbols when they were large and specially decorated. They were components of pot-

30. Sauk–Suiattle longhouse (under construction), Sauk–Suiattle Reservation, Washington. Reservation resident builders, 1992.

31. Canoe shed, Upper Skagit Reservation, Washington.
Reservation resident builders, 1988.

latch giveaways and served as funeral vessels. The revival of long-canoe building and decoration, as well as of races and ceremonies connected with canoeing, is an aspect of the contemporary regeneration and strengthening of Native American culture. Several new sheds were built in the 1980s—for instance, at the Upper Skagit Reservation after residents obtained federal recognition for their small nation.[27]

* * *

The Hoo-Hoogam-Ki Museum on the Salt River Pima–Maricopa Reservation near Scottsdale, Arizona, preserves a distinctive regional technology in a rectangular building with a projecting entrance and a ramada, or arbor, shading an outdoor restaurant at the rear (32). The building was originally a residence for children in community care. In 1987, the house was doubled in size at the left of the entrance to accommodate cultural displays. Construction is "sandwich-style"—metal supports with applied saguaro ribs filled in with saguaro and ocotillo stalks cemented with adobe. Inside, mesquite trunks with forked branches hold the beam and plank ceilings. Reservation residents gathered the natural materials and erected the museum. The construction method was cheap, and it offered good insulation properties. Rubber covers the roof

and metal nails replace the traditional wooden pegs, but the industrial components are concealed to give the impression of a building connected to the past. Tribal member Alfretta M. Antone*, who hoped to teach Indian cookery, dances, songs, and basketweaving there, feared the loss of culture if efforts were not made to preserve it; this explains why she said, "We are trying to get the building to look as close as possible to a traditional Pima–Maricopa house."[28]

Wood and branch shelters are found in many places. These temporary and renewable constructions keep the summer sun from participants in ceremonies, from vendors of food or tickets, from speakers and judges at contests, or from families working and dining outdoors. These ramadas can be seen in many parts of the country. Sometimes they are made permanent in metal, like the one near the Ottawa tribal headquarters in Oklahoma, or the one at Fort Belknap that cost $65,000 and replaced a brush and pole predecessor rebuilt annually.[29]

Not every tradition dates from the precontact period. When European practices suited Native people, tribes incorporated them. Log buildings are less vulnerable to extreme weather and wind conditions than some aboriginal structures, for example, and that is why they are still used for housing in northern tier states. The Stanley Red Bird Lakota Studies Building at Sinte Gleska University on South Dakota's Rosebud Reservation, finished in 1991, was therefore made of logs by a crew of Lakota builders under the supervision of tribal member Jim Stands-and-Looks-Back* (110, 111). Jules Obomsawin* and his fellow Oneida built the Shako:wi Cultural Center of logs near Verona, New York, in 1993 (125, 126). Stands-and-Looks-Back sees log houses as part of the Lakota past. The college's building is longer than the 18 feet in which logs are cut, so the design includes a break in the lecture room wall where T-shaped logs anchor the next stretch of wall. Doors and windows were built to withstand the drop expected from green logs. These are today's additions to older log building methods, but any living culture allows for change.[30]

The inclusion of the nineteenth-century Native past also explains the presentation as authentically Indian of the fire station (1987) (33), casino (1990), library (1992), and Living Arts Heritage House (1985) for the Bad River Band of the Lake Superior Band of Chippewa at Odanah, Wisconsin. Tribal members Richard Ackley*, planner; Dana Jackson*, education director; and John Blanchard*, construction expert regard these buildings as part of the local aesthetic, giving a sense of warmth. Working with logs is familiar to the Ojibwe.[31] The resulting buildings are durable. Log construction uses building methods without ruining the group's own cultural values. Ackley tries "to pull together various influences and present them to the tribe," as he, like the Pima–Maricopa, sees a "need for fusion between ideas taken from tradition and modern means used" to realize them. The Heritage House accommodates youth activities and traditional funerals. Ackley would like to see arts and crafts practiced there as well. He does not object to having this facility near the casino, because he conceives all the activities of the band as a unity.

The casino was built by students at the Bad River Training School as a construction exercise, and later converted to a casino, the only one in Wisconsin made of logs. It was "designed to our own aesthetics, not a Las Vegas casino" by joining two vacant log buildings. Ackley was pleased that this was done, because the band did not want outside management or, for that matter, "domineering" architects who would offer standard efficiencies but uncongenial buildings; he also disliked ambitious architects "who try to rip off the tribes." Richard J. Coker & Associates, interior designers from Syracuse, New York,

32. Hoo-Hoogam-Ki Museum, Salt River Pima–Maricopa Reservation, Scottsdale, Arizona. Jack Gauman (construction supervisor), 1987.

33. Fire station, Bad River Reservation, Wisconsin. William Turner of Stubenrauch Associates, 1985.

replaced architects, giving the band more opportunity to make its own decisions. Ornament refers to the buffalo and other indigenous forms and species. An impression of rusticity is imparted by the visible wood and the open timber roof of the upper floor. The building's nickname—"Log Vegas"—emphasizes its difference from more glamorous rivals in the West.

Another use for traditional buildings is in tourist facilities, which usually are sponsored by Anglo businessmen who erect more or less authentic historical structures in outdoor settings and who sometimes employ Native guides. By contrast, when state governments reconstruct historic architecture or build visitors' facilities near ancient mounds or historic settlements, they consult with appropriate tribes in hopes of offering accurate interpretation. Native American festivals, races, and other activities are often held on these state-sponsored sites, as at Chaw'Se or in Yosemite National Park, both in California. The Yurok Sumeg village erected in 1989 and 1990 at Patrick's Point State Park near Trinidad, California, under the direction of Walt Lara* is meant for tourists, for instructing schoolchildren, and for ceremonial dances to be performed by tribal members; traditions recounted by tribal elders, and old photographs, made this reconstruction possible. Old ceremonial sweathouses there are cordoned off from tourists, segregating the vernacular structures from the

reconstructed ones.[32] In North Dakota, On-a-Slant Village near Bismarck, created in the 1930s, is an older reconstructed settlement where staff readily point out departures from ancient mound construction, offer information about restorations and alterations, and accommodate current Native American cultural activity.

Villages sponsored by tribes may be regarded as most authentic, although their construction and presentation may reflect only the interpretations of some tribal members. These villages show the sponsors' desire to offer an Indian understanding of past and present, unlike the derogatory impressions of Native America given by ignorant or hostile purveyors of mass culture. To be sure, in any culture, interpretation of the past has tendentious aspects.

The Cherokee in both Oklahoma and North Carolina have the most complete historic-building parks. Tribal members practice traditional crafts and perform dances or music, and the Eastern Band has long been active in marketing Native heritage. At Tsa-la-gi in Oklahoma, there is not only a traditional village through which one is guided by well-informed Cherokee college students, but also a village set up to show Cherokee life in the nineteenth century, the first major era of interaction with Euro-Americans. The aim is to demonstrate the richness of the past and the adaptability of the people to historical change, freeing the Cherokee from exclusive association with aboriginal ways. This is a statement that the Cherokee are progressive, as the term is understood by the majority population, and reference to the Euro-American designation of the Cherokee as one of the "Five Civilized Tribes" appears frequently in Cherokee statements about their history, even now when others have questioned white-oriented ideas of progress.

Other groups such as the Lumbee and Seneca hope to establish educational villages in the future. The latter, working with consultants Molinaro/Rubin, received a grant in 1990 from the Administration for Native Americans for three years of planning and development. The present museum, erected by inexperienced workmen, suffers from poor construction and inadequate temperature and humidity control; it must be replaced. As usual with tribes' public projects, the new center will preserve and interpret the Seneca heritage, while also offering opportunities for economic development through attractive tourist facilities. Among the many components of the cultural center are a museum and shops, an arts and crafts area, an outdoor amphitheater, a hotel and conference center, a transformation of the present museum for archives and research or for visitors' reception, and a reconstructed traditional Seneca village. This would be archaeologically accurate, with the buildings showing life at a specific period; it would not be an ahistorical grouping, like that of Colonial Williamsburg.[33]

Tourist-oriented historic-building parks have already been established by the Alabama–Coushatta in Texas (34) and by the Miccosukee in Florida, among others.[34] They all include restaurants or inns, craft shops, and cultural displays. The Gila River Arts & Crafts Center near Sacaton,

34. **Alabama–Coushatta Museum and Village (ceremonial building), Livingston, Texas. Barry Moore, 1972. (Rick Gardner Photography [Houston])**

Arizona, operated by the Pima and Maricopa, maintains an outdoor museum with houses from those two tribal cultures as well as examples of Papago, Apache, and ancient Hohokam dwellings. No attempt is made to construct a village or to provide context, so this complex features curiosities, however accurate the reproductions may be. Nevertheless, they may inculcate more history and knowledge than most visitors absorb in school books or from television programs. Given that tourism is one of the few industries from which Native Americans can hope to profit on often isolated reservations, a focus on tourism makes sense. Not all tribes have the internal personnel or expert advisers to produce entirely authentic villages, and even villages erected on a scholarly basis inevitably lack the true atmosphere of a past in which one saw more people and activity. George H. J. Abrams* cautions also that "poor administration, and the reluctance to place qualified non-Indians in high-profile and relatively high-paid positions, results in poorly run institutions."

An unusual privately sponsored project is the "Structures of the Ho-ho-kam" on 20 acres of "Sacred Grounds" established by a retired judge, C. Lawrence Huerta*, a Pascua Yaqui. Nine pit houses, two sweatlodges, a healing pit, a kiva, a burial platform, a mound, and other structures compose the project, located near Huerta's home. He used no historic models and made the building walls of wood, although he feels that he "should put stucco on them." He designed the pit houses from his memory of such buildings, knowing that these do not go as deep into the ground as historic ones did; he calls his examples "symbolic." Although the project is commemorative rather than archaeological, the time, funds, and devotion involved satisfy the sponsor's deeply felt needs and bear public witness to the power that tradition has in the life of someone able to succeed in "Anglo" society for many years.

Sweatlodges of regional or tribal types are in wide use wherever Native Americans live, erected on tribal land by community groups or on private land by individuals. They are used in preparation for religious and other meaningful activity. Sweatlodge experiences purify the body, subjecting the participant to intense physical changes that remove him or her from ordinary experience. At the Kullihoma alcohol- and drug-treatment center in Oklahoma, the ritual cleanses the body and the emotions to allow room for the patient's insight into his problems.[35] In this case, culture and medicine are intimately allied to assist Native Americans today. Unassuming as sweatlodges are in physical terms, they contribute greatly to individual and community well-being. They appear above and dug into the ground, are covered with wood or earth or fabric, and vary with the sponsor and the nation. Confined and thermally efficient, these structures suggest that some of the most meaningful architecture for Native Americans today may also be the most modest.

8

Paraphrases

It is one thing to build a new longhouse, but quite another to build a glass and steel longhouse at twice its original scale and to surround it with corridors and offices. Practicality and logic limit the utility of purely traditional buildings today, so some contemporary Native American architecture must paraphrase historic building types, and other architecture modifies pure forms from the past.

The long, low rectilinearity of the Chickasaw Nation Headquarters (1970) persuades Glenda Galvan*, director of the museum housed there, that the building relates to the activities of her ancestors in their winter lodges. Ray James, the architect, made no such claims. He was more concerned with providing opportunities for Native Americans to work on the building, as only four of thirty-seven workers came with appropriate skills. Tilt-slab concrete construction allowed James to use unskilled labor to sandcast the walls. Glue-laminated beams were made locally, and the construction crew could be trained to shingle the roof. Local stones are embedded in the walls, in a pattern that James calls "not Indian but sensitive to nature" (35). And although the architect disclaims any intent to have the battered walls evoke Meso-American architecture or to see small polygonal cupolas as tipi-like, tribal members might

make the connections. The relationship may, then, seem to be based on wishful thinking, but building forms have often—and why not?—evoked ideas beyond those that their architects intended; the most famous example is that of a long church with a transept, commonly supposed to imitate Christ's cross.

Glenda Galvan is correct in saying that the Chickasaw Trading Post along Interstate 35 near Davis, Oklahoma, recalls a dancehouse; this convenience store, craft shop, and filling station is a wide polygon, partly stone faced, with sloping supports and a sloping low roof with a central skylight.[1]

Many other examples are even more obvious. The long rectilinear lodges of the Northwest Coast lend themselves easily to modern uses. Phillip Norton and Richard Mettler at the Fred Bassetti architectural firm said that the Makah Cultural Research Center at Neah Bay, Washington, was "designed to replicate roughly the sense of the board longhouse on the exterior," although the structure is made of concrete up to roof level for the sake of protection against fire (36). It is not a pure rectangle, as the entrance angles outward, but the long and proportionately low contours immediately suggest a longhouse. The building was designed from the inside out by Jean Jacques André, a museum consultant, who prepared seven plans to accommodate the Makah's desires as they evolved, but the final plan fit into the architects' shell.[2]

The center, perhaps the "first large scale tribal museum,"[3] owes its origin to the discovery in 1966 of Ozette, an ancestral Makah site. In 1970, in order to prevent further vandalism and theft there, the tribe decided to permit excavation and to remove the objects to the reservation; some young Makah joined the dig. The tribe approved the idea after long deliberation about opening a museum, some members having opposed tourist services while other needs were more pressing. Although the Makah spent years dealing with the BIA and National Park Service, the EDA found the BIA plans "unacceptable and unfundable"[4] and required the employment of independent architects before funding the project. The architects believe that they were given the job because they were known to the tribal chairman, who worked as a parking-lot attendant next to their offices.

André organized the displays around the four seasons, and the Makah—including some trained for museum work

in a BIA–National Endowment for the Arts program—elaborated on the idea. They wanted to be able to see canoes first, and a diorama of the Ozette site. The Makah wanted to display a longhouse; it took several months to build, including weathering, and three potlatches were held in it before installation.[5] Tribal cultural authorities even considered it important to make the correct odors of smoked food palpable in the longhouse.

Asking themselves whom the museum was for, the Makah concluded that it was for themselves, as they use it in four seasons, while tourists—albeit more numerous than local residents—come only in summer. For this reason among others, the Cultural Research Center includes signs in the native language, maintains records in Makah, and offers language and crafts lessons. Its board of directors includes representatives of the twelve major family groups that composed the pre-1936 government system.[6] This institution's primary function is to maintain everything possible about Makah culture, and the only reasonable form for it was one related to traditional architecture, even if the wood is only cladding over concrete.[7]

35. **Chickasaw Nation Headquarters (detail of exterior), Ada, Oklahoma. James–Childers, ca. 1970.**

36. Makah Cultural Research Center, Neah Bay, Washington. Fred Bassetti, Architects, 1979.

Other evocations of indigenous Northwest Coast architectural tradition can be seen throughout the area. The Lower Elwha Tribal Center (1979) for the S'Klallam at Port Angeles, Washington, is a modern longhouse with a central corridor and offices on the sides. Ceilings are higher than they would have been in older times, and the technical installations suited an era of plentiful electricity, but they are encased in an oblong form clad in wood. The Squaxin Island Tribal Center, which contains offices and a gymnasium in one building—this has to do with intricacies of funding—is also built on the longhouse model.

Like the Makah Cultural Resource Center, the Suquamish Museum on the Port Madison Reservation in Washington was in part a response to archaeological discoveries. A structure over 500 feet long, known as Old Man House, was excavated in 1974 and 1975, and in 1976 Bicentennial funds aided the renovation of an old cemetery. To record and preserve cultural heritage, planning began two years later, motivated in part by the idea that "essential to the concept of self-determination is the ability of tribes to determine the use and development of cultural resources." The museum staff was "to record the Tribe's past...[and] to educate the present and thereby preserve and perpetuate the heritage."[9] Other aims were promotion of mutual understanding between Native and other peoples, and support for tourism.

One problem was that insufficient funding made a separate building impossible. Coincidentally, a fire in the community center, 90 percent completed in 1979, engendered a rebuilding there by the Arai–Jackson firm in Seattle, but inflated costs prevented the finishing of the second floor. That was eventually made into the museum, with annexed spaces for archives and storage (37). In a second phase of building, the architects added a ramp for the disabled, while Rod Slemmons with Stan Smith and Dins Danielson of the Argentum design firm in Seattle laid out the exhibit area. Tribal members constructed the display spaces under the direction of W. W. Platt.

Although the building is two storied, it has the long shape and high-pitched roof of a longhouse, the roof sloping to a low eaves line facing the parking lot, where two totem poles show local pride in the culture. The cedar planks on the exterior have grayed with the weather, as they have on several of the other modern longhouses and on historic buildings of the area.[10]

The Swinomish, in addition to their great smokehouse, have a Social Services Building, which opened around 1982. It also paraphrases a traditional structure. Within the long rectilinear building is a central room with carpeted steps used as benches, surrounding a central floor. A long central skylight is equivalent to the smokehole (38). The architect, Bailey Behm of Edmonds, Washington, claimed to have placed function before form, but it proved possible to combine traditional references with offices, a library, and other modern services.[11]

The Confederated Tribes and Bands of the Yakima

37. Suquamish Museum (detail of exterior), Port Madison Reservation, Washington. Arai–Jackson, 1983.

38. Social Services Building, Swinomish Reservation, Washington. Bailey Behm, 1970s.

Clients, Architects, and Design Strategies

39. **Yakima Nation Museum (ceremonial building), Toppenish, Washington. Doudna–Williams, 1980.**

Nation erected a national cultural center and tribal buildings between 1977 and 1979; it officially opened in June 1980 (39). Plans developed as early as the late 1960s were activated when the tribe received a legacy of books and artifacts from Nach Tum Strongheart*, a film actor who died in 1966. His gifts were stored until 1973, and then catalogued before a museum was planned by Doudna–Williams, which had designed housing for the tribe; Pietro Belluschi provided a preliminary consultation.

Within the tribal building complex, the most prominent structure is a 76-foot-high winter lodge used for meetings and ceremonies for up to 550 people. (It is not called a longhouse because that word refers to a setting for tribal government rather than for community activities, but it is a greatly enlarged version of the traditional structure erected inside the museum by Yakima member James Selam*.) A direct axis runs from its east side to Mount Adams, a revered natural landmark. The large structure is not simply a magnified replica of a winter lodge, as it is made of

durable materials, including stone, and is covered with a wood-shingle roof. Parquet floors, several windows, and large light fixtures are not traditional elements, either, nor are modern wall panels colored a warm red, and oversized ornamental bands. Nevertheless, the elongated polygonal plan and the tapering silhouette are unmistakably related to historic models. Because the lodge is closed to the public, visitors are made aware that this is a special part of the Yakima building complex. This suggests respect for the Yakimas' privacy and sovereignty, and implies that the building form carries significant meaning for the people who use it.[12]

Farther south, in Oregon, the museum at Warm Springs paraphrases a lodge, a tipi, and a travois on a reservation that is home to three confederated tribes with differing traditions (40). As early as 1983, architects in Portland, Salem, and Bend submitted proposals for a museum near the tribal resort hotel. One was a crescent-shaped group of pavilions; another was split in two parts by a meandering

Paraphrases   **85**

40. **Warm Springs Museum (plan), Warm Springs Reservation, Oregon. Stastny–Burke, 1993. (Courtesy Stastny–Burke)**

path; a third, roughly T-shaped, had a central round room; a fourth based its imagery on the trapezoidal tule backrest, ceremonial staffs, pipes, hand drums, and other artifacts known within the three cultures.

These were responses to the Confederated Tribes' plans to rescue their material heritage from dispersal and destruction. A collection formed in 1955 was flooded and injured by mold in 1957. In the 1960s, Chief Delvis Heath* observed that "we could see that the old ways were disappearing, the old language was disappearing, and that pretty soon none of our young people would know where they came from, or who they were. That's when we decided to build a museum." Early in the following decade, the leadership realized that components of family and group history were passing from Native hands to those of collectors and curators, and that few people could make replacements. They voted for the first $50,000 allocations in a total of $875,000 to buy artifacts, photographs, and documents. They chartered the Middle Oregon Indian Historical Society to develop and build a museum. In 1988, reservation residents voted 60 percent to 40 percent to devote $2.5 million of tribal money for construction, an amount later augmented. Several foundations contributed to it, being impressed by Native Americans' willingness to sacrifice for the project.

In 1987, Warm Springs authorities decided to build along Highway 26, not near the more secluded resort, thereby directing the museum to the general public as well as to tribal members. Formations of Portland advised about displays, but Stastny–Burke designed the museum; the firm was chosen after a limited request for proposal was offered to seven Anglo firms, as no Amerindian ones were known to be available. The architects think that a photograph of partner Donald Stastny in Native dance clothing may have helped them gain the commission; Stastny had been deeply interested in Klamath culture since boyhood and had even toured with a Native dance group. Carol Mayer-Reed is the landscape architect.

The designers were open to clients' suggestions. Bryan Burke and Christopher Boothby, the project architect, described themselves as novices in "Indian country" but were eager to "make a concerted effort to do something suited to Native Americans," although they knew that "it's always difficult to design a building for a culture that you can never hope to understand." They remained aware that most architects tend to produce "an appropriate or a superficial statement, based on [their] own ideas" rather than those of the client. To forestall this, they held a week-long charrette at Warm Springs rather than making a single, perhaps authoritarian, presentation. They met with residents to ask how they envisioned the museum. They brought samples of rock and timber, cut as they were to be in the finished building. Design staff made drawings and models in the interviewing room. The architects were asked to produce something with a "unique quality" reflecting the physical environment and natural materials such as basalt and timber, but they were not asked to make the buildings "look Indian per se. We were told that they didn't want a simple box. We utilized aspects of their culture as we understood it" to convey the idea of unity on the reservation created by three groups that retained distinctive identities.[13]

The museum's literature describes the ensemble as a "stream-side encampment," an effect given by the rooflines. A paraphrased tule-mat longhouse of the river-dwelling Wasco tribe houses the administration wing (41); a modified tipi of the hunter-gatherer Warm Springs people covers the temporary-exhibitions gallery; and an evocation of the Paiute travois rises above the permanent exhibits. Enclosing these three main elements is a curved wall of basalt, the stone of the nearby valley rim.

The architects had connected their circular enclosure to the medicine wheel, but one of the Confederated Tribes does not include the wheel in its traditions, "so we backed

41. **Warm Springs Museum (administration wing at right).**

off and just said there was a round form. We've learned that the best thing to do is take your best shot even at a sub-conscious level and let tribal people interpret the result," said Burke. Pointed and curved roofs appeared to one resi-dent as the wings and head of an eagle, although the sug-gestion was unintended. Interwoven designs, used by the architects to make brick look like thin skin rather than mass, was seen as basketweaving, as fishnets, and as shadow patterns on local cliffs. Burke says, however, that "if you pick one reference like fish nets, you end up with kitsch."

Boothby noticed a tendency among reservation resi-dents "to expect a literal image of some sort. I'd be asked, 'What does this mean?'...We wanted to be less literal" and hoped that "people of different perspectives could be able to read different things" in the buildings. That is why the allusions to traditional architectural forms are only allu-sions, not replicas.

Brick bearing walls and heavy timber on the interior are not part of local tradition, but the Confederated Tribes know that while they care intensely about cultural preser-vation, new ideas must be added. As Burke put it, "The whole idea of a building in which to put Indian objects is a contradiction, because all the building processes and mate-rials, etc., are Anglo. So the problem is how to create

something grounded in that, and not have it look as if it is a white man's building plunked down on a reservation." The sequence goes from the surrounding landscape to a berm—the museum is built in a flood plain of the Deschutes River Canyon and had to be raised by about 5 feet—to basalt from the reservation, and then to the brick and industrial-steel structure topped by galvanized-steel shingles: "We have not reconciled them [the Native and Anglo elements] but we've straddled them. We hoped for some expression of culture."

The architects also drew ideas from the landscape and from Native artifacts. Beyond the steel circle-topped stan-chions that delimit the museum grounds, an entrance path leads along steps, rocks, and a stream. The real stream changes to a rivulet of green slate cut into the gray stone of the lobby. A stone door opens to the 50-foot-long lobby, where five fir columns suggest the local woods (42). The ceiling is sky blue, and the upper part of the walls is dark green, like leaves. Below that, amber evokes the arid land of this part of Oregon. The fir columns suggest to Boothby that the "building is similar to an oasis where cultures come together....All species cohabit at oases." As irregular cohabitation can lead to confusion, the exhibition areas have been placed under the tipi and travois; the offices, in

42. **Warm Springs Museum (lobby).**

the longhouse. Among the details evoking Native tradition are entrance-door pulls and metal forms outside the lobby that can be interpreted as feather bustles or sacred eagle feathers.

Among the exhibits in the 25,000-square-foot museum are replicas of tule mats, a wickiup, and a plank house (albeit made of milled boards); these are important in traditional architecture. A display about reservation residents in the armed forces from the 1860s to the 1990s shows that here again, modernity and patriotism accompany tradition and group self-consciousness.

Carol Mayer-Reed, as landscape architect, faced the problem of giving significance to a site without previous cultural resonance. She thought of the Fire Place, a salmon bake or picnic area for small groups that might not have barbecued food in the past but are as likely as anyone else to do so today. She had the idea for the Treaty Oak Place from an older woman who suggested planting a tree and establishing a sitting area near it. The Apple Tree Place might commemorate a generous woman who had

helped start farming at the reservation, and who traded her orchard's yield with hunters; as some tension persists between hunters and farmers, this area might have special meaning for residents. At the Creek Place might be a sweatlodge. Mayer-Reed also used native plants, just as the architects employed local stone and wood.[14]

Other versions of traditional buildings have been evoked in contemporary Native American architecture. The Hoopa administration building in central California, with its long, sloping profile, magnifies and modifies the indigenous pitched-roof buildings, some of them semisubterranean, that one can visit at the cultural grounds a short distance down the road. On the same reservation, Loren Norton*, who was learning to be a building contractor, erected a split-level house on a hillside at the direction of his mother, Marcellene*, a crafts expert seriously concerned with tribal culture. It shows clear ties to the Hupa pit house of the past, even though Marcellene Norton had not seen photographs of historic examples when she conceived the house plan. The cedar-plank structure has a sunken round living room, 4 feet deep as in Hupa lodges, with a ledge or deck that is usual around the top of the pit. The kitchen opens into the living room, while an added structure, having nothing to do with ancient pit houses, accommodates a bathroom and utility room.[15]

The Hoopa Library by D. Phillip Holcomb, completed in 1992, uses cedar planks donated by the tribe. These are becoming rare and therefore precious, and their use in this building shows the high regard of tribal members for the idea of a library. Working with a tight budget and charging low fees, Holcomb was able to use only the building shapes of the reservation era, but that is part of Hupa history, too. Nevertheless, being interested in historic tribal architecture, he tried to use "traditional dwelling shapes" to make something "evocative of them ... taking forms and materials and trying to evoke the feeling. A technological solution would not have worked." For this reason, the sides exposed to the public were bermed, recalling the old houses dug into the ground. The other sides, however, are concrete to deter vandals, and cedar shakes on the roof replaced "old cedar plank roofs [that] were leaky in the rain."

Long buildings of various types are found elsewhere— for instance, as evocations of the longhouse or later board-covered structures in New York State. In Basom, the Tonawanda Seneca community cultural building and clinic, built under the WPA between 1936 and 1939, is a two-story long building of cypress logs. John Teich, an architect in Cazenovia, added a wing in 1977 under instruction to "retain the longhouse idea." For the addition, reservation members cleared stone from their yards and donated it for the foundation. While neither part replicates old Seneca structures, the cultural center refers to traditional longhouses and local materials, and both sections were built by Amerindian labor.[16]

More obviously a paraphrase of an older building is the Iroquois Indian Museum (43), opened in 1992 at Howes Cave, New York. Although some Iroquois now live in other states and Canada, New York was a historic focus of their activity, and anthropologists there are prominent in Iroquoian studies. The museum was planned by scholars and is run by a cultural anthropologist, but Iroquois are trustees and staff members, the displays are exclusively of Iroquois cultures, and the museum has been blessed by spiritual leaders. It is based substantially on Native suggestions, it displays their donations, and it hosts Iroquois performing and fine artists, some of them highly critical of the Anglo impact on Native peoples. John P. Ferguson, chairman of the board of trustees, knew no Iroquois who were happy with the personal dissension at the "Turtle" multi-

43. **Iroquois Indian Museum, Howes Cave, New York. Banwell White Arnold Hemberger & Partners, 1992.**

44. DNA Legal Services Building (lobby), Window Rock, Arizona. Hemsley Martin Lee*, 1985.

latter permits repeated hammering of nails. They avoided an architect whose glass wall had "cooked" a valuable collection elsewhere, and kept in mind that those who design buildings do not have to work in them later.

Thanks to its situation on a slope, this modified longhouse can have a second, lower level with a rear door leading to a tent-covered outdoor performance area. The ends are open porches because C. Treat Arnold, architect with Banwell White Arnold Hemberger & Partners of Hanover, New Hampshire, understood that in historic longhouses "the ends were often lightly built, where expansion took place." Cedar shakes, some stained red and laid in horizontal bands, reflect the scale of the elm bark originally used by the Iroquois. The shingles cover plywood framed in steel that forms a single large interior room with subdivisions, an idea based on principles of the longhouse. The curved roof recalls bent-sapling construction, but off-the-shelf lumber-yard trusses bear on parallel stud walls for the sake of economy. The mezzanine is the modern replacement for the upper tier of living spaces in a genuine longhouse.

Circulation is counter-clockwise, as Arnold learned it was in older Iroquois buildings. A central skylight reminds us that aboriginal longhouses had smokeholes. Museum offices are aligned at the sides, like sleeping areas in a longhouse. Living tradition is emphasized, so that contemporary Iroquois artists have a central place. A sculptured turtle, supporter of the Iroquois world, floats in a pond, recalling the metaphor of Earth as Turtle Island. Images of geese from the creation story have been placed in the stairwell. In the grounds stands a nineteenth-century Iroquois cabin, moved from Canada by an Iroquois. Any additions to the museum will be similar buildings aligned with the first, as they would have been in an Iroquois village.

Arnold had known Ferguson, but had to compete with other architects for the commission. Arnold earned approval for his research on earlier Iroquois museum facilities. He had also learned about the practice of building new longhouses over burned ones—by extension, new museums to replace predecessors. The trustees welcomed his proposal for a tent-covered performance space.

The architecture is unusual enough to prompt questions from virtually everyone who passes the site, and many will quickly remember schoolbook pictures of Indian dwellings. It satisfies functional requirements well, even with only a third of the square footage envisioned in the first planning stages, and it does so in a building that shows respect for traditional architecture as well as ingenuity in its partial adaptation for current use.

tribal cultural center in Niagara Falls, which had contributed to that facility's physical problems. Part of the Native American population may therefore have been glad enough to see Euro-Americans take responsibility for funding, administration, and construction supervision at Howes Cave. White settlers had drawn the existing images of ancient Iroquois houses; their descendants paid for a longhouse museum.

The building is a rectangle 40 feet wide, 156 feet long, and 20 feet high—double any historic dimensions—evocative of a longhouse but not imitative. Ferguson and his fellow trustees wanted "something that evoked traditional architecture and also that was modern, not just a reconstruction," and did not want a rustic Adirondack lodge. They were concerned, too, with humidity control, with modern interior fittings, and with other practical matters important to museum professionals, having been alerted them to during visits to Native American and Canadian museums. They learned, for instance, to avoid half-inch sheetrock and to use plywood for display walls because the

The Winnebago of Nebraska may build a new office building for which Bruce Knutson of Minneapolis prepared a design (19). He intended it for the Wisconsin branch of the tribe, but they decided not to use it and sold the design to their compatriots farther south. Hoping to create something culturally sensitive, the architect consulted Dallas Whitewing* in the tribal executive office, who described longhouses. Knutson drew a double oval to attain desirable proportions and covered it with a barrel vault, creating a two-story interior atrium flanked by wings that contain work spaces. Longitudinal and transverse struts that seem to wrap around the building come from indigenous building methods. The architect proposed a terrazzo floor, with one design option being Winnebago symbols cast in place. Nearly everyone in the tribe admired the design, but a few elders thought it sacrilegious to replicate a longhouse, although the building avoided literal copying, being clad in brick and glass.

The Pamunkey Indian Museum and Cultural Center near King William, Virginia, was built in 1979 as a series of longhouses. Reservation residents owned artifacts and had been talking for some years about building a museum. "It was my idea to connect the longhouses," says museum official Warren Cook*. "The architect and designer were told we wanted an Indian motif, to show the culture of the area." With money from HUD and EDA, the tribe commissioned the Richmond architects Strange, Boston to execute the building. Funds obtained under the Comprehensive Employment and Training Act helped to pay for interior work. The tribal members, inexperienced at museum design, also received help from Eric Callahan, an anthropologist in Lynchburg.

In the Southwest, it is common to paraphrase historic architectural forms because Native peoples created stable structures of durable materials that can be used as models. The Navajo have several contemporary polygonal buildings, polygons alone sufficing to suggest hogans. Hemsley Martin Lee* designed the DNA Legal Services Building and the Navajo Education Center, both in Window Rock, Arizona. The legal-services facility has a polygonal lobby with skylights (44). It is colored dark rust outside and embellished with geometric designs around the roof edge; the entrance is at the east, following hogan tradition. The education building, built two years later, is a pair of enlarged russet-colored hogans joined together. The interiors suit office and legal work, and are not based on tradition.

At Navajo Community College in Tsaile, Arizona, other polygons designed by Chambers, Campbell & Partners of Albuquerque reflect differences in function and in representative purpose (45, 46). Raymond Nakai*, when

45. Ned A. Hatathli Center, Navajo Community College, Tsaile, Arizona. Chambers, Campbell & Partners, 1973.

46. Dormitories, Navajo Community College, Tsaile,
Arizona. Chambers, Campbell & Partners, 1973.

seeking the office of tribal chairman, pledged to build an
"academy" of Navajo-centered studies. It first offered
classes in 1969 and expanded into its present form in 1973
after funding came through the Navajo Community College Act of 1971 (PL 89-192). The college's first president,
Robert Roessel, married to a Navajo, selected the firm of
Douglas Campbell, who understood that the design
should reflect the Navajos' own surroundings and culture.
At the time, this was an unusual idea.

The preeminent structure is the Ned A. Hatathli Center (45), at the east side of the campus, named in memory
of the college's second president. It houses administrative
and public facilities in a glass-walled octagon of reinforced
concrete that rises from brick supports resting on a berm.
Low concrete steps ascend to the octagon. In the center of
the ground floor, a circular area is used for meditation.
Board meetings and other important events are held in a
room with an earthen floor. Chant rooms for community
religious purposes were planned for the second story. Part
of the building was intended as a cultural center (although
it now houses administrators), and as part of an art collec-

tion begun in 1983, the college commissioned murals of
Navajo subjects for each floor, fourteen of which were
installed in 1985. Near the building stand a hogan and a
brush shelter.

The rest of the Tsaile campus is laid out along a circular road opening only at the east, with buildings placed to
match the functions within a hogan. Near the center, in
the hearth position, stands the dining room, with food prepared on the southeastern side and consumed in the southwest. Classrooms are in the east, the side associated with
learning. Dormitories are in the west, the direction of
sleeping, while vocational and professional education are
offered toward the south, the direction of daylight, which
helps one in knowing how to earn a living. In the north are
the gymnasium and student union. These ideas came from
traditional healers, assembled from the entire reservation.
Not all their ideas were used, but they blessed the result,
inventing a ritual based on the act of planting by Changing
Woman, which created the Navajo people.

The educational and social activities are carried out in
low polygonal buildings of domestic scale, evoking hogans

to the satisfaction of local observers (46). Dormitories are sixteen-room "hogans" with baseboard heating instead of traditional fireplaces. Other structures are faculty houses that have required extensive retrofitting to conserve energy; before the oil crisis of 1973, few architects gave extended thought to this matter. Through both curriculum and architecture, the institution fosters self-esteem.

References to the culture are found at three levels. The most serious was the relationship of the overall campus plan to activity centers in hogans. The most obvious was provision of centrally planned, multisided buildings for all purposes, altered in size, height, and finishing materials to suit the building type. The least convincing is the elevation of a Navajo building high above the ground and the cladding in reflective glass. The Hatathli Center was, however, erected early in the new movement toward culturally appropriate design; there had been few previous attempts. In addition, it was to be the home of essential campus functions in the first tribally controlled college. Both architect and client must have found it desirable to have at least one imposing structure on the campus; other college campuses have bell towers, domed administration buildings, and turreted Alumni Halls. At least the glass

reflects the sky, bringing the Hatathli Center into a new relationship with its natural surroundings.[17]

Other recent designs come closer to the original model. On the campus of the University of Colorado at Boulder, Charles Cambridge*, while a doctoral candidate, and architect Dennis Holloway, then at the College of Environmental Design, built three experimental hogans that used various types and levels of energy (47, 48). Cambridge had been thinking of a project of this kind since 1977, but only in 1988 did the collaborators receive a grant from the Colorado Office of Energy Conservation; funds from the university; and materials and services donated by local businesses, 260 students, and 35 other volunteers. On October 6, 1989, George Bluehorse*, an elder, inaugurated the buildings in a Navajo blessingway ceremony.

These are not traditional hogans but energy-conscious ones, built within HUD cost guidelines, provided with windows, and intended to help the Navajo become self-sufficient in domestic energy. They were also meant to show federal authorities that Indian housing could be energy-efficient yet entirely different in appearance from the usual HUD designs. Cambridge intended that some of the units be for Navajo who want to live on the reservation

47. Solar-heated hogans, Boulder, Colorado. Dennis Holloway and Charles Cambridge*, 1989. (Courtesy Tom Noel, 1990)

in their old age, but for whom struggling with harsh weather conditions and the absence of electricity or running water constitute hardships that few people today can endure, however traditionally inclined they may be. The hogans at Boulder use electricity from solar panels. Waterless toilets evaporate waste. Propane fuels cooking, and water is hauled to the site. The north walls are doubled, with insulation between them. Sensors in the walls monitor energy use, each hogan being wired to a computer that measures thermal changes inside and out.

The first unit is 16 feet in diameter, domed, with a smokehole in its cribbed log ceiling that rests on walls of local sandstone (47). Weeds grow on the roof in summertime, possibly aiding insulation. The second unit has a flagstone encircling wall with eastern and western windows. The wall protects a space on the south that can be used for outdoor living or for planting. The three south-facing walls hold glass-fiber glazing material developed with Arnold Valdez of Ghost Ranch, New Mexico. It reflects the sun's heat and becomes the main heat source so that less wood-burning is needed indoors.

The third unit is a three-bedroom house built into a hillside (48). The lower level has 1600 square feet of living space, including the bath and kitchen. The upper level is a hogan with a separate entrance from a terraced walk. On the southern side, large windows of insulated glass are set at an angle that receives the winter sun and bounces away the rays of the summer sun. An active solar system beside the hogan heats a hot-water tank, with the water pressurized by a solar-powered pump. Water used for bathing and dish-washing is meant to be recycled for use in the garden. Photovoltaic cells track the sun, fueling electric lights and small appliances, while the stove and refrigerator use propane.

These experimental buildings have had some problems. Under Navajo chairman Peter MacDonald*, the head of the Navajo division of HUD did not support this effort. The smallest unit used earth with an insufficiently high clay content, so that the building retains water and

48. Solar-heated hogan, Boulder, Colorado. Dennis Holloway and Charles Cambridge*, 1980. (Ed Kosmicki; courtesy Office of Public Relations, University of Colorado)

has had to be covered with tar and plastic roofing. The log hogan suffered rotting from water damage, again owing to the use of the wrong kind of earth. All were meant to be used as dormitories, especially for Native American students, but they are now used by New Agers and by an alcohol-rehabilitation group for Native Americans. The university covets the isolated site on which the hogans rise, and occasionally, young vandals attack the buildings.

They have, nevertheless, survived, and may have inspired the solar hogans near Window Rock on the Navajo Reservation, executed by an architect from Gallup at the behest of Chevron Oil, which had to rehouse a woman displaced by one of the company's projects. While Cambridge was building his experimental houses, Save the Children Fund supplied money for fourteen solar-fitted houses in Cottonwood, Arizona; by the end of 1988, about 150 Navajo homes had been fitted with solar panels under a program at Northern Arizona University in which student engineers applied their knowledge of solar energy to Navajo dwellings. Unlike the examples at Boulder, however, these were not hogan-shaped.[18]

Because the Navajo Reservation is very large, social services are offered within buildings known as chapter houses. They are located near water sources and other community facilities in various districts. Each has an assembly room, a conference room, and a kitchen, and some have a laundry, a sewing room, and other facilities. Chapter houses can be polygonal, or consciously hogan-shaped, some of them with sloping roofs to recall the contours of the hogan. There is no standard model. Among the examples built since 1985 are those at Chichiltah, where older women measured the dimensions according to the length of their own feet and where a Navajo blessing initiated the building activity; at Alamo (1985–1987) by David Sloan* & Associates, where an octagonal skylit multipurpose room is nearly encased in a rectangle and where Isaac*, a Navajo artist, executed murals with local subject matter; and at Steamboat, where the Sloan firm simply created a fifth side on the gray concrete building to break from a pure rectangle. This attractive small chapter house has a metal roof and other details colored bright blue, a symbolically referential color.[19]

Housing for older Navajo, proposed by the TM Group in 1991, provided for the eastern entry seen in hogans and for a fireplace located slightly off center, as it is often placed in hogans. The circular form was intended to evoke both the polygonal building type and a sundial. Beams were to radiate outward from the fireplace area, an inspiration from the tribal buildings of the 1930s and the National

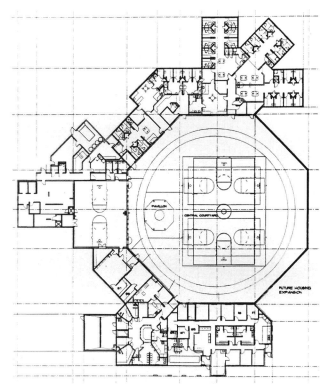

49. **Juvenile detention center (plan), Tuba City, Arizona. Arctic Slope Consulting Group, 1993. (Courtesy Winton Smith, ASCG [Albuquerque])**

Park Service architecture at Grand Canyon. The buildings were to be stone-faced, which the architect saw as "essentially Navajo," and to be built by the nation's excellent stone masons. Seeing the principles of geometry and symmetry as characteristic of the culture, the same architect proposed a prefabricated senior-citizen-center model with a fireplace, the axial formality of rugs, and an evaporative cooler to balance the fireplace visually and functionally.[20]

An unusual use for the hogan form is a pair of juvenile-detention facilities on the Navajo Reservation, one with thirty-six beds at Tuba City (49) and the other with fifty beds at Chinle. They were designed in 1993 and 1994 by Winton L. Smith of the Arctic Slope Consulting Group, a firm owned by Inupiat Alaskans, assisted by architect Randal Blair, mechanical engineer Bob Bassett, civil engineer Dan Cook, and structural engineer Kenton Steiner. Robert Montoya* was project manager for the BIA. Bureau of Indian Affairs Superintendent Ed Carlisle wanted an arrangement of spaces recalling the "different areas of responsibility based on the different directions," an idea he might have adopted from a planning committee

50. Visitor center, Chaw'Se Indian Grinding Rocks State Park, California. 1974.

including elders and spiritual leaders of the local Navajo communities; this type of committee has recently been introduced for BIA projects.

The plans include eastern entrances; separate areas for male and female inmates and for overseers; and administrative, classroom, and service areas around central courtyards with multipurpose sports courts. The architects describe the arrangement as being "very much the way extended family dwellings have been organized traditionally," a reference to the independent but coordinated structures of a family settlement. At Chinle, there is a smokehole in the center, omitted at Tuba City, where the authorities were concerned with leakage and preferred a sloping roof. Both buildings include traditional blanket patterns woven into the exterior masonry and interior spaces, and finishes that match earth tones were selected.

A good deal of hope is invested in cultural reference. According to Theodore Evans*, former Navajo council member from Chinle, "if it doesn't bring back meaning, then it's just kind of a real detention center," a jail rather than a rehabilitative facility.[21] The central courtyard for gathering the inmates and for performing ceremonies reflects the "intent...to take them back to their roots" and to increase "the strength they get from their culture and beliefs."[22] The goal is detention leading to rehabilitation, employing aspects of culture to make a better lifeway apparent.

* * *

The roundhouse presents the same opportunities for cultural identification as the hogan does, although both may be parodied by fast-food shops and highway attractions that trim polygonal or circular plans with Indian-inspired decoration. North of Albuquerque, on land belonging to Sandia Pueblo, the Bien Mur Indian Market Center of about 1980 is an enlarged and much-heightened roundhouse, based on a model from California rather than Sandia. It suggests an exotic place enticing to tourists; in its context, that would mean generically Indian rather than something expressive of a specific Native culture. If the original owner was in fact an Anglo banker in Albuquerque, that could explain the appearance of an incongruous roundhouse on a highway in New Mexico.

The Miwuk visitor center in Chaw'Se Indian Grinding Rocks State Park, by contrast, had a tribal origin and purpose (50). The Miwuk had maintained an annual celebration in a roundhouse, dedicated in 1969, within the reconstructed village in this park, but in the late 1970s, with the help of the California Department of Parks and Recreation, they lobbied the state architect's office for a cultural center where their artifacts could be housed. They hoped for $1 million but were given half that, for a smaller building than they had planned; money for staff, displays, and a parking lot was added only several years later. The building may have been designed proportionately taller and narrower than a traditional roundhouse to distinguish it from the traditional structures close by. Its back porch, overlooking the rebuilt village and grinding rocks, would not have been found on a traditional roundhouse.

The visitor center is a polygon, faced in wood, with a sloping roof and freestanding internal supports. Using some metal and plastics made practical sense. The two windows result from a compromise between the Native Americans, who wanted none, for greater authenticity, and the architect, who originally designed more. The Miwuk supported it until disputes over administrative and commercial matters strained their relationship with the state's parks department.[23]

The health center for the Round Valley Rancheria is a wood-surfaced building of central plan under a low, sloping roof with an overhang, generally reminiscent of the low roundhouses in central California. Other small buildings for tribes in California also occasionally evoke the roundhouse, but religious connotations of the roundhouse may limit its use for purposes other than those related to spiritual or physical health.

Perhaps cultural knowledge was associated with spiritual matters in the case of the Pomo Cultural Center at Lake Mendocino, dedicated in 1982 (51, 52). It is also possible that the collaborating architects looked for an identifiably Indian form to emphasize that the building lies on land taken by the state from its Native owners; the center represents partial compensation, and it is operated by the Pomo. This beautiful small modern version of a roundhouse, used for exhibitions and teaching, was designed by the Army Corps of Engineers and the Promontory Partnership.[24] The architects were selected in open bidding. They developed the design in concert with Native Californians who exercised enough control to prevent the employment of one contractor. The Native representatives were originally members of the Mendocino Lake Pomo Council, but are now from the Coyote Valley Band, as some tribes find it difficult to work together or with the government.

The building is circular, with auxiliary spaces stretching out on three sides, and buttresses arching over curved benches at an outdoor assembly space. The eastern side facing the lake has large windows in the shingled walls. Small windows open to the north of the northeastern entrance. A central chimney occupies the heart of the building, much as the stepped tower does at the Pyramid Lake Cultural Center in Nevada, where one also sees ceiling ribs radiating from the center. The Lake Mendocino building is discreet, its shingles weathering to a subtle gray of an intensity matching that of surrounding trees, so that the eastern side seems almost to fade into the landscape. The assembly space is surprisingly bold, given the reticence of the most visible eastern side, but it ought to be, to enhance people's expectations of presentations held there.[25]

Another central plan, an octagon, defines the small, grayed wooden Upper Sioux Community Tribal Office, on Highway 67 east of Granite Falls, Minnesota. An eastern door leads to offices surrounding a skylit central meeting room.[26] Here, a traditional ceremonial building is transformed into offices—a difficult feat from a conceptual

51. Pomo Cultural Center, Lake Mendocino, California.
Promontory Partnership, 1982.

52. Pomo Cultural Center (outdoor performance area).

viewpoint, but easy enough if form alone is considered meaningful and if it suits the modern program.

Bonnie Tehm Wadsworth*, active in cultural affairs at the Fort Hall Shoshone–Bannock Reservation in Idaho, finds that suitable form and meaning suffice to give Native Americans "an idea of older buildings." She discussed the reservation museum, based on a district meeting place built in 1934, itself based on the polygonal form of local lodges. The museum is made of two attached hexagons enclosing 2640 square feet. The larger one is the display area; the second, a support building. The sixteen reservation members concerned with the museum, working with a Native American architect employed by a firm in Washington State, would have preferred a two-story museum, but the existing structure satisfied the desire to "represent part of our history.... Some people notice it could recall sundance lodges," although neither the building technique nor certain details copy those of historic architecture. Cost-reduction measures required a post in the center to ensure sturdiness, but "when a Native American does come in, he gets an idea of older building."

As in many Native museums, displays here inform local people of their heritage, and also attract tourists and dispel stereotypes; "that's how you get rid of prejudice," as Bonnie Wadsworth points out. Historic presentations are shown in clockwise order, from the origin story to the present. But while Shoshone–Bannock people move around a tipi or sweatlodge by first turning toward the left to start a circular movement, most visitors start at the right. A sign is unlikely to change habitual behavior or the common desire to wander at will, so the displays will be shifted in position.

A tipi is sometimes placed in the center. Its opening faces east, but the museum door is at the west, making the tipi opening invisible from the building entrance. Elders advised reversing the tipi, finding that the orientation matters to tipis outdoors but not to those on display. In ways such as these, Native tradition flexibly accommodates contemporary necessity.

Other modern centrally planned lodges are found in the Dakotas. Knife River Indian Villages National Historic Site near Stanton, North Dakota, has a visitors center finished in 1992 to the design of Surrounded-by-Enemy* (102). The exterior is a striking zoomorphic invention, but the principal interior space resembles an earth lodge in having four supports hold a domical roof, here a skylit cupola. The warm color of wood reinforces this association. The surrounding walls are not solid, as they would have been in the past, but are broken by doors and parti-

tions leading to a cinema and administrative spaces at the sides. Opposite the entrance, broad glass windows afford a view toward the mounds and the path that leads to them.[27]

The Harry V. Johnston Cultural Center in Eagle Butte, South Dakota, was built in 1973 as an octagon partly surrounded by auxiliary spaces, funded by the foundation that gave the center its name (53). The Anglo architect may have been inspired by ideas from a reservation resident. The building was intended to be like a shingled sweatlodge, considered similar in having a community purpose and in being supported by eight verticals that bend and meet at the top, about 30 feet above the floor. The building accommodates small powwows, naming ceremonies, giveaways, and traditional "feeds." A facade added in 1977 features two concrete pylons and battle scenes painted in 1978 by M. Running Wolf*, a tribal member. Three artists, including Matthew Uses-the-Knife*, director of the facility, painted additional murals on the walls of the octagon.[28]

Newer, handsome examples of centrally planned buildings are found at two separate districts of the Mille Lacs Reservation in Minnesota, where Cuningham Hamilton Quiter architects in Minneapolis, designed ceremonial structures that opened in 1993 (54–57). These and five other buildings, including two schools and a clinic, were financed by tax-free bonds backed by revenue from two profitable casinos. The ceremonial buildings have won awards from the Minnesota chapter of the American Institute of Architects and from the Interfaith Forum on Religion, Art and Architecture. Neither imitates precisely a nineteenth-century antecedent known from a photograph and one differs from the other, but both are creative versions of older drum-ceremony buildings in which thanks are given to the spirits each spring and autumn. At the Mille Lacs District near Onamia, the building is a 30-foot-high octagon within a square (54, 55); this was the form known from the early photograph. At Lake Lena, the two-story octagon alone has a dramatic interior congenial to that independent-minded community (56, 57).

The three-tiered octagon in a bowed square (technically a dodecagon at ceiling level) was the first of several new buildings to be erected at Mille Lacs. One elder pointed out that without this one and the rituals it housed, there would be no need for the others. The architects attended ceremonies to learn how many people to accommodate, and then recommended an appropriate size without prescribing or insisting on their figures; partner John Cuningham and Robert Zakaras, Team Leader for Native Projects, learned quickly the importance of listening and of being directed by the band.

53. Harry V. Johnston Cultural Center, Eagle Butte, South
Dakota. Paintings by M. Running Wolf*, 1977.

The clients wanted buildings oriented to the lake and
woods, taking advantage of important locations or topo-
graphical features. They considered economy of materials
and the use of natural ones to be important; they allowed
concrete block and stucco along with wood as being of the
earth, and preferred cedar or even asphalt roof shingles textured and colored to recall the forest setting. Strict orientation to the cardinal points was required in ceremonial
buildings. They preferred forms that were often "softer"
than those in other buildings, with low sloping roof lines
and canopies at transition points. Cuningham came to
understand the importance of "the absence of an ego in a
building. It would be puzzling to them to do a building
that had an ego."

The architects worked with a contractor from another
band. The Mille Lacs building emphasizes wood—fir
structure, cedar-log walls, rough-sawn-cedar shingled roof
with broad overhangs, maple floor, and laminated wood
beams and columns. Nature is further evoked by ceiling
fixtures recalling birds in flight. Light enters through a
central clerestory and door transoms, but as with many
Native American buildings for religious and ceremonial
activity, there are no low windows on the surrounding
walls; attention must be focused on the community and its
actions, now as in the past.

At Lake Lena, where the ceremonial building overlooks the lake, the same materials are seen, as well as the
kitchen, toilets, and storage areas needed in both ceremonial structures (56, 57). At 3400 square feet, this is 100
square feet larger than its sister building. Here the glue-
laminated structure radiates from the core, creating a striking form that seems to reach out toward the participants on
benches around the perimeter. In the center is a small area
of earthen floor, reflecting the community's strong wish to
make contact with the earth during the ceremonies, a
desire common to most Native American ritual activity.[29]

The Mille Lacs District is also the location of a house
based on a round wigwam, but entirely of this century (58,
59). It is comparable in section to Le Corbusier's galleried
apartment plans or to Ralph Erskine's hemispheric house
for an engineering-company director on the Swedish
island of Lisö.[30] The home of Don and Joycelyn* Wedll,
respectively Natural Resources Commissioner and Site
Manager/Curator of the Museum for the Mille Lacs Band.
The house was conceived independently of the European
examples, but like them has a bedroom gallery raised
above a lower level. Distinctive in this house is the wood
surface of the walls and the rough stone cladding on a flue
at one edge of the living room.

Don Wedll, a student of mathematics at college,

54. Mille Lacs Ceremonial Building, Onamia, Minnesota. Cuningham Hamilton Quiter, 1993. (Courtesy Cuningham Hamilton Quiter)

55. Mille Lacs Ceremonial Building. (Courtesy Cuningham Hamilton Quiter)

56. Mille Lacs Ceremonial Building, Lake Lena, Minnesota. Cuningham Hamilton Quiter, 1993. (Courtesy Cuningham Hamilton Quiter)

57. Mille Lacs Ceremonial Building. (Courtesy Cuningham Hamilton Quiter)

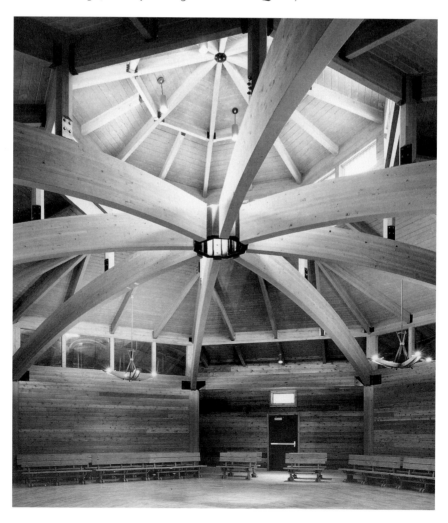

58. Wedll house, Onamia, Minnesota. Don Wedll, 1980.

59. Wedll house.

understood, as Erskine did in a similar climate, that a hemisphere is the most efficient space to heat, and Wedll knew how to cut the spherical triangles that cover the house. His inspiration came when he noticed plans to build a simple wigwam of ironwood for the reservation's Head Start program. Observing the structural strength of the wigwam, he reasoned that using contemporary materials might produce an exceptionally rigid structure suitable for a dwelling. R. Buckminster Fuller's ideas for geodesic domes seemed to require many seams or large pieces of building material. Wedll's procedure, suggested by an elderly inventor, was to laminate small curved pieces of wood to form beams, a method common in old barns. Having previously built another house, Wedll had learned how best to raise the rafters, and knew that the curve should start not at the ground but above walls about 4 feet high, allowing for eaves. The exterior is asphalt shingled. Wedll began to build in July 1980, and moved in that October, having even built the kitchen cabinets by then. The materials, common at any lumber yard, were cheap, costing $6800; a well cost about $1200. If a contractor had built this for a client—perhaps a tribal housing authority—the costs would probably have doubled, but they would have remained substantially lower than those of HUD houses.

The long, low Menominee school at Neopit, Wisconsin, has been described by a neighboring Ojibwe as "strikingly similar to a lodge in shape." A rectangular masonry base supports a curved roof framed in wood, reflecting the general form of longhouse or wigwam. Over the entrance, a cantilever echoes the protective entrance of historic lodges, while the cafeteria has round vaults like those of a wickiup. Contractors used lumber from Menominee land. Murals on the school were designed by a reservation artist. Given the Menominee history of termination and revival, the emphasis on local sources and tradition is a positive element in cultural revival. Indeed, the "mission of the Menominee Indian School District is to establish an educational program compatible with Menominee Indian heritage and with community involvement."[31]

* * *

It is easier to paraphrase pueblo architecture for modern purposes than it is to vary the hogan, roundhouse, or central-plan lodge, since those are single, enclosed shapes while the pueblo is a flexible composite of many smaller, generally rectangular elements, sometimes varied with circular ritual spaces. In an unbuilt design for the Museum of Fine Arts in Santa Fe, Edward Larrabee Barnes proposed to combine hogan and pueblo for the display of both Navajo and Pueblo works (60). He saw Navajo culture as centrifugal, and referred to its "restless, episodic history which is reflected in their art by stylistic changes." This seemed to require showing Navajo "cultural evolution…in a linear fashion, chronologically" in a series of separate galleries along a square outer wall of the building and in "the circle enclosing the Pueblo area…. As one proceeds through this space, the rooms pinch in and open out, suggesting the fluctuating fortune of the tribes." By contrast, he found the Pueblo peoples centripetal, "agrarian, rooted, timeless," with villages centered around the kiva but looking outward to four sacred mountains. Accordingly, he designed the central circular area to be entered from below, so that one could see on the upper walls photographs of the four mountains. Cases in a maze-like pattern were to hold displays; this pattern was probably derived from plans of historic pueblos. Even if Navajo and Pueblo peoples dispute his interpretation, it was ingenious and several conceptual steps beyond the smooth walls and rounded corners that constitute much pueblo-style design.[32]

The Hopi Cultural Center at Second Mesa, dedicated in June 1971, originated with the desire of Fred Kabotie*, artist and cultural affairs director, to have a museum, library, and craft workrooms (61). Under Hopi chairman Charles Hamilton*, a development corporation was established to promote economic benefits and jobs; the cultural center was to help fulfill these goals. As financing through a bank loan posed risks, owing to difficulties over reposses-

60. Indian Arts Museum (addition to Museum of Fine Arts, unbuilt project), Santa Fe, New Mexico. Edward Larrabee Barnes, 1979. (Courtesy Edward Larrabee Barnes)

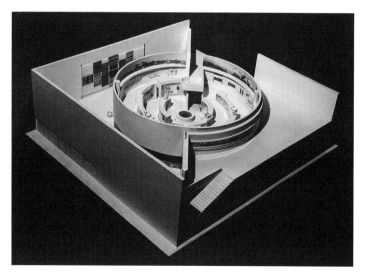

61. Hopi Cultural Center, Second Mesa, Arizona. Bennie Gonzales, 1971.

sion, the Economic Development Administration funded the project.

Bennie Gonzales, well known in the Southwest for his buildings in regional style, submitted the winning response to a request for bids. He had worked for the BIA on several Navajo projects, and credits the bureau for promoting his selection. At Second Mesa, perhaps because of cost constraints, the results have been described as "debased copies of a generalized Hopi village."[33] From an archaeological viewpoint that may be true, but from the viewpoint of function and tourist appeal the judgment is harsh. The cultural center is made of several small buildings grouped around courtyards that evoke the general arrangement of a Hopi village centered on a plaza. Performances are held in the open spaces. Breezeways and small patios link craft shops on the west. The complex includes museum and shop spaces. A successful restaurant, eventually enlarged, is a focal point, and behind it, motel units offer simple but comfortable accommodation in rooms decorated in styles associated with Pueblo design. The limited budget, the remote site, and the expertise of Hopi as masons determined the use of concrete block. As many Hopi as wanted jobs on the project were able to get them, but a shortage of skilled labor meant hiring other workers also. Reservation officials, Hopi intellectuals, and university anthropologists find the forms appropriate, and one hopes that Hopi youth derive from it the inspiration that Kabotie hoped to create.[34]

It is unusual for pueblo-like buildings to be circular, recalling kivas in plan, but one example is the Santa Clara Senior/Community Center, planned in 1993 by Arctic Slope Consulting Group working with tribal planner Mel Tafoya* (62). Like most such facilities, this one is to have dining and meeting areas, a kitchen, offices, and other services, as well as rooms for craft work and for transmitting culture through storytelling and reading. The architects describe the design and function as "reminiscent of the Grand Kivas of pueblo ancestors with tall spacious circular

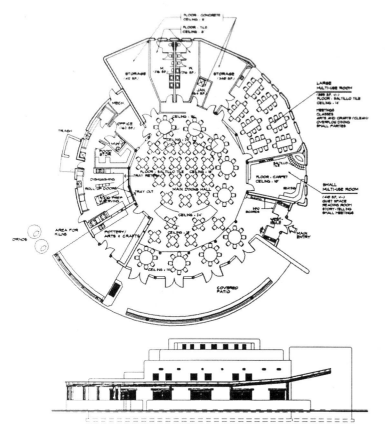

62. Santa Clara Senior/Community Center (project drawings), Santa Clara Pueblo, New Mexico. Arctic Slope Consulting Group, 1993. (Courtesy Winton Smith, ASCG)

gathering spaces filtered with natural light and surrounded by smaller rooms.... Exterior spaces are equally important in pueblo culture; a ramada on the south side invites the use of an open grill and adobe bread ovens for the preparation of traditional foods." The external treatment shows stepped walls with softened edges, rising from the perimeter rooms to a clerestory above the central space. Vigas protrude from the lowest walls. The smooth spaces of the entrance side may receive mural painting. The architects speak of active community participation in the planning, and of construction work by reservation residents. While pueblos of the past would not have accommodated these purposes in a round, kiva-like building, and would not have had all the windows that modern life demands, the effect is convincingly traditional by the standards of today.

Older traditions did not allow for the splitting of large multifunction rooms, nor were there houses for nuclear families or rooms and special buildings for people of specific ages. Rina Naranjo Swentzell* of Santa Clara Pueblo,

architect and writer on Tewa culture, finds these subdivisions to be evidence of the Americanization of her people, clearly evident in the restricted uses of space; she writes of this phenomenon as the "secularization of life." [35]

Other recent architecture reveals this combined culture, now current in the pueblos. The Jemez administrative offices occupy a massive structure with the rough planar walls and softened edges of historic local architecture, although its isolation from any context shows that the building is modern. For the Jemez elementary school, Neal McCaleb* juxtaposed rectangular earth-toned prisms, and let the roofs project to provide shelter from the sun (63). Finding the pueblo traditional, he tried to approximate the appearance of older architecture by using a stucco finish over concrete block. No one seems to have wanted to imitate a historic model, however. A tiny shaded garden near the entrance is backed by a wall with symbolic reliefs, and a metal sculpture of a family hangs on the broadest wall plane of the facade; the relief and sculpture were designed by Jannita Complo*, the former principal.

San Juan Pueblo's Oke-Owe'enge Crafts Cooperative and Cultural Center, dedicated in 1973, is comparable to the Jemez school in using long, horizontal forms with smooth surfaces and a certain amount of modern glass, and in creating a sheltered pocket of space inside the building line, here without plants. Andy Acoya* worked with Chambers, Campbell & Isaacson of Albuquerque, assisting the co-op with schematics and helping the architects with documents; Acoya knew the firm from its earlier work at Laguna Pueblo. For this project, members of the cooperative contributed ideas and spoke about cultural appropriateness, being aware of the other architectural styles used on the same plaza. The interior spaces radiate from a fireplace, a familiar image for pueblo residents. David Saile, a sensitive observer of regional tradition, found this, the San Felipe tribal office extension, and the Eight Northern Pueblos Indian Council headquarters to be "fine efforts to accommodate new functions without undermining the architectural continuity of their settings." [36]

One of the handsomest paraphrases is the school at San Felipe Pueblo by Mimbres Associates, designed in the early 1980s (64). Robert Montoya*, who supervised the work of Michael Doody, the designer, spoke of the building as being based on a "pueblo theme." Val Cordova*, former principal, admits that he "drove the architects crazy" by offering suggestions, as did parents, the teaching staff, and the tribal council, but they got most of what they wanted.

Here again are juxtaposed geometric prisms, softened

63. Jemez elementary school, Jemez Pueblo, New Mexico. Neal A. McCaleb*, Jack Nusbaum, and Robert L. Thomas, 1980.

64. San Felipe elementary school, San Felipe Pueblo, New Mexico. Mimbres Associates, 1982.

slightly at the corners and varied with surfaces in muted yellow and orange. As at Jemez, the forms seem to become smaller and more intimate as one approaches the entrance, a good idea in a building that welcomes children. And here, too, there are plants, this time in front of the enclosing wall, and then inside it, near the entrance. Between the wall and the school proper is a play area, separated into areas for different age groups, and there are trees for shade. The kindergarten teachers were especially active in assisting the design process for their area. As at Jemez, the administrative rooms were designed to be visible (although a later principal installed shades for privacy); this may reflect the desire for communal openness often described as characteristic of Native American public life.

San Felipe parents and staff consider the design appropriate, and although Cordova was not pleased with one feature, the multipurpose room, he realized that the budget had not allowed for ideal solutions everywhere.[37]

Architects Wayne Lloyd of McHugh Lloyd Tryk and Dennis Holloway, at the direction of George Rivera*, a Pojoaque Pueblo artist, designed the Poeh Cultural Center to evoke Spanish-influenced form and then pueblo forms alone (65, 66). Having been drastically reduced in population, but having increased recently, pueblo members investigated their cultural heritage, established a community building by 1970, and revived their dances in 1973. The traditional offices of war chief and captains are once again filled, to reconstitute lost practices. Poeh planners

65. Poeh Cultural Center (model), Pojoaque Pueblo, New Mexico. Dennis Holloway. Under construction, 1994. (Courtesy Dennis Holloway)

conceived a cultural center where the combined drawing power of several pueblos could make the facility more significant for all Tewa people and more attractive to visitors. Since 1989, they have resolved to conduct archival research and to promote participation in cultural activities. The Northern Pueblo Arts Council will have its offices there; it is meant to be a model of cultural revitalization and intertribal cooperation, where natural vegetation and land will be respected.

Holloway hoped to evoke a pueblo in the "design of space, the buildings in the plaza, the size of the buildings, changes in levels of the rooftops and parapets." The buildings are also designed to keep people cool by traditional means. Rivera hopes to build a pueblo for the present, finding it "crucial to incorporate [the past] because it is the identity of the people." Modifications will make "it functional for today and for the future," so that, for example, reinforced concrete would be allowed for structural purposes although not for exposed surfaces. Only one building is to be traditional in construction and form, an exhibit in itself with stone foundations, adobe above, and no nails. Rivera anticipated that the construction workers here and on the whole project would be "99 percent Pueblo."

A first construction stage features a symbolic building, a four-story tower, inspired by Alfonso Ortiz*, an authority on Tewa culture and adviser to the Poeh project. Holloway proposed a building with a functional kiva in the basement, and with windows in the tower opening toward each of the existing eight pueblos. Other windows are to face ancestral ruins at ancient Chama and Ojo. Windows at the top open to the sunrise and sunset, as these directions are important in Pueblo corn-planting rituals. An account of this project given with Rivera's approval offers additional details and, more important, sets the project in its context of Pojoaque revival (see Appendix).

This comprehensive conceptual effort is unusual, because most modern pueblo design deals with individual buildings or small groups of houses—usually not attached, as they were in the past. There has also been restoration with infill at historic locations; one example is Tesuque, where Arctic Slope Consulting Group has designed some new buildings. It appears to be the especially intense desire for regeneration that has driven the Poeh project. Especially if revenues from the Cities of Gold casino prove sufficient, the Poeh Cultural Center is likely to be built and to draw a considerable audience from those who come at first only for entertainment.[38]

Another approximation of a historic model is the Indian Pueblo Cultural Center in Albuquerque, planned

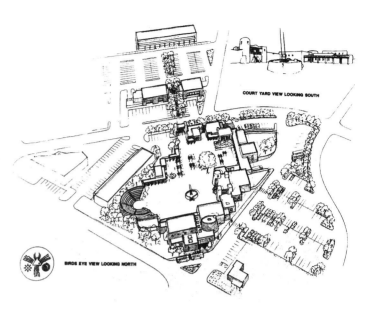

66. Poeh Cultural Center (preliminary plan). McHugh Lloyd Tryk. (Courtesy McHugh Lloyd Tryk)

around 1970 and built in 1975 and 1976 to the design of Hoshour & Pearson of Albuquerque (67); later, David Riley* designed a wall and an identifying sign at the edge of the property. The building incorporates the functions of a museum of Pueblo culture, shops selling Indian-made products, a venue for Native performances, and a social meeting place. Funding came when Senator Joseph Montoya lobbied for money to increase tourism, appealing to the EDA for $800,000, which the Native sponsors supplemented with $200,000 worth of land. The center provides about forty to fifty on-site jobs.

Joe Sando*, a Jemez historian and storyteller, said that "it comforts me to have the center here. When I feel city-bound and out of touch, it provides me with a quick, sure reconnection to my heritage."[39] This was a grass-roots project, not one created and run by professional curators or anthropologists. In this facility, "the Pueblo Indian himself will present the reality of his history and the facts of his present existence."[40]

The plan is approximately semicircular, with a straight entrance arm and curved spaces devoted to the shops at ground level. Between the shops and on the inner entrance wall are huge murals by several Pueblo artists, including Robert Montoya* (also an architect) and Pablita Velarde*. Near the entrance is an information desk, and the ground floor also accommodates an auditorium, a restaurant offering Native foods, and a plaza for dance per-

67. **Indian Pueblo Cultural Center (interior court),**
Albuquerque, New Mexico. Hoshour & Pearson, 1976.

formances and ceremonies. On an upper level are admin-istrative and conference rooms, while underground are museum displays; a library and a radio and media center were also planned below grade. Display cases fit the period of the artifacts shown in them, changing, for instance, from cavelike surrounds to those in imitation adobe brick.

The semicircular form with its rough-textured, adobe-colored surface is often said to be based on Pueblo Bonito at Chaco Canyon. The present Hoshour staff says so, as does Andy Acoya,* who worked at the Hoshour firm in the past. So does a typescript account produced by the center itself. Harvey Hoshour denied any conscious connection (as architects often do), saying that as he had often visited the canyon, perhaps the ruins had "some effect on my design, if only an unconscious one."[41] The architects would have preferred to design rooms on several levels, creating something closer to ancient pueblo form, but the present simplified elevation is due to cost constraints.[42]

The form gathers people into a coherent space, pro-vides both flat and curved backdrops for performances, allows spectators to spread out or to group themselves informally around a broad curve, and makes all the shops visible to anyone entering the premises. The solid walls screen out traffic and external noise, and the high walls make people more aware of the interior space. The south-eastern orientation captures the winter sun.

Native Americans know enough about their own heritage to appreciate both Chaco Canyon and the In-dian Pueblo Cultural Center in separate ways. Visitors appear to be persuaded that the center is pueblo-like for Pueblo people, and seem to entertain positive feelings about Pueblo culture and craftwork after spending a few hours on the premises. That is an acceptable result for a building conceived for economic rather than purely cul-tural purposes.

The flexible "adobe style" suits many kinds of build-

110   Clients, Architects, and Design Strategies

ings. Edward Norris of the University of New Mexico's community planning assistance department reported to Santo Domingo Pueblo about using the style for an arts and crafts facility, a museum, housing, commercial premises, a health-care building, and even a meat-processing plant. A filling station might have a sympathetic appearance with solid walls and vigas on the office, and a gymnasium/swimming pool, although steel-framed, could be built of concrete block stuccoed over. Convection, cross-ventilation, and building mass can control climatic variations now, as they did in the past. Even in a homogeneous setting, however, certain buildings might be designed to stand out. A restaurant, for example, might have distinctive details to make it conspicuous. Nevertheless, to limit the buildings to adobe construction, wooden vigas, and native landscaping "would not be truly representative of a people who are seeking to integrate their traditional lifestyle with a modern approach to living, exemplified by the desire for a commercial development." This concern accounts for the presence of contrasting materials to project a progressive image on some buildings.[43]

* * *

The flexibility of the tipi is limited by the central plan, as is the case with the hogan and the roundhouse, but the tipi is even less adaptable because it tapers toward the top. All the same, versions of it have been made for special purposes. A Native American Church congregation may, for instance, prefer to worship in a building reminiscent of the tipi because this Plains building type is commonly used for their prayer services, even in southwestern hogan and pueblo country (68). Joel Davy, architect with Anderson Wade Barsness & Walter, calls the preschool on the United Tribes Technical College campus in Bismarck, North Dakota, a "takeoff" on a tipi motif, with beams recalling tent poles. The Saint Labre Roman Catholic Church, serving a Plains population, rises to a point from a broad base, and although its angular forms faced with stone bear little overt resemblance to a lightweight circular tent of skins or fabric, the pointed form and protruding beams seem to be modifications of a tipi model. Architect Ron Hernandez* prepared designs for the Wakpamni district center at Batesland on the Pine Ridge Reservation, including extended poles rising above the log building with asphalt-shingle roofing; a starburst design that he had admired in a magazine photograph was planned for the roof. He also envisioned the Porcupine College Center for the same reservation as a series of hexagons, a form that easily accommodates additions; the college authorities, however, eventually decided to use other designs.[44]

In 1985, the Shakopee Mdewakanton of Prior Lake,

68. **Church of God, Wounded Knee, South Dakota.**

Minnesota, completed a shingled cultural center and youth facility, with space for a shop, small restaurant, and meeting room, and an upper-floor balcony facing east. Tribal chairman Norman Crooks* wanted it to give the young people among the reservation's approximately sixty families a recreational space on the reservation rather than in unwholesome locations nearby. The landscape architect was of part Native ancestry, and Johnson, Sheldon & Sorensen was selected as the architectural firm because the contractor introduced it to the tribal chairman and council. Crooks asked the architects to create an architectural element resembling a tipi; it was to be the visual focus, with the youth center subordinate to it (69). This explains the prominence of a proportionately huge concrete-framed "tipi" above the shingled building. Eventually, Hickey Thorstensen Grover of Edina remodeled the youth center into a bingo parlor. It is now a small casino,

but plans are to turn it back into a cultural center, since most of the gambling at Prior Lake is done at the enormous Mystic Lake Casino just over a ridge. That is probably the best known tipi variant, in which light beams create the lodgepoles that rise from a solid sloping circular base.[45]

A more serious interpretation of the tipi is found at the Chief Gall Inn near Mobridge, South Dakota, designed for the Standing Rock Sioux by Harrison Bagg of Billings, Montana. This is a fifty-six-unit motel, restaurant, conference center, and campground, complete with covered swimming pool and a museum, financed by the EDA and opened in 1972. Less than twenty years later, the buildings were vandalized empty shells (70).

Management problems caused some of the decline in the inn's fortunes. In addition, the motel is located on a windy, treeless rise above Lake Oahe. Although walleye pike fishing, boating, and camping offered recreational

69. **Shakopee Mdewakanton Community Hall (now small casino), Prior Lake, Minnesota. Johnson, Sheldon & Sorensen (phase 1); Hickey Thorstensen Grover (phase 2, 1985).**

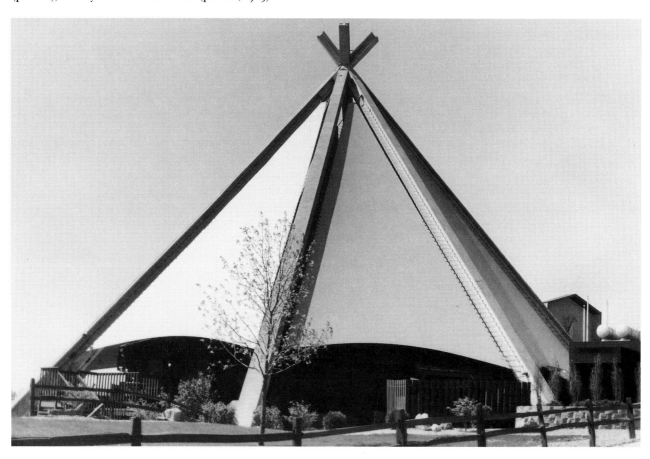

70. Chief Gall Inn, Standing Rock Reservation, South Dakota. Harrison Bagg, 1972.

potential, there is no shelter from sun or wind, and the wind makes boating difficult, if not treacherous. The shoreline fluctuates, so that it is difficult to establish good permanent beaches and docks; in addition, the Army Corps of Engineers, which holds jurisdiction over the waters and shoreline, created obstacles to the development of tribal beaches. As the lake is the product of damming, the water rises above old forests, and stumps under the water may damage boats. This seems to have been a risky project for both the Standing Rock people and the EDA, but it has been said more than once that some EDA projects were instigated to create construction and administration jobs in the short term, with the long term left for an indefinite moment's consideration.

The buildings, even in their present condition, are remarkably attractive. They are polygons made of natural stone, wood, and glass, some clustered in a rough circle, others set apart for special uses. Aaron Swan*, an architect in the region, liked the complex because it was a kind of village, embellished by the tipi motifs. Beams evoking tipi poles meet above the center of each polygon and then spread outward. The largest polygon has a skylight in its roof, supported by versions of these tipi poles; this building held the swimming pool, and must have been a delightful place when it was in use.

There are plans to rehabilitate the buildings, and to rehabilitate young men in them. Proposals have been made since 1981, at least, for a facility for substance-abusing youth. George Barta, director of the Native American Alcohol Treatment Center in Sioux City, Iowa, said that "a cultural approach would most likely be used to help teens recover from alcohol and drug use."[46] What better setting could there be for this purpose than buildings evoking the best known homes of Plains people?

* * *

The varied Native cultures in Oklahoma include that of the Osage, whose council house–IHS center--BIA office in Pawhuska reflects the ancestral lodge. A spacious council room has a pyramidal high ceiling with exposed wood. The entrance is a square porch lined with wood and shingled, rising to a central skylight (71).[47]

An impressive modern mound is the Muscogee Creek Independent Agencies Building at Okmulgee, Oklahoma, by Ragsdale, Christenson, and Everette (72). The motive for this design was cultural, with energy conservation secondary.[48] Ocmulgee National Monument in Macon, Georgia, the original home of the Muscogee Creek, is a mound field, including an underground council house, framed and then dug out, and provided with a smokehole; the entrance is at the east. Robert Trepp*, a tribal official,

Paraphrases **113**

71. Osage Council House, Pawhuska, Oklahoma. Neal A. McCaleb*, Jack Nusbaum, and Robert L. Thomas, 1977.

72. Muscogee Creek Independent Agencies Building, Okmulgee, Oklahoma. Ragsdale, Christenson, and Everette, ca. 1980.

says, "So when we got federal money for public works construction, we wanted a mound." He hopes also to see a future cultural center in similar form, although it need not be circular, as the agencies building is; mounds can also be square. The modern building has a recessed entrance leading to a lobby, and then an annular aisle with offices on one side and a central auditorium where council meetings and ceremonies are held, as in a council house.

Not every attempt to build in a culturally relevant way meets with success. The Tunica–Biloxi Museum in Louisiana, meant to evoke an ancestral temple on a mound, suffered from a host of problems. It was built to house Native and European trade artifacts known as the Tunica Treasure and aboriginal human remains. These had been stored for some years at Harvard and Louisiana State Universities, where the materials languished, slowly decaying. Tunica–Biloxi chairman Earl Barbry, Sr.*, felt it appropriate to establish a museum where the few remains

could be preserved; as they were not intact, they could not easily be buried in the customary way. They were to go into a cavity in a diorama, with a guard mannequin watching over them.

The museum building received funds from HUD as part of a regional Indian center offering job training, help to the aged, and other assistance. Jerry Neal of Alexandria, Louisiana, was the low bidder for architectural services. He built a rectangular pyramid flattened at the top and lit by clerestory windows. To form the slope, compacted earth encased a rectangular foundation, and staggered hollow concrete blocks outlined a mound. In the hollows, small-leaf ivy covered the concrete, looking like grass from a distance. The result resembled a southeastern temple, but a real temple on a mound was out of the question, because a ramp for handicapped access would have had to start at a great distance, and an elevator would have been too costly.

Tunica pottery inspired decorative motifs on a railing;

73. Sac and Fox National Public Library, Stroud, Oklahoma. MNT Architects, 1988.

74. Sac and Fox National Public Library (metamorphosis from older building form). Watercolor by Bette Hubbard. (Courtesy Bette Hubbard at Marguerite Studio [Oklahoma])

other ornament depended on nature and animal symbols, such as a pileated woodpecker announcing the dawn, or a hawk, a snake, and red and blue alligators symbolizing the new emergence of the tribe. Inside the museum, dioramas showed a historic house and the Sieur de Bienville trading with the Native population (to emphasize the early interaction of peoples). Digitized wax–cylinder recordings made early in this century were to provide background music.

Ingenuity played a part, too: The conservation and storage rooms are made of two steel and thick-gauge aluminum refrigerated trailers with 3 inches of insulation to keep stored objects at 65°F. William Day, museum director, took laboratory tables from the school board's junkyard, obtained two old Kentucky Fried Chicken fires for boiling microcrystalline wax, got a rainwater tank from a farmer friend to use for electrolysis procedures, and obtained Smithsonian surplus mannequins.

The building, however, experienced problems. The earth berm rested on river sand that washed out in the rain, as the seams of an impervious membrane covering the sand had not been lapped. Resulting instability led to the roof caving in. Day found no structural engineer's stamp on the building's blueprints, a lapse that could help to explain how all this could happen. The blocks sagged, and some collapsed. The ivy died in two exceptionally cold winters. Moisture caused the growth of fungi that ruined the backs of display cases. Repairs will cost over $100,000, but Day expects the remodeled museum to look less "like an ammunition bunker and more like an Indian mound."

* * *

Modest examples of paraphrase appear in many other places. The Morongo Indian Bingo Palace in California is a wide, low building with a pitched roof, and a front porch with emphatic verticals faced with stone. It resembles, probably not coincidentally, a Mojave dwelling, although the old house form was wooden with a thatched roof and log uprights that rose through the roof.[49]

Perhaps the clearest example of a paraphrased older architectural form is that of the Sac and Fox National Public Library in Stroud, Oklahoma (73). The tribe's own brochure, *Jim Thorpe's People*, says that the Sac and Fox people "enjoy the reputation of being one of the most progressive tribes in Oklahoma" in their "business practices, conversion of tribal land for industry, and careful investment of capital." All the same, they stress cultural retention. A watercolor by Bette Hubbard makes this plain (74) by showing the metamorphosis of a traditional rectilinear structure into its slightly modified form, well suited to a small library. Slender cylindrical piers hold a steeply pitched roof, elements known in older tribal buildings. HNT Architects of Edmond understood the need for windows in modern times, but also understood that this home for history and archives, above any of the others in a small group of tribal administrative and commercial buildings, had to be culturally referential.[50]

9

Symbolic Forms

Plans and elevations based on symbols reflect the perception that symbolic content is more potent and enduring than literal content. The architect's challenge is to find symbols that will resonate profoundly—that will not be merely simplistic shapes decorated with allusive details. Symbolism is often thought to be superior intellectually to practicality, just as architects separate themselves from builders in part by pointing to their academic training and ability to conceptualize. Perhaps this helps to explain why clients seem to ask for symbolic content less often than architects think about it: The clients often focus on a problem to be solved within a prescribed budget, and put aside the abstruse speculation preferred by professionals with learned inclinations.

It is not for an outsider to assess the power of the symbolic designs produced for Native Americans, but the proposals can be described and local opinions can be recorded. Most solutions fall into two broad categories: the diagram and the zoomorph. Many of the diagrams include a circle—seen as the circle of life, medicine wheel, wind rose, and cosmos. The zoomorphic shapes tend to be those of the birds, serpents, and turtles important in Native narrative.

One of the few realized diagrammatic designs is the Four Winds School at the Fort Totten Reservation in North Dakota (75). It is a three-story concrete cylinder 350 feet in diameter, quadrisected by corridors that meet in a central room, a plan related to the wind diagram or medicine wheel. Following tribal demands, the architects were all Native American, albeit from different nations—Neal McCaleb*, Charles Archambault*, and the designer, Surrounded-by-Enemy*.[1] The school committee and the tribal council were determined to build something "different from the usual school" and wanted a design that would represent the tribe.

Planning began in 1972 with a survey of needs, construction began in 1978, and a sweatlodge ceremony accompanied the opening in 1983. The BIA review committee, with no Native American members, balked at the idea of a circular building, but backed down when tribal participants threatened to approve no school at all. School personnel were not on the tribal committee, which was criticized for planning an unusual building in which none of its members had to work. Tension may have increased, too, because the budget did not allow all needs to be fulfilled, the library being reduced by about 25 percent along with athletic facilities.

The plan is circular except for a rectangular extension

for the gymnasium. Surrounded-by-Enemy refers to the circle as a concept rather than as a rigid model; he points out that even if Indians speak about sitting in circles at meetings, they really distribute themselves in a roughly circular pattern. Moreover, everyone willingly accepted a structural system based on a rectilinear grid for the sake of economy. Those planning the building saw tradition and practicality as compatible.

The four corridors lead from entrances at the cardinal points to the central cultural "heartroom" space; a yellow lifeline runs throughout the school to represent the continual gaining of knowledge. In the heartroom, murals of semiabstract animals surmount display cases for cultural artifacts. All children must pass through this space between the classrooms and the library. Overhead, skylights cross in four directions, and a light and sound fixture with four branches suggests an eagle hovering above; lights shine from the eagle's eyes (76). McCaleb finds a reference to a smokehole and converging tipi points in the ceiling, but these seem not to have been consciously planned.

The central room now houses a solid-walled tipi in what was once a sunken performance space (77). The tipi is about 20 feet high with a 19-foot base diameter, containing two carpeted levels in which children with problems are counseled in a culturally supportive physical setting. The core can no longer be used for presentations and assemblies, and the tipi overwhelms the displays in the vitrines. The tipi's purpose, however, is considered of primary importance; the sunken circle was rarely used as intended in any case. Surrounded-by-Enemy would have preferred to build a sweatlodge—a place of community and of spiritual change—but a firm in Bismarck, called in to work quickly, decided on the more obvious but less conceptually suitable tipi.

The school's exterior has no windows, a measure taken to conserve energy in winter, although the interior is hot in warm weather. Berms allow the building to be entered at any of its three levels. Embedding the building was meant to be culturally sensitive, but it is more appropriate to the history of the Mandan and other earth-lodge builders than it is to that of the Dakota. Surrounded-by-Enemy designed vertical concrete signposts at the entrances. Each shows an abstraction of an animal or a natural spirit important to one of the four cardinal direc-

75. Four Winds School, Fort Totten Reservation, North Dakota. Charles Archambault*, Surrounded-by-Enemy*, and Neal A. McCaleb*, 1983.

tions—buffalo, bird, elk, and thunder—and each emphasizes a color associated with one of the winds. Those who associate black with death and, by extension, with chaos in the school opposed the use of that color, although other elders and Surrounded-by-Enemy attach no negative connotation to it.

More obvious and literal images have been added, such as murals of animals in the gymnasium by Kinney Gray Wound*, a tribal member. Photographs of students who have joined the armed forces testify to more than youthful patriotism: The dropout rate at Fort Totten is so high and the future on the reservation so bleak that the former superintendent encouraged military enrollment so that pupils might obtain at least high-school-equivalency diplomas along with other training and, eventually, pensions.

The symbolic entrance signs, the heartroom with its tipi, the literal murals in the gym—all must play some part in raising consciousness about identity. So far, the building

has not had a noticeable effect on the dropout rate, but it is one tool in an educational process geared specifically to Native American students and their cultural needs. Even if it elicits only a delayed response, the effort to design a school building sensitive to the children's heritage has surely not been in vain.[2]

Surrounded-by-Enemy also designed the unexecuted Temple for the Sacred Pipe of the Sioux, for Green Grass, South Dakota, where the pipe is kept. He will not ask for money if the temple is built, as the project is religious and communal. The temple will stand on a peninsula formed by a river. Sweatlodge purification rites will be held there. The building will be circular, with a tipi-like structure of concrete slabs. The concrete surface should be packed with clay under a finish of natural materials brought from the nearby hills, the building thereby suggesting an earth mound. A buffalo skull on top, facing east, represents prayer offerings. The architect marked the cardinal directions on the enclosing circle, emphasizing them with sym-

76. **Four Winds School (eagle light and sound fixture).**

77. Four Winds School (counseling tipi).

bolic sculpture, as at the Four Winds School. Participants will enter through an underground passage at the east, reaching the tipi-like temple. The earthen floor will have a smaller round central area covered with sage. There, a holy man is to sit, guiding those who place themselves around him. Natural sun- or moonlight will illuminate the building. As this is not meant to be a tourist destination, those who come will understand the references to earth, the four directions, and the cosmos.

The architect has long been concerned with symbols. For his thesis project at North Dakota State University School of Architecture, he designed an unexecuted monument to Lewis and Clark's guide, Sakakawea*, for Bismarck, North Dakota, that reflects the plan of a circular earth lodge. Her statue points west from a hill, with native plants gathered at the statue base. A circular ceremonial area, approached from a sunken pathway at the east, is cut in tiers into the hill. Around this, curved subterranean corridors lead to arts and crafts areas, to a restaurant and bookshop opposite, to classrooms and a library, and to an information area and toilets in the center. A sweatlodge occupies a separate area. The references embodied in a circle dominated here, even though a linear design might have reflected Sakakawea's journey.

Among the many Native peoples who find the circle an essential symbol are the Seneca of New York State. In connection with a proposed cultural center, tribal officials, museum personnel, and Native experts from elsewhere expressed their desires to Molinaro/Rubin, consultants in Columbia, Maryland. It is not clear why the previous museum administration was not included in the planning process. The Seneca expected investment in the cultural base to help ameliorate the difficult social and economic conditions now prevalent, but for the moment, the project has been suspended.

The center, when built, will allow visitors to leave the dominant society behind once they enter the multiple-acre site. The museum displays go farther back in time as visitors penetrate deeper into the museum grounds. At the end will be a traditional village, presented as it would have been at a specified date, not a conglomerate invention meant only to amuse. Auxiliary facilities are to include a museum and shops, a dining area, an arts and crafts center, memorial gardens, an outdoor amphitheater approached along a running stream, and a visitor orientation center. The museum is to have a central glass-covered passageway about 300 feet long and 40 feet high rising above treelike wooden columns, to recall Seneca longhouses. The symbolic element here is a circular configuration encompass-

ing many of the parts of the complex, a reference to the circle of life. Specific Indian references are absent from the other building designs because these are different in time and purpose from those of the reproduced village.[3]

At Haskell Indian Nations University in Kansas, plans have been made for a 4-acre medicine-wheel earthwork, to be "a symbol of healing and a gift to the world from Native Americans." This is connected to a ceremony held there in October 1992 to reconcile Native Americans and the rest of the residents of this continent. Leslie Evans*, an art teacher, and Stan Herd, a field artist in Kansas, explained that earth art was found throughout the Americas. This is to reflect Native American spirituality and provide an alternative response to Columbus, showing hope for the future rather than protest. Those involved did not claim to be speaking for all indigenous people, some of whom find that interracial communication remains inadequate.[4]

Circles here show how "we are all related and are dependent on each other." A large circle represents the power of spirituality. Four spokes refer to thunder, to ancestors, and to paths through the circle of life aligned to the solstices. A central circle contains the sacred fire. To the east, a thunderbird flying toward the center and "etched on the grass," as if flying toward the center of the circle, represents "knowledge and the connectedness of all things." To the west, a bear claw symbolizes the "sustaining strength of cultural traditions for generations." The symbolic content here appears to have been invented for the occasion, although parts relate to tradition. If it were any more complicated, it would probably soon be forgotten.

Intricate symbolism informed the competition entry for the Navajo Supreme Court building submitted by David Sloan* & Associates in 1991:

> We took the idea from the past, where the Supreme Court is seen as a place to balance out justice. In the Navajo tradition…you would have an elder, chief peacemaker…to resolve the dispute…. They used to have two different clans, and then leaders who would resolve disputes, sometimes under a shade structure…. Other things also, the Long Walk tradition; we played with that. Also, you have a Greater Being overlooking the court, so the principal judicial room would have an opening to the sky.

The design was based on a Navajo basket unraveling toward the east, implying a womb and umbilical cord. The architects thought it might also be seen as a disassembled ye'i figure and a hogan.

The outline, a chord of a circle, has a round ye'i head room for hearings at the western end. A concrete cone rises above it, with an oculus open to Father Sky. One steps down from this to support offices, the womb in the building's center. The secure corridor, a circulation system, curves north of the womb, and the public corridor runs in a line on the south. The eastern, entrance, end is marked by an octagonal ramada. "Feathers," or rooms north of the secure corridor, are offices for judges and a library. A southern retaining wall might have relief sculptures showing ideas about emergence and the concepts of the future. It is unusual to incorporate so many diverse ideas into the design for a single building, but Sloan and his associates agreed to "shoot for something we feel is a statement from our end, even if it is difficult for others to understand."

Just as the Navajo would be the principal people to comprehend the Supreme Court imagery, the Cheyenne would be the main audience for the Northern Cheyenne Heritage Center (78). Since 1991, architect Peter C. Kommers has collaborated on this project with William Tall Bull* of the tribe. The center is to house sacred and community-held objects—some of them repatriated—and will provide areas for displays, a book and craft shop, and rooms for meetings, administration, and counseling. Outside, an arbor and concentric tiers of seats define a ceremonial area. The spaces and the activities housed in them are all clearly related.

To prepare for his task, Kommers listened to tapes of a conference held at the Wheelwright Museum where Native Americans offered many perspectives on architecture. The building form is a drum connected by a vestibule along the east–west axis to a quadrisected rectangular prism. The most important space is the stone-faced cylinder at the east, with its own eastern entrance. Here is a form of sacred space, because it is "the vessel for the important tribal artifacts of the Northern Cheyenne, some of which they hope to repatriate from museums." Here people may "learn how to properly care for the objects, and conduct family rituals to renew the power of family artifacts," since the power must be strengthened periodically. Shamans and spiritual leaders will offer instruction here, surrounded by displays of the community-owned artifacts. Here, too, the "six warrior societies would have a place to display elements unique to their identity. Some objects might change, and some would be permanent."

A vestibule at the west leads into the rectangular part of the complex, but does not afford entry into the drum, which must be approached from the east. The western building is for the instruction of tribal members and

78. **Northern Cheyenne Heritage Center (model), Lame Deer, Montana. Peter Kommers, 1993. (Courtesy Peter Kommers)**

visitors. Walls here are straight to allow the installation of display cases in the four broad corridors and in the gift shop–bookstore. Photomurals and photographs will line the halls, so that the past will accompany those who walk there. The three other quadrilateral spaces are destined for archives, meetings, and administration and counseling. Counseling not only is psychological, but includes instruction in Cheyenne ritual and in methods of making important artifacts. It could hardly be clearer that traditional cultural knowledge is meant to provide support for healing.

The functional rectilinear block is a formal foil for the drum, but more important, it is, like the cylinder, related to Northern Cheyenne cosmology: "While the whole spectrum of mineral, plant, and animal life is important to their symbol system, they have a particular reliance on color, number, and geometry.... The Morning Star, for instance, is shown as a square oriented so that its points face north, east, south, and west, and in its quadrants are locations of the guardian spirits." Stone piers inside the drum are set in a square, as there is more emphasis among the Northern Cheyenne on geometric formalism and less on organic fluidity than one finds in some other northern Plains cultures. Nor is this a simple emphasis on the cardinal points. Instead, "the quadrants take on importance because they refer to landscape elements" in the vicinity. The Northern Cheyenne "have a vertical order, too. Some southwestern tribes think of the bowl and basket image, with a bowl for the earth and a basket above it for the sky. The Northern Cheyenne image is more…complex. You can go from the topmost Deep Sky to the Deep Earth" along a path with such demarcations as Trees and Plants, Small Animals, and Roots, with subordinate elements in each. Horizontal grooves in the stone exterior of the drum are "an attempt to demarcate these regions horizontally: while its interior vault is painted blue to refer to the Deep Sky." In addition, the angular rooflines are derived from landscape forms, echoing subtly their rise and fall.

Symbolic elements of various kinds are found in several other sites. Todd County Middle School (1992) on the Rosebud Reservation in South Dakota, by Hewitt*–Drapeau*, includes a plaza in the shape of a medicine wheel, with black, white, yellow, and red concrete quadrants that point to the school's wings. The colors reappear throughout the school, as does ornament based on beadwork and on star-quilt designs. A tile eagle is inlaid on the art-room floor.[5] Lydia Whirlwind Soldier* and Albert White Hat* explained the symbolic references to the architects and to

fellow Lakotas who did not know them. The projected Big Foot Memorial Building for Pine Ridge Reservation is to be a twelve-sided housing unit, its top twisted like a tipi.[6] A seven-sided building for the seven Omaha clans was built about a decade ago by the Dana Roubal Larson firm of Rapid City. Although the building suffers from poor lighting and acoustics, maintenance problems, and shallow symbolism, some tribal officials must at first have found number references better than no Omaha elements at all.[7]

At Lac du Flambeau in Wisconsin, the Ojibwe Band commissioned Dreger & Associates of Ironwood, Michigan, to design a museum that opened in 1989 (79). Funding came from state and federal sources, and from foundations. Verdaine Farmilant*, the director, explains that "it's an octagon and built in a circle because everything in our culture seems to be in a circle." Ben Guthrie* of the band wanted the building to have an Indian theme and was instrumental in winning the approval of the tribal council for the plan. Farmilant points out that the building is not a replica of anything in the past, as it is not made of

79. **Lac du Flambeau Chippewa Museum and Cultural Center, Lac du Flambeau, Wisconsin. Dreger & Associates, 1991.**

birch bark, but the central plan is both formally reminiscent and symbolic. The simple wooden museum has two stories, the lower one concealed in the slope of a hill. This level is used for classes and meetings. Participants see the lake through large windows, and can enjoy the murals painted by local children, showing symbols and beadwork designs. On the wood-framed principal floor is a central display below a skylit ceiling. Each of four compartments holds a diorama of a season. Eight clan totem medallions adorn the ceiling panels, painted by Nick Hocking*, a band member (80).[8]

Gregory Adams of the Native American Resource Development Association in Pueblo, Colorado, has also alluded to traditional symbols in his proposals of late 1988 for a museum and arts facility serving visitors to Wounded Knee on the Pine Ridge Reservation (81). There, in 1890, the Seventh Cavalry massacred Lakotas, including infants and the aged. In 1973, members of several Native nations who opposed the Pine Ridge government of the time occupied the land.

Adams suggested a circular museum, 130 feet in diameter, in the center of four additional buildings shaped to curve around a quadrisected circle. The central building would be domed and surmounted by a cross of pipestone at its core. The peripheral buildings would be a gallery for Lakota arts, a restaurant and gift shop, a motel, and studio–living spaces for ten Lakota artists. The plan suggests a medicine wheel, and the four sacred colors of the cardinal directions above the doors allude to it also. The glass block shown in elevation drawings would be laid in a geometric pattern based on quill and beadwork traditions. Statues of spiritual healers would face the cardinal points. Adams envisioned construction in adobe block covered with cement stucco under metal roofs. To be sure, these materials are not indigenous, but the local soil is suited to this kind of construction. Adobe offers security, low maintenance costs, and excellent thermal control. For short stays, tourists could be sheltered near a powwow arbor to the south in 20-foot conical lodges recalling tipis.

For the same reservation, Patrick Cudmore proposed eight low-cost houses for an extended family, to be widely spaced around a circle so as to avoid interfamily disputes. One house lot would remain empty at the east, as camp circles and tipis were open in this direction. All houses would face south, taking advantage of the passive solar possibilities found in much Native building. The center of the circle could contain a huge communal garden to promote self-sufficiency in certain foods, and to provide a rehabilitative focus for people recovering from illness, alcoholism

80. **Lac du Flambeau Chippewa Museum and Cultural Center.**

in particular. Cudmore imagined the houses as built of stuccoed mud brick over rigid insulation; on the ivory-colored stucco, occupants could paint individualized images, such as pictographs or scenes of family history, and a Lakota artist, Martin Red Bear*, would assist them. Cudmore is interested in "the symbolic meanings in astronomy, myth, and geometry," and tries to make the heritage of ancient knowledge of these matters bear on the present.

In 1991, this architect also proposed the Black Hills American Indian Center for Rapid City, South Dakota, to be designed with Ron Hernandez*, a Lakota architect. Cudmore wants the visually exotic, mysterious elements in Plains art to be cultivated here, intending his visual imagery to "revolutionize the architecture of the United

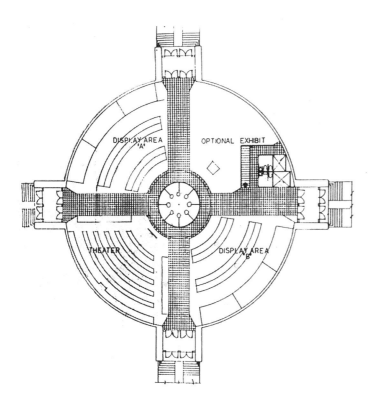

81. **Wounded Knee Visitor Center (proposed plan), Wounded Knee, South Dakota. Gregory B. Adams, 1988. (Courtesy Gregory B. Adams)**

States as a consequence of the revival of shamanism and traditional religion." His serpentine design incorporates three layers of symbolism—celestial, terrestrial, and intellectual—the first based on a circumpolar star map, the second on a model of the Black Hills, and the third on the thought of Black Elk*. This Lakota philosopher and Christian catechist predicted that his people would turn from hunting to agriculture; Cudmore envisions terraced gardens to realize this idea.[9]

Simpler in concept is the symbolism of Red Lake School #1 in Minnesota (1993), by Dale Sickles of A&E in Grand Forks, North Dakota. The architects held a three-day charrette listening to the Ojibwes' ideas on education. Sickles recalls "several hours where we discussed the aspects of culture they wanted to preserve." The planners, representing the school board and school staff, wanted the building to "reflect some of the meaning of the growth of the Indian." This is accomplished in part by imitating the Ojibwe diagram of human development as it relates to the cosmos: One enters the teaching lodge "on the east, and as

you grow, kindergarten and first grade are on the south, second and third grade on the west," and the upper grades on the north—"laid out in the way of growth through life," as Sickles explains it. Each direction is associated with an animal, so the committee planned sculptures—including an eagle, a bear, and a marten—on posts, colored symbolically and placed outside the building. They refer also to the seven-clan organization of the people. Sickles says that the school's center "is the media area. They see it as the heart, and also it's where elders teach. So we designed an oval in the center as reflective of the lodge with a vaulted ceiling." Other culturally appropriate aspects are display cases for Ojibwe artifacts, and rooms for teaching of language and beadwork. A firepit must be outdoors to conform with safety codes, but it will be close to the building. Judy Roy*, Chairwoman of the school board, explained that these measures are to inculcate affirmative attitudes among the children to help them avoid self-destructive activities, particularly those connected with drugs and alcohol.

Ancient traces also inspired the Education Building on the Tohono O'odham Reservation, built by Mike Enriquez & Company of Tempe, Arizona (82). The former education director, Sister Kateri*, proposed that the building have the form of a maze. This image was found on a rock cliff on the reservation, and tribal members believe that it predates the Spanish arrival. This treasured image is appreciated as a diagrammatic approach to understanding life. It is said to illustrate the complicated and puzzling way that people must travel to find fulfillment, located at the center. Education helps people to evaluate alternatives, so important in a maze, and to find the proper path. The maze plan is therefore particularly appropriate to this building.[10]

This maze is a simple one. Concentric steps approach the cement-block structure. An outer ring partly encloses a central curved-wall library that looks square, as it is supported by four square pillars and has a paneled ceiling. The idea of the maze underlies the building, however, and governs people's descriptions of it, despite the simplicity of the plan.

Symbols govern the plans in Michael Trujillo's* master of architecture thesis for the University of New Mexico (83). He designed a museum and research institute for an endangered site with precontact petroglyphs on the Los Metates escarpment west of Albuquerque, locating his building where the summer and winter solstice rays intersect. The "lava tubes and mythic meaning of the rock art spirals...become a symbolic sipapu" passage,

82. Tohono O'odham Education Building, Sells, Arizona. Mike Enriquez & Company, 1971.

83. Visitor center (proposal), Petroglyph National Monument, New Mexico. Michael J. Trujillo*, 1994. (Courtesy Michael J. Trujillo)

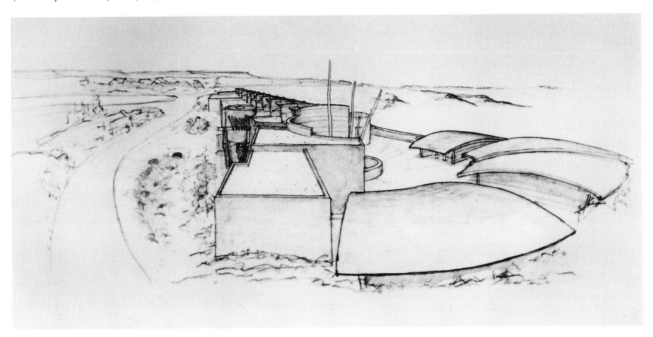

not to the earth's inner spirit world but to knowledge and appreciation of the petroglyphs. From the center of a spiral at the start of the educational center, curved walls faced with local sandstone continue the contours of the cliffs. The roofs are covered with black metal to represent molten lava.

Seven, the number of the Cherokee clans, governs the plan of Charles Chief Boyd* proposed in the 1960s for the Cherokee National Archives in Tahlequah, Oklahoma. Boyd describes the plan as a re-creation of the Cherokee council house, although its three stories would have been exceptional in the past. The building is to be near the Cherokee Museum, surrounded by seven fingers of parking lots, and located among trees. A core will rise higher than the surrounding aisle. The building is to contain originals or copies of everything ever written about the Cherokee and to provide secure facilities for storing documents. Accommodations for researchers in a library and carrels are included.

The architect believes that some tribal members thought of all the buildings within the museum and traditional village grounds as tourist attractions, and as this one did not relate to tourism, they declined to invest in it. Boyd, however, thinks of this as a kind of spiritual investment. An alternative idea, mentioned by Duane King, an anthropologist who specializes in Cherokee studies, envisions the archives building as a re-creation of the nineteenth-century Female Seminary, a highly respected institution of learning of which several columns survive at the entrance to the museum.[11]

In Seattle, the Daybreak Star Indian Cultural and Arts Center (1977) refers to a distinctive symbol (84–86). The supratribal facility has four large pavilions radiating from a core. The form and the name of the center come from Black Elk's* vision of a sheltering tree and a daybreak star dropping to earth and rooting. From its single stem sprouted four differently colored blossoms, each now associated with the four principal architectural divisions.

84. Daybreak Star Indian Cultural and Arts Center (aerial view), Seattle, Washington. Arai–Jackson–Reyes*, 1977. (Courtesy Clifford Jackson)

85. **Daybreak Star Indian Cultural and Arts Center.**

Lawney Reyes*, a Colville sculptor active in designing the project, understood the star as giving wisdom and knowledge to human beings. The four blossoms connect four colors, seasons, races, and directions. Upper-level entrances at the east and west, and grade-level entrances at the north and south, respond to demands of the site but also refer to the cardinal points emphasized in many Native American religions. Each indicates a cultural area: the Pacific Coast and Alaska, the Plains and Basin, the Southwest, and the eastern woodlands. The arrangement that suggests rotation around a core relates to those aspects of Native American art that include revolving patterns.

The building exists as an indirect consequence of the Department of Defense's abandonment in 1970 of 390 acres at Fort Lawton. Native Americans in the Seattle area asked for the land, pursuant to laws governing federal appropriation and release of Native American property. A demonstration followed, perhaps inspired by the Native American occupation of Alcatraz Island near San Francisco a year earlier.

Taking a position on behalf of the approximately 17,000 Native Americans in the Seattle area at the time, a group incorporated as the United Indians of All Tribes Federation to sponsor a cultural center. Eventually, they obtained a ninety-nine-year lease for 20 acres of fort grounds and secured financing for a social-service facility in downtown Seattle. The master plan described the goals: "to provide a place for recognition of Indian self-esteem and an awareness of a submerged society again emerging into a position of high regard," and "to develop and sustain the sense of Indian identity among Indian people." The cultural center was to "strike at the root of social problems caused by separation from...Indian identity," and "build understanding of Indian concepts and culture in the non-Indian community." Once again, culture was to foster social goals rather than purely aesthetic or recreational ones.

Support came from tribal governments, federal agencies, forty non-Indian organizations in Seattle, the city government, and the National Congress of American Indians, among others. The city required the center to be economically self-sufficient, and the Native Americans agreed, as they had conceived the center as a means of promoting self-determination.

Jones* & Jones, architects and landscape architects in Seattle, prepared the first site plan and had the idea for the

86. **Daybreak Star Indian Cultural and Arts Center.**

building between 1972 and 1973. Robert Small of the University of Washington put his graduate students in architecture to work on proposals. The commission went to the firm of Arai–Jackson–Reyes*, which won a competition in 1975. Partnership with Lawney Reyes* was a factor in the decision, according to Clifford Jackson, as Reyes is said to be the half-brother of Daybreak Star's director, Bernie Whitebear*; the sculptor had collaborated earlier with his architect partners. Arai–Jackson–Reyes held charrettes with the clients, and presented their own ideas while learning about Native opinions and stories during interviews with people of all ages from many tribes. Jackson praises Reyes for being instrumental in forming the building concept. Reyes saw the building settling into the landscape like an eagle landing, and collaborated with his associates to make the landing smooth.

Excavation was done by a Native American subcontractor, and a predominantly Indian crew carried out the landscaping. The Yakima, Quinault, Makah, and Colville tribe donated logs to the site, as did owners of timber businesses. Haida, Tlingit, and others—George David* is mentioned especially—hand-adzed the 50-foot fir beams

that rest on cedar posts; some of the work was done without pay. The city's lighting department gave an $80,000 grant for permanent installations, completed by 1980, by Native American artists from several tribes. Marvin Oliver* carved the massive wooden doors, now flanking the entrance to artists' studios.

Jackson speaks of the building as having local flavor, but not imitating a local tradition in shape or material. The metal and reinforced concrete used here show that Native Americans welcome technological innovation when doing so is appropriate. The master plan suggested that "the exterior architectural form will be essentially inspired by a traditional shelter form but designed to complement the natural setting and present a low silhouette of earth berms and continuous structural beams." The designers did not want the building to dominate the park. They were eager to afford views into the land and seascape, the northern view to Puget Sound being particularly impressive. To incorporate natural elements into the building, they originally proposed reflecting pools on the upper-level plaza that would echo the roof forms.

The cultural center includes a preschool program,

social-service agencies, and vocational preparation, all run by the foundation though not all in the four-part building. In the grounds are buildings representing various Native cultures, such as a pueblo house and a partly completed longhouse erected for the Goodwill Games in 1990. Arai–Jackson is now trying to build a "people's lodge" of 140,000 square feet to show historic and recent Native artifacts and works of art, thereby breaking down intercultural barriers. When this is completed, Daybreak Star will be used for displays and for sales of contemporary work. A Grand Hall or Hall of Ancestors will be included later (87).

The master plan had also called for a circular Flowering Tree Center representing "the spirit that sustains the universe." The approach to it passes a carved entry gate and some of the twelve carved structural posts, one for each month. Here the symbolism is more conventional than that of the Daybreak Star. A suggestion that the exterior would merge "conical sectional forms (teepees)" suggests an even more literal approach to Native American design.[12]

The 74-acre Phoenix Indian School site will be remodeled by the city's Parks, Recreation, and Library Department. "To respect the past of the Phoenix Indian School," the agency used a design team from the Navajo Nation when creating a master plan in 1992, and praised its members for "providing the spirit of the design." Among the symbolic features will be a governing circle "of life," for which a Hopi artist provided a symbolic explanation; an emphasis on the cardinal directions and on solar considerations; an ethnobotanic exhibit; and forms important to the Navajo. A path will be straight on one side, wavy on the other, reflecting a tribal idea about human relationships. One lagoon will have the contours of a hummingbird, while another will be shaped like a fish. Ten landscaped acres will be based on Hopi ceramic patterns and Pima basket designs. While Native Americans are not the official clients, they will be among the park's users and have a historic interest in the site. It is to the city's credit that it took seriously the need to retain a focus on its indigenous population.[13]

The next step beyond the literal images in these two buildings is the suggestion or depiction of symbolic animals in architecture. These symbols can impart a sense of distinctive identity, but only if the intended audience recognizes and understands them.

The first zoomorphic building was the serpentine Gila River Arts & Crafts Center near Sacaton, Arizona, built with the help of EDA funds (88). Working with Richard Roth, a developer in Phoenix, Hemmingson, Durham & Richardson of that city designed it to be an outlet for artistic work by members of several southwestern tribes; the architects also worked on road design and environmental assessments for Gila River. A small museum presents the history of the Pima and Maricopa. Dancers perform at the arts and crafts center, a restaurant provides food, and near the principal building, a "Heritage Park" contains an outdoor exhibit of building types from five Native nations.

The principal building curves around an almost-complete circle, the gap serving as the entrance. In the enclosed court, a tapering cylindrical tower at one side evokes an ancient Near Eastern ziggurat. John Long*, director, says that the ensemble is meant to resemble a coiled rattlesnake, with the tower as the tail it raises while rattling. He does not know why this shape is significant for this building, but he points out that all desert tribes have

87. **Daybreak Star Indian Cultural and Arts Center (proposed Hall of Ancestors). Arai–Jackson, 1993. (Courtesy Clifford Jackson)**

88. **Gila River Arts & Crafts Center, Sacaton, Arizona.**
Hemmingson, Durham & Richardson, 1971.

some cultural relation to the snake, and some of the artifacts displayed came from the nearby Snaketown excavation, although that name was given by Euro-Americans who saw reptiles there.[14]

The architects wanted to suggest continuity from the past. Recent historic houses of the Pima–Maricopa were rectilinear, but earlier nineteenth-century dwellings were round or were made of several round forms.[15] Otherwise, there is nothing specifically Native American about the design. The crafts center has a deep overhang shading large glass panes that form the walls around the interior courtyard. The stucco finish on the buildings was formerly beige, but is now bright white for greater visibility from the nearby highway.

The arts and crafts center is attractive, but probably not meaningful. Indeed, in the early 1970s some elderly tribal members associated it not with their own architecture but with the city of Bethlehem, because they thought the new building resembled Sunday-school textbook images of sites associated with Jesus.[16]

Another symbolic form of questionable effectiveness can be found at the Pine Point School in Ponsford, Minnesota, a distinctive building that won an honor award in 1985 in its state. Architect Thomas Hodne says that it was designed as a result of an "experimental, tribally generated program." It "pleases its users," providing a "focal point"[17] that has become not just a school but the "center of the community, the heart of the community."[18] Sara Loe, an architect of part-Ojibwe descent, found that "the staff and children seem very comfortable in it."[19] It is, in short, successful from the aesthetic, social, and functional viewpoints (89, 90).

The problem is that children were unaware of its symbolic references, which ought to be evident even if their teachers neglect to discuss the building and its meaning. It is unlikely that the staff will provide this instruction, because some of them "thought the building was based on southwestern design, which they did not know much about."[20] The architect, however, reports that at the dedication, a spiritual healer who lives nearby said that she had not been sure about the school until she heard the voices of her ancestors during the previous night. She arose and went outdoors, where she saw her ancestors dancing on top of the building. This convinced her that the beaver and the earth lodge were elements of her culture embodied in the school.

The White Earth Reservation residents asked Hodne–Stageberg Partners for a school addition "designed around some earth-lodge concepts. We tried to see how to do it [and tried] to learn their most revered images."[21] The Ojibwe said that they had "learned from beavers how to make earth lodges,"[22] and the architects eventually produced a design variously described as a "beaver leaving its lodge of sticks and earth"[23] or as a beaver settling into the earth, with its projecting concrete entrance representing "a beaver on its back playing with the circular symbolic sun image punched into the entrance's concrete banner." Thomas Hodne refers to a beaver floating on a "lake of grass; the banner is his tail." The shifting interpretations probably explain the students' and staff members' inability to see symbols: They have not been made clear enough to apprehend. In addition, references to the earth lodge and the beaver as its originator are puzzling, since the Mandan rather than the Ojibwe were earth-lodge builders. Perhaps Gerry Backanaga*, whom Hodne describes as a "strong" and "bright young educator" and who was important in formulating this idea, was as concerned with practicality and with embedding the school in its natural environment as he was with reflecting a specific tribal building form.

The Pine Point School consists of an older classroom wing to which Hodne and his colleagues Gerald Johnson ("my right hand on this project" and many others) and Dennis Sun Rhodes* were asked to provide additions. They designed a large, central-plan multipurpose room, a skylit walkway to the older wing, and a concrete projection from the multipurpose room to the front of a paved entrance court; this is the "banner" that recalls the raised head of a beaver emerging from a round body. The multi-

89. Pine Point School, Ponsford, Minnesota.
Hodne–Stageberg Partners, 1978.

90. **Pine Point School (multipurpose room).**

purpose room is made of concrete outside and heavy glue-laminated wood inside, left unfinished, with some solid wood elements. An aisle encircles a slightly sunken central space for community and cultural activities such as powwows for as many as 500 people, school-opening assemblies, and even bingo and boxing matches. Diane Lehse*, the principal, listed the features that she finds appropriate to the White Earth residents: the round room; the use of natural wood and not just concrete; paintings by students on pillars and walls using indigenous and original designs; some landscaping, although there is no garden; and a summer program to train youth in maintenance and groundskeeping.

The school succeeds in its mission of nurturing and educating children with a strong sense of their Native American roots. The school's business manager, when asked why there were not more references to Native American culture, quoted a band member. He said that the community's beliefs were so strong that no building had to show or reflect them; the sense of nationhood was more

spiritual than physical.[24] If that is so, symbolic architecture was not essential to the mission of the school.

These architects have designed several other symbolic forms pertinent to the clients. In the case of houses along old logging roads at Nett Lake for the Bois Forte Ojibwe, Dennis Sun Rhodes* "took the lead in identifying the symbolic spirit" and in being the client liaison, according to Roger Kipp of Hodne–Stageberg Partners. Sun Rhodes learned that this band regarded "the loon as their educator," which led the designers to think of the houses as located in a "sea of earth rather than...water." They created protruding side walls seen as protruding bird breasts (91), and in an early conceptual stage included a flue with a red eye, like the eye of the loon. The reference need not be obvious to outsiders; those who understood it were the Bois Forte Band members.

The aboriginal Ojibwe had not had "separate rooms but one space with sleeping on the edges, a ritual area in the middle, and of course, traditionally, personal hygiene out on the prairie....We developed...a woodland cultural prototype" suited to modern times.[25] It was necessary, however, to compromise with tradition by building the individual rooms that the Department of Housing and Urban Development knows how to approve, and this inevitably diluted the specificity of the symbol.

The architects emphasized the kitchen as central to the house. Openings to allow the passing of dishes through to the living–dining room kept women from being isolated while they cooked; this was one response to characteristics of Ojibwe social life. A stove in the center, with a duct to the roof, reflects the ancient central ritual area. Several models and colors of paint avoid institutional monotony, and landscape architect Ron Melchert* sited the houses among trees so that one family cannot see into the windows of another. Adults and teenagers were invited to inspect the plans, sections, and models. When the houses were first occupied, they were well received.

They have not, however, stood up well. Within a decade, they had become decrepit and some were vacant.

As one person connected with the housing office put it, "it was a nice design, but not for here." Building the bottom half of the house with treated lumber suited drier areas than Nett Lake, where high humidity and frigid winters made walls perspire and mildew. The kitchens were partly enclosed and were considered small. Single mothers were unable to maintain their houses. Since the houses lacked garages or storage rooms, residents stored many belongings in their yards. Even the display of plans and models could not guide the design because, to have useful comments from the residents here, "it's best to go to their homes and sit and visit individually, one on one.... Discuss their lives and families."[26] This case forms an exception to Sun Rhodes's idea that "if you do things from the people's cultural perspective, or you solve their problems in the design, then it's going to be more useable to them. Then if you give them something even more special in a symbolic sense, it becomes their own blood, so to speak, and so they take better care of it."[27]

91. HUD house for Ojibwe, Nett Lake, Minnesota. Hodne–Stageberg Partners, ca. 1979.

Little Wound School at Kyle, South Dakota, on the Pine Ridge Reservation, has been less problematic since its opening in 1982 (92). "It was conceived from the heart," said H. John Haas*, now the superintendent, and many teachers contributed ideas. They tried to incorporate Lakota designs while keeping within the traditional educational setting of classrooms, cafeteria, and gymnasium. Hodne–Stageberg designed the building for between 250 and 400 children in kindergarten through twelfth grade.[28]

The entrance of the Little Wound School, faced in red ceramic tiles, curves around a plaza on which stand four pole-like sculptures conceived by Gerald Johnson, project architect, to represent parents and children (92). Above the door, a room with windows on two sides protrudes, looking like a head with eyes—the head of a buffalo that embraces the plaza. This animal, essential to Lakota life in the past, is embodied in the building and is said to give strength through education, just as the real buffalo gave it in other ways. In the upper room, children are instructed in Lakota studies and such traditional values as responsibility, generosity, courage, and wisdom. On either side of the entrance area are the gymnasium and the cafeteria, neither one confined by walls. Behind the entrance, a corridor, closed by gates forming a pattern described as

symbolizing a buffalo spine, leads to classrooms and also to a central round room that Hodne likens to the hump of the buffalo, used for "oral teaching, well used for speeches and meetings." It is skylit, with glazing held in stick-like mullions that hint at tipi poles. The corridor curves around a core of rooms for science, home economics, business, and the library. Birgil Kills Straight*, former executive director, saw the hallway as reminding students of the Lakota sacred hoop, which teaches about the ebb and flow of existence. The BIA, pressing for a building cheaper than the $6.2 million that this one cost, was uninterested in the instructive potential of a school seen in Kyle as a "victory for Indians over the federal government" that had formerly built only "square buildings" for them.[29]

The mechanical system recycles heat from the sun on the south and east. Vent pipes, grates, and exposed girders painted in warm colors recall the prairie sunset. Students can make computer-generated Lakota designs and read explanations of the forms. They study the earth science of the Badlands. The home-economics room has microwave ovens but also wood, electric, and gas stoves to match conditions on the reservation rather than a remote authority's notion of what ought to be there. Academic trophies as well as athletic ones stand in a display case, and sculptures of a

92. Little Wound School, Kyle, South Dakota.
Hodne–Stageberg Partners, 1982.

93. Piya Wiconi building, Oglala Lakota College, Kyle, South Dakota. Hodne–Stageberg Partners, 1979.

bear and an eagle by Fools Crow*, a Lakota artist, stand near them. Problems such as water seepage behind some of the red facade tiles are considered minor when balanced against the overall success of the school as a building and an educational institution, although more serious problems of funding and maintenance arose by 1995.[30]

The same architects designed the main building of Oglala Lakota College after Dennis Sun Rhodes* introduced them to the tribal chairman. The college, chartered in 1971, lies at the center of the Pine Ridge Reservation; it was being designed by 1977, and took sixteen months to build using local labor. It was not, however, originally conceived for the college but was intended as the reservation's chief administrative building. Chairman Al Trimble* hoped to move the tribal offices out of the town of Pine Ridge, which he saw as dominated by the BIA and other outside forces. He dreamed of an entire new village, called Piya Wiconi (new life), the name now of the college building alone. The city of Brasília was new at the time, and it may have inspired Trimble's thinking—of course on a smaller scale.[31] Piya Wiconi was supposed to be watered by an aqueduct and to have common gardens, and it was to be the home of tradition, albeit financed by the EDA.

When Dick Wilson* replaced Trimble as tribal chairman, the new leader wanted the government back in Pine Ridge, where the architects built a new office building and converted Piya Wiconi into the college center.

Frank Fools Crow*, a spiritual leader, staked out the site, setting the main axis; his own house in the new village was to have been within a sacred medicine Sun Dance circle. The building is earth-sheltered on three sides and rests on a slope. A Native American construction crew built reinforced-concrete walls and columns under a heavy timber and wood deck roof. The approach side looks like many modern buildings with some straight and some curved parts; a bridge connects a main wing to a small one that houses a laboratory below a guest apartment.

The back is entirely different, its wall designed like an eagle with its talons poised facing a virgin field (93). The eagle appears to recline, and water—that is, tears—pours from its eye into a ritual canal planned around a Community Council Circle and along the summer solstice axis. Eagles and their feathers are sacred to the Lakota, so that the building refers to an image known universally on the reservation. The college's literature says that the eagle symbolizes great courage and accomplishment. These are characteristics of the students, most of whom must overcome hardships to earn their general education diplomas, vocational certificates, and associate or bachelor degrees. Arthur Zimiga*, Vice President of the college, hopes that the institution can help people solve various kinds of problems, and mentioned the suicide rate among the young as something that might be changed by cultural reinforcement combined with practical education.

The building functions well and is dramatic in appearance. A central well employs the circular shape common in Lakota symbology. Zimiga speaks of the circle not only in connection with the medicine wheel and wind diagram, but also as a reflection of the clockwise motion of the sun and as a means to achieve harmony, as in a sweatlodge. Lakota artist Marty Red Bear* has provided images for the lobby, including stars, the life sign, and shields, to enhance the sense of rotation. As is appropriate for a space in which work is done and conferences are held, it lacks the dramatic force of the exterior. The interior is crowded in some parts but wastes space near the curved walls, and although

air enters through operable windows, it is not well vented. A circular room with a balcony, meant as a council chamber, is now a lecture hall. Despite acoustics imperfect for lectures, the shape of the room reinforces the idea important for a tribally sponsored college that one must seek wisdom from Mother Earth, from whom all come and to whom all must return.[32]

In 1991, Ron Hernandez* designed an addition to Piya Wiconi; construction documents date from 1993. This is to be a library, archives, a computer center, and an audio-visual studio for the production of Lakota language and history resources. The design has nothing to do with the original eagle, but is small in scale, with four almost domestic pavilions on the entrance side, and larger in scale, faced in shaded glass, on the prairie side. The college's students of carpentry and electrical work will erect the building under the supervision of the same contractors who executed the first phase.

As this reservation spreads over many miles, it is useful to have governmental subdivisions; they are housed in

94. Chapter house, Pine Ridge Reservation, South Dakota. Hodne–Stageberg Partners, 1979.

95. Native American Center for the Living Arts, Niagara Falls, New York. Hodne–Stageberg Partners, 1981. (Alice Krinsky, 1993)

"chapter houses"—identical buildings of 3400 square feet erected to Hodne–Stageberg's design, again with Gerald Johnson as project architect and with the collaboration of Dennis Sun Rhodes* (94). They are circular two-storied structures of reinforced concrete, with walls extending from one side to form a sheltering barrier. They contain central raised crowning features in which mechanical services are housed.

These buildings are known as Prairie Falcons or Hawks. Thomas Hodne's literature says that they "symbolically portray the proud Prairie Falcon, master of the prairie winds, poised for flight or nurturing its young." The reference shows again the architects' and clients' desire to build something unlike anything the BIA had provided earlier, and something with symbolic reference to Lakota culture. The buildings were to "incite curiosity, psychological stability, and stimulate pride and identity across the Pine Ridge reservation...[to] encourage community involvement in the tribal government process at the local level."[33] They may fulfill those goals despite the uncertain symbolism; even Hodne was unclear about whether the bird is about to fly or is caring for its young.

The most dramatic of Hodne–Stageberg's works is the Native American Center for the Living Arts, commonly known as the Turtle, in Niagara Falls, New York (95, 96). This animal sustains the world, according to the Iroquoian tribes of the United States and Canada, who sponsored the building. As cultural issues and a world view are coterminous, it is symbolically appropriate to use this form for a facility in which culture is sustained. The turtle also carries associations with the earth, with power, and with long life or survival, the last being especially important to Native Americans concerned with their culture. Sun Rhodes feels that architects have persuaded Native Americans to accept their Euro-American ideas, but that Native people should seek their own new "emergence, and bring it to life."[34] This building attempts to do that with its unusual symbolic form. One wonders why it has never been discussed at length in the architectural press; the designers attribute this to editors' unease with a building so overtly different from those in the mainstream. Those who do not admire it may also have hesitated to offend sponsors who are members of a minority group.

The elevation presents semiabstract references to a

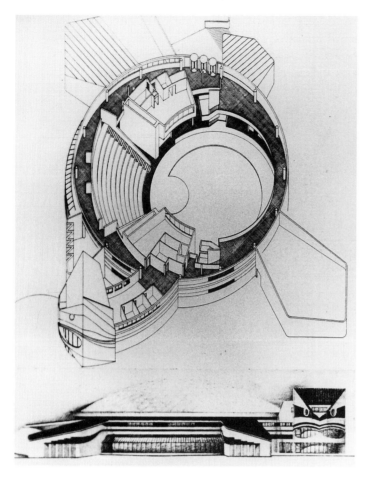

96. Native American Center for the Living Arts (axonometric view). (Courtesy Thomas H. Hodne, Jr.)

The center, originally in a storefront, was to be relocated to the Art Park in Lewiston, New York, but in 1976 it obtained money to erect a new building a few blocks from Niagara Falls. Construction money came from the EDA; the National Endowments for both Arts and Humanities, state and city agencies, and foundations contributed to other parts of the program. Wilson knew Sun Rhodes, who had worked in 1972 on a design for a new center; this may explain why Sun Rhodes's employers, Hodne–Stageberg, became the architects.

The building has at its center the turtle's body under a kind of carapace made of a geodesic dome 182 feet in diameter; Hodne had studied the work of R. Buckminster Fuller while in architecture school. Performances and ceremonies are held there. The architects worked hard to make the legs and head suit a gift shop, a gallery, service areas, and rooms for archaeological and anthropological study. "We had to justify it [the plan] and make it an integral part of the interior."[36] The tail was reserved for a teenage center, studios, and community rooms. The tail is somewhat enlarged, to accommodate all the spaces needed, so Hodne relates this turtle to marine rather than to land-based types; Sun Rhodes identifies it with a snapping turtle.[37] Wilson wanted to have people enter through the turtle's mouth, which Sun Rhodes likens to "something at Disney World," so the architects designed a raised head, as if it were looking toward the falls, which are sacred to local Native people.[38] The head contains a restaurant on a balcony above administrative offices. Other parts of the building, around the carapace and on a lower level, house museum exhibits, a kitchen, service rooms, and a residence for a visiting artist.

Problems of insufficient maintenance and conflicts within Native groups have affected the Turtle. It has been so closely associated with Wilson and his family that others have remained at some distance from it. While funds sufficed for construction, the center has never been able to raise enough operating money from admission fees to provide adequate upkeep. Until 1988, it received between $500,000 and $700,000 each year from New York State, but now the grant is only $20,000 to $26,000 from the National Endowment for the Arts, supplemented by small amounts for folk art projects.[39] The building costs $400,000 annually to keep open, and the quarterly publication and artist-in-residence programs require about $1 million a year. Deeply in debt to the city and federal government, the Turtle is in danger of closing as of early 1995. Native Americans have little lobbying power, so they do not expect any windfalls from New York State. This

turtle through a design apparently based on northwest coastal defined color areas rather than on northeastern Native imagery. Sun Rhodes says that turtles come in many patterns and colors, and that in the thinking of his own Arapaho people, the turtle is considered to own color. He finds that this "actually looks like a turtle, but in essence, what it is was a special symbol for the Iroquois confederacy."[35]

The building owes its inception to Duffy Wilson*, a Tuscarora sculptor who had long dreamed of a giant turtle along the shore of the Niagara River. He was the director of the center, which was incorporated in 1970 in New York City. It moved to Niagara Falls perhaps because of Wilson's dream and because the center would be more accessible to about 35,000 Native Americans and Native Canadians. It could also benefit from a tourist market eager for attractions other than the falls.

explains much about the physical condition of the building today, although it continues to make a dramatic impression on visitors.[40]

A better fate may be anticipated for the turtle-shaped Oneida tribal school built in 1994 near Green Bay, Wisconsin, because schools are the hearts of defined communities. The architect, Richard Thern, is experienced in school design, having designed about 300; this one covers about 160,000 square feet and cost about $14 million. He had worked for the Menominee and prepared for his interview with the Oneida by extensive reading, knowing that he was short-listed in competition with two Native American architects. On the selection committee were Maria Hinton* and Amos Chrisjohn*, elders deeply concerned with cultural and linguistic preservation. Artley Skenandore*, Oneida director of development, and Ernie Stevens, Sr.*, school program director, suggested the plan of a turtle because—in the words of a typed statement by the architect—the animal "represents the birth of the Oneida Nation and is the base of the Oneida Cultural Tree" (97, 98). By extension, it "depicts the rebirth of education for the Oneida children," whose previous training was hampered by inattention to their cultural heritage. Stevens and Skenandore saved the symbolic plan when a contractor proposed a commonplace rectangular school. It probably helped that Thern, who had built about a dozen circular schools, knew that round schools cost about $1 less per square foot than rectilinear ones do.

Native Americans participated in the project, among them Ron Skenandore*, the general contractor; Stevens; Ronald Hill*, school board chairman; about 80 percent of the construction force; and Nancy Redeye* of Flynn Battaglia Architects in Buffalo, New York. This firm designed much of the interior, chose the color scheme, and introduced details such as tile designs derived from wampum belts.

Thern believes that schools "should be as pleasant as a home," a place conducive to learning. He likes quiet schools, with materials to dull the noise and reduce hyperactivity. A conversation area has carpeted floors and walls as well as subdued lighting to foster restful intimacy and provide suitable acoustics. Early-childhood classrooms

97. Oneida tribal school (aerial view), Oneida, Wisconsin. Thern Design Center, 1994. (Courtesy Richard Thern)

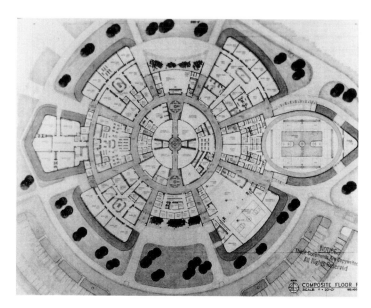

98. Oneida tribal school (composite plan). (Courtesy Richard Thern)

located in the turtle's tail have carpeted curved and stepped storytelling corners. Custodians prefer hard floors, but Thern does not "build schools for the custodians."

The architect fit the program with apparent ease into the turtle shape. In most schools, the library and media room are in the center, but the Oneidas' desire to have the language and cultural center there took precedence. Where four corridors cross, an octagonal room opens to windows in classrooms at the angles and to the sky through a skylight. The suggestion is clear that this is the place of illumination, a climax of the educational experience based on culture and nature. Ben Cannon*, an Oneida artist active in school affairs, says that the language and culture lessons are highlights of each day for his young nephew. Classroom displays, bilingual signs, and library posters make the emphasis on Oneida heritage visible throughout the school.

The head houses a huge balconied gymnasium, large enough for assemblies of reservation residents. Two legs hold classrooms for specified age groups, while the other legs contain the cafeteria and the elementary-school gym, along with rooms for special subjects and projects. Connecting the legs are administrative offices and nurse's premises, music practice rooms, a fitness room, and lockers. The school appears to be unusually well supplied with spaces for small groups to engage in varied activities. It provides special premises for the learning-disabled in the same legs as classes for unimpaired children of the same age. Cultural references such as Flynn Battaglia's wampum-based tile designs adorn corridors and are installed in such unexpected—and perhaps inappropriate—places as locker rooms, over toilet fixtures, and on the kitchen floor.

The building combines practicality with a clear reference to a cultural symbol, but the building design—low and expansive, rising from an insulating beam—is unobtrusive. This is unlike the Turtle at Niagara Falls, which was meant in part to attract paying visitors. In this way, the school conforms to the discreet design approach seen in recent Oneida architecture (apart from the new casino, but even that is half-hidden behind the tribally run hotel). The Oneida build modest buildings made of wood and local materials when that is possible.[41]

Apart from the examples in Niagara Falls and near Green Bay, the turtle has only rarely appeared in architectural plans. Its shape was proposed for an unbuilt sports center for the Mohawks near the Canadian border. The potential users wanted it to be functional, but also asked the architectural consultants, Wang Gregorson of Toronto, for culturally referential design. In housing for the Turtle Mountain Band at Belcourt, North Dakota, architects Zejdlik & Harmala thought that the clients ought to live in something different from HUD boxes, but did not know what to do that would be appropriate. The results were houses with double-pitched roofs divided into compartments that might be seen as the patterns of a turtle's carapace. The solution, known as "little turtles" in the office, was not appropriate to this tribe's heritage, but at least the architects made an effort to consider something specific for their clients.[42]

Hodne and Sun Rhodes* have incorporated other symbolic forms into the buildings they have done independently. Using Community Development Block Grant funds, Sun Rhodes designed ten houses for the Las Vegas Band of Paiutes (1986). Tribal members explained their traditions and contributed to the design during discussions with the architect and with the master planners, Design Concepts West of Carson City, Nevada. The houses were based on the form of a wolf, an important image for the band. The front represented the head, the body made up the living quarters, and the tail contained a heating and cooling system. The design included an elevated wind catcher to move wind through an underground tunnel for cooling or warming, to foster harmony between people and nature. HUD would fund only more ordinary houses and cheaper infrastructure, so the wolf houses were never built.[43]

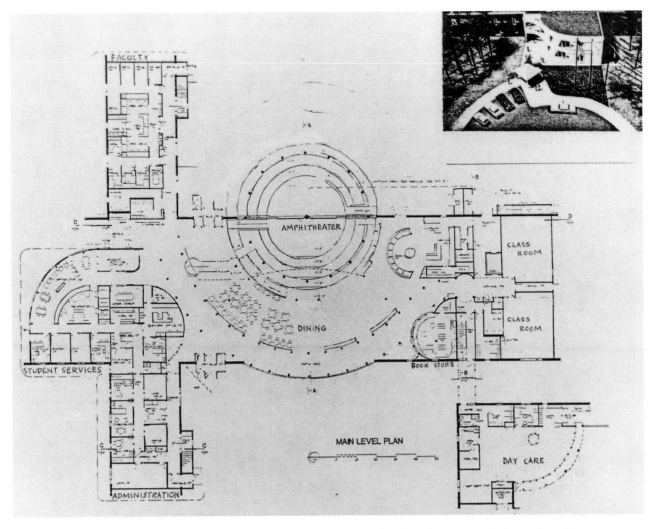

99. Fond du Lac Community College (plan), Cloquet, Minnesota. Thomas H. Hodne, Jr., and Damberg, Scott, Peck & Booker, 1992. (Courtesy Thomas H. Hodne, Jr.)

For the Division of Indian Work Building, under construction in late 1994, Sun Rhodes and his partner, Daniel Feidt, are using less obvious symbolism for an urban social-service agency. Seventeen thousand square feet of program and meeting premises include a library, offices, and a community room. A donation for construction came from gambling proceeds at the Shakopee Mdewakanton Dakota casinos about 30 miles away.

The doorway, centered between two broad planes in the facade, contains an inverted crescent moon, considered female in many cultures and used here because women, and this agency, are "providers of nourishment for survival." The idea for the moon image came from a "cul-tural design workshop" attended by female "pipe carriers in the Sun Dance." They told Sun Rhodes that 1993 was the year of the wet moon, an indicator of favorable weather for growing things. The community room for ceremonies and assemblies is to be circular, a form considered sacred. Designs both traditional and interpreted will be shown on the surface materials outside.[44]

Thomas Hodne, working with Damberg, Scott, Peck & Booker, designed Fond du Lac Community College in Cloquet, Minnesota, outside Duluth, inaugurated in September 1992 (99–101). This institution is tribally sponsored, and its board of directors is composed of tribal members, but it is the only tribal college to be also a public institu-

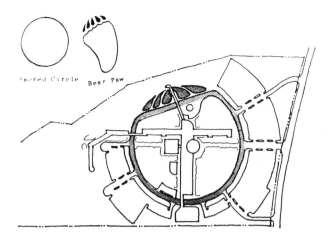

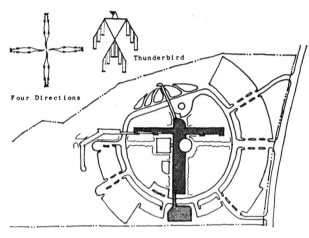

100. Fond du Lac Community College (conceptual plans). (Courtesy Thomas H. Hodne, Jr.)

101. Fond du Lac Community College (amphitheater under construction).

tion receiving full state financing. Most of the students are Anglos, in part because only 11 percent of the population within a 40-mile radius is Amerindian and so far there is no campus housing for those beyond commuter range; the college hopes to add it soon, using a line and spiral plan that Hodne likens to a shaman's yoyo. That may help overcome the immediate appeal of jobs in casinos sponsored by the Fond du Lac Ojibwe and other bands.

The site of over 30 acres is a former tree farm of red pines, given by the Potlatch Corporation, a wood-products business that is the county's largest employer. This enabled the college to move from an abandoned school in Cloquet, where instruction began in 1987. The aim was to inculcate among Indian students a sense of prideful ownership of their college as a way of averting their high drop-out rates in other colleges. The curriculum includes courses directed toward Native American concerns, such as Ojibwe language, fish and silviculture, and addiction and substance abuse. The state legislature funded the first construction phase by a bonding bill, the city and county contributed water and sewer service, and the state continued grants to Native American students in higher education that it initiated in 1957.

The award-winning building is located in a firebreak in the planted forest. Only thirty-seven trees had to be cut to allow the college to be built, and some of them were used as posts in the construction. The design began with consideration of cultural issues; Hodne believes it is essential to hold design workshops to elicit his clients' ideas—here, those of reservation residents and members of the college's planning committee. Using 40-inch-wide brown wrapping paper posted on the walls, the workshop participants produced such images as the thunderbird, the bear's paw, a circle representing the continuity of life, and a heart circle marking the spiritual core of the community (100). Providing drawing materials while discussing cultural form will inevitably lead some participants to design literal images, but Hodne—and Sun Rhodes—had been seeking them for about twenty years in any case.

The architects considered the square footage, the perimeter, and environmental and cultural issues. They produced a cruciform plan for the college's first construction stage. It is about 90 feet from head to foot, with a cross arm of about 60 feet. The head of the cross is rounded to the east, and below the cross arm, half of a rotunda projects outward (101). A gymnasium occupies the foot, while a rectangular wing for fine arts and performance, and a separate structure for day care of students' children, complete the present building.

It is possible to see the form as that of a thunderbird as well as a Christian cross; doing so would suit the mission of the college, which is to unite the two cultures. Gail Thomas, secretary to the board of directors, says that some of the design ideas were intentionally left ambiguous. Hodne sometimes speaks of the surrounding ring road as a sacred circle. At the north, where the land slopes to break the circle, plantings are laid out like bear claws, each claw representing a clan. The rotunda, where cultural activities and assemblies take place, is a sky-blue domed heart for the bird. Here, rustic posts stand near columns clad in stainless steel. The glass wall that bisects the rotunda can move upward to allow free passage from the interior to the half that is outdoors. The glass wall here and the many windows everywhere counter the usual practice in designing colleges for northern climates, but the outward orientation characteristic of Native culture dominated the planning; when heat loss proved too great, some windows were halved diagonally to produce triangular openings. The exterior cladding of corrugated metal is colored white, yellow, red, and black, representing the four directions that symbolize harmony of life in Ojibwe culture. In the classrooms, chairs are placed in curves, not rows, to promote equality in the Indian manner. An archives room with curved walls has a round table, windows on several sides, and embellishment of bowed drum spindles; Ron Gittings, a faculty member, quoted one Mdewakanton Dakota visitor who said that in this room, "the spirits are pretty strong."[45]

At the Knife River Indian Villages National Historic Site, Surrounded-by-Enemy* designed for the exterior a semiabstract eagle, sacred to the Native peoples of the area (102). This is not simply painted; the architect believes that decoration must be intrinsic to the structure. The eagle's head projects from the building, but its body is indicated by various textures in the concrete block used in the construction. While this building is owned by the North Dakota Parks Department and not by a tribe, the clients wanted the architect to express fully ideas that were appropriate for the people who had built the nearby earth lodges.[46]

Animal symbols inform the design of the North Carolina Indian Cultural Center, to be on 500 wooded acres near Pembroke, North Carolina. This will show the heritage of southeastern tribes in a visitor center, an Indian village, arts and crafts display and sales areas, an outdoor amphitheater, and a museum. Wilbur Smith Associates of Columbia, South Carolina, prepared a feasibility study in

102. Visitor center (under construction), Knife River Indian Villages National Historic Site, North Dakota. Surrounded-by-Enemy* and North Dakota Parks Department, 1991.

103. Pascua Yaqui Ceremonial Building, Tucson, Arizona.
Anselmo Valencia* and reservation residents, ca. 1973. (Kathy
Ann Valencia, 1993)

1981. Incorporation in 1985 and an archaeological survey in 1986 preceded any further moves. Yelverton & Stone, selected in 1988, prepared a preliminary plan, and then sixty architects responded to questions based on desirable program components devised by Native Americans. Former governor James Hunt wanted a tourist facility along Interstate 95, and appointed a commission to plan it in December 1990. Beyond the educational and job-generating purposes of the center, its program emphasizes building in harmony with the natural beauty of the site, reflecting Native American connections to the earth, water, and celestial bodies. The planners chose NBBJ of Morrisville, North Carolina, working with design consultant James Mahoney, and met with them fifteen to twenty times during the first fifteen months of their association.

The designers were asked to help correct stereotypes that show Native Americans as primitives mired in ancient ways, or as people whose history began with European contact. They were asked to help counter even positive stereotypes, such as the myth that every Native American was an ideal environmentalist. The advisers did not want a park with only native plants; today's Indians adapt to the world as it is now. They were asked to show differences among Native groups so as to counter pan-Indian ideas. They were asked to learn from historians of all races, not from indigenous people alone "and an anthropologist or two." Native Americans living in cities were also to be consulted, as they are often overlooked. North Carolina had a special history as a border between two Native culture areas and as a place of great variety among tribes. The displays were to address conflicts frankly and were to admit gaps in knowledge. These are unusual considerations, formed by clear-headed and honest people. Perhaps debate and difference can be acknowledged in a multitribal facility on state land, whereas in comparable centers for a single tribe, local considerations and specific philosophies may prevail.

The visitor center combines a bird and a serpent in its plan. Two wings extend along a hypostyle hall made of heavy timber columns. On one side will be exhibits; on the other, administrative and educational services. The building is to have rugged wood siding and rough shingles, to evoke Native American construction. But it is not overtly a bird or a serpent; it is a modern building with some culturally meaningful overtones, and in that respect suited to the program. David Francis of NBBJ said that although the bird and serpent were on historic Native medallions, "we didn't want a Venturi duck." The overall concept, said Francis, "is like a village," although the scale is different from that of a traditional settlement, and little information was available about the settlements in any case. The Native advisers insisted, however, that the roofs be curved like those of indigenous lodges known in old drawings; this was done despite the architects' objection on practical grounds. The result embodies symbolism subtly. It should be possible here to reflect on the bird and serpent as historic images and to address the more immediately meaningful exhibits about history, culture, and modern identity.[47]

A more private project is at the same time more universal in its references. About twenty years ago, the Pascua Yaqui Yoemem Takia Foundation established a 2-acre cultural area on its land near Tucson. It is focused on a plaza, with a church and a domed building nearby to represent the sun, the Father-Creator in precontact times, and sign of the cycles of life (103). This area is important for Easter ceremonies, which relate to rebirth, joining Yaqui and Christian belief. The domed building contains 4100 square feet under its octagonal dome. The eight sides recall the eight pueblos of Rio Yaqui. The walls are made of curved radial steel beams supported by reinforced-concrete piers, while acoustical materials sprayed on expanded metal lath form the dome. On the exterior are seven murals showing historical events and images related to Yaqui beliefs. Local children who write graffiti on other buildings do not write on this one, showing that its special character is understood and respected.

The dome has been supplemented at the south by rectangular additions, at best suggesting the juxtaposition of round and rectilinear forms in the houses and kivas of pueblo villages. In about 1985, a large gymnasium was erected about 10 feet from the northern wall of the dome, and athletes enter on the gym's southern side. The gymnasium was built there because people "wanted to offer access and activity to the youth... near their repository of history, language, and culture." A preschool is nearby for the same reason: Culture begins at birth. These buildings obstruct the view of the dome from several sides, reducing its symbolic impressiveness. The domed structure is not, however, used for its intended purposes today, but for the tribal government office. It is to become a museum when the Pascua Yaqui erect a new office building.

Anselmo Valencia*, a religious and governmental leader, was instrumental in asking architect Don W.

Ryden to adapt the building for reuse as a museum and visitor center. The architect suggested that outdoor exhibits replicate traditional houses and gardens where classes and demonstrations would be held. A desert garden could symbolize tribal beliefs, and a circular observatory for skygazing might also include a meditation room. A path along a stream could symbolize the Rio Yaqui and eight pueblos along it. The tribe could build a a gift shop and food ramadas or a restaurant for visitors who came to see the new cultural attractions. The kitchen should, however, keep its traditional earthen floor, even if the walls are made of concrete block.

Ryden feels that the rectangular additions have so muddled the power of the circular geometry that a site plan alone can remedy the situation. He prepared development concepts for the tribe and foundation in early 1994, proposing that "site features and landscaping...reinforce concentric patterns on the ground plane emanating from the Dome... to draw attention to the sacred geometry of the natural world and to contrast it with the irregular geometry of man's creations." His plan envisions concentric circles visually strong enough to contain the disparate elements, existing and proposed. In this case, the locally acknowledged importance of the domed building with its solar symbolism is likely to reassert its importance at the center of a circular, cosmic, plan.[48]

* * *

Is explicit symbolism effective as a way of embedding the buildings into their cultural context? Does it help to make the buildings and their purpose important to their Native American sponsors and public? Both answers may be yes, but only when the symbols are widely known and immediately appreciated. Diagrams that are too intricate for easy remembering, or symbols developed by a small group, are unlikely to find a receptive public and probably will not be understood twenty years after their invention.

Perhaps some designers and clients try too hard to make their buildings symbolically impressive. Their exertions may not be necessary. After all, Chartres Cathedral impresses even those who do not know that its plan is cross shaped, and Nôtre Dame of Paris is inspiring even though its plan is not cruciform. Must it be only minorities who use symbolic forms to assert their identity boldly against public indifference or hostility?

10

References to Nature

Many Americans, whether of Native or other descent, agree that American Indians have a special relationship with nature. The relationship may be hard to define, but the opinion is widespread, and it has affected a number of recent buildings.

The American school system generally attempts to present all human groups as worthy of respect, but as Native peoples are also discussed in the context of defeat, something must be said to compensate for that. If the defeat occurred because the victors were superior in number and in military and other technology, Native peoples must be connected to alternative positive values, unrelated to number and technology, if their heritage is not to be thought of as outmoded and incompetent. In this context, the antonym of technology is nature. When teachers explain Native peoples' intelligent use of all parts of the buffalo, their knowledge of animal tracking and of nourishing or medicinal plants, and their ability to create ingenious dwellings in forbidding locations, these examples suggest something larger—the environmental interests of people who stand apart from modern Western practices.

The Native American relationship to nature can also be seen as morally valuable and as connected to the spirit, in opposition to the machine and its materialistic exploita-tions. Joseph Laban*, executive director of the Hopi Housing Authority, said that Anglo "society is about convenience," whereas "Indian society is about the effort to achieve harmony with Mother Earth." Native peoples are usually described as exceptionally sensitive to the land, animals, and seasons, and as having unrivaled standing to discuss ecological balance. This way of seeing Native cultures situates other people as respectful observers who cannot appropriate the indigenous material.

Native American astronomical knowledge has been recognized in learned articles and by archaeologists such as those who study the ruins in Chaco Canyon, New Mexico, where door openings are aligned with the sun at the solstices. Anna Sofaer, now president of the Solstice Project to study, document, and preserve the Sun Dagger there, notes that this ancient Pueblo celestial calendar marks with precise light patterns the solstices, equinoxes, and nineteen-year cycle of the moon. Other solar markings nearby record solar noon, the solstices, and the equinoxes. The project's participants suggest that Chaco roads expressed symbolically the culture's cosmology and that the major ceremonial structures had astronomical and religious importance.[1] Astronomical reference points are important to many tribes, not only those in the Southwest.

The orientation and internal alignments of the new

Institute of American Indian Arts may reflect these relationships, as Al Qöyawayma* of the planning committee expressed great interest in them. This pantribal school, federally chartered under private leadership, was established with federal funds and BIA encouragement in 1962. It had been on the Santa Fe Indian School campus, where Paolo Soleri designed an amphitheater, finished by others, in 1966. Pueblo governments wanted the site back, and the school left for barracks and mobile-home classrooms at the College of Santa Fe.

The architect for the new campus is Douglas Cardinal*, working with other Native professionals, including Johnpaul Jones*, landscape architect; Donna House*, a Navajo botanist; David Sloan* & Associates, architects; and Edmund Gonzales*, project manager. The building committee, over half Indian in membership, employed indigenous talent whenever possible. The planning documents emphasize also that the building must support personal and group values important to many Native Americans, and encourage reverence for nature and the Great Spirit behind it. Orientation, relationship to nearby landscape features, and solar-energy considerations are all discussed.

Qöyawayma, an engineer and a renowned potter, hopes to incorporate an orientation to solar and lunar axes into the plan, and particularly into that of the central structure and adjacent walkway. He and other committee members also want to reflect the Pueblo cosmology inside the buildings. These planners hope to use knowledge of aboriginal celestial learning to embed the new buildings in their setting, just as ancestral pueblos were linked to the earth and cosmos.[2]

Native astronomy also underlies the plans by Gregory Adams at the Native American Resource Development Association in Pueblo, Colorado, for remodeling an unfinished cement-block office building at Sinte Gleska University on the Rosebud Reservation. A year after plans were drawn by the Nance Company of Omaha, the project lost its funding, leaving a fragmentary rotunda with a deck for an upper story and wings. Adams conceived three circles, the central one a lobby open to a raised skylight through which teachers could bring students to study the night sky. His proposal envisions four openings to the building, facing each cardinal direction. Adams is seriously interested in Lakota culture and proud of his close relations with Rosebud members, so he incorporated as much of their worldview as he could in a preexisting shell and within financial limits. He is aware, however, that important elders may object to the materialization of spiritual beliefs in a building.[3]

A proposal by Marley Porter in 1991 for the Navajo Supreme Court envisioned a circular courtroom with openings at the equinox points to make the building like a solar clock. The sun would illuminate motifs of planting and harvest on stone walls. The rest of the building would have been composed of several wings radiating from the courtroom, thus keeping a central element comparable to the hogan but not imitative, and allowing for expansion and for specialized spaces hard to achieve with a purely central plan.

Amerindian cultures, like other preindustrial societies, organized planting and harvest festivals, calendars, and other important aspects of life around the equinoxes and solstices, responding also to comets or stellar and planetary alignments. Although Jewish and Christian feasts such as Passover, Christmas, and the Annunciation are also tied to solar phenomena and seasonal change, members of technological societies often regard Native Americans as the people most intimately allied with the cosmos.

It is not possible here to resolve disagreements about the accuracy of these perspectives. Simplistic statements abound. As though to dismiss those Native Americans who speak with sincere reverence for nature's forces and about their own spiritual connection to them, cynics name tribal officials willing to accept nuclear-waste dumps in exchange for payment. Those who regard Indians as model ecologists meet opponents who claim that Native peoples were as ready as any others to exhaust nature's abundance and then move elsewhere.[4] Here it is important only to recognize that in recent decades, many Native Americans and their admirers in other cultures have accorded to Indian nations a special standing in considering humanity's relationship to the natural world.

A direct way to suggest the Native connection to nature is to add murals of animals and landscapes, as Johnson Loud, Jr., did at Red Lake IHS Hospital and nursing home in 1980 and 1991 (113). Another straightforward way is to use a shape, materials, and colors that blend with the natural surroundings, placing trees and bushes adjacent to the building or vice versa. The Karuk Tribe of California Community Service Center at Happy Camp (1981) refused to approve a less costly and simply utilitarian building than Environmental Harmonics eventually designed. The one they accepted is set among trees, keeping a low profile. Warm in color and with a band of ornament evoking woven baskets around the top, it seems to be almost absorbed within its forest setting.[5] Inside, skylights as well as windows admit natural light, skylighting often being found in tribal civic buildings and schools of the past twenty years. The Agua Caliente Tribal Office and Building in Palm Springs, California, similarly uses dark wood and horizontal lines, adding deep overhangs for shade and some rough stonework, all encased in dense plantings of trees, shrubs, and flowers.

Evoking landscape forms is another way to connect architecture to nature. Robert Cain, designer at Six Associates for the Museum of the Cherokee Indian in North Carolina, said that the "building concept was meant to echo the form of mountains, rising and falling in peaks and valleys" (104). The materials are natural—wood, stone, and copper—and used in the past by the Cherokee. There is no obvious ornament, but a border of banked earth, leafy plants, flowers, stones, and a small stream reinforce the connection to nature.[6]

Charles Chief Boyd* conceived his design for the Cherokee National Museum at Tahlequah, Oklahoma, as an earth mound, although it is made of cast concrete and stone (105). Boyd sees the museum as an emanation from nature. The building—lengthened now—is a long, low flat-roofed quadrilateral. It blends into the slope of a hill to the right of the original entrance, near a reconstructed historic village. The museum seems to be an extension of the hill, or a kind of cave dug into a rise in the landscape. Faced with stone, surrounded by trees and plants, it is subordinated to nature and barely intrusive. The Cherokee National Historical Society, its sponsor, thought of the museum as "rising from the ground [and] using nature's materials," like council houses of the past.[7] Funds to build the museum came from admission fees to the reconstructed village (1967), so a reference to older architecture was well placed. The design, reflecting "the feeling of being Indian," was intended to foster knowledge and pride in Cherokee heritage and to wrest control of historical presentations from the "limited part-bloods" who had controlled it earlier.[8] The interior displays, by Sphere, exhibition consultants from Chicago, were encased in glass-fiber partitions which the tribe now proposes to replace with others made of natural materials. If references to a mound and to a council house confuse the antecedents, it is nev-

104. **Museum of the Cherokee Indian, Cherokee, North Carolina. Six Associates, 1976. (Paul Brezny [Asheville, North Carolina]; courtesy Robert Cain)**

105. Cherokee National Museum, Tahlequah, Oklahoma.
Charles Chief Boyd*, 1975.

ertheless clear that the sponsors and designer all wanted a building related both to nature and to Cherokee architectural traditions.

Geological strata helped to inspire the facade of the Salish Kootenai Cultural Center (1994) in Montana funded by the reservation treasury and designed by Paul Bishop of Paradigm Architects in Missoula, who responded to a request for a proposal. Flanking a cylinder that houses the entrance and the heart of the building, symmetrical walls are faced in bands of buff granite and dark gray quartzite, separated by thin lines of flagstone. The contiguous but distinct materials represent the confederation of Salish who came from the Bitterroot Valley, where Bishop found the granite; the Kootenai who knew the quartzite at Flathead Lake; and the small Pend d'Oreille Tribe from the center of the reservation, where there are flagstone beds.

The cylinder, its round form echoing an outdoor dance arbor, is also to be explained by the government-instigated occupation of one reservation by three tribes. The cylinder, or gathering space, responds to the tribes' agreement on one major element—the drum at the heart of their cultures. Eight log supports, 17 feet tall, four of them carved by Dwight Billedeaux* and Chey Brown*, surround this inhabited drum. The carvers created designs of animal tracks, leaves, bird tracks, and aquatic life, conceived in spirals. These pillars sustain a flat ceiling; piercing its center is a domical skylight made of diamond-shaped double-paned polycarbonate translucent plastic, admitting the kind of clear light that filters into a tipi. The white, green, red, and blue allude to snow, the earth, blood, and the sky—all natural phenomena. Planters near the entrance contain mountain plants on one side and prairie plants on the other.

The cultural center was not meant to be overtly referential, as the tribes had no historic permanent architecture. "Tule tipis and skin lodges are hard to transfer to buildings today," said Shelly Fyant McClure, museum

References to Nature **151**

106. A-Shwi School, Zuni Pueblo, New Mexico.
Gregory Hicks & Associates, 1991.

director. They did want something different from Anglo building, but left the visualization of this desire to the architect, offering little direction because doing so had not previously been possible. The feeling of the building rather than the shape was of chief significance. The four cardinal directions are respected, with an entrance at the east, education at the south, exhibits at the north, and collections and a gift shop at the west. The architecture was meant to support the message of the building that is a gathering place for the people. To be sure, the sponsors and architects hoped that it would be attractive, but a ceremonial arbor between the approach and the museum is of even greater significance.[9]

Among pueblo peoples, Hopi High School (1980), long and low atop a mesa, almost seems to be another stratum of earth and rock, although the Hopi did not ask Barnes, Landis, Goodman & Youngblood for that specifically. Zuni Middle School (1986) by James Rowland is made of concrete block colored to imitate the local red-brown stone, and shaken in the mold to produce the slightly sagging appearance of raw adobe brick. (This continued the approach of the Zuni school built in 1939, in which quarried stone and logs recalled earlier house-building materials.)

The attractive A-Shwi School for the Zuni Pueblo school district (first phase, 1991) refers to the strata of red and white sandstone in the nearby cliffs by alternating red and white concrete-block stripes on the facade, and by having several steps within the silhouette (106). A third color of concrete block closer to the base recalls the somewhat purpler red sandstone used on reservation buildings of the 1930s and 1940s. Hayes Lewis*, school superintendent, hoped that the school buildings would look somehow Zuni, while serving contemporary functions; reference to natural building materials must satisfy the request because the schools could not be made to imitate pueblos within the available budget.[10]

At A-Shwi, Gregory Hicks & Associates also designed a long wall with many windows to reflect the caves in the sides of mesas along the Gallup road and on a mesa leading toward sacred Corn Mountain. Interior colors are based on those used in Zuni jewelry—coral accents and turquoise trim and casework accenting the walls, painted off-white to substitute for silver. Unfortunately, the plan was reversed from its original orientation because a local owner would not sell the land needed for access to the correct side. The architects "fixed what we could," but the entrance now faces northwest, the source of unpleasant prevailing winds that blow trash around the entrance. This disappoints the architects and those who stress Native sensitivity to nature.[11]

More successful from the ecological viewpoint is the Zuni Arts and Crafts building (107). Adobe blocks and conventional construction were too costly and would have to have been erected by non-Zuni workers. Jim Ostler, director of the facility, chose machine–rammed-earth blocks so that Zuni labor could be employed almost entirely. The laborers earned praise for workmanship, morale, and collaboration, and two Zuni became supervisors, working with the architect, Joseph Brawley. Two walls of rammed-earth blocks are connected by Dur-o-wal 6-gauge-wire reinforcing bars, with insulation and electrical ducts placed in the cavity. The wall has an insulation rating of R-30 for excellent thermal control. Passive solar heat could be introduced in the future using the broad south window. Flagstone flooring allows for radiant heating in plastic tubes below it and could be installed by Zunis unskilled at laying con-

crete. It cost only about three-quarters of what it would have if outside labor and material had been used, and Ostler expects the building to last for 500 years.[12]

Bill Chaleff, of Chaleff & Rogers in Bridgehampton, New York, is designing a museum and cultural center for the Shinnecock Tribe of Long Island (108, 109). It may be constructed in pressed-earth bricks. The material is locally abundant, and Shinnecocks can be trained to work with it. Current plans are to build a sample house of this material to test its suitability for the museum and for tribal housing in the future. At the end of the project, tribal members will have acquired both skills and products that can be employed off the reservation, thereby increasing the Shinnecock economic base. No aboriginal building can be replicated for the museum, so that the design draws on soft natural curves and maintains a modesty of scale suited to its surroundings, while looking distinctive to attract notice.

Planning documents are increasingly concerned with energy efficiency, use of local, natural materials, and conservation. Raymond Obomsawin*, an Oneida official, points out the possibilities for reviving tradition in an ecological framework. His people cannot restore longhouse life because the nuclear family is the standard today,

107. **Zuni Arts and Crafts building (under construction), Zuni Pueblo, New Mexico. Joseph Brawley, 1993. (Dale W. Anderson/ Aztec Media [Aztec, New Mexico]; courtesy James Ostler)**

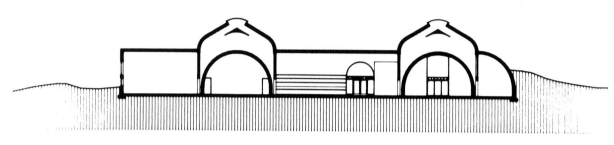

EAST ELEVATION
4 2 0 4 8 16 24 40

108. Shinnecock Nation Cultural Center and Museum
(proposed east elevation and section), Shinnecock Reservation,
Long Island, New York. Chaleff & Rogers, 1994. (Courtesy
William Chaleff)

but they can revive communal gardens. They can participate in the construction of their houses, perhaps using
rammed earth because the Oneida Valley soil has a high
clay content.

When plans were made for the Beeline Highway
through Arizona's Fort McDowell Reservation, the Yavapai
Apache asked the architectural firms of Don W. Ryden
and Wyatt*/Rhodes to prepare guidelines for developers
who want to build industrial and commercial facilities
along a 4.5 mile stretch of road. The goals are environmental and aesthetic: preventing erosion and loss of plant
and animal life, minimizing pavements to restrict solar-
heat absorption, and creating a style responsive to landscape and climate. There is no Yavapai Apache architectural tradition apart from brush shelters and wickiups, so a
new architectural image will be established; the clients
want a "timeless vernacular" based on their culture to produce a sense of place. This is to be achieved by stressing a
pueblo-inspired style of grouped, compact buildings usually in a 1 to 1:3 proportion, faced in stucco or stone, surrounded by wooden fences, and looking into closed, land-

scaped areas. Guidelines call for varied building heights,
an 80-foot length limit to preserve human scale and to create good relationships among buildings, and desert plants
or landscape features. Battered parapets will soften the profile of masses. Vertical windows will balance the prevailing
horizontality. Shade will come from walls and porches,
ramadas, trellises, pergolas, and gardens. For a harmonious
effect, only approved materials and pigments will be
allowed, the colors based as far as possible on those of old
baskets.

Conservation of "materials, labor, energy, and the natural environment" is a major goal. Natural drainage, parking along existing earth contours, changes in surface-water
patterns allowed only if they affect no one else adversely—
these and many other provisions should ensure a development that respects the site. Rustic materials are desired,
and the planners propose restrictions on rooftop equipment, neon lighting, signs, and ornament. There is hope
that developers will see this as an unusually well-planned
enclave, and that the buildings will fit into their setting
instead of violating it.[13] When proposing provisional

designs for the Satwiwa Native American Cultural Center in Newbury Park, California, University of California students emphasized similar ideas. They paid "tribute to Native American values toward Mother Earth" by having a display shelter, a demonstration village, and a circle of stone seats around a firepit "sit lightly on the land" and incorporate both active- and passive-solar-heating techniques for environmental control.[14]

On the Rosebud Reservation, Jim Stands-and-Looks-Back* and Charlie Garriott, husband of a tribal member, collaborated with reservation residents to erect the Stanley Red Bird Lakota Studies Building at Sinte Gleska University, using advice from David Howard, a specialist in log buildings (110, 111). A consultant from Wisconsin instructed the builders in indigenous ponderosa-pine expanded-log construction, a technique that compensates for tapered and twisting trunks. The building recalls nineteenth-century log architecture. This type of construction gives jobs to Rosebud workers, helping the local economy, and uses indigenous resources, especially renewable wood, following the Native philosophy of seeing the earth as related to human beings.

Classrooms and offices occupy the main floor, and auxiliary rooms fill the timber-framed basement. The builders tried to embody environmentally sound principles, although they had to use carpeting with some toxic material in it, standard paints and varnishes because of budget constraints, foamboard insulation, and propane heating. They had to use some plywood and truss construction rather than only timber from the Rosebud sawmill. All the same, even with a limited budget and a relatively inexperienced, changing work force, they found many ways to achieve their goal: photovoltaic cells to provide between 30 and 50 percent of the electricity, efficient fluorescent bulbs, flow restrictors on faucets and toilets, an on-demand hot-water heater, dampers on fans to prevent air leakage, double thermopane windows, logs and rough siding from the tribal sawmill, unbleached and recycled papers in the washroom, a carpet sweeper rather than a vacuum cleaner, leather and solid wood for much of the furniture, cedar shakes for the roof, slate and quarry tile for the floor, and, usually, nontoxic cleaning materials. Heating and air-conditioning are 94 percent efficient. Native plants will provide additional landscaping. Some of the

109. **Shinnecock Nation Cultural Center and Museum (proposed plan). (Courtesy William Chaleff)**

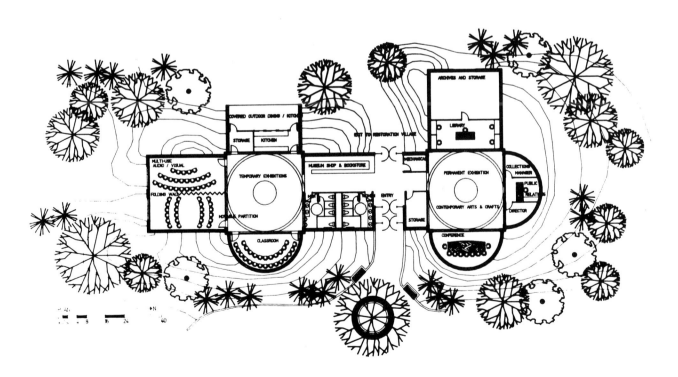

110. Stanley Red Bird Lakota Studies Building (side and back), Sinte Gleska University, Rosebud, South Dakota. David Howard and Jim Stands-and-Looks-Back* (construction supervisor), 1991.

methods used to promote energy conservation and environmental health are costly, but the university made a serious commitment to these ways of living in harmony with Mother Earth.

A housing cooperative to which Garriott belongs has experimented with concrete-strengthened rammed earth, mixed in wooden forms. Board-and-batten siding covers the rammed earth, and an insulated metal-covered timber-frame roof covers the two-story building. Although this construction material needs no insulation and retains heat in winter, heating is costly in South Dakota, and most people want to use wood, as logs are locally available and much cheaper than other fuels. But wood stoves made of iron or steel create pollution during their manufacture. Catalytic burners use a great deal of energy in the production stages and cannot tolerate the glossy colored paper of magazines that owners sometimes put into them. Garriott learned that the best way to obtain efficient heat from wood—about 97 percent efficiency compared with the usual half of that—is to use it in masonry heating stoves. These stoves originated in Siberia, were known in Europe, and are a specialty of Albert Barden, an expert from Maine, who advised the builders at Rosebud. Masonry

stoves are massive and intensely hot inside, but cool enough outside to make accidents to children unlikely. And while they are costly, they could be made locally. They last for more than two and up to four times longer than catalytic iron or steel stoves. Whether the residents prefer round buildings to recall tipi plans or rectilinear ones based on square altars, the heat source can be in the center, as it was in a tipi. Energy efficiency and Lakota tradition can therefore be combined.

The Oglala Lakota of the nearby Pine Ridge Reservation lack adequate housing, have few native building materials, and command insufficient funds to build what they need. To begin to address winter heating and other problems, eight families working with the intertribal Ta S'ina Tokaheya Foundation and Mike Sierra*, a Lakota, decided to develop a community that hopes "to live lightly on the land and its resources."[15] They "will reintroduce native tribal patterns within a village model that puts the Sioux in greater control of their own resources and gives dignity to their people by making use of new takes on age-old technologies that benignly use nature." They will train "Sioux to design and build their own houses using adobe brick made from local clay and local timber....Many buildings will be sited directly into local hillsides in order to optimize solar heat retention." Double-thick adobe walls and special glazing will add to the insulation. The aim is to get off the electric-power grid, off "reliance on the white man's world so that they can go back to relying on the natural world."[16] Strong plains winds will generate electricity for pumping well water and for lighting houses, agricultural buildings, and a community center. The architect, William McDonough, is known for environmentally sensitive work, including dwellings for formerly nomadic Bedouins who are now sedentary and the expanded offices of the Environmental Defense Fund (1986), where indoor pollution is minimized.[17]

The tribal headquarters of the Wampanoag of Gay Head, Massachusetts, was completed in 1992 by ARC Design Group, whose goals included using low-impact technologies to minimize adverse environmental effects. The building is set into a south-facing hillside, ideal for passive-solar-heating design. Two-thirds of the windows are on the south. The insulation levels create a "tight" building. Lights dim and brighten depending on available sunlight; plant beds process "gray" water, and the Clivus Multrum composting toilet system produces material that can be sold

to farmers. The architects used recycled wood where they could as well as ceramic tile made from broken car windshields. Even doormats are made of recycled truck tires. The building, which was meant to look more like a home than an institution—it recalls old Cape Cod hotels—uses colors related to those of the Gay Head cliffs.[18]

On the opposite coast, Native American groups in Portland are collaborating in plans made in 1994 for the American Indian Cultural Center, with Stastny Architects as designer and Brian McCormack as landscape architect. Funding began with a large contribution from Arthur W. Bresciani, a real-estate executive in New York who learned of the need for a facility of this kind. A committee with members ranging widely in age decided to erect a cultural center rather than a tourist facility, although they hope to share their culture with others.

The committee chose a site in Delta Park, and even though other locations were quieter—this one is near a freeway—this place had accommodated powwows in the past. A cultural center at one end of the property and a visitor center at the other end anchor the project and will deflect traffic noise up and over the buildings. A large central open space is a third element, as important as the

111. **Stanley Red Bird Lakota Studies Building.**

112. Turning Stone Casino, Verona, New York.
David Smotrich & Partners, 1993.

buildings. Native plants will be used for cooking demonstrations. A slough will be reclaimed, and it may be used to grow plants important in rituals.

A large gathering hall is located away from roadway sounds; a smaller one can be used for weekly potluck lunches served to the elderly; auxiliary rooms will be used for offices and craft-work studios, while a circular enclosure outdoors will accommodate performances and meetings. Most of the symbolic references—suggestions of a large bird in the roof of a gallery and the emphasis on circles indoors and out—are based on natural elements and astronomy, although a pyramidal form housing administrative offices may be regarded as a literal reference to a tipi. Visible from Interstate 5 between Portland and the Oregon–Washington border, the pyramid will be a signpost, although its real purpose is to segregate administration from meeting spaces; after the normal workweek, some parts may be used while the pyramid is closed and not heated. Throughout, the emphasis will be placed on a habitable environment.[19]

Unexpected results of characterizing Native Ameri-

cans as sensitive to nature are the windows and glass domes used in tribal casinos of the 1990s. They overturn standard practice in the gambling industry, which keeps casino halls windowless to prevent customers from sensing the passage of time, and keeps the rooms dark, lighting only the machines. It is increasingly important, however, for tribal casinos to distinguish themselves from ordinary ones, lest pressures to limit their activity or to tax their revenues become even more intense than they are now. In the 1990s, several casinos are being conceived as part of resorts, even family resorts, with motels and recreational amenities. This is as true for Las Vegas as it is for tribal casinos, but the Native Americans can present their casinos as more wholesome by letting in the light of day, having nothing to hide in the dark, and providing a cheerful as well as perversely stimulating environment. The Oneida near Verona, New York, even prohibit the sale of alcoholic drinks, making their casino a comfortable destination for folks who just want a little excitement now and then (112).

Some other tribally sponsored casinos have made other references to nature. The Morongo Indian Bingo

Palace combines wood and rough stone facing on the pillars of the entrance porch, suggesting something rustic. Ray Byron Frogge, Jr., in designing gambling halls in 1991 for the Creek, Shawnee, and Chickasaw of Oklahoma, replaced the ramps that his clients requested and proposed berms instead, recalling ancient mounds. To solve flood problems on the site, he suggested digging out some earth to create a marsh, and then bridging it (13). He describes himself as being "extremely into the energy side of a building," and employs active and passive solar heating, geomass, and heat pumps using the earth's temperature. He "soften[s] any style with organic" because "Indian or white, we all like to relate to nature."

Two of the largest and most profitable tribally sponsored casinos—Foxwoods for the Mashantucket Pequots in Connecticut, and Mystic Lake for the Shakopee Mdewakanton Dakota southwest of Minneapolis near Prior Lake, Minnesota—have interior landscaped areas with real or artificial rocks, pools or rivulets, and foliage to suggest that in tribal casinos, values are being honored that are ignored by ordinary sponsors of gambling halls (149). Adjacent to Mystic Lake's artificial landscape is a café where people can sit under natural light and contemplate these natural features, the antitheses of the machines that they had been staring at moments before. At Foxwoods, the landscaping descends to the basement, as though the artificial rock were a natural outcropping included in the building by people who could not bear to disturb Mother Nature by cutting it away. Beside the base of the "rock" is the entrance to a museum room in which the tribe presents its history and offers information and displays about the present and plans for the future. No casino in Nevada or Atlantic City could offer a serious presentation of this kind, but a tribally sponsored casino can suggest that the gambling activity is a means to a higher end, while being diverting in itself. The more elevated posture of Native Americans with regard to nature can be maintained, then, even in a casino.

11

Embodiment of Values

A good many projects and realized buildings incorporate references to Native American concerns, but they do not copy older buildings, extract or evoke parts of traditional forms, or symbolize anything specific. Instead, the architects try to express Native American values even if there is no immediate appearance of Indianness. Buildings of this type may convey the impression of being at least unusual, if not specific to one group, or they may subtly incorporate responses to cultural requirements within a laconic outer form.

The Ne Ia Shing clinic (1993) at Mille Lacs by Cuningham Hamilton Quiter of Minneapolis has a circular lobby, a form often associated with Native sacred beliefs. The most sensitive part of the plan is a curving corridor, requested by the tribal planning representatives although the architects at first thought it superfluous. It leads from the lobby to examining rooms for physical diseases on one side and examining rooms for mental and addictive disorders on the other. Only gradually did the architects grasp the point of designing a long curved hall with doors to either side at the ends and center: Patients could vanish immediately into and emerge quickly from their examining rooms with little chance of being seen by acquaintances. As reservation members are discreet about psycho-logical and addictive problems, this arrangement corresponds to an important cultural requirement, even though nothing "looks Indian."

In other places, indigenous approaches to family and health have led a few hospitals to include rooms for Native healing ceremonies, and others have rooms in which an extended rather than just an immediate family can visit a patient.

Mark Wirtanen of Architectural Resources in Hibbing, Minnesota, talked to the coordinators at the Red Lake IHS Hospital about "what Native people wanted in health care facilities and were not finding." Family gathering rooms, abundant natural light, floor lines in meaningful colors to guide senile patients, and a center for making crafts were among the features mentioned. He had not expected a preference for lively colors rather than "the white man's pale colors" or the browns and greens that he proposed as being related to nature. The clients did not reveal what they wanted immediately, in order to avoid hurting his feelings. Brightly colored murals now adorn the central octagons of the two main wings, which opened in 1980 and 1991 (113). Mike*, a custodian in 1992, expressed his pleasure at working in such an attractive building; he had sought this job after returning from the

113. Red Lake Indian Health Service Hospital, Minnesota. Murals by Johnson Loud, Jr.*, 1980. Architectural Resources, 1980.

114. Lac du Flambeau School, Lac du Flambeau, Wisconsin. Seymour, Davis, Seymour, 1992. (Courtesy Mike West, Seymour, Davis, Seymour)

Twin Cities, where he feared that his city-reared sons would never know how to hunt and fish, and where Mike never felt at home.

The Euro-American architect of the Lac du Flambeau School (114) also changed his preconceived ideas about what contemporary Ojibwe want from an educational institution. Mike West of Seymour, Davis, Seymour of Eau Claire, Wisconsin, specialists in school design, prepared his approach. He

> did a great deal of research into the culture, and I naively moved into the first meeting thinking I would demonstrate how sensitive I am to their culture. But I was surprised to see that...their first comment was about wanting a school that was first class in terms of the latest educational thinking....I had done my research and I expected to go in with my feeble knowl-

edge of their culture and give them a nudge and then they'd take over and say, "This is what our culture means and we want to show it." If I hadn't [prodded], they'd never have brought it [cultural aspects] up. [Instead] we got into budgets, the media center, how big the gym is.

While West was interested in "pushing the symbolism as hard as we could..., it's hard not to be heavy-handed. Ultimately, it was a blessing to me that they were looking for more subtle expressions of a culture. I've seen very few examples where the Native American" aspect was emphasized but where the result "didn't look forced....As the design developed, I realized that to base the design on what for most people in the tribe was fairly obscure symbolism would be a waste of time."

For a $7 million school of 100,000 square feet, West thought it inappropriate to translate small, organic, impermanent materials into steel I-sections, brick, and glass. The school includes a large round room used for drum ceremonies, an example of the effort "to provide spaces which would facilitate the ceremonies, rather than make spaces overtly symbolic." In addition, "we adapted colors and patterns from their beadwork for designs on the interior and exterior. We're working...with the Indian artist community to integrate some artwork into the building. There's a problem, though, of people who have the most knowledge of symbols [but] may not be the best artists....The school is also more colorful than schools for your typical Germans and Norwegians here." These features suggest that the school belongs only to the Ojibwe, but they do not imitate or even paraphrase ancient building forms.

One of the earliest buildings in which architects learned to listen to Native American clients is the Minneapolis American Indian Center, which opened in 1975 (115). Thomas Hodne and his partner, Gerald Johnson, had completed the design work by 1971, having studied and reflected for almost two years.[1] They had to prepare well because this was the first purpose-built urban Indian community and social-service center. The building was intended to "help spur a renewed sense of identity, a truer self image...[through] a physical form that would proclaim to the Indian community and the rest of the city an emerging pride in the Indian heritage"[2] while fitting in with the varied buildings along the main street of an Amerindian neighborhood.

Since this was a multitribal facility, it could not imitate the architecture or planning of one culture alone. The clients requested natural materials and open spaces for gatherings. For this wedge-shaped building, Hodne proposed that a part of the performance, dining, and office wing project toward the street, as though to join the other citizens of Minneapolis; that is why a glass-walled fin can be seen at the left side.

Hodne had promised to take a Native American architect as his associate if one could be found. Two were, in fact—Surrounded-by-Enemy* and his employee at the time, Dennis Sun Rhodes*. By the time Hodne met them, the design work was almost finished; they contributed ideas for the auditorium, for some landscaping and a ceremonial arbor, for the colors and a concrete "banner" in a children's outdoor play area, and for a large cedar mural in a crow-quill pattern, designed by George Morrison*, an Ojibwe artist, for the facade of the gymnasium wing.

The building's referential characteristics are evident, despite its generally modern appearance. Wood is used outside and in, with glue-laminated unfinished fir beams and purlins, among many other features, although the architect now regrets the use of so much wood outside, because it rots. Abundant natural light enters through window walls and skylights, as the users wanted to see and be seen, even though the city fathers protested that public buildings should have small windows to keep heating costs down. A small wigwam occupies one side of the principal room. Outdoors, an amphitheater accommodates ceremonies. The children's play area is circular. Spaces have been allocated for the exhibition and sale of works of art and craft; one is known as the "glass wigwam" because of its curved roof. Circles are used in ornamental forms, and murals showing indigenous life were painted by Native American artists inside and out. The eastward orientation of the whole building is another element traditional with many Native nations.

The essential Indian feature is less obvious—a ramp that zigzags along one side of the principal ground-floor room, leading to offices and other rooms upstairs (116). Hodne learned that local Native Americans do not like to

115. Minneapolis American Indian Center, Minneapolis, Minnesota. Hodne–Stageberg Partners, 1975.

116. Minneapolis American Indian Center.

sit in rows; they prefer to gather informally at good vantage points around the edge of an event. The ramp allows people to choose their own places and clusters of companions while they look down at speakers and performers. Here Hodne addressed aspects of inner comfort and behavior, as the Cuningham firm did in the Mille Lacs clinic. Doing so requires familiarity with and sensitivity to indigenous lifeways, and this familiarity may take years to attain; few architects have the time for the process, which must be repeated for each separate Amerindian group.[3]

The less specific aspects of the Minneapolis American Indian Center are probably related to the time when it was conceived; the movement toward cultural specificity or even separatism in design was only in its first stages around 1970. But modernity in design reflects the truth: Urban Indians are not leading traditional lives. There may be members of many tribes in a city and few of one's own relatives. People may have inner conflicts about the attractions of the reservation as compared with those of the city. One cannot even build an urban center with logs because most are too small to use as beams in large buildings.

Many other materials are ephemeral or unsuited to the area. Traditional buildings had no rooms for record keeping and refrigerators. Moreover, it strains credibility to associate job-training and adult-literacy classes with old patterns of cultural transmission or to draw parallels between soccer and ritual ball games, although promotions at bingo games are associated with traditional giveaways.

For the pantribal Native American Preparatory School proposed for Rowe, New Mexico, Richard Yates Architects in Santa Fe had to consider a wide range of Amerindian values, since they could not imitate any one Native style (117). Judges of a competition for the school commission wanted more than "cultural wallpaper," and this firm, which won the competition, wanted to avoid a "Disneyesque" hogan or tipi. When looking for ideas common to all indigenous American nations, they reflected on the common elements in much traditional architecture throughout the world. Jon Dick of this firm says that they considered the environment and allowed the site to inform their work; in this respect, Native Americans were comparable to architects in Greece, ancient Ireland, or Stone-henge. They found a "certain level of spirituality" in older forms and saw "something haunting, simple, and beautiful about ancient architecture, worldwide." When addressing their specific problem, they noted a frequent interest in the circle among Native Americans—in igloos, tipis, hogans, pueblos—and designed their school around the curve of a semicircle.

Architects realize that not all values held by Native Americans are ancient (although for Amerindian clients they tend to look far into the past more often than they do for Euro-Americans). In connection with civic buildings for the Tohono O'odham, Gibbs & Vint in Tucson hoped

to assist "cultural strengthening" by giving "voice to…the Tohono O'odham's current values, which include both traditional and Catholic beliefs," even though they wanted to help their clients "recover the loss" of their traditional architecture. Gibbs & Vint were attempting, in fact, to "reconstitute Native American design for the Tohono O'odham," but understood that they were not working for a group living in precolonial times.[4]

The Fort Yuma Quechan are among the many tribes sensitive to the fact that their postcontact history includes centuries of interaction with other cultures. This understanding informed a master plan for practical, educational, and recreational facilities, including a museum. After the

117. Native American Preparatory School (project), Rowe, New Mexico. Richard Yates Architects, 1992. (Courtesy John Dick, Richard Yates Architects)

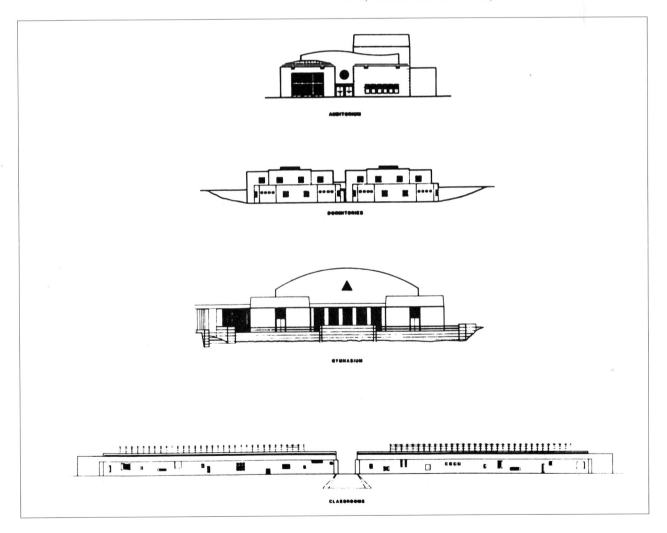

EDA commissioned a master plan from consultant Hunter Johnson, the tribe asked BRW and Don W. Ryden for a second one, presented in 1990. This called for a museum that "would be visually compatible with the historic fort and school buildings" of the nineteenth century, "yet not try to replicate them." They wanted the museum to show local history and culture at various periods of the past, to emphasize their continuity and flexibility. A village reconstructed along a slough and an amphitheater would, for instance, be more closely related to the earth than would the recreational vehicle park—or a museum of the 1990s.

Barry Patterson, an architect in Yuma, was the successful bidder for the museum design, a circle with an eastern opening. The tribal members did not specify what they wanted, preferring to evaluate his presentation. The architect based his design on "their interest in the power of the circle...the power of the sun rising at the east" and on the need to find a form that could be built in stages because the tribe had little money for the project. Patterson and his clients understood that a museum cannot be made of the wattle and daub used earlier for tribal buildings, so the architect proposed slump block covered in mortar wash with adobe. The pleasant reception of his ideas suggested a realistic accommodation to present economic and practical necessities on the clients' part.

New values must substitute for old ones in many current buildings, whether urban or rural. Edward Norris, when advising his students at the University of New Mexico, finds some who think that Navajo architects must design hogans, but feels "there's more to being Navajo" than that, even if some students have asked how they would explain any other designs to their parents. James N. Rowland has the answer: When Navajo clients asked him to design a high school at Tohatchi in hogan form, he convinced his clients that it could not be done by inviting them to help design one. David Sloan* adopted such features as stone veneer, thick piers, and admiration of massive curved walls from the pueblos at Chaco Canyon, but could imitate nothing directly in his designs for the Crownpoint Shopping Center of 1986.

Traditional values still affect architecture. Alfonso Ortiz* described a project by the Ute Mountain Utes to reconstruct cliff dwellings authentically, even though their ancestors lived in other building forms. He emphasized that those in charge of the project were "not letting architects walk all over them." Self-determinative independence is the value emphasized in this case. In 1992, a bill was introduced in Congress to establish the Big Foot National Memorial at Pine Ridge and Cheyenne River to commemorate tragic events of a century earlier. Tribal members would be offered jobs, fees paid by visitors would finance scholarships for tribal youth, and no American or Canadian Sioux would have to pay admission. Nevertheless, some people, including members of the Wounded Knee Survivors' Association, objected to a plan conceived by the government rather than by local people, objected to moving a Roman Catholic church and some houses, and criticized charging fees at a gravesite. The Oglala Tribal Council wanted joint management by the tribes and direct control over contracting, refusing to have this work done by the National Park Service alone. This dispute over jurisdiction can be seen also as a quarrel about self-determination, with implications for the nationhood of the tribes.

Values pertaining to religion and to customs affected the Tohatchi school, for as foundation digging began, a backhoe operator uncovered a freshly killed pig, placed there by a spiritual healer for reasons unknown to James Rowland, the architect. People then refused to build on that site. The frequency of eastern orientation and incorporation of circular forms, often mentioned in this book, is only the most obvious manifestation of this, but the Tohatchi case indicates the presence of less visible religious and customary determinants.

Old ways found in domestic behavior, including deference and constant contact, inspired Dennis Sun Rhodes's* designs for a culturally sensitive prototype house for Plains people. The plans adapt the tipi's zones for men and women, ritual, honor, and work, but use wooden rectilinear forms suited to modern building methods (118).[5]

Not every tribal planning group or Native American individual has the same ideas. Some Native people want buildings with explicit symbols; others think of more abstract ideas, such as embodying mutual respect and sharing in communally undertaken structures, or looking to spiritual powers or those in nature for good models for building.[6] Richard Ackley*, planner at the Bad River Band, feels that while architects and historic preservation specialists care about buildings, the Ojibwe are interested in space. He finds that visual and spatial values are prominent in Native American thought and that the "visualization of space" is an Amerindian characteristic and a way of thinking. It is not clear whether this is a common perception. Some Native people—Ackley is one—object to right angles, which he sees as a legacy of the alien Beaux-Arts training of architects; other Native nations build willingly with right angles. While most Native Americans profess interest in significant landscape elements, astronomical systems, and cycles for time and for living creatures, any architect, Amerindian or not, must address each client or group separately without preconceiving a single "Indian way" of life or the values held by all indigenous people.

Nor are there uniform perceptions about suitable architecture. Don Jiran is designing the tribally controlled Fort Berthold Community College in North Dakota in a wide U-shape because residents of this reservation associate separate houses and other buildings with Euro-Americans. They find that connected buildings give a better sense of community.[7]

At Tuolumne Rancheria in California, Chairman Sonny Hendricks* praised Charles Young, architect with Keeline Pizzi Young in Redding, who designed a tribal hall and health center in 1976 using EDA funds. The clients wanted the new buildings to match their roundhouse, which stands immediately to the east. The architect used dark wood, shingles, and sloping roof forms that relate to historic roundhouses, but without Hendricks's

assurance, an observer might not see the old building as a model for the new ones. Apparently, the architect and the rancheria residents reached an understanding about these matters that went beyond the literal. Good interpersonal relations may also have played a role in the warm reception given to Young's work.

An architect may be given permission to exercise his imagination freely if he is a fellow Native American. People who have no training in design may not object to leaving decision-making to someone who they believe will not impose on them coercive Euro-American forms. This may more easily occur when there is no usable local architectural tradition, as happens with tribes whose traditional architecture consisted of brush shelters, cave dwellings, or other constructions hard to reconcile with twentieth-century standards.

At Pyramid Lake, Nevada, the Hopi architect Dennis Numkena* designed a striking cultural center and mu-

118. Plains house prototype. Dennis Sun Rhodes*, ca. 1990. (Courtesy Dennis Sun Rhodes)

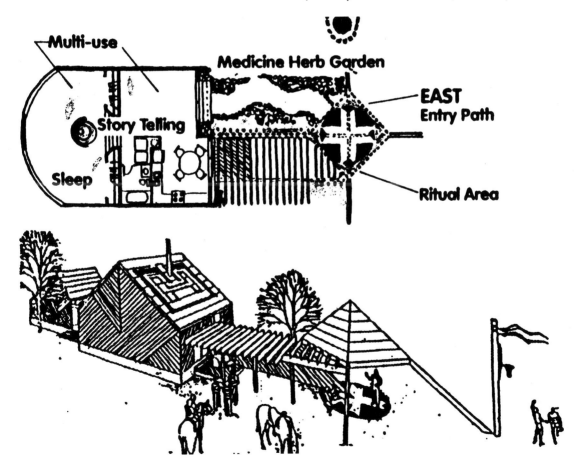

119. **Pyramid Lake Cultural Center and Museum (approach side), Pyramid Lake, Nevada. Dennis Numkena*, 1976.**

seum for the Paiutes (119, 120). He had entered a competition against four other firms, including the Taliesin Associates, successors to Frank Lloyd Wright. In a burst of inspiration, he designed the building during a stay of just over three weeks in a motel in Reno. It had to be an original form, because the Paiutes had had only ephemeral buildings in the past.

The cultural center, never completed, stands on a slope covered with colorful small stones—tufa, marble, and others. They reappear on the outer and inner surfaces of the building, making it seem like a form finally realized from the rough potential of the site. The shape is that of a broad cone, with a projecting fanlike entrance canopy at the front, and the back provided with a low shelter for performances. The plan is a circle, universally intelligible, centered on a dance area with stepped seats around it. Thin wood beams rise to a skylight. Most dramatic are two

large stone-faced piers that ascend to help support the roof, and that frame a tower perhaps related to Numkena's own heritage of kiva ladders. In the absence of a usable historic model, the architect designed a building accessible to Native people of many nations: Rooted in the land, it also aspires. It is one of the most imaginative designs in contemporary Amerindian architecture, even in its present incomplete and neglected condition.[8]

Other factors can make individual Native Americans feel comfortable. One is having a personal experience in common with the architect. An Amerindian intellectual, charged with conceptualizing his tribe's new buildings, appreciated the efforts of an earnest Euro-American middle-class designer, but felt that the architect "didn't get it right" in an undefined way. The speaker preferred the work of Frank Gehry, not on formal grounds but because "Gehry also grew up poor."[9]

It may be difficult to do everything right, even when designing for one's own culture, but the level of success can be high. During the past twenty years, an entire Native community has been built, largely in modern form but incorporating culturally sensitive ideas. The Upper Skagit were recognized in 1974, with about 500 members, approximately 200 of them living on the 74-acre reservation near Sedro-Wooley, Washington. These Coast Salish people had been dispersed from the land in the second decade of this century, but returned annually and kept permanent settlement on the land as their constant goal. In 1980, they bought the 74 acres and converted them to trust status. In 1987, HUD built fifty houses there. The residents have revived important aspects of culture, although they live in a setting that looks entirely up-to-date.

An 80- by 30-foot smokehouse, built in 1985 by tribal members, a massive canoe shed erected in 1988 (31), and a salmon barbecue pit in front of the community center address religious and cultural concerns overtly. It is less immediately obvious that the village was designed "to accomplish social engineering" for the sake of reconstituting the formerly dispersed Coast Salish. Tribal officials, working with Don Frothingham of Architectural Resources Collaborative in Seattle, created a plan that promotes walking and thus contact with the reservation and its people. The plan is dense for the sake of efficiency and to encourage interaction, but buildings are situated to give the illusion of privacy: "Because of dispersal, everything we do must attract them home. We've been designing things with that mission in mind, to re-create the Upper Skagit community."

120. **Pyramid Lake Cultural Center and Museum (lake side).**

121. Community center, Upper Skagit Reservation, Washington. Architectural Resources Collaborative, 1982.

Frothingham "came to listen and help us design a building." His respect for tribal decision-making was evident to his clients: "He brought us his paintings and we sat talking philosophy. He understands that you have to begin [by] listening. Then there was a tribal committee of nine people [who took] a long time designing. ARC helped us design." After some deliberation, "we threw out the book and asked, 'If this were your own, how would you do it?' We wanted the right thing for the tribal members"[10] rather than for an architect thinking of himself.

The plan itself helps to create a communal sense. The houses are developed along three roughly circular greens. The lots are about 30 by 60 feet, but they are wedge-shaped in some cases to be less rigid than uniform rectangles. Each living room looks toward the green, so that people can watch their children at play there, but no one can see into his neighbor's living room. The houses are set among trees, because the planners left as much existing vegetation as possible. The tribal members wanted to "re-create the

feel of an old Indian Shaker church, which people used to visit every year, twenty miles east, surrounded by old cedar trees.... Scent and sound are very important" to tribal members concerned with sensitive design.

Architectural Resources Collaborative worked with Steve Duncan, a builder who had a reputation for efficient building in Alaska. They brought the project in under budget, so ten extra houses could be put up. The houses are built to a standard considered unusual for HUD. Their style, however, is based on a northwestern camp town of about 1900, unrelated to anything specifically Salish. The houses were originally colored identically, but a repainting in the early 1990s "changed the design so each family had different roof tones of the shingles," allowing for some individual choice within the group setting.

The community center (121) opens to a fine panorama with a fire circle, a pond, a landscaped area, and a valley below. It was built with advice from young and old: "When designing [the kitchen], we paced off areas to make sure things were in good relation to each other." The building originally ended at the kitchen, but was later enlarged for a housing office.

Wood is seen everywhere, in cedar siding and cedar-shingled piers: "Shingles in different colors were used on the roof. Traditional baskets show ziggurats and a similar shape is seen on mussels. So we used two tones of dark sienna and black on the community center." The floors were grooved like those of the Shaker church that had been the former community meeting place, but the wood shrank as it dried, creating grooves that require painstaking vacuuming; this is the only problem with the building.

Inside are offices, a library, and a preschool pending construction of a separate one nearby. The rooms stand on three sides of a centralized space in the middle of one side. A wood stove on a platform marks its center under a clerestory. In this hearthlike area, trees used as pillars support the ceiling. Upholstered chairs and a couch make it comfortable for gatherings.

* * *

The buildings discussed here make it clear that sensitive and culturally appropriate design can be created for modern purposes without recourse to overt symbols or to imitation. One solution is not universally preferable because different tribes, and responsible individuals in each, will have varied opinions about each type of building. People's opinions change over time, and new ideas come into play as a consequence of political, social, and economic changes.

12

Appropriate Processes

ppropriate design processes enhance indigenous values in new buildings for Native Americans. Any architect must listen closely to his clients, but for Amerindian commissions, he may sometimes listen for longer periods. Even a Native American architect may not have known any of his clients in the past. He may be from a different tribe and culture. He may want to wait and listen. Thomas Hodne reflected a widespread impression when he said that "Indians don't live day by day—they live generation by generation."[1] To foster a collegial planning process, the clients may expect the architect to exchange social courtesies, such as dinner invitations, although an architect from a large town or city may be accustomed to separating personal and professional contacts. In some Native American cultures, direct eye contact is seen as disrespectful and people feel uncomfortable shaking hands. They may shy away from an architect who approaches them in the hearty way favored in Euro-American society. While many people like to be asked their opinions, which they then give freely, some Native Americans reserve their opinions until they are fully formed and may volunteer comments only when the time seems right. That time may even be after the close of a meeting, while an efficient Anglo architect may be eager

for answers. Tribal clients may not criticize directly, and some do not welcome forthright challenges. An indirect approach may call for telling a story, apologizing in advance, or asking questions rather than making statements. Well-brought-up Native Americans of many nations are instructed since childhood to read silences and body language, not to speak or ask; information will explain itself to the attentive observer. A person who feels no need to introduce himself will not do so, and someone who feels that his presence is not needed may leave a meeting without interrupting to offer an excuse. Architects may have to adjust to unfamiliar ideas about courtesy, instrusion on personal space, speed of decision-making, and the need for consensus or for obvious consideration of each person's opinion. Since there is no single standard of behavior, architects must learn in advance about the ideas embraced by their clients.

Some indigenous people will speak openly about an objective matter such as the placement of a school cafeteria, but will not reveal aspects of group belief or behavior to a new Euro-American acquaintance, even one hired to offer practical expertise based on that information. It is often expected, or at least hoped, that the outsider will, like a courteous Amerindian, become a patient observer, to whom things will become clear in time. Native reticence does more than protect the group's knowledge from further potential Anglo exploitation; it is a deeply held value in many cultures.

Misunderstandings inevitably occur among human beings, but some can be avoided by mutual honesty and careful explanation offered according to the client's standards of courtesy. Marge Anderson*, chairwoman of the Mille Lacs Ojibwe, looked architect Robert Zakaras "straight in the eye and asked, 'Will you cheat us?'"[2] Ron Hernandez* says that because tribes usually go to a contractor and explain their needs, they may be reluctant to pay for an architect's services, at least until they see the improved product that they receive. In addition, he finds Native clients willing to pay for bricks and mortar—or even to build a wall themselves to show to their grandchildren—but unable to understand paying for paperwork, filing fees, and other administrative tasks.

To be culturally appropriate in most Native nations, the design process is usually a communal one. An architect is hired for his specific skills—and because laws require certified people to prepare documents—but he is rarely hired to be the sole design authority. D. Kristine Woolsey, who designed the Ak-Chin Eco-Museum for the Tohono O'odham in 1991 and conducted a design studio for a Salt River Pima–Maricopa museum in 1994, said, "I learned so much about how to do collaborative design. I started out thinking that I was going to be the master builder, like a god, but ended feeling blessed" (122, 123).

Eco-museums are new phenomena, and not yet a sin-

122. Ak-Chin Eco-Museum (south elevation), Maricopa, Arizona. D. Kristine Woolsey, 1991. (Courtesy D. Kristine Woolsey)

123. Ak-Chin Eco-Museum (section showing roof terrace). (Courtesy D. Kristine Woolsey)

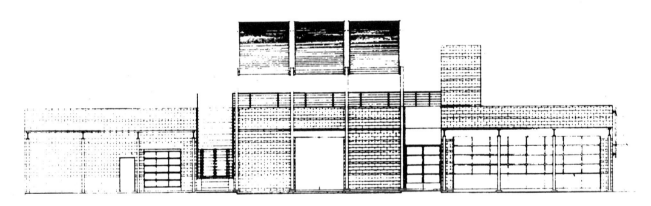

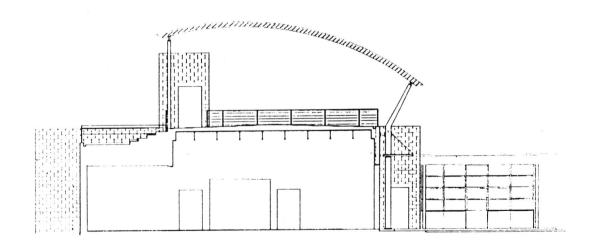

gle type of facility. This one is "really a service center, not a museum," a tool for community growth rather than for tourists. It stores materials, provides a venue for continuing cultural activity and meetings, houses an office for an archaeological survey, and increases cultural awareness for Tohono O'odham of all ages. The displays may include few historic artifacts. There may be audio-visual materials, papers, even ceremonies. Some exhibits may be presented on people's porches or in their yards. The modest masonry and frame buildings form a compound focused on a central zone where historical objects are displayed, but the architecture is barely intrusive in the landscape, and "a public space is created in the Ak-Chin way, by gently capturing edges and implying rather than dictating closure."[3]

The idea of an eco-museum was introduced here by Nancy Fuller of the Smithsonian Institution, who has made helping Native American museums a mission, not just one of her tasks, and who maintains files about many of them. "The Smithsonian was incredibly supportive," said Woolsey, and it helped one tribal member to become a historian, and others to obtain training in archival and museological record-keeping. Six active Tohono O'odham constituted a committee that supplied information to the Anglo architect and advisers.

The planning process was a long one, including travel by the committee members, Woolsey, and Fuller to several other tribal museums where the Tohono O'odham asked about dealing with sacred items and the architect asked about how much storage was needed. On returning to Arizona, Woolsey prepared small-size scale models and supplied extra cardboard for modifications at meetings attended at various times by children and adults. Once the Tohono O'odham "realized that they could unpin the walls," they made modifications readily. "Eventually, we built a large model—half an inch equal to one foot—and we had barbecues" at which the model was exhibited and altered. "That's how you do things there, with barbecues." A consultant archivist, Shayne Del Cohen, also offered technical assistance in assembling and caring for archival materials. "She shows up with a crock pot," said Woolsey, and she teaches while it bubbles away. Over the course of almost two years, a congenial atmosphere encouraged reservation residents to participate in design.

Outside the historic displays area, the eco-museum includes a floor for dances that must be performed on earth; around it is a red concrete sidewalk with handprints of all the children in the Head Start program. A silhouette on its door represents Kokopelli, the flutist, and stylized images of this figure form door handles. Railings and gates

screening the mechanical systems are of .25-inch steel plate incorporating designs made at a barbecue by reservation residents. The designs include baskets and scenes in photographs. But Woolsey had only one-third of the panels made up this way because the tribe decided to do parts of the rest every ten years. The "central zone is topped by an observation deck, allowing views out to the farming operation which will carry Ak-Chin successfully into the next century."[4]

Charles Cambridge* and Dennis Holloway also emphasize "meeting user requirements." In the spring of 1989, they took a computer to the Navajo Reservation and conducted workshops for adults and children on solar-powered hogan design (47, 48). Similarly, Stastny–Burke held a week-long studio at the Warm Springs Reservation before attempting to design the museum (42). During their stay, they elicited residents' reactions to their drawings, and learned which materials were considered suitable and which were not.[5]

Ron Shaffer, chief designer for Chambers, Campbell & Partners at Navajo Community College, spoke about values important in Navajo school design around 1970. He was told that having many corridors displeased Navajos, who were accustomed to the free movement found in the unified space of a hogan. When the interior had to be divided, openings were preferred to doors. The main entrance had to be at the east. The clients wanted a central fireplace for heat and as a focus for learning. Since people sat on goat pelts on hogan floors, low tables, cushions, or carpeting could be used for seating rather than chairs alone. They requested natural materials, colors, and lighting.[6] These features need not lead to historically referential design, although they did at the college (45, 46).

For the Mounds Park All Nations American Indian Magnet School in Saint Paul, Minnesota, director Cornel Pewewardy* spoke of many doorways as promoting the idea of a "family of learning" and wanted chairs that could be moved into a circle. He preferred earth colors that encouraged harmony and referred to the natural environment. He also advised against having clocks, because there is no set time for learning.[7] These recommendations are not universal, but they suggest ways in which planning can be related to the culture of particular groups.

Like D. Kristine Woolsey, John Cuningham, of Cuningham Hamilton Quiter, believes in "intensive user participation." He says, "We had certain preconceptions about decoration, and they [Native American clients] weren't interested. . . . If possible, their input supersedes ours." A good example is the Pejuta Haka Center at Oglala Lakota

124. Pejuta Haka Center, Oglala Lakota College, Kyle, South Dakota. Ron Hernandez*, 1991.

College (1991) planned by college officials and Lakota architect Ron Hernandez*, and built by Lakota vocational-education students (124). Another example is the Shako:wi Cultural Center for the Oneida in Verona, New York, opened in 1993 (125). This was paid for entirely by the Oneida from bingo receipts, and was erected by Jules Obomsawin*, expert in an exceptionally beautiful Scandinavian log building technique. He and his wife, Robbin, planned the building because the Oneida had no specific idea in mind. She explains that they hand-picked white pine from reforested Adirondack farmland as symbolic of the healing powers; white pine also recalls the Tree of Peace. The steam-bent oak staircase and the granite fireplace lintel are also made of natural materials. The building, "when it returns to Mother Earth, will not corrupt her," as no chemically treated wood was used and each log was scribed to fit the one below it, avoiding the use of nails (126). This is not typical of Oneida historic architecture, but hand-crafting is. The work was executed by almost all Oneida builders.[8]

Consideration for the users can be included even when a non-Indian architect is asked to remodel an existing structure. In 1990, Peter Kramer transformed a former telephone-book warehouse in Minneapolis into the AIOIC, a job-training agency directed by Mike Bongo* and William Means*. The clients wanted to "make people feel good coming in" and include aspects of "cultural appropriateness." They therefore worked closely with Kramer so that the result could represent "the contemporary environment that students would be moving into, but it is combined with traditional elements, especially earth colors." A large curved landscaping element outside is also a retaining wall. Inside the concrete block building are pleasant colors; abundant lighting, including skylights where corridors cross; textural changes in the structural material; glass walls to expand spaces and eliminate visual barriers; and practical, inexpensive materials.

On another occasion, Cuningham said that architects "cannot dominate or steer Indians to specific schemes, pretending to have all the answers.... You cannot prescribe

125. Shako:wi Cultural Center, Verona, New York.
Jules Obomsawin* (master builder), 1993.

solutions unless the Indians direct you."[9] Robert Zakaras, who supervises much of the Amerindian work for Cunningham Hamilton Quiter, says that "we show a range of building types, materials, etc., to get them to elaborate on what feels right to them.... [We then work in] small groups. We try to get the scale of discussions one to one, to get feedback."

Thomas Hodne invites his clients to draw their ideas, encouraging them to think about the natural setting and their responses to cultural traditions and values. He tries to elicit strong visual symbols that will express something important about the culture and that may harmonize with existing historic structures, but "if they move away from symbols, okay." These procedures have contributed significantly to the design of Fond du Lac Community College (100) and the Mille Lacs Museum (127). The museum is sponsored by the Minnesota Historical Society but is on the reservation, and tribal members are part of the planning team. Hodne and his colleague Don Vermeland, and their associates in the firm of Bentz Thompson Rietow, wanted to respect the sacred character of the lake and

woods, and "tried to do something spiritual with nature and the walkways, but this wasn't Indian land" in times remembered clearly, so the Ojibwe invested less emotion and spiritual meaning in the site. The clients were interested in protected storage for objects, which meant a largely closed perimeter to avoid sun damage. They wanted an entrance near an old trading post, a diorama of older Indian life inside, and a cultural circle outdoors. The final design resulted from repeated meetings with the museum representatives, during which they discussed and sketched their ideas.

"You can't design buildings for Native people," says Hodne. "Architects must learn from what the Indians have to teach us. We are only their interpreters." When asked to design an Indian house, one participant named "Ken*" designed a rocket. So this said to me that we didn't have to design a bear [or another obvious image] in order to be Indian." People began by drawing diagrams of the four seasons. Both Native Americans and Euro-Americans drew circles, some with porches. A curator suggested a circle with extensions. A staff member drew wolf paws projecting

126. Shako:wi Cultural Center (detail of log construction at corner).

127. Mille Lacs Museum (rendering), Onamia, Minnesota.
Thomas H. Hodne, Jr., and Bentz Thompson Rietow, 1994.
(Courtesy Thomas H. Hodne, Jr.)

from a ring. Tipis and wigwams, whole or halved, were among the other designs, and Charles Nelson, an architectural historian, proposed a village. Joycelyn Wedll's* sketch "gave us the heartbeat" of the design with its reference to the heart of her people, family, and home. Rachel Tucker's drawing showed a wedge with a dome near the intersection of the two legs and a curved outer wall in front of the dome; this is the general scheme of the final design, with the dome over the diorama. Another woman participant had earlier suggested a drum over the diorama to serve as a kind of "banner" from outside, but the form looked like a water tank and was replaced by a dome. The planners evaluated flow diagrams and advised about all aspects of disposition and design. The museum may, then, be considered an Indian design, despite the work of Euro-American architects.[10]

Dennis Sun Rhodes*, an advocate of symbolic form, advises studying a "tribe's hierarchy of animal and natural symbols and its four-directional color code." He has "found many symbolic messages by examining the historic record." He advises architects to read about Indian "symbology, or visit museums that display hide paintings." He tries to extract meaning even from the location of a fireplace: In the Division of Indian Work Building constructed in 1994 in Minneapolis, the fireplace is freestanding "because you need to go all around a fireplace for the full spirit circle. The fire will be touching the earth." His firm,

"AmerINDIAN Architecture, strives for a consciousness of symbols among all the firm's native clients," although he ruefully acknowledges that some are not interested, wanting either two-car garages or simple log cabins.[11]

Sinte Gleska University on the Rosebud Reservation asked partners Craig Stevens and Michael Rotondi of the Roto firm to design a multipurpose building. The architects began by asking the clients to think about the curriculum, not about form. What did they want to teach? What ideas did they want to communicate? "Where do you want to be in the next generation, in thirty years, if all goes well?" The architects circulated a questionnaire to help structure and stimulate responses. They hoped that the clients could work back toward the goal of a spatial experience consistent with the answers. The resulting building could then support essential aims and not only satisfy specific immediate needs.

At Sinte Gleska, the officials "had never done any real planning" because they never expected to be able to. They could not answer certain of Roto's questions, and were encouraged to formulate new ones. During discussions, the school's representatives began to think not of one multipurpose building but of a new campus. The architects also asked people to sketch their ideas. One man drew a bustle, which suggests both centrality and extension from a core, unlike the finite quality of a circle. The Roto partners were puzzled by the clients' tendency to translate ideas that are abstract into concrete images, whereas Hodne and Sun Rhodes* welcome them; Stevens doesn't want to "risk creating one-liners....A circle is good. Boom! Design a circle." He finds more depth in the Lakota philosophy, numerological systems, and star knowledge, and hopes that these can lead to a richer formal solution than a pure imitation of a circle or bustle: "If we can help them to say what's critical about traditional values...that's what's unchanging." The architects hope to embody that in the building rather than an obvious form, especially because forms have changed when the Lakota moved from one natural environment to the other, or when they adopted new things such as the horse.

Stevens also understands the dangers of preconceptions on either side. Anglos may tend to overstate the spiritual aspects of their Native American clients. When consulting several elders, the architects asked ninety-one-year-old Paul Leader Charge* how the Lakota knew it was time to move camp and how they chose a new site. Leader Charge replied, "We Lakotas are clean people, a sanitary people." When the rubbish pits and latrines were filled, his ancestors moved! Clients, too, may have preconceptions about the result to be expected from a firm known for design more than for planning.

Richard Brittain, who teaches architecture at the University of Arizona, studied Tohono O'odham architectural traditions but discarded his ideas about what clients might want when he assisted with the Baboquivari District Building (1983) near Topawa, Arizona. According to a survey conducted in 1976 by Father Richard Purcell of the Covered Wells Roman Catholic Church, the Tohono O'odham preferred adobe to cement and wood to gas heating, wanted separate buildings for cooking and sleeping, and thought that sanitary facilities should be separate from their residences, but they also regarded modern technology and plumbing as progressive. The process of design involved repeated meetings, building a model before disturbing the ground, and setting out saguaro ribs, sticks, and rocks to denote walls and fireplace and windows. The design process also involved a change of plan.

The project began when the clients asked the university for help in developing alternatives to HUD housing and contracting. Brittain and his colleague Matts Myhrman, who builds in natural materials, tried to design federally funded housing for which money for materials and labor would be spent on the reservation. The houses were to respect cultural heritage and the desert environment. The tribe selected the site, and made decisions by consensus at their own pace, a procedure that the archi-

tects found essential to the successful result. Brittain made conceptual drawings and a cardboard model in 1981, but despite the tribe's approval HUD did not fund the project.

At that point, Tribal Councilman Ed Kisto* thought of building a prototype house as a district office, and obtained money for that. The building could show an appropriate kind of housing, and people might decide that they wanted its features in their own homes someday. The structure uses 10- by 14- by 14-inch blocks of sun-dried asphalt-stabilized adobe made in Pisinimo village on the reservation. Workers from Topawa either knew how to lay them or could learn quickly. The stabilized mortar is made of local adobe soil and emulsified asphalt. The materials provide good thermal mass for passive-solar-heating design, require little maintenance, and look traditional. Solar-energy provisions include southern windows, and heat storage in the brick floor and massive walls; open fireplaces and a stove supplement the heat in cold or cloudy weather. Part of the ceiling over the main meeting hall is made of dried saguaro ribs nailed to the joists in a herringbone pattern. Outside, a ramada of mesquite posts has a covering of laced ocotillo stalks and flooring of flagstone from hills nearby. An outdoor fireplace burns mesquite bought from reservation woodcutters. The sanitary facilities are in a separate building. The building has performed well, but the happy ending would have been even happier if the housing had ever been funded.[12]

Some tribal clients, like a good many elsewhere, lack experience in giving directions to an architect, although they can often say what they do not like. At Mille Lacs, the band members could not describe the desirable size for the new ceremonial building, so Cuningham Hamilton Quiter's staff counted the people attending the drum ceremony and drew their own satisfactory conclusions (54, 55). Since the federal government had told them what to do for a century or more, the clients did not realize that they were encouraged, not just allowed, to make choices. To overcome this problem, which has particularly serious consequences for housing, Chester Sprague and John Steffian prepared a report for HUD in 1970 proposing an advocacy team and a housing coordinator at the local level.[13] One person would transfer skills to the Native population while the other would draw from the Native group. This would help to develop locally trained people who could help create housing. This plan was not implemented, however.

At about the same time, Charles Albanese, professor of architecture at the University of Arizona, became aware of processes needed to create successful housing for Tonto Apache families who had won federal recognition on their

73-acre reservation near Payson, Arizona. The group was stable, with fourteen family men, almost all employed. They were then living in houses made partly of sheet metal and cardboard. The BIA offered them housing of the kind that HUD had funded for the Camp Verde Apaches at White River, who accepted it because it was free. The Tonto group refused, and continued to live for three more years in houses appalling on the outside but tidy inside.

Albanese brought his students to visit the community, by then consisting of twenty families, in hopes of designing houses that would satisfy the residents. The architects presented no solutions, but asked questions. The residents expressed a preference for a housing type new to them — one with separate bedrooms for parents and for children. Albanese and his team returned with a model kit that allowed people to see or make styrofoam miniatures at .25-inch scale; this allowed even illiterates or people hesitant to draw to visualize their ideas, and about a dozen families used them. Only after the residents had shown what they wanted did the architect and his students create house designs. Of the four types presented, almost every family with children chose the model with a master bedroom and two children's bedrooms, and older people chose a one-bedroom model. They evidently found it possible to live comfortably in modern houses while carrying on essential cultural traditions. Choices about where to live within the new settlement reflected matrilineal kinship relations.

The residents performed a siting ritual, and then the houses were laid out in a meander uphill from a grant-funded masonry community building used as a church, group dining hall, and common storage room. The houses are wood framed, with unfinished board and batten overlapped outside; the grayed color suits the forest setting. High foundations permit storage under the house. Each dwelling has a porch, where wood that is cut all year long can be kept dry. The porch is used for talking with friends who respect spatial segregation and approaches, much as they used to when socializing in pickup trucks. In the yards are places for 20- or 50-gallon drums, used for cooking in summertime, and animal shelters (which conform to Anglo rather than Apache ideas about housing pets).

As in the houses on reservations in Washington State designed around common green spaces by Don Frothingham and his colleagues at Architectural Resources Collaborative, these houses and their arrangement helped to confirm a sense of community, and they satisfy the wishes of the occupants. Standardized solutions imposed from outside, whether for housing or for other architecture, rarely achieve either goal, so that the users do not adopt the results as their own. "Imposed" (by coercion or by benevolent bribery in the form of a free house) is the important word here, because Native Americans should be as free as other people to accept a standard HUD or Habitat for Humanity house if the occupants consider them suitable.[14]

Community-based planning processes help to lock buildings into their culture. Officials of the SIPI vocational–technical school begun in Albuquerque in 1964 attempted to solicit ideas from a variety of Native groups for a school serving all tribes. So did Rough Rock Demonstration School which opened in the 1970/1971 school year on the Navajo Reservation, funded first by the Office of Economic Opportunity in 1965. An old BIA school of beautiful red rock, with hogan-shaped dormitories for children from families on remote sites, had become obsolete and was replaced by a new structure. The community then decided to offer education for grades seven through twelve locally and obtained federal funds, but not from the BIA, whose Facilities and Management staff proved uncooperative. Much more help came from Chester Sprague and John Steffian and their students in the architecture department at the Massachusetts Institute of Technology.

Like Albanese's students in Arizona, those from MIT were brought to the site. They interviewed about one-third of the Rough Rock residents, mostly through interpreters so as to strengthen the concept of community control. The school was Navajo-run through a nonprofit organization called DINE ("the people" in Navajo). Local residents preferred small buildings in a loose plan reminiscent of a Navajo camp settlement with hogan-like buildings and ramadas. A street-like arrangement gives visible organization to varied elements and some protection against the southwest wind, and it is compact enough to be coherent but spread out enough to let the landscape be "part of the school's resources."[15] The orientation is to the cliffs, a canyon, mesas, and the desert. People approach from the east, and a meeting hall faces east. The materials are local fire-resistant wood, stone, and adobe. Some of the construction workers were local, too. The consultants from MIT, and Pacheco & Graham, executing architects, hoped to use as little heavy machinery as possible, as it would have to be brought in from far away and probably operated by non-Navajos. Furniture and textiles were to be made locally. Navajo aspects of the interiors include using areas rather than separate rooms, separating spaces by level and height rather than walls, and avoiding corridors.

The buildings were products of compromise with the BIA. Local people had wanted hogan shapes, but they settled for rectilinear buildings. At least there are many exposed wood beams. A school is by definition not Navajo in that it promotes individual and competitive rather than group achievement and is oriented toward progress in the future, but modern Navajo children hear about alternative values on television anyway.

Sprague mentioned a problem in connection with community control of architecture: The architect wants something over which he can claim authorship, and he wants to be sure that the product will not hurt his reputation. Sprague also identified a more serious problem—the difficulty of sustaining community participation. "They don't believe it's theirs to run," he said, but that was in 1972 and a greater self-awareness has spread widely in Indian country since then. Some Native Americans now hope to be the exclusive directors of all reservation institutions.[16]

At about the time that the MIT consultants were working in the main part of the Navajo Reservation in Arizona, the Gallup–McKinley School Board decided that building deficiencies required the closing of Ramah High School, which served Navajos on the separate and smaller New Mexico reservation. The parents, however, wanted the children to stay close to home and in 1970 elected their own school board. They sought their own high school and, hoping to evade BIA planning, appealed for help from the Ford Foundation. At one point, a group of parents staged a sit-in at the BIA office in Washington in order to get permission to contract for their own school. (This was before the Indian Self-Determination Act of 1975 made contracting common.)

It was probably in 1972 that someone suggested to the Ford Foundation that Sanford Hirshen of the Hirshen, Gammill, Trumbo & Cook firm in Berkeley, California, be asked to consult with the people at Ramah. Franklin Thomas, the foundation director, had been Hirshen's classmate at Columbia University, where the architect had, as he puts it, been "radicalized" by the sociologist C. Wright Mills. Hirshen had a long-standing interest in working with poor people, having been born in New York to immigrant parents. He had designed shelters and clinics for migrant workers and homes for recent immigrants. The firm developed sophisticated programming methods at a time when formal programming was fairly new.

Hirshen went to Ramah for what was to have been a brief consultation. Not knowing that a friend of the school board chairman had a financial interest in a certain site, Hirshen declared it unsuitable, but the chairman welcomed the bearer of a truth that others had not dared to utter. He asked the Ford Foundation to send the architect

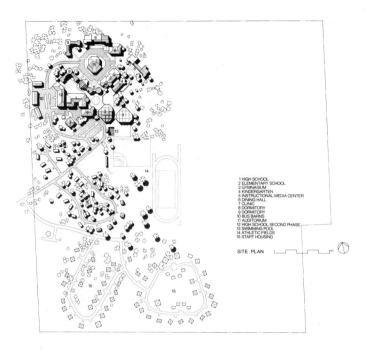

128. Pine Hill Navajo School (site plan), Ramah, New Mexico. Hirshen, Gammill, Trumbo & Cook, 1975. (Courtesy Sanford Hirshen)

back to find a new site and help with the programming. Among the Navajo leaders of the meetings were Gloria Emerson*, an artist who is now an educational planner at the Institute of American Indian Arts in Santa Fe, and Abe Plummer*, an educator. Another participant was Michael Gross, a lawyer from the East who had begun to work in legal services for Native Americans. Joseph R. Harding, a social anthropologist, elicited cultural concerns, interviewing every member of the community. The board then hired the Hirshen firm to design the school, and Dennison Cook, Hirshen's partner in charge of the project, lived at Ramah for two years, although the production work was done by firms in New Mexico (128–130). Hirshen believes that the BIA expected the Navajos to fail to produce a school, but hadn't counted on college-educated Navajos or committed professionals.

The site was chosen in part because near it was the last stand of ponderosa pine in the area. Although the site was isolated in 1970, it now has about fifty units of housing, some apartments, shops and a filling station, as well as a polygonal clinic, the last done to the Hirshen firm's design.

The Pine Hill Navajo School buildings were erected

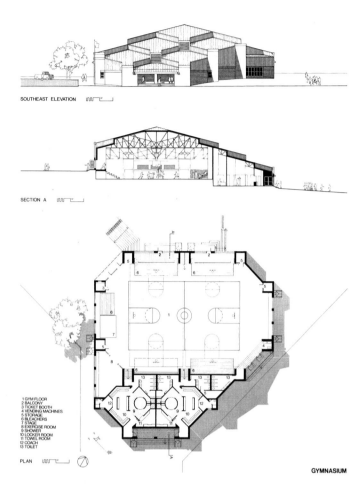

SOUTHEAST ELEVATION

SECTION A

1 GYM FLOOR
2 BALCONY
3 TICKET BOOTH
4 VENDING MACHINES
5 STORAGE
6 BLEACHERS
7 STAGE
8 EXERCISE ROOM
9 SHOWER
10 LOCKER ROOM
11 TOWEL ROOM
12 COACH
13 TOILET

PLAN

GYMNASIUM

129. Pine Hill Navajo School (gymnasium, southeast elevation and section). (Courtesy Sanford Hirshen)

in two phases: the elementary and high schools and gymnasium by 1975, and the kindergarten, clinic, and library–media center from 1976 to 1980. Plummer and Gross had done an "end run around the BIA" by persuading Senator Joseph Montoya to sponsor a bill for direct funding from Congress. Some buildings were extended later and supplemented by additional ones. The board decided to have separate buildings despite temperatures that range from -30°F to 100°F, so that the children could experience nature as they walked from one to another; eventually, covered walkways were added for some relief. The buildings had all-electric services, then the most reliable on a remote site. The buildings were made compact to comply with a cultural preference for central plans and for economy in heating and cooling. The roofs slope to shed snow. Wood-burning fireplaces with chimneys in all

the major spaces are seen as related to Navajo dwellings. The clients asked for bright colors, seen especially on the light blue roofs, which may relate to turquoise as the color of learning.

Gloria Emerson recalls that they

spoke in generalities [about]...using Navajo materials...cozy spaces and open spaces...saving the environment....We didn't talk about the rooflines, whether it would reach into the sky or things like that. We were conscious of the need to include the cardinal directions [and]...the holy placement of mountains.... We explored colors from gemstones....I don't recall [using] Navajo philosophical creation stories that might have helped give us guidance. We spoke about the... "beauty way."

The buildings do not look identifiably Indian, but they are products of a planning process dominated by Navajos and they are symbols of community victory over federal and county domination.

In retrospect, Emerson perceives that the planners from "Big Navajo"—the Arizona reservation—came from an area where the promotion of traditional values was more highly regarded than it was at Ramah. The "picture was complicated" by the distinctions among several small communities at Ramah, such as the Mormon Navajo, the Pentecostals, the traditional people, and the "Mormon white Anglo rancher who has been there for a long time..., white teachers from all over the country...[and] nine or so interns from an eastern university who were looking for a new experience." Some southern white male staff members "were having trouble accepting direction from a Navajo woman [Emerson]. There were a lot of cultural shock waves, one after the other." They did not, however, ruin the work as architecture.

Marley Porter, who has been the Navajo Nation architect, is critical of some polygonal buildings, seeing the form alone as an "anemic and poor attempt to be Indian." A polygon, he finds, "is one of many 'in-search-of' graspings at what is almost lost in Native architecture—the spirit of connection to [the] natural cycle of growth and decay....Anglos especially, but now also natives, see polygonal geometry as a quick fix to that which is lost." Nowadays, "the oneness of space and its understandability have been ignored. This is the lost essence of the polygonal shape; the figural memory of mother's womb. A cave, not a carved-up 'token pole.'" He would like to see hogans used as homes and meeting rooms, but for other purposes build-

130. Pine Hill Navajo School.

ings "can be anything. It's a foreign environment anyway. Just use natural materials" for Navajo clients.[17]

Porter was writing twenty years after Hirshen, Gammill, Trumbo & Cook were called in as consultants to the Pine Hill Navajo School. Earlier, the idea of building anything sympathetic to Navajo culture was still new. Nevertheless, the architects did not erect the more obvious, less modulated polygons of the Navajo Community College (45, 46). The Pine Hill Navajo School responded to what local people wanted, and was more subtle and more sensitive to varied demands of function. It was also intended in these ways to be a prototype, being with Rough Rock among the first schools based on principles of self-determination. Porter's observations about the essence of space may, however, be applicable to designs conceived for Navajo clients in the future.

The Pine Hill Navajo School may be faulted for other things—wasted space in the high volumes under the complex roofs, some hard-to-use irregular spaces, noise in open classrooms, an imbalance between administrative space and that available for other needs, clumsier parts added

later by other architects. But some of the flaws come from a method of planning still new to Ramah residents at the time, and from some probably inevitable conflicts between pure practicality and fine design. Gloria Emerson says that the Navajo people involved considered the building culturally appropriate. Ramah residents found the school beautiful, and thought that it gave a sense of place. It fits its site. There is abundant natural light. And it is well kept, suggesting respect by the pupils and good work by the maintenance staff.[18]

One school initiated without federal help or control is the Akwesasne Freedom School (131), which is being built adjacent to the Mohawk Reservation at St. Regis, New York, to replace an older school on chemically contaminated ground.[19] Volunteers, mostly Mohawks, are building it as funds become available, on land bought by the Viola Whitewater Foundation, of which Jimmy Little Turtle* is director. He used his own house as collateral for the mortgage, an act of true commitment. Jonathan Post, a doctoral candidate in English education, represented Barn Raisers, a not-for-profit construction company that assists needy

Appropriate Processes   **183**

131. Akwesasne Freedom School (roof under construction),
Mohawk Reservation, St. Regis, New York. David Seaman,
Barn Raisers, and reservation resident builders, 1994.
(Jonathan Post)

clients in upstate New York. Inspired by Chief Sakokwe-nionkwas (Tom Porter*) at a lecture, Post welcomed his invitation to help. David Seaman volunteered his architectural services. Michael Pettica, a computer instructor, taught his students to produce the drawings. These outside participants, and Quaker volunteers, learned to work according to the Indian way of making decisions, involving extended discussions for the sake of promoting consensus.

The school, established in 1979 and on its current site since 1984, is independent of state control. It has its own curricular base that incorporates tradition "into everything, including administration and discipline." There is no principal; the parents meet weekly to run the school. Children are taught in Mohawk up to the fifth grade, when English is introduced. Speeches of thanksgiving at the opening and closing of school remind children of Mother Earth and responsibilities toward her. Each child gets a chance to offer thanks. Traditional songs and dances have been led each week by an older person or chief. Dan Benedict*, the office manager, says that "the only way the children can learn about tradition is if it can be mixed in with every-

thing else." Benedict reports that the community's planners intended the school to "be like a longhouse...although we could've [gone] with other designs. Some people were thinking circular." The shape was important, but not of primary significance. As Jonathan Post put it, "In building this school, we like to think of process more than product."

The building is simple in appearance; reservation residents do not use house designs to display wealth or earn prestige. Blessings by chiefs have been given at significant points during construction, and there will be appropriate rituals when the work is completed. The building is one story high, as longhouses were. Three classrooms and toilets in each wing flank a central area; a utility room on one side balances a kitchen on the other. In the center, behind offices and a waiting area, is a room 62-feet square where the thanksgiving ceremonies and meetings will be held. The parents wanted a wooden floor and a "cathedral-type ceiling." When the architect proposed bench seating around a lowered floor, the parents questioned the idea because, Benedict says, "in a longhouse, everybody is on the same level. So we stress a flat floor," although James W.

Ransom*, a parent, said later that the floor would be lowered after all. (In fact, some longhouses did have tiered seats.) Families would sit there according to their membership in the clans. Provisions for passive solar heating are being made for the sake of economy and to support respect for nature. Classroom doors will open to the outside in warm weather, partly to foster awareness of the natural environment.

The most obvious Mohawk feature is a design in the roof shingles showing the Tree of Peace, the central symbol of the Iroquois Confederacy. This might seem to be simply an ornament, but it has serious meaning for the Mohawk, who hope to reinvigorate tradition, and for the school specifically. The parents had the idea to include it, and suggested that it face Route 37, so as to be seen by passersby. At a meeting with the nonprofit construction consultants, Chief Porter said that there had been a prophecy that the tree would die, but not completely. It would be held up by people who would come from out-side—perhaps Barn Raisers, who had come to help build the school when a previous architect had stalled the work by engineering the log trusses incorrectly. The tree has four white roots on the bottom. Under the tree are buried weapons. Above it, an eagle keeps out intruders who might fell the tree or bring weapons. These aspects use traditional images to convey ideas to reservation members who have disagreed intensely about subjects ranging from religion to gambling. In the center of the school site will be a tree to be blessed by Chief Jake Swamp*, and the Mohawks hope to plant another one each year.

At this school, tradition and community work serve education, politics, and intergroup communication. Chief Porter spoke for the committed parents and for the parents and cultural leaders on many reservations when he recalled that "the prophecies say that the time will come when the grandchildren will speak to the whole world. The reason for the Akwesasne Freedom School is so the grandchildren will have something significant to say."[20]

PART III

Specific Building Types

13

Housing

When shelter is perfected for need, it
is not in material terms alone.

Paul Oliver, in
Habitat International

ousing on many Indian reservations is shockingly inadequate.[1] Because few Native Americans have access to the private mortgage market, those with low incomes often accept whatever is available from federal housing programs: "About 44 percent of Indian homes are financed by the Department of Housing and Urban Development."[2] Federal housing programs do not begin to meet the need, so that people put up their own homes, which often decay rapidly because of inadequate materials and building procedures; others live in trailers; some double- and triple-up with relatives. Even Henry Cisneros, Secretary of Housing and Urban Development, stated that "American Indian housing is some of the worst in America."[3]

This situation has come about for many reasons; these include widespread poverty, greater demand from a rising population, a larger number of nuclear (rather than extended) families, a greater frequency of divorce, and a backlog in demand created before 1961, when federal housing programs authorized under the Federal Housing Act of 1937 did not serve reservations. It took six more years to establish Indian Housing Authorities on reservations to receive funds and supervise projects, and no HUD houses were actually built until 1968. Private mortgage lenders

cannot take over land held in trust in case of default. The Federal Housing Administration's Section 248 Mortgage Insurance Program has been used by banks in Boise, Phoenix, and Sioux Falls, which have found remedies for default through tribal courts, but these examples are few.[4] Hardly any use has been made of Section 5(h) of the Homeownership Program, added in 1974 to the Federal Housing Act, which allows public-housing tenants to buy their units, and lets HUD continue to service the debt on various costs. By the end of fiscal year 1990, not one mortgage had been insured under the new federally guaranteed Single Family Mortgage Insurance Program enacted in 1987 to deal with this problem.[5] Under PL 102-547, signed in 1992, the Veterans Administration may make loans to Native Americans on trust land if they are otherwise eligible, provided that a memorandum of understanding is signed between the tribal council and the Veterans Administration; the law contains provisions for waivers of usual rules to account for reservation conditions. The law, however, was signed only in late 1993.[6] The Indian Housing Loan Guarantee Program passed as part of the Housing and Community Development Act of 1992 was to begin only in fiscal year 1995. The Farmers' Home Administration has financed relatively few houses for Native Americans. Raising income limits in July 1994 offered help only to those with incomes sufficient to make home ownership or repair possible. The HOME program of block grants allocated about $15 million to tribal housing in the 1993 budget, but that pays for fewer than 200 houses in the entire country.[7] A guide intended to help build and improve housing "on Native lands by promoting an increase in the availability of conventional credit" addressed only those with the ability to obtain that credit.[8] Others could simply hope to be given one of the dozen or two houses that HUD allocated even to large tribes in the course of a fiscal year.[9]

To make matters worse, presidential budget requests since 1981 omitted funding for Indian and Native Alaskan housing; it has had to be restored at the present meager level by members of Congress. The largest number of Indian housing units erected in any one year was 6000 in 1978, but in each fiscal year from 1985 through 1990 the average was only 2673;[10] to relieve the Navajo shortage, the total for four of those years should have been allocated to that reservation alone. In addition, toward the end of the Carter administration, fewer units were allocated to Native Americans, and HUD tried to stretch the available dollars. Administrative costs, and those resulting from small-quantity purchases, should have been cut, but the quick solution of reducing house size was adopted for several years.[11] In 1993, $100 million was authorized for housing homeless people and those with AIDS, but tribes and their housing authorities had to compete for the funds against private nonprofit organizations and community mental-health associations in urban and rural areas throughout the country.[12]

In 1972, the approximately 420,000 Native Americans living on reservations needed about 62,000 housing units,[13] and more are needed today, even though HUD has built more than 70,000 units since 1968 and about 80,000 units have been rehabilitated or built under the Bureau of Indian Affairs Housing Improvement Program.[14] In 1969, "only 3 percent of the houses on Cheyenne River [reservation] could be classified as suitable for human occupancy," according to the National Study of American Indian Education, and in mid-1992 a HUD draft report estimated that about 35 percent of houses in areas under tribal housing authorities was substandard, requiring major repairs.[15] As late as 1991, Alex White Plume* of the tribal government at Pine Ridge estimated that "each house here has five families living in it." Carmel Richards*, financial officer of the tribal housing authority, had "2000 families on the waiting list, and those are the ones who haven't given up waiting," as people often do. The Navajo need 6000 homes

immediately for families who have none; 500 to 1000 new households are created each year; annual current production from federal and local sources is only 250 to 300. Cherokees in Oklahoma face forty years of waiting if the present pace of building continues.[16] In smaller Native American communities, the numbers are less stunning but the proportionate needs are the same.

Problems are built into available housing programs. A tenant who must pay 30 percent of his income may not be eager to increase his earnings lest almost one-third be taken away. This accounts for some people's occupancy of their own trailers, if they can afford them, rather than HUD houses. Planning processes can take so long that contractors may tender higher bids than they would under more efficient and thus more cost-effective conditions; some delays even extend past the limits of contractors' warranties. Clear lines of authority are needed, as shown by the problem of access roads: HUD may build an adequate road, but one smaller than a certain size is ineligible for the BIA's maintenance services. Mutual or self-help building projects have run into such problems as the tribal members' reluctance to work with those not their relatives, their preference for wage labor rather than for the reward of a good water or sanitary system, lack of sanctions against the lazy, and the need to use inferior workers if abler ones hold daytime jobs when the self-help crews are active.[17]

Until PL 101-235 separated Indian from other public housing in 1988 through the HUD Reform Act, the former tended to get lost in the larger field of low-income housing. Government departments assumed too much—for instance, that novice housing officials knew about requiring performance bonds from contractors. When builders were unscrupulous or incompetent, there was often no recourse. If a crooked contractor ran away, unpaid subcontractors tended to blame the tribe, a convenient target. When reservation residents saw tribal officials receiving new houses first, they resented the housing as well as the process.

Regional offices of HUD and the BIA tended to approve identical plans and contractors for tribes in vastly different climates and geographic situations, and for people of widely differing culture; the officials—even Native American ones—mistakenly assumed that whatever aroused few complaints from needy people of other races would suit all Native Americans as well. Inexperienced housing authorities, or those who wanted no arguments with the regional offices, sometimes used the inappropriate plans. Since standard HUD houses are based on a certain type of society and economy, the house may be automatically unsatisfactory for other kinds. Occupants may then use the spaces differently from the ways the planners intended, perhaps to the structure's detriment. The National American Indian Housing Council, founded in 1974, began in 1993 to offer technical assistance to the 187 Indian housing authorities so that the weaker ones could obtain and make better use of housing opportunities.

Indian Housing Authorities, like most offices whose work is evaluated quantitatively, tend to want the largest number of units for the limited funds available, whether or not they are suitable. One architect says that he is told, "We need 150 units. Here are six plans. Here's the budget." If an architect wants "to change this and say 'What if...?' it's almost literally an Act of Congress to get them to change," although he realizes that some Native Americans resist being subjects of innovations; it's as though they were saying, "Don't experiment with *us!*" Untrained in home maintenance, many renters cannot prevent problems from developing and cannot fix them; they must ask the local Indian Housing Authority, which may have no money to do it for them. They can then only watch their houses or the infrastructure deteriorate.[18]

While doing research for her master of architecture thesis at the University of Wisconsin, Tari Rayala learned that Indian Housing Authorities are often understaffed and inadequately skilled, and that they may not always work closely with the tribal and outside governments.[19] Some either do not know how or do not take time to investigate extra funding opportunities. Unable to assess the virtues and flaws of technology, some tribes resist using new, economical materials; to keep jobs for tribal members, reservation officials sometimes ignore new machines and labor-saving measures.

Anyone concerned with Native American well-being can recite at least one sad story. An architect in California designed housing in which there was an efficient counter for eating in the kitchen, but never learned that her clients eat in groups at large tables or seated all around a room, and that meals are important social events. Cooking is often a group activity for women, and small kitchens cannot accommodate that. In some cultures, the women are not supposed to touch one another, but they will have to if they work together in cramped quarters. The problems are typical of those caused by the architect's ignorance of Native American lifeways.[20]

At Shiprock on the Navajo Reservation, Fairchild Instrument and Camera sponsored housing for 1500 people in 1965 for completion in 1972. The Shiprock Nonprofit Housing Corporation tapped BIA, Indian Health Service, Economic Development Administration, and Federal Housing Administration funds for a total of 255 units. Architect Bennie Gonzales recalls that the wife of Vice President Spiro Agnew intervened, believing that the Navajo "needed what the rest of us have. So we put carpets in, and window curtains. She wanted to have walls or fences around each house. But the Navajo didn't know about such things, and they ended up using the bedrooms for weaving."[21]

Inflexible rules create other problems. Native Americans who do not belong to federally recognized tribes cannot obtain home-related services from the BIA. Some families ineligible for mutual-help houses must be placed in them by tribal officials who have no other shelter to offer, while other poor tribal members must live with relatives in already overcrowded quarters. In many pueblo cultures, it is common to add rooms when children or adults come into the family and to let rooms crumble when they are no longer needed, but houses in home-ownership programs may not be altered for at least ten, and usually twenty-five, years—until the residents gain full possession. This means that expanding families that begin in small houses must squeeze into inadequate spaces, and parents in larger houses whose children have become adults and have left cannot use all of their rooms. Few will risk homelessness by giving up even an unsuitable house. It has been difficult to get permission to alter a house for a newly disabled family member who needs a ramp, wider doors, or a remodeled bathroom. HUD has strict rules about the number of rooms given to new tenants, but does not consider an extra bedroom for an old person's attendant, space to accommodate the frequent long-term guests expected in most Indian homes, or the unanticipated presence of relatives' children who need shelter. HUD's standards ignore such common matters as the moving between reservation and city of many working-age people who therefore lack reservation homes of their own, and the dislocations common in families affected by alcoholism. Until recently, it was impossible to build houses at standards below the locally acceptable norm, even if tenants wanted it. Federal officials understandably feared an outcry from local well-meaning "friends of the Indian" if the Navajo, for instance, were given the outhouses that some traditionalists want instead of indoor bathrooms.[22]

So few building professionals live near remote reservations that those who are willing to go to them must travel long distances and may therefore increase their charges. HUD's standards produce houses that require maintenance that occupants cannot always afford, but if people in home-ownership programs refuse to meet their financial obligations for houses built on trust lands, HUD cannot always enforce penalties against them because this land cannot be alienated.

Fortunately, beginning in 1993, new standards and greater flexibility were promised by those HUD officials who had long been aware of and distressed by the problems. Home-ownership equity accounts became usable for home-improvement loans, so that problems could be fixed before they worsened. Tribal housing authorities were given the opportunity to build houses that did not meet HUD standards for sewage connection, for instance, if the future occupants requested it.[23] Senator John McCain proposed a bill to integrate repair and other services of the BIA into the HUD programs, and Secretary Cisneros planned more decentralized decision-making. He spoke, too, of providing culturally sensitive designs and houses that respond to the often harsh climatic conditions of many reservations. The Indian Housing Act of 1988 (PL 100-358) had already ended some restrictive cost-containment provisions, and for some years Dominic Nessi at HUD has advocated good design, as it is more durable and is likely to be better kept by its occupants.[24] HUD began to award prizes for good design and gave its Cultural Design Consultation Award for 1994 to the Southern Utes for housing designed by Reynolds/Larsen of Durango, Colorado. These architects acted "more as technical consultants to the tribal council, the Housing Authority Board of Commissioners, groups of elders," and the future residents, assisted by the engineers, the IHS, and BIA representatives. Reynolds/Larsen even took into account the experiences of previous HUD housing residents. The design used more flexible plans, passive-solar-heating features, attractive clerestory and corner windows, and vaulted ceilings, and it allowed adequate storage areas. The synthetic stucco finish accords with other architecture in the area, while it resists cracking and minimizes maintenance requirements.[25]

Earlier, new houses were so often considered unsuitable that some people preferred to live in miserable conditions, hoping for improved offerings later. Besides, self-built housing is free. At Fort Washakie on the Wind River Reservation in Wyoming, tenants refused to move into apartments, as they could not abide living so close together. The Lower Brule in South Dakota had a similar experience, rejecting the standard spacing of houses, which they regarded as far too close, while Pueblo people found the same spacing uncomfortably distant. Some Native Americans dislike the many walls and partitions in Anglo houses. Some Shoshone in Nevada refused to live in HUD houses, and some southwestern Indians are said to live in hogans and adobes, using HUD houses for storage or for shelter only in certain weather conditions. Some southwestern people ignore kitchens and cook outdoors under ramadas, even though the space between houses may put the fires dangerously close to dwellings that are no longer built of fire-resistant adobe. In cultures in which all family members sleep in one room, or in which prepubertal children and parents do so, the Anglo idea of separate bedrooms segregated by sex and used mainly for sleeping has seemed odd and unwelcome until recently, and this idea persists in traditional households. Some of the families that prefer single-room dwellings, which HUD's standards will not allow (in part because subsequent occupants might reject them), use bedrooms as workspaces or storage areas. Elsewhere, a man who knew that he could not repair faulty plumbing wanted an outhouse, not an indoor bathroom; of course, he got one anyway but built an outhouse, ripped out the bathroom fixtures as soon as the pipes clogged, and made practical use of the space for skinning deer, butchering cows, and storage.[26]

Other conflicting values are less tangible but no less real. Architect Rina Naranjo Swentzell* finds housing in the Western world to be isolated, built by males who specialize in one profession, using linear forms made of industrial materials in standard measurements fostered by codes and regulations. By contrast, at her own Santa Clara Pueblo, people build connected, communal spaces that are thought of as born and that must be blessed. Old houses and disused rooms can therefore be allowed to crumble and die, but Anglos prefer historic preservation. Joseph Laban*, executive director of the Hopi Tribal Housing Authority, knows that many modern Hopi have learned about and want Euro-American values and features in their houses. He feels that the difference in the cultures has to do with the "lack of challenge, suffering, hardship to put value into the society. Anglo society is about convenience" while "Indian society is about the effort to achieve harmony with Mother Earth." Indeed, clan leaders in the Hopi village of Mishongnovi rejected federal housing, as it would have made the land unfit for sacred ceremonies.[27]

Ray Halbritter*, who manages much of the New York Oneidas' business, has different ideas about housing. A casino's revenues might be used to build large suburban-style houses like those near Mystic Lake Casino outside Minneapolis. While Halbritter hopes to "maximize attractiveness and design quality of the territory and housing," he wants to reflect the individuality of each Oneida. "There is an image of us as communal, but we are very much individual," he says. While some Indian leaders "live in a pseudo-native theme," he "won't build a design that's Indian. We may like *no* design.... not have your own government decide." If people who do day work in nearby Syracuse want to imitate their employers' houses, Halbritter wants them to be free to do that.

He is equally firm about tribal members' responsibility for their own housing: "We're thinking of having people pay half the cost of the home. They have to have some feeling that a thing, if it's broken, affects them.... A free house is not going to help" people who need discipline in their way of living. Halbritter is not in favor of payment through sweat equity. "How are you going to count the hours?" he asks. Besides, "a housewife will get hurt by an electric saw; people will put nails into a window instead of a door."

The most difficult problem will be that "they won't pay, and you have to evict them. The first person who doesn't pay is out. There will be Indians with a gun saying 'This is our land and whites kicked us out and now Indians do, too.'" Halbritter knows that people will find his viewpoint "harsh, Republican, white," but he wants his fellow Oneida to be independent and self-sufficient, educated and hard-working. Far from welcoming per capita payments from the casino, he likens them to heroin.

Other Native Americans seek to balance tradition with the economy and technology of modern America. Wayne Newell*, assistant principal of the Indian Township School and a Passamaquoddy leader in Maine, says that "nobody here is suggesting that we send back our new houses or that we disconnect all of our utility poles, but there's a real search for perspective on all of this."[28] Larry Edmondson*, an architect, says that while Indians in Oklahoma "are pretty well integrated and look on the past as past," people attending housing workshops in Oklahoma City and Seattle showed interest in "planning for the extended family, in the kitchen as the central part of the house and [in] recollection of its past religious tradition, with other rooms around it as in a hogan or tipi. You would normally try to have space flow from the living room to the dining room to the playroom" rather than build tightly segregated spaces that many people regard as specifically Euro-American.

The shift from subsistence to wage economies has inserted new factors into housing. In wage economies, untraditional building types such as shops and offices will intrude on settings of houses and corrals. The private car or pickup truck will need a parking space; highway access and roads will become important; a filling station may interrupt the edge of a settlement.[29] House-building skills once universally taught are more often reserved for specialists, so that funds must be reserved for home buying, renting, and repair.

* * *

No building material is optimal everywhere. Balloon-frame construction is familiar and quick to produce, and therefore can reduce labor costs. Some Native people consider it culturally alien, while others resent the fact that it is usually non-Indian workers who erect it. The preference for indigenous materials may therefore have both cultural and economic motivations. That the motivations are not purely economic is seen when the Navajo, for instance, show little enthusiasm for the adobe that many nearby Pueblo people use and hope to see in more HUD housing.

Native Americans disagree about the desirability of various materials. The Jicarilla Apache prefer metal-sided and -roofed housing because they regard it as durable and quick to construct. The Pascua Yaqui chose split-faced and smooth concrete block, both because it is durable and because varying its texture allows for the design of surface patterns. Although both these groups live in the Southwest, microclimatic variations mean that some have to think about problems associated with snow and cold, while others deal with dry land and intense heat. The common practice of building houses on concrete slabs is good only in warm climates.[30] In strong winds or where sandstorms occur, applied surface paint may be whipped off in a short time.[31]

It is sometimes said that Native Americans should live in houses made of natural materials, but the Jicarilla Apache and Southern Ute seem not to agree. Even members of cultures that had permanent architecture of local materials may disagree, as did the late Abbott Sekaquaptewa*, former Hopi chairman. He rejected the idea of rammed earth as alien to Hopi tradition, and recognized the increased strength given by metal bars to buildings made of concrete block, which may be stronger and quicker to build than structures of adobe or small stones. One also should not romanticize the expertise of all ancient hogan builders or all who work in log construction today; when the Christian Relief Fund built a log house at Pine Ridge, it was so badly constructed that it needed repair immediately,[32] and while the log technique employed at the Shako:wi Cultural Center in Verona, New York, is beautiful (126), it is a Scandinavian one that Jules Obomsawin*, an Oneida builder, learned in British Columbia. Local and renewable materials are generally desirable, and they use a reservation's own resources, but glass fiber is a better insulator than wood. Realizing the utility of combining materials kept separate in the past, in 1993 the Oglala Lakota Tribal Housing Office evaluated proposed log houses, with adobe covering used for insulation rather than for a southwestern appearance.[33]

In much of the Southwest, adobe is praised for its low cost, its use of local labor, its heat absorption, and its cultural heritage. HUD resisted authorizing its use because without a standard brick, its stability was open to question. Establishing a standard increases its cost, as does adding asphalt for waterproofing. HUD found that adobe's resistance to temperature change was less than that of standard insulated wood-frame walls (ignoring adobe's ability to store heat at night). HUD also was afraid that the increased building time would raise labor costs, since even unskilled reservation residents must be paid prevailing local wages on projects large enough to be governed by the Davis-Bacon Act. In about 1980, HUD finally collaborated with the University of New Mexico and the Eight Northern Pueblos Council to establish performance standards and develop prototypes. San Juan Pueblo received an adobe-making machine whose success depended on requests for its products, to be anticipated mainly from HUD itself. Several years later, the pueblo sold the machine, as running this kind of enterprise was not part of the pueblo government's mandate. All the same, the viability of the material and its potential for use in HUD housing had been demonstrated.[34]

As one aspect of the performance testing, Tesuque Pueblo sponsored a demonstration project in 1981 to turn a mobile home into an energy-efficient solar-heated house. Dale F. Zinn & Associates of the Architecture Planning Group in Santa Fe designed the transformation with Edward E. Smith, geologist and planner with the Eight Northern Pueblos Council. The manufactured house was covered with stuccoed adobe block to give it a "hacienda-like appearance"; this can be done with concrete elsewhere. All the components used are found in hardware stores, and a semiskilled person can create similar changes himself. More houses were not built in this way at Tesuque because the real purpose of the project was to demonstrate adobe technology and to help produce standards for adobe construction. "The concept wasn't new," said Zinn. "Lots of people encapsulate mobile homes in New Mexico, Colorado, and so on. We documented and validated the methodology of doing it, with more insight into how solar and mobile homes work.[35]

Some natural material is unfamiliar and meets resistance partly for that reason. Straw bale covered with cement stucco outside and adobe plaster inside is much more thermally efficient than standard insulated wood HUD houses if the roof is properly insulated. The material is cheap because it is widely available, even burned as waste in many parts of the country. The mass and surface material combine to eliminate the threat of fire or instability, and the high fiber content and plastering remove the potential nuisance of insect infestation. In 1993, a Navajo family of six helped the tribal architect's office and builders make an experimental house—of straw, boards, mud, and custom-built windows and doors—that cost $20,000.[36] Given the unmanageable costs of heating poor Native people's homes in cold climates, this kind of construction ought to be widespread and welcomed, but people worry about flimsiness or flammability.

Marley Porter, formerly with the Navajo architectural office, describes other culturally sensitive aspects of the building:

> Four pendentive lofts in the hearth room meet to form the traditional eight-sided hogan. Sleepovers and additional family can sleep there. The stove is in the northeast corner, the greenhouse to the south, mom and dad's bedroom to the west where sits always the head of the family.... We used a green roof and red walls to invert the surrounding vegetation to the mountains and thereby lock the home and the land together. It is so quiet and warm inside. Building it was like a birth reversed.... Even though many do not know what they think about the structure, they feel something special.... We have received no less than twenty requests to come and teach them how to, well, go home.[37]

Even the most natural and traditional material needs maintenance, and residents need training to do it. Adobe must be resurfaced annually, for instance. Renters may need incentives beyond knowing that other housing is not available, as many Americans without equity in their homes are thought to be less attentive than owners are to repair and upkeep. Preventive measures may be economical as well as aesthetically and socially desirable. As Larry Sanchez* at the Nisqually Reservation puts it, "If you can't afford caulking and stapling to repair leaks in your plywood siding when it separates, you're going to see it get worse, or else someone will spend twice as much to contract out" the remedy.

Cost considerations among needy people tend to focus on the charges for utilities. People formerly in hogans and pueblos and log cabins who receive HUD housing now also receive bills for electricity and fuel. In Yerington, Nevada, a member of the tribal housing staff was faced with a $400 electric bill, which prompted her to buy a wood stove for heating. At Pine Ridge, residents had to pay $300 to $450 a month, and Navajos were paying $250 to $300. While some people reject wood stoves as smoky and messy and as health and fire hazards, and while wood is not available everywhere, when it is free for the gathering it is understandably popular and must be taken into account in plans for housing. Many Native Americans in new HUD homes have not been trained to fix houses that lack heat, so that it is especially important for these houses to be thermally efficient. Some provisions for solar energy take a long time to amortize, however, and this must be factored into budgets. In addition, residents may not be able to afford new batteries for certain solar installations or know how to install them properly. Funds for replacements and training also need to be included in house budget calculations.[38]

All families need storage space, but it is proportionately more common in Native American homes to need a place to store donated commodities or economical quantities of foodstuffs bought on payday, to keep homemade crafts for later sale, and to store fishing and hunting gear and to process the catch. People without basements, attics, or garages who must salvage parts from old automobiles and machines store these in the yard, contrary to common Euro-American custom.

In order to deal effectively with problems related to materials, energy use, and storage, site planning is important although not adequately considered everywhere. To be sure, every building ought to harmonize with the landscape and should include energy-efficiency measures, but these considerations have special significance for Native Americans who believe that they "live as a part of the land, not merely on it."[39] To facilitate this, Edward Norris, director of the Design Planning and Assistance Center at the University of New Mexico, cautioned against disturbing drainage channels and arroyos at Santo Domingo Pueblo, suggested that all fronts face south to maximize solar orientation—an arrangement made possible because house entries would be on the sides—and wanted work and private spaces to be both outdoors and in.[40] It is also important to take account of Native Americans' intangible knowledge: Ron Hilbert,* an artist, sensed something amiss about the first site chosen for houses for the S'Klallam in Washington State, and the houses were then relocated to everyone's satisfaction.[41]

* * *

Alfonso Ortiz* says that Tewa and other Pueblo people tend to define as normal the things of symbolic value that lie closest to the village or group of villages; this may affect the siting of houses, schools, and hospitals.[42] Norris's students recommended placing houses near existing villages, and hoped to preserve family unity by not segregating young and old. New religious buildings should be placed along traditional sacred axes. Forms traditionally doubled or opposed should find their echoes in newer buildings, lest their power be suspect.[43] Traditional associations of gender location and activities proper to certain directions are still made—for instance, among the Lakota and Navajo, for whom an eastern entrance has attained religious significance; it is more than just a way to let morning sunlight into a windowless dwelling.

Houses paid for by outside sources tend to be spaced more closely than many Native people would like. When the Kinzua Dam displaced Allegany Seneca into two new communities, residents were forced to live too near one another and were not resettled according to kinship and community ties.[44] The Navajo and others who own livestock must be situated farther apart than pueblo dwellers, and tightly spaced Navajo projects tend to turn into slums.[45] The Stockbridge-Munsee Mohicans in Bowler, Wisconsin, turned down the offer of a trailer park because the dwellings would have been unbearably close to one another. Infrastructure costs more to install over greater distances, but proximity creates its own problems: When feuding families and clans are too near one another, community life is endangered. If that is likely, "first come, first served" rules should be modified.

Some problems are caused by bureaucratic tangles. According to Peter Pino* at Zia Pueblo, "HUD gives money for housing, the [Indian] Health Service gives you money for water lines [and] sewers, and the BIA gives you money for street paving. . . . If you talk to HUD, they say, 'Where's the infrastructure?' so you go to the IHS and they say, 'Where's the housing?' and the BIA says, 'Where's the housing and the infrastructure?'"

Some safety matters are especially important in planning for Native Americans. In wooded areas, houses need to be separated by some distance from trees, as municipal fire departments are usually too far away from reservations to offer immediate help in case of forest fires. It is unwise to leave just a few trees standing unless drainage areas are thoroughly investigated, because trees newly isolated may fall over.[46] Remote Indian lands may have been requisitioned for artillery ranges with unexploded shells, for toxic storage, or for other activities that make them unsuitable for housing. George H. J. Abrams* reports that a housing complex for elder Allegany Seneca collapsed, having been built over an abandoned tannery in which the foundation had merely been filled in, a fact that the contractor failed to investigate.

A study in 1992 for the matrilocal Navajo Nation included suggestions about village planning for family clusters of four to seven dwellings for parents and the families of their daughters. Each cluster would have a pasture or garden of 2 to 3 acres, a ramada 24-feet square, and a concealed sweatlodge about 6 feet in diameter. Eight to ten such clusters form a village. Each would have about a dozen cars and additional parking spaces, a day-care or preschool building, a chapter house with a hogan, a building for elders, and a structure to shelter vendors. This plan is reasonable for a nation with enormous acreage; by contrast, the Wampanoag Tribal Council in Gay Head, Massachusetts, recognized in 1987 by PL 95-100, adopted a master plan by Forrest Cuch for only 47.5 acres. Thirty houses planned by Larkin/Tenney on culs-de-sac left culturally sensitive sites undeveloped. The master plan included a cultural center, an outdoor amphitheater, and features directed at visitors as well as at Wampanoags; this is a different approach from that of the remote and private Navajo.

A cul-de-sac can create a sense of place and neighborhood, and it uses land economically, also saving paving, curbs, and sidewalks; these are values admired by three tribes in Washington State whose members like the houses built for them around circular open spaces by Architectural Resources Collaborative.[47] The spirit of community was deemed more important than the individual buildings, just as among the Navajo the settlement pattern seems to be more important than the house form.[48] The cul-de-sac plans should, however, vary the buildings to take account of winds, solar orientation, or sacred meanings given to the four directions when tribal members are concerned about these issues. Critics prefer street connections to the center of the reservation to make communal activities convenient and to avoid having to drive great distances on perimeter roads to visit close relatives, to attend religious services, or to confer with children's teachers.

Technical installations can be sensitive to the environment and to cost constraints. The Navajo housing study of 1992 recommends grouping power sources for mechanical equipment or using windmills for pumping water. Small-scale enterprises reduce the need for cars and fuel to reach distant workplaces. Local expertise should be developed in building and for maintaining solar water heaters and small

photovoltaic systems. A central-plan house minimizes the surface-to-volume ratio, and promises economies in winter heating.[49] For Pueblo peoples in the sunny but cold upper Rio Grande Valley, J. Douglas Balcomb of the National Renewable Energy Laboratory in Boulder, Colorado, recommends that houses have foot-thick high-density black double-glazed concrete-block (trombe) walls on the south for delayed solar-heat transfer to the interior, a clerestory for direct gain to rooms that face north, and good insulation for passive-solar-heating benefits. This type of house should be comfortable, and should create only low bills for winter heating.[50]

Several architects hope to create defined outdoor spaces to relieve the stark rectangularity of the typical HUD house or to establish a place for ritual. Native Americans in the Southwest often cook outdoors to avoid adding heat to interiors, and include spaces for ovens, food preparation, laundry, and storage when building their own houses. One proposal made at regional housing-design improvement workshops sponsored by the National Endowment for the Arts envisioned a house with main and subsidiary parts connected by a cover that could shade a car or outdoor craft work. An experiment (1980) at the University of Arizona for the Tohono O'odham at Sells, Arizona, envisioned houses made of three small structures and a central courtyard; one would be for beds, another for storage, and the third for cooking.[51] For woodland peoples, architect Tari Rayala recommends using trees to define spaces to occupy, pass through, or dream about. She hopes to connect houses to the earth by surrounding them with beaten earth, brick, or gravel—materials intermediate between the purely natural and the entirely artificial. She thereby makes ambiguous the boundary between house and earth.

There may be little need to provide space for ornamental gardens, as many Native Americans regard open space around the house as best suited for practical purposes such as vegetable-growing, storage, or public passage. While Euro-Americans feel that everyone not invited is excluded from their property, Native Americans let outsiders into their space as long as they do not change anything. There is usually scant interest in the Euro-American drive to tend lawns and bushes that denotes respectable status; some Indians think that this activity is "a concern for the idle."[52] Ron Hernandez* and Dennis Sun Rhodes* worked for Hodne–Stageberg Partners in the years around 1980 when it received commissions for housing the Omaha at Macy, Nebraska; the Dakota at Hastings, Minnesota; and the Santee Sioux at Flandreau, South Dakota.

For these projects, the architects set aside private gardens for agriculture rather than ornament, clustered the buildings when that was accepted, and added graphic ornament to the sides or facades of houses.[53]

Several other designs attempt to incorporate cultural and environmental concerns in housing, including the low-income population served by HUD—sometimes with special consideration for the elderly. Around 1980, Surrounded-by-Enemy*, when designing for older residents in the three affiliated tribes at Fort Berthold, North Dakota, around 1980, raised the earth in berms around the houses to add insulation. Covered breezeways with benches link pairs of houses, protecting stored objects and affording shade in the summer. Log siding covers the houses and breezeways, using locally available material related to past building tradition. Community space opens at the center of every group of four units. Ten-foot-square cultural emblems introduce the houses from the road, abstracting a Mandan earth lodge, the eagle's eye and talon for the

Hidatsa, and the buffalo and horse for the these tribes and the Arikara. As the plans were not uniquely suited to older people, the units could be allocated to small families when relatives invited their elders to live with them, as is usual in Native American communities.

Even within cost constraints of $54 a square foot, it is possible to build useful indoor and outdoor spaces. When houses on the Salt River Pima–Maricopa Reservation had to be demolished for highway widening, about sixty new houses were planned to replace them. The residents did not want standard HUD boxes or "suburban Spanish" styles. They expected energy efficiency as well as a blend of Native culture and lifeways with modern materials and methods. Charles Robert Schiffner, an architect in Phoenix, designed several house types, the most innovative being a rectangle with its roof extended to form a ramada and carport (132, 133). A central wall holds most of the house's weight, supporting inverted roof trusses that create a triangular attic for insulation and ductwork and for orna-

132. HUD house for Pima–Maricopa Reservation, Scottsdale, Arizona. Charles Robert Schiffner, 1991. (Mark Boisclair, 1991 [91-51-6]; courtesy Charles Robert Schiffner)

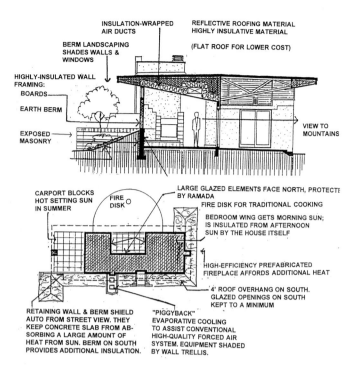

INSULATION-WRAPPED AIR DUCTS

REFLECTIVE ROOFING MATERIAL
HIGHLY INSULATIVE MATERIAL

(FLAT ROOF FOR LOWER COST)

BERM LANDSCAPING SHADES WALLS & WINDOWS

HIGHLY-INSULATED WALL FRAMING:
BOARDS

EARTH BERM

EXPOSED MASONRY

VIEW TO MOUNTAINS

CARPORT BLOCKS HOT SETTING SUN IN SUMMER

FIRE DISK

LARGE GLAZED ELEMENTS FACE NORTH, PROTECTE BY RAMADA

FIRE DISK FOR TRADITIONAL COOKING

BEDROOM WING GETS MORNING SUN; IS INSULATED FROM AFTERNOON SUN BY THE HOUSE ITSELF

HIGH-EFFICIENCY PREFABRICATED FIREPLACE AFFORDS ADDITIONAL HEAT

4' ROOF OVERHANG ON SOUTH. GLAZED OPENINGS ON SOUTH KEPT TO A MINIMUM

RETAINING WALL & BERM SHIELD AUTO FROM STREET VIEW. THEY KEEP CONCRETE SLAB FROM AB-SORBING A LARGE AMOUNT OF HEAT FROM SUN. BERM ON SOUTH PROVIDES ADDITIONAL INSULATION.

"PIGGYBACK" EVAPORATIVE COOLING TO ASSIST CONVENTIONAL HIGH-QUALITY FORCED AIR SYSTEM. EQUIPMENT SHADED BY WALL TRELLIS.

133. HUD house for Pima–Maricopa Reservation (energy-conservation provisions), Scottsdale, Arizona. (Courtesy Charles Robert Schiffner)

mental designs, if desired, at the ends. Above the ramada and carport, the trusses are left visible, offering an increased sense of volume and a sense of expansion in the living spaces. This structural method allows for an inexpensive reflective roof. More important, the plan is expandable, stretching from a one-bedroom, one-bath model to one with six bedrooms and three baths. It has the additional advantages of being attractive in appearance and different from standard low-income models, although its unconventional aspects may have made some residents hesitate to choose it.[54] Those who did had participated in deciding the style, orientation, and materials, and in setting priorities for budgeted features. Schiffner developed a new appreciation for joint activity and for offering choices. "The greatest ideas are those that synthesize the greatest amount of elements. The more issues, the greater the concepts." Now he is eager to make his procedures available to others. He found the challenges of the Pima–Maricopa work to be instructive to him as a person trained in the Frank Lloyd Wright tradition, which emphasized solutions

by an individual genius. Here he put as little as possible of his own personality into the work, and at the end was proud to have been of service.

Don Frothingham of Architectural Resources Collaborative managed to complete houses for the Upper Skagit Reservation on time and under budget, using 10-inch floors, 6-inch walls, oak trim, solid oak for stairwells, and even insulated draperies. This feat is hard to duplicate with shrunken budgets, when bidding is done in periods of inflation, and when tribal building officials or architects are less expert. Architectural Resources Collaborative also split the work into small contracts to avoid having to pay tribal workers generally prevailing wages, as required by the Davis-Bacon Act; this law is often blamed for making tribal workers uncompetitive with more experienced outside labor.[55]

Occasionally, however, other good results have been achieved despite the undesirable effects of rules and laws, as with a log house at Fort Berthold or a house designed by David Sloan* on the Hopi Reservation (11, 12). This is a modest building, well regarded by officials concerned with HUD housing. A simple rectangle, like many pueblo dwellings, it rises from a cement block foundation and is faced with local stone. Many Hopi consider various types of cement block to be like stone; cast stone with a rough surface is a popular building material. The house has the flat roof seen in older Hopi villages, and the ceiling in the front room is made of the vigas and thinner poles (latillas) familiar in the Southwest. The tenant, who previously lived in a nondescript modern house, was enthusiastic about the prospect of living in a new building that related to her ancestral traditions.[56]

There is no universal standard for placing such features as entrances or storage areas; each culture group has its own traditions, although some are the same. For the woodlands Ojibwe, Tari Rayala sensibly suggested storing at the north of the house things that need no sun, such as wood, skis, or cars. Dennis Sun Rhodes* thinks that Plains peoples should store things indoors at the west, using the perpendicular axis for gardens and a ramada (118). The Navajo housing study of 1992 recommended that spaces for food preparation and hygiene be at the north to provide an energy buffer on that cold side; these activities had been traditionally conducted there, but often outside the hogan. Some of the conclusions reached by each group, tribal member, or architect will depend on the relative importance of symbolism or practicality.

Native Americans, for whom hospitality is usually centered on the kitchen, overwhelming support house plans that emphasize large kitchens connected to dining and living rooms or areas. A large table may be prominent in many houses as the focus of social life, as in the novels of Louise Erdrich* about twentieth-century Ojibwe. The kitchen and big table are important also to the Lakota, and Ron Hernandez* connects them with the essential elements of fire and water.

There is also broad interest expressed in plans with bedrooms and bathrooms radiating from the main living–dining–kitchen area, omitting corridors. Ramona Bennett*, a social worker and former tribal chairwoman in Washington, conceived a plan for her house in which small rooms would surround a central skylit area, to let her supervise all the spaces, foster group activity, allow for privacy, and give easy access to all parts without wasting space. On contemplating this practical solution, she suddenly exclaimed, "Check it out! This is a longhouse, the best plan for a great big Indian family!"[57]

Architect Miles Yanick worked closely with Port Gamble tribal members and the planning department on Bainbridge Island, Washington, producing ten units of prize-winning self-help HUD houses with two to five bedrooms. The squarish houses have open interiors and no halls. The main room has a wood stove in the northwest, following the local longhouse tradition; the chimney area is open to the second floor. This produces a central well with balconies, akin to the longhouse arrangement. An added feature is the provision for exterior art, here by Ron Hilbert*, a Tulalip painter and storyteller. He asked each family to request an image of its own "spirit power," resulting in a scene of a bear, hunting canoes pursuing a whale, and other identifying forms.

An intelligent plan for Navajo housing also emphasizes a hearth. In the square core room, a circle is defined on the floor to evoke a hogan; a stove stands in one corner. Doors lead from each side of this room to modular bedroom, kitchen, and bathroom units, which can be made of local or synthetic material in various patterns (134). Additional rooms or such groups as an extra bedroom and kitchen can extend the house beyond a centralized form, if that is desired.[58]

For the Ojibwe, Tari Rayala advocates continuity inside, with the open circulation of people, sounds, and smells to enliven the home and promote social interaction. She wants the heart of a house to be tangent to the main circulation paths rather than a crossing point, and finds a fireplace psychologically necessary. There should be a secondary focal point for times when the fire is not lit. This room should be visible from the adjacent kitchen, which

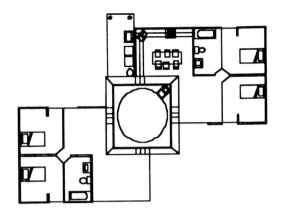

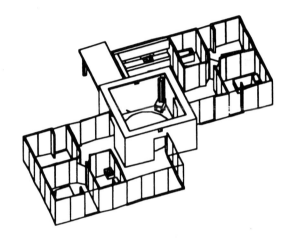

134. Modular house for Navajo (prototype plan). Tommy Yazzie* and Marley Porter, 1992. (Courtesy Marley Porter, from Navajo Nation, *Navahomes*)

should also be spacious with room for a table and chairs used by diners and observers.[59]

Some groups or individuals are content to have small bedrooms, especially if they are not used in conventional ways. Charles Archambault* noticed that some people sit on the floor while creating crafts; they would like lower windows to afford views outside. Flexibility in sleeping arrangements is important to the many Native American families whose hospitality extends to those in need of shelter, whether relatives or not. Some traditional people want toilets apart from the house or at least at the perimeter of the building rather than at the core. Those who want fireplaces tend to mention them for symbolic associations with the hearth rather than for effective heating; health officials dislike the attendant smoke, and fear their hazardous potential.

Ron Hernandez* makes practical suggestions—using wood stoves of cast iron and soapstone where wood supplies are adequate; using snap-out screen doors because when those fixed in place tear, they cannot easily be replaced; making heating units easily accessible for maintenance. He emphasizes proper commodities–storage areas and places for home-canned and dried food, for firewood, and for work equipment, especially in houses for large families. Children's rooms should have durable walls instead of the flimsy, penetrable ones sometimes used. Archambault thinks that modern wall finishes may be unnecessary, as people could suspend blankets and hangings on plain wooden walls.

The Student Design Studio led by Ron Kasprisin at the University of Washington assisted the Swinomish with planning, and recommended building both apartments suited to the special needs of the aged and "grandmother apartments" connected to standard single-family housing. The students also took into account the varied planning needs of families with distinctive characteristics: extended families that may need larger communal spaces and smaller bedrooms or more than one kitchen and/or living room; families that might find shared facilities useful for several households at once; families that need space for crafts activity; families that would benefit from having rooms that could be closed off or attached to other units as people leave a household or are added to it.

The Oneida, assisted by Ron Baba and his students of environmental design at the University of Wisconsin, proposed housing in 1993 to include sleeping, bath, and living rooms attached to a family house, for the use of elderly relatives who wanted some independence but who cook and eat with the others. Recent housing suggestions for the Oneida have included a principal room easily visible from the kitchen. The Oneida stress efficiency and affordability in housing, including professional management, follow-up studies, and tenant accountability, but they also pay attention to the direction of the sun and to tradition that makes it culturally unacceptable to relegate elders to congregate housing and old-age homes, especially when they are far from other family members' houses.[60]

Elsewhere, for older people without families, or for those who live in cities, other house types have been designed. At White Earth Reservation in Minnesota, polygonal buildings have lodgepoles rising at the center. (The reservation residents, although in the woodlands, use tipi shelters during wild-rice-gathering season.) On each face of the polygon is a compact apartment.[61] In Saint Paul, Minnesota, the Earthstar Elders' House, planned in 1993 with funds from several sources including the Wilder Foundation, envisioned a multiuse community room with a capacity of 150, and then small apartments for each resident. The potential occupants approved these plans, which call for a single living area that can be divided with a movable wall to form a bedroom area acceptable to HUD.[62]

The Wampanoags in Gay Head, Massachusetts, broke ground in June 1994 for twenty-five three-bedroom and five four-bedroom houses funded by HUD. They are going up along culs-de-sac on 6.5 acres, leaving about 40 more acres as open space. No building will enter the swamp or rise over threatened plants, a burial ground, or areas with archaeological material. In December 1992, the tribal members selected the design from two models submitted by Larkin/Tenney architects of Cambridge, Massachusetts, which had answered a request for proposal (135). Tribal members appreciated the architects' research into the Native past. The architects learned that Wampanoags had lived in clusters, practicing communal farming near wetlands, and had built round-roofed, additive buildings focused on central fires.

One model looked like a two-story fisherman's house of the area, and the other had a curved roof. While the architects regarded the latter as emblematic of shelter, they had been asked to recall traditional Wampanoag architecture, and the curved roof could be interpreted as a response to Native American building forms. Upon seeing the curved-roof designs, some people expressed doubts, suggesting that basements might be damp or that a central skylight evoking a smokehole was not needed; they may also have felt uneasy at having houses different from those of other householders in Gay Head. Most Native Americans today would like to have their distinctive heritage acknowledged visually, but their models for success come from the surrounding society, so that some ambivalence is to be expected. The architects were pleased that the Wampanoags approved the curved-roof design, having decided that "the house represented what they were after." They "realized that the house was not going to be typical even with a gable roof."

In designing the houses, Larkin/Tenney wanted "to do a scheme that paid tribute to [the tribe's] aspiration" to establish a homeland, something the Wampanoags had been denied until they won a land-claim settlement and federal recognition in 1987. The housing "would be representative of Native Americans building for themselves," even though assisted by outsiders who included Mark

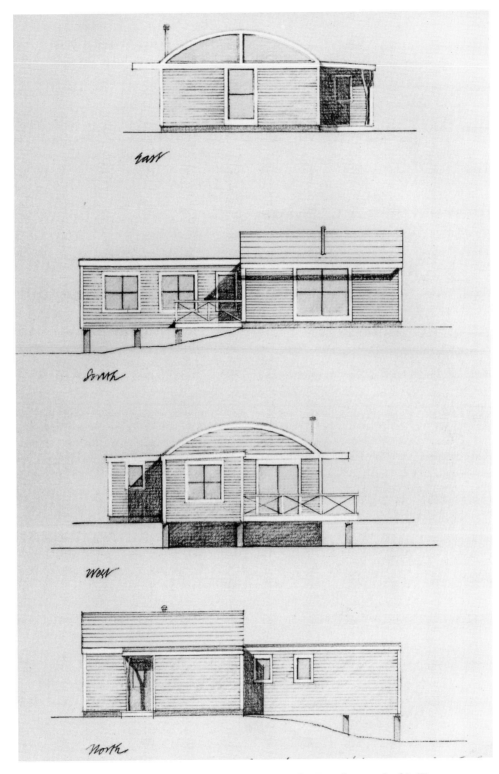

135. HUD house for Wampanoag Reservation, Gay Head, Massachusetts. Larkin/Tenney, 1994. (Courtesy Celine Larkin)

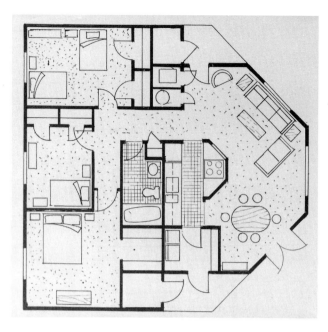

136. HUD house for Navajo (plan). AICAE workshop, modified by David N. Sloan*, 1991. (From AICAE, *Our Home*)

137. HUD house for Pueblos. AICAE, 1991. Walls are thick adobe or stucco. (From AICAE, *Our Home*)

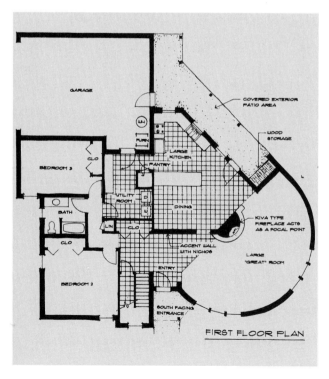

Three Stars*, a Lakota raised in the Southwest who was on the architects' staff. During the building process, the architects met with the tribal housing authority and with Wampanoags who expressed their desires and opinions. A mail poll solicited everyone's vote on the final plan. Tribal members and their relatives were active in the construction work that began in the summer of 1994.

Celine Larkin says that "we felt that it was important not just to put a few arches in. We needed spatial relationships that mattered, and we had to try to transform them for today." The combined living room and kitchen came from the idea of a central hearth in a wigwam, which had an open plan. This was placed in one block as close as practical to a square. Despite some objections to the skylight, she promoted the idea, as she "felt that it showed the primal connection to the hearth and the wigwam as the center of the family." The proposed central stove had to be abandoned, as the tribe would be liable in case of fire, and stoves emit unhealthy particulates.

The living-room–kitchen unit is the only part of the house with a basement; other rooms can be aligned in various ways or stacked along the sloping land. Linear additive plans characterize both longhouses and Euro-American farmhouses in New England. If pillars support rooms above a slope, outdoor protected storage is created, although the undersides of these rooms must be insulated. Some people feared that animals would nest under the houses, an unlikely eventuality on gravel surfaces.

Each house within its group of four to nine dwellings fronts on a common public space, but has views to uplands and wetlands. Decks to capture solar gain are directed to the south. In collaboration with BSS Design landscape architects, surveyors, and civil engineers in Falmouth— Larkin/Tenney proposed to "renaturalize the landscape," making walkways of quahog shells and landscaping with native plants. Four community gardens will reflect historic common gardens. Two landscaped areas for gatherings are included among the reserved open spaces, the replicated or preserved wetlands, and old walking trails. Celine Larkin explained that "if we took something out of nature, we had to give it back." HUD gave the houses its Cultural Design Award for 1994, although tribal authorities substituted inferior components and unsuitable details for those that the architects specified.[63]

The idea of incorporating regional culture into modern housing motivated Dennis Sun Rhodes* to design a Plains house prototype (*118*) based on his analysis of historic dwellings, including his grandmother's one-room log house at Wind River, Wyoming.[64] While working with

Thomas Hodne, Sun Rhodes also devised a round wood-land and a pyramidal square Plains "tipi" housing proto-type, and then, apparently independently, an "American Indian Cultural/Solar Heated House." He explains that his own work is based on his understanding of the way people move and use spaces—in a tipi, moving to the left toward the south, the woman's place where cooking is done; to the west, where the most important man sits; to the north for male guests and activities; and to the east for the door-keeper.[65]

Perhaps the most potentially important recent efforts in design are those made by the American Indian Council of Architects and Engineers (AICAE) following workshops held in eight locations, primarily in the West and Alaska. Its publication, *Our Home: A Design Guide for Indian Housing*, is available through federal government sources and is thus likely to be widely distributed. Directed by Louis Weller*, an architect in Albuquerque, and assisted by southwestern architects David Sloan* and Burke Wyatt*, the workshops were funded by the National Endowment for the Arts and encouraged by the Indian housing office at HUD. These studies complemented J. Douglas Balcomb's excellent work on energy efficiency in housing design.

The publication offers a model for culturally suitable housing in each of three areas (136, 137). One is the pueblo-style structure, with light-colored, rough walls, solid geometric forms, and a stepped parapet rising to the upper floor, where a master bedroom and bath open onto a terrace that forms a roof over the principal room down-stairs, a semicircular one with a kiva-style fireplace at the center of the implied circle. Bob Gachupin*, a participant in the Albuquerque workshop, proposed a linear house with a round kiva-like living room appended to one side (138); inverted and reversed by Balcomb, it provided a cul-turally suitable and thermally desirable dwelling. For a northern woodland people, the Forest County Potawatomi, the workshop participants approved a rectangular plan with utility and garage space perpendicular to the living quarters. A metal-roofed round-vaulted ceiling covers the latter, recalling the cover of a longhouse. The slightly sunken floor is another traditional reminiscence. The AICAE gave credit for the overall idea to Katharine Clute*, at present a student of architecture in Wisconsin. For the Navajo, the plan incorporates bedrooms in a rectangle,

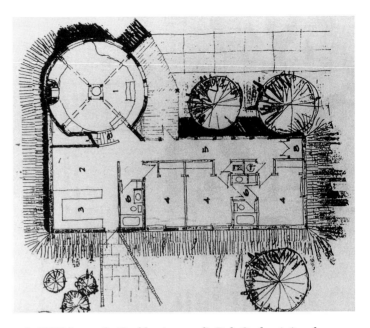

138. HUD house for Pueblos (proposal). Bob Gachupin* and David N. Sloan*, 1991. (From AICAE, *Our Home*)

with mechanical and plumbed spaces along its inner side. A living room extends on three sides of an octagon, recall-ing the polygonal hogan but doing so by using shapes and dimensions that accommodate modern life. The eastern entrance is essential, fitted into one side of the living room.

* * *

Today's houses with segregated spaces for bedrooms, televi-sion-watching, and hygiene cannot be traditional no mat-ter what veneer of style is applied to them. They cannot always use certain older materials that decay quickly but used to be just as quickly renewed; government housing agencies must be especially attentive to durability because, lacking other housing resources, reservation families are likely to remain in federally supplied housing forever. To be sure, the buildings discussed here do not intend to be traditional. They are evocative. They are signs or simply bear signs in the form of ornament. They are responses to cultural evaporation, pouring at least a few old resources into new vessels. They reinforce a sense of identity, even of ethnic pride. And if they can help to build or rebuild Native nations, the best examples will have fulfilled an essential mission in contemporary Indian America.

14

Museums

We tend to think of museums as places to exhibit either art or natural or national history. An art museum holds well-lit original and usually handmade objects owned by the museum itself, while a gallery, whether in a museum or elsewhere, normally offers temporary or borrowed displays. Museums of natural history and ethnography exhibit aspects of nature and of the vernacular environment of people around the globe—in the United States, frequently deemphasizing Europe and North America apart from peasants and atypical groups such as Romany, Lapps, and Native Americans. By implication, the majority population identifies itself as having a distinctly different culture, one taken for granted as normative for most of its visitors; it therefore marginalizes the others.[1] In any type of customary museum, the objects are identified by labels giving name, date of execution, and provenance, frequently supplemented by explanations of significance and of function or method of use.

The contemporary Native American museum may not adhere to these norms, although Amerindians seem to think that despite being a Western institution, the museum can present their partly non-Western cultures. The Native American museum today is often primarily a place for the sponsors' cultural self-definition.[2] A national or government-sponsored museum may empower even a nation's least favored inhabitants by displaying their history in the kind of institution associated by the powerful with high culture. The intent is to present history within a generally triumphant narrative and to demonstrate unity despite diversity. Three examples are the Museum of Canadian Civilisation, in which every identifiable ethnic group is presented to a nation of immigrants; Mexico's National Museum of Anthropology, where descendants of indigenes and conquerors can come to greater understanding; and the coordinated museums of Tarnów, one of them even showing the history and artifacts of the Jewish and Romany minorities in southern Poland. These museums, although sponsored by government entities rather than by immigrant or minority groups directly, are conceptually parallel to many tribal museums (most of which depend on federal government funds to some extent).

The Native American museum may mix art, natural history, and ethnography. Sometimes it is promoted as an economic catalyst. Unlike most museums sponsored by larger and richer governments, one built by a tribe may have under its roof a senior citizens' center or a job-training program, or it may be housed more predictably with a school, a library, or archives. The motivation for establishing the museum may include therapeutic support, as described in the 1970s by Herbert Fowler, a psychiatrist, in supporting the Yakima Nation Museum (39); he felt that Indians "fear that if they are forced into American culture they are forced into non-culture.... It is necessary to resurrect Indian history, languages, songs, folklore and dances to erase anxiety and its self-destructive symptoms."[3]

The Molinaro/Rubin consulting firm identified at least forty-six tribes that were planning museums for the years 1991 to 1996. In contemplating one for the Tulalip Nation, planner Henry Gobin* told landscape architects from the University of Washington of his hopes to "bring Tulalip people closer to who they are: Would the architects' plans do that, or bring them farther away?" The question was important because the museum would "impact the Tulalip people's way of thinking about themselves."

Increasingly, Native Americans expect to make the decisions about museum operations and content, and they intend to have the museums enhance life for their own communities. The Buffalo Bill Historical Center in Cody, Wyoming, engaged Native American consultants when a new section for indigenous displays was built in 1979, and so did the director of the Iroquois Indian Museum at Howes Cave, New York (43). Most southwestern museums now "have involved Indians in collecting, documenting, exhibiting, and interpreting collections," as have the Arizona State Museum, the Milwaukee Public Museums, the Field Museum in Chicago, the National Museum of American History, and the National Museum of Natural History, both in Washington, D.C.[4]

The Arapaho Cultural Museum at Wind River, Wyoming, used not anthropologists but spiritual healers and tribal historians as consultants. Indian labor renovated an older building for this new use. Native American artists adorned the interior, and the building supervisor, Dennis Sun Rhodes*, is an Arapaho with a bachelor of architecture degree. In other cases, tribal members have little choice, as hiring outsiders is too costly; moreover, outside labor deprives local residents of the chance for even temporary employment. When tribes employ outsiders for special expertise, they now usually insist that the architects listen to them closely and follow their orders carefully. Only in unusual cases do the tribal clients look for a famous architect who is well known for pursuing his personal vision.[5]

Like Native American museums, public museums present the sponsors' interpretation of history. Public museums often do so unconsciously because their procedures have become widespread, therefore seeming objective and traditional. Natural history museums are associated with science; art and history museums, with university-level education. Both associations suggest truth.

That museums are unobjective and contrived, not neutral at all but in fact ideological, is an idea that has lately received increasing attention.[6]

When the Museum of Modern Art in New York exhibited works of non-Western art out of context to show the sources of early-twentieth-century Primitivism, the curators acknowledged the Eurocentric milieu of the artists but were criticized for displaying Southern Hemisphere works as mere contributors to Northern Hemisphere ones. Well aware of this practice, Fred Wilson, an African-American artist in New York, when asked to create an installation at the Maryland Historical Society, overturned the traditional view of local history by displaying items never shown before: He placed slave shackles in a vitrine along with fine eighteenth-century silversmiths' work, displayed a slave whipping post in the woodwork section, and confronted portraits of famous whites with those of famous blacks. Native Americans also feel that they have the right to present their views of history, and intend to do so as much as possible in tribal museums and at the National Museum of the American Indian in Washington, D.C.[7]

Some Native Americans believe that Anglos still picture them as living in tipis, wearing buckskin garments, and speaking halting English, as Tonto did to the Lone Ranger. They want tribal institutions that will enlighten the ignorant and present a positive contemporary image. Clarinda Begay* of the Navajo Nation presented the primary function of her museum as promoting "sovereignty among our people," while William Day, director of the Tunica–Biloxi Museum, stated that it aimed to educate Native Americans and others while giving tribal members pride in being Indian.[8] Ideally, tribal members would have arrived at a common view of these matters, although in some cases the view of only one group prevails—perhaps a group concerned with particular ideas of cultural preservation and contemporary identity, or perhaps the only tribal members who understand the social roles of a museum.

Many popular books and films still give the perspective of immigrant settlers. White-sponsored museums before the late 1960s emphasized at their worst the savagery of aboriginal people or displayed human remains in ways intolerable to descendants. At other times, these museums created romantic visions of unintelligible pagans leading Bronze Age lives in the Railroad Age. Museums initiated by missionaries tended to emphasize the gradual acceptance of Christianity as part of a missionary's success story and as a narrative of increasing "civilization" of the aborigines, thus fostering an ideal of assimilation; they tended to overlook recidivist tendencies and syncretism.

Tribal museums usually offer different views of these matters, and emphatically present Native American life today to counter any idea that Indians are all dead or that they are en route to assimilation. It is useful for everyone to hear alternative ideas about what is regarded as sacred, what kinds of family structures have supported group life for hundreds of years, ways in which people interact with varied natural environments, and values in indigenous literature that offer parallels and additions to what others regard as canonical.

A desire to present tribally oriented material does not, however, mean that all available information will be offered. Some things are kept in reserve, not for lack of space—the usual excuse in other museums—but for reasons particular to Amerindians. Tribal curators will not always tell visitors or even all fellow Indians everything that is known about certain objects and their use; this knowledge is reserved for leaders, especially religious leaders, who have a need to know. Pueblo peoples conceal religious information from the general public. Others, including the Makah, do so as well, sometimes because the information is meant to be known only by communally designated and trained people, sometimes because outsiders have caused harm by misusing the information, and sometimes, it seems, to frustrate intruders because too many of them have altered every aspect of Indian life to which they have gained access. The excuse offered at the Makah Cultural Research Center (36) for the inexplicit labels is that the Makah want unanimity of opinion when questions arise about the material on display, although one may doubt that unanimous interpretations are often made.

The center has a spacious, sophisticated, and somewhat abstract interior design that is probably unfamiliar to the local population. The laconic labels and the installation may have been designed to mystify outsiders in order to replace Euro-American analysis and reason with a new form of response.[9]

The Makah now insist that no photographs be taken inside their Cultural Research Center, and other tribes require visitors to obtain permits for photography on reservation land. The Allegany Seneca do not intend to display medicine bags because they are considered sacred,[10] although certain other ritual artifacts may be shown. The Hopi allow no photographs to be taken of ceremonies, Acoma Pueblo sharply restricts photography, and Zuni will not display certain historic photographs in their collection because the information in them is considered private. Some Native informants require prepublication submission of material written from interviews with them

(ostensibly to avoid distortions of fact), and several tribes will not divulge the location of sacred sites.[11] Objects seen by the general public may be only copies of original work. Some Indians reject the idea of museums entirely: "We're pulling back into our own life, trying to revive what we have left. It's ours, not something to put on display."[12] In October 1992, fifteen pipes had to be removed from a quincentenary exhibition at the Minneapolis Institute of Arts when midwestern Native people claimed that showing seven pipes of catlinite, a stone they considered to be the blood of Mother Earth, was like revealing photographs of white people's "companions in intimate settings...before strangers." They maintained this position even though Mother Earth is not an ancient concept, even though the pipes were not ceremonial but had been made for nineteenth-century tourists, and even though they were to be shown respectfully—dismantled, and lying on a bed of sacred sage.[13]

Indian museums may consider materials to be cultural or spiritual beings, to be used and not simply stored. Some Native people believe that they receive "supernatural favor through the 'gift' of Indian wealth," whereas "non-Indian museums buy artifacts and own them as physical inventory." Curators must learn the specific tribal belief system to avoid malevolent supernatural powers.[14]

The establishment of tribal museums is related to several tendencies in American society.[15] As the ideal of the "melting pot" began to disintegrate within the last generation, increasing numbers of ethnic groups inaugurated or enhanced their own museums. For many people in dynamic societies who no longer adhere automatically to traditional religion, a museum offers a connection to aspects of spiritual heritage and to culturally elevated messages, or even to propaganda that people see as important for guiding the group's future. Museums, then, have proliferated recently in industrialized, secularized nations such as the United States, Germany, and Japan. A museum is often seen by its promoters as a mark of having arrived socially or intellectually, or as denoting a community's aspirations to do so.[16]

As Native Americans acquire increasing education in the mainstream, usually having to separate themselves from traditional and locally based life and then return to it, they need to document their heritage and use reinforced cultural knowledge to sustain them through new challenges. In this respect, Amerindian museums parallel those of developing countries, which are often inaugurated by leaders who hope to show through these institutions that they "have their own intellectual models and will no longer be dealt with as simply quaint, exotic, or primitive in other people's museums."[17] In addition, tribal members seek increased control over the research questions being asked, the types of information sources used, and the interpretations given in their own and in mainstream museums. They expect Indians to be docents, to take charge of repairing artifacts that they may understand better than outsiders do, and to become curators and directors, as some already are.[18]

Another way in which Native American museums differ from those of the majority society is that they may be comprehensive cultural centers, where displays represent only one aspect of a drive toward cultural preservation. The Mid-America All-Indian Center in Wichita, Kansas, proposed a museum in 1976 in which "concepts expressed will reflect the Indian viewpoint," suggesting that there was only one. This plan followed the establishment of social and health services at the center, and the recognition that both flesh and spirit need attention; the disruptions of urbanization had made cultural and heritage activities essential for understanding Native ways of life. The sponsors hoped to collect objects of high quality and to keep them accessible. They promised not to buy, and to reject as gifts, any material objectionable to the culture concerned. They hoped to conduct workshops in crafts and Native arts, to continue work with Native artisans being trained with federal funds, and to have programs for schoolchildren.

Recording and use of the native language is a major activity for the Makah, who even maintain the museum catalogue in their language. Elsewhere, curators are sometimes required to learn the ancestral language. The maintenance of Tohono O'odham archives is central to the Ak-Chin Eco-museum. A tribal library rather than a library concerned primarily with art or ethnography is often incorporated within the museum facility. Community meetings may be held at the museum, close to religious and historic artifacts. Celebrations take place in tribal museums, including some forbidden to tourists. Elders may be invited there to transmit traditional lore and language to children. Training is offered in dance and music, sometimes in cooking, and in the traditional use of plants.

This combination of offerings is especially useful when the number of available artifacts is limited, as it often is for formerly migratory peoples, or for those whose ancestral lands have been buried by cities, dams, or slag heaps. In such cases, displays concerning language, oral history, traditional stories, music, dance, lifeways, and the group's relation to nature can replace artifacts. By contrast, in large mainstream museums, accounts of these subjects complement the artifacts.

More unusual are museums to which extraneous facilities have been attached, such as feeding and nutrition centers or vocational-training facilities. These and other quarters may surround the museum because funds are available for those purposes rather than for cultural expression alone. If the latter is presented convincingly as an appendix to the former, funds may be given for both. Several dozen tribes have obtained money for museums and cultural centers through the Economic Development Administration within the Department of Commerce, because the museum is meant to increase tourism and to stimulate the provision of related services. The Administration for Native Americans is another source of funding to plan cultural centers.

It is unlikely that tribal museums in remote locations can be self-sustaining, let alone income generators, but tribal politicians expect them to bring in revenue.[19] Lakota artist and gallery owner Vic Runnels* has been the primary Native American to work with local businessmen in Hill City, South Dakota, who agreed to donate a 13.5-acre site, 1.5 of the acres destined for a museum. The institution intends to show Lakota history, to present traveling exhibitions from the National Museum of the American Indian, to promote knowledge of Lakota tradition, and to sell contemporary art and crafts. The sponsors envision a theater, concerts, a research facility, a mall with "upscale businesses," and a motel and convention center. All are to be designed by a Lakota or part-Lakota architect.[20] This is one of several museums promoted as economic catalysts, bringing jobs in construction, maintenance, museology, and craft work, and attracting tourist revenue. Owing to the lack of endowments, or viable economic bases, some tribes are unable to keep their facilities open and in good repair, but at least construction, service, and curatorial jobs will have been created for Indians in the meantime.

Tribal museums set up for their economic potential contain shops. While gift shops in major urban museums stock merchandise appealing to the upper middle class, Native American museum shops cater to varied tastes, selling handmade products of the reservation perhaps along with handmade products of other tribes, books, greeting cards (at times showing fair-skinned maidens wearing buckskin dresses), inspirational plaques recording a text erroneously attributed to Chief Seattle, packets of dried foods gathered nearby, and clothing and scarves with local or supratribal motifs. Raymond Thompson, an experienced museum professional, writes that "museums have

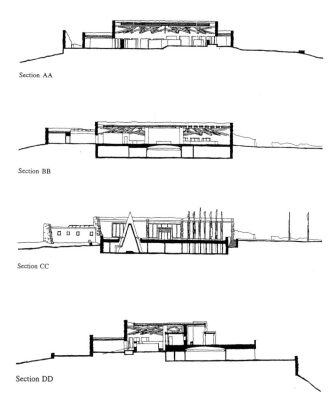

Section AA

Section BB

Section CC

Section DD

139. Omaha Interpretative Center (project), vicinity of Macy, Nebraska. Mark Hoistad, 1993. (Courtesy Mark Hoistad)

helped Indian artists and artisans revive old designs, improve methods, maintain [high] quality production, market their products, and exhibit outstanding examples."[21] They generally do not offer painted Indian heads on velvet, although these are found at nearby tourist traps. George H. J. Abrams*, former Seneca museum director, was adamant about having none of these, nor images of "The End of the Trail" in the Seneca shop, and felt that selling artifacts of other tribes was also improper. If, as he pointed out, a tribal museum established to attract tourists is to some extent "an exploitation of culture,"[22] a bit of reverse financial exploitation of the tourist is appropriate, especially as the visitor is not forced to buy anything.

The Oneida of Wisconsin have only a constricted shop, however, because their museum—to be replaced—was designed too quickly by inexperienced Oneida participants who did not heed all the advice given by consultants. It was put up in 1977, in only one year after the Oneida obtained a Bicentennial grant without yet knowing what they wanted in a museum, or how to make use of one; they had simply been encouraged to apply to the EDA, a move

that seemed sensible in terms of its economic potential. The two-level building of concrete block faced with diagonal tongue-and-groove wooden siding is covered by a hipped roof, embellished by a central cupola and skylight. It is built into a bank, or has had earth banked around it, and is less noticeable than the reconstructed longhouses erected outside. The building suffers from insufficient supporting services, the absence of wheelchair access, poor security, and vermin in the inadequate storeroom. Casino revenues should help to support a new museum, of which a drawing was displayed in 1992; it showed a rectilinear building with piers around the perimeter, perhaps alluding to longhouse framing, and a main entrance under glass barrel vaults perhaps meant to recall curved roofs of wigwams and longhouses.[23]

A specific impetus to the creation of several Native American museums came from the repatriation of those tribal materials that had been taken dishonorably from Native owners and housed in mainstream museums. In 1970, wampum belts were removed from the New York State Museum and returned to the Onondaga. The Colville plan a repository for repatriated artifacts and an associated educational facility near Nespelem, Washington, as a way to sustain the objects and traditions.[24] The Field Museum in Chicago returned excavated remains to the Winnebago. In the 1980s, the now-disbanded North American Indian Museums Association published a directory including "Suggested Guidelines for Museums in Dealing with Requests for Return of Native American Materials." The Native American Grave Protection and Repatriation Act of 1990 obliged federally funded public repositories to take inventory of their Native American holdings, to inform Native people about them, and to settle claims to human remains, funerary objects, other religious artifacts, and objects considered tribal patrimony. Settlement required the expeditious return of these materials. Tribal claims to artifacts and human remains "make manifest the historical and political reality of Indian revival and resurgence."[25]

A good many Native Americans are tired of having their ancestors' bones displayed. Some oppose archaeological research, feeling that enough human remains and artifacts have been dug up already and treated disrespectfully too often; they maintain that Indians in a given area are descendants of all those whom the Creator placed there earlier, and that their ancestors, like those of any white scientist, are worthy of respectful reinterment and undisturbed rest.[26] An impressive automobile convoy traveled more than a thousand miles in 1991 to escort the bones of

Sisseton members to resting places more dignified than urban museum storerooms.[27] Those asking for repatriation of remains in the 1970s tended to be urban, university-based, and militant;[28] now the petitioners are more broadly based. While some advocate repatriation even without adequate homes for the material—one person complained that rules requiring museum-standard repositories were "shoving the white man's paradigms down our throat"[29]— they appear to be in the minority. Some returned materials such as Zuni statues of war gods may be destroyed because their original purpose requires their exposure to nature and eventual return to the earth.[30]

The Omaha plan an interpretative center, having repatriated a sacred pole and other objects from the Peabody Museum in Cambridge, Massachusetts. The objects are stored temporarily in repositories in Nebraska. A program for community projects at the architecture school at the University of Nebraska led the tribe to Mark Hoistad, a faculty member who had been inspired by a video about the pole's return. He devised a plan, guided by Dennis Hastings*, tribal historian, who said that Hoistad gave the project "130 percent," although Hastings still had some doubts about building it (139).

The Omaha are not primarily interested in attracting tourists, although crafts and food will be sold at the center; funding might be available through the BIA or the Administration for Native Americans if this were an economic development project. Both Hastings and Hoistad regard the center as a place for preservation and learning. They designated the 600-acre site as a culture and wildlife preserve, regarding it as sacred because it lies on the edge of the religious road, a bluff where chiefs are buried. Hoistad designed a line of seven totems evoking warriors, one for each surviving clan, with three other now-extinguished clans having shadow representatives disappearing in the woods. He was told that a camp circle reflects the cosmos and the framework for housing in Omaha culture. When bisected by the sun's path, it can represent, in the north, the sky people clans concerned with spiritual matters and masculinity, and, in the south, the earth people clans concerned with daily life, including farming, war, and governance. In the circle stands a conical container for the sacred pole, regarded as "an icon of woman" and as "a living being, the oldest Omaha." Hoistad saw his task as making a home for a myth, not creating something showy, while Hastings did not "want to see a building that's non-Indian and we're housed inside" or a building "with just a bit of exterior ornament." Hoistad kept the building partly underground to reduce its impact on the landscape; plants

140. Sequoyah Memorial Museum (plan), Vonore, Tennessee. Brewer, Ingram, Fuller, 1984. (Courtesy Lee Ingram)

will grow on the earth-covered roof. Displays about history and modern life are to line the circle's rough stone walls which refer to the bluffs. Around the perimeter will be rooms for instruction, meetings, and archives. These are intended to reinforce Omaha knowledge and to teach language students, those intent on self-discovery, and children, as "people age 44 or less are 80% of our population." Hastings wanted "generations to come [to] feel part of the culture."[31]

Discoveries of unknown materials also lead to museums because tribes now usually insist on keeping newly excavated material found on their land. This has been the impetus to creating museums for the Makah and the Tunica–Biloxi, among others.

Destruction of Native lands led to the creation of the Sequoyah Memorial Museum in Vonore, Tennessee, opened in 1986 (140, 141). When the Tennessee Valley

141. Sequoyah Memorial Museum, on opening day, 1986.
(Courtesy Maxwell Ramsey)

Authority (TVA) announced plans for its Tellico Dam despite the pleas of environmentalists and Cherokees in 1966, it admitted that abandoned Indian village sites and burial grounds would be drowned. Remains of over 12,000 Native Americans were exhumed and reinterred. Their civilization is presented in the museum that the TVA chose as the best of eighty options for commemorating the losses. Through a trust fund, the agency donated $640,000 and 47.4 acres for it at the western end of Fort Loudoun Island, where Sequoyah, the half-Cherokee inventor of the Cherokee syllabary, was born. Carroll Hamilton*, a Cherokee museum official, calls the institution the "brainchild of Dr. Duane King," an anthropologist whom the tribe respected enough to have as the former museum director, even though he is Euro-American.

The Eastern Band of Cherokees owns and operates it as a satellite of its museum in North Carolina, and band members told the architect what they wanted. Lee J. Ingram, David Roberts, and Elizabeth Kremmer Pogue designed it in 1985. The architects earned praise for having provided maximum square feet for the money, accommodating exhibit space, offices, a gift shop, and a visitor reception area.

The museum is simple in form and easy to maintain. Its east–west axis is intersected by a north–south lobby. The center of the facade evokes a traditional winter house with wood supports and a pitched roof. Seven supports, one for each Cherokee clan, hold the entrance porch, which continues through the structure to create the tall lobby. Flanking the entrance is a landscaped area marked by walls of staggered-height poles, recalling the building material of Sequoyah's time. Behind them, the museum's walls are punctuated by designs in tan and brown brick suggesting basket patterns. Seven columns inside the lobby and a seven-sided audio-visual room allude to the seven-sided Cherokee council houses of the eighteenth century. At certain hours, sunlight falls on the place where the chief would have sat, although Ingram had not consciously planned this effect. Natural materials are used, and the seven-paned windows were designed to diminish the use of fossil fuels.[32] The references are easy to understand, as might be expected in a project conceived in a short time using limited funds and intended for tourists as well as for Cherokees. Working for a single tribe simplified the architects' task, which becomes complicated in cities or on reservations inhabited by members of several Native nations.

Another impetus to museum foundation has been achievement of federal recognition. The Mashantucket Pequots of Connecticut, federally recognized in 1983, will build the largest and most expensive tribal museum. Polshek and Partners are the architects, Timothy Hartung and Susan Rodriguez being especially concerned with the project. It will rise on a north-facing slope near a cedar swamp surrounded by a maple forest that is laced with rocks and outcroppings, where Pequots settled in the seventeenth century. Because this band owns Foxwoods, the most successful Indian casino in the United States, it was possible to engage prominent architects, selected from a distinguished group—Kevin Roche, Antoine Predock, Douglas Cardinal*, and the Cambridge 7.

A Bicentennial grant in 1976 had funded a preliminary tribal roll of the widely scattered Pequots, and in the early 1980s HUD provided homes for some of them. They obtained federal recognition through congressional legislation in 1983,[33] after four years of planning following earlier research by graduate students and particularly by Richard Hayward*, who became tribal chairman. Knowledge of history, essential to the group's formal existence, is an important part of the museum's mission to the Pequots and also to the general public. A suit to recover lost land provided $900,000 for additions to Pequot territory, at first 214 acres and now 3072; the museum design will emphasize the terrain and afford views of it from windows and a rooftop terrace, while displays will present the results of research.

After attaining recognition, the tribal council introduced small-scale industry and businesses but not enough to make the approximately 300 Pequots self-sufficient. Prosperity came only with a high-stakes bingo hall in 1986, and then a casino. As Hayward had always been eager to have a museum—imagined at first as a 20- x 20-foot log cabin, and then as a reconstructed village—a percentage of each of the tribal enterprises was allocated to a museum fund. A more impressive museum than the one now contained in the casino's basement will help the Pequots to overcome their current image as gambling promoters.

Gambling revenue made it possible for the Pequots to have Jack Campisi and William Starna, scholars of Iroquoian peoples, accompany Hayward to other Indian museums to learn how to achieve his goal of revealing

Pequot history, values, and present condition to those who rejoined his nation and to outsiders. The museum will help Pequots "to understand what it means to be a sovereign tribal nation." It will embody expectations of tribal affiliation, for as the blood quantum is inevitably diluted, it will be increasingly essential to remember that being a Mashantucket Pequot is a "conscious decision," not merely a function of descent.[34]

In 1991, architect Tony Atkin in Philadelphia heard about the museum plans and set the museum design as a problem for a studio at the University of Pennsylvania School of Architecture.[35] The class read Kenneth Frampton's essay "Toward a Critical Regionalism" and Christian Norberg-Schulz's *Genius Loci*,[36] as well as publications about Native Americans, the Pequots in particular. They visited the reservation twice, met the residents, and learned from Kevin McBride, an authority on archaeological remains and the museum site. The students understood that the museum as a central element in the community would house many activities rather than the few surviving ancient artifacts, and they saw the museum as capable of adaptive growth. They hoped it could engender a kind of cultural self-invention—that the right form or architectural idea could become more meaningful over time as a repository for a positive cultural identity. In the absence of a usable architectural tradition, the students concentrated on stone remains of earlier occupation and on the topography, walking across the site to observe the slope, solar orientation, vegetation, and "feel," as well as the local geology and seasonal variation.

Lisa Dustin's grouping of discrete building elements suggested movement along the earth, and showed parallels between the geometry and variety in nature and those in architecture. The visitor would proceed from geometric enclosed museum elements of concrete on solid land to a more fragile and stick-like group of wooden elements as the museum extended to a viewing walkway onto the swamp near the site (142). She opened the research and scientific departments to view, providing windows from the public space into the laboratories.

Brian Johnston's design also emphasized the change from dry land toward the water, by designing part of the building in stone, and part in wood or metal. Part of his building sank within a south-facing slope where the subterranean spaces recalled archaeological trenches nearby. He spoke of his design as being related to the invention of the cultural self—one purpose of a tribal museum after centuries of cultural repression and destruction.

In Seung Bom Roh's design, a ramp descended into

142. Mashantucket Pequot museum (proposal). Lisa Dustin, 1991. (Courtesy Tony Atkin)

the site, as if to engage the topography with the architecture. He translated into metal and glass a wigwam of bent saplings that had once stood nearby. Emphasizing the visitor's first impression, Roh juxtaposed a central fireplace near the entrance with the glass wigwam cover that allowed a panoramic view outward. Farther down the slope, a rock-like lower wall anchored the building to the ground. Tribal members who attended the student presentation in May 1991 found this image immediately understandable, although University of Pennsylvania critics had found the symbolic references too obvious.

Paul Cuta recalled past occupation of the land by basing part of his design on remains of straight stone walls at angles to each other that had proved the Pequots' earlier possession of the site (143). The resulting trapezoidal spaces provided a suitable shape for an auditorium. A trellis allowed some natural light to enter the museum, while controlling its intensity. Like several others, his proposal

afforded views of the land in several directions, and allowed visitors to see the research and scientific personnel at work.

David Ashen allowed views from a tower above the museum space (144). One tribal member compared the tower favorably to a perch in a tree, from which one can see without being seen; others also admired it as an orientation point within the reservation. A short distance away, Ashen provided a round amphitheatrical meeting space, marking cardinal points and extending pointers into the natural surroundings, a feature appreciated by Pequots who foresaw a feeling of serenity in the amphitheater and a closeness to nature in that excavated space. They liked Ashen's idea of building a tunnel from the amphitheater toward the swamp, thereby connecting high and low, tower and tunnel, view and experience.

Plato Marinakos designed a building to attract the sun and to embody aspects of the calendar year important to indigenous people who live intimately with nature (145). His building was to be a kind of giant sundial, with light at the solstices entering through slots in the walls. From a modest entrance, he initiated a procession along a ramp into the land, placing the most recent parts of the Pequot story at the top, the earliest at the bottom, recalling the process of archaeological excavation but in a way different from Johnston's. An outdoor gathering area, envisioned as a kind of stage, stood between the building and the woodland beyond. His ideas for incorporating the sun and building a ramp down into history won particular approval from tribal members.

The intelligent solutions by Atkin's students could not all have been built without modifications for climate control and other considerations beyond those of their studio. The museum commission went to Polshek and Partners, which was then working on the study and storage building for the National Museum of the American Indian in Suitland, Maryland, a suburb of Washington, D.C. The tribal mandate was "to create a powerful three-dimensional image that will forever represent, validate, and celebrate the history of the Mashantucket Pequot Nation; . . . to create a structure that will respect the ecological and archaeological value of the site; [to show] the historic dependence of the tribe on both inland agricultural and aquatic zones; [and to use] the plan of the original Mystic Fort (site of the 1637 massacre [of Pequots]) as a symbol of the rebirth of the Mashantucket Pequot Nation."[37]

Susan Rodriguez spoke about the architects' desire to have the museum emerging "from the place instead of imposing our own formal preconceptions," using the "discipline that comes from the analysis of the locale, the site

143. Mashantucket Pequot museum (proposal). Paul Cuta, 1991. (Courtesy Tony Atkin)

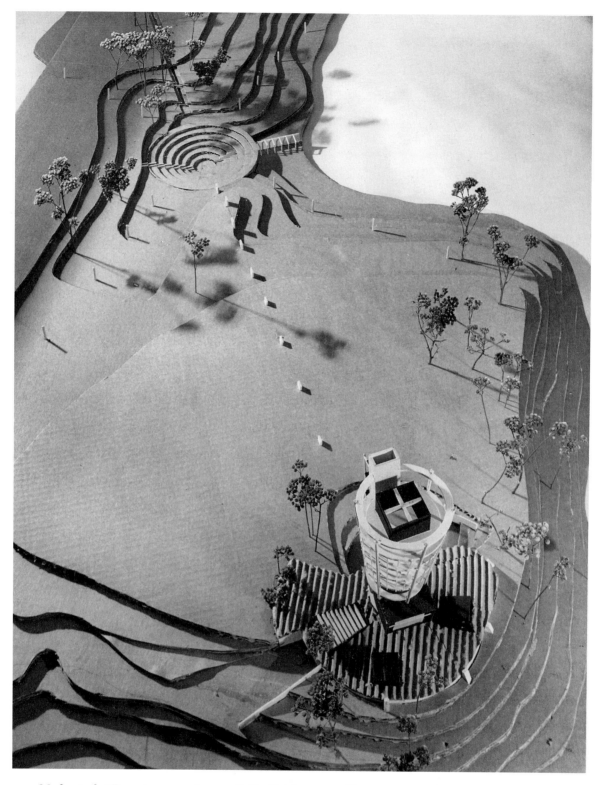

144. Mashantucket Pequot museum (proposal). David Ashen, 1991. (Courtesy Tony Atkin)

145. Mashantucket Pequot museum (proposal). Plato Marinakos, 1991. (Courtesy Tony Atkin)

as a physical thing, the program and exhibitions, circulation and movement, the formal inspiration," and other aspects of museum design. The conceptualization of their task was made more difficult because the architects were not designing the entire museum; DMCD, exhibit designers, prepared the displays to be encased by the building.

The museum envelope has roughly the form of the letter D (146). A tower marks the way to the entrance on the ground floor, near the base of the straight shaft of the D. The tower will draw attention to matters of greatest importance to the Pequots rather than to the casino. The entrance wall continues to a multistory hall faced with sloping glass; rooms for research open along it. Jutting out from the curve of the D, a library will have the world's largest collection of print and nonprint materials on Native Americans. A curved balcony will allow views back to the hallway.

The D-curve is irregular, created by a planted roof terrace designed by landscape architect Dan Kiley above exhibition areas. Glass walls in these areas afford views to the swamp. The display spaces were adjusted to make the interior plan efficient yet spacious enough to accommodate several groups visiting simultaneously, and to allow visitors an easy return to the entrance. Displays will present such subjects as Native horticulture, the making of wampum, interaction with Europeans, and the changing environment from the glacial ages to the present. Some participants suggested moving the lower exhibition area below the upper one, but then the building would have risen to urban scale, and the architects had been told to

Museums   **215**

146. Mashantucket Pequot museum (model), Ledyard, Connecticut. Polshek and Partners, 1993. (© Jack Pottle/ESTO 93JP 58:7; courtesy Polshek and Partners)

make it as low as possible. In addition, independent cores can be placed unobtrusively where they are needed in the research, entrance, and display spaces. Had different functional areas been superimposed, the cores would have intruded on exhibition areas.

Hayward wanted a space for banquets. A path will proceed upward to it, with displays placed along the way. While those who want to find symbols in buildings for Native Americans have spoken of a chambered-nautilus plan, Rodriguez says that the plan is simply a spiral. Eighty thousand square feet of exhibit space require about 12,000 feet of gathering space for what James Stewart Polshek calls "anticipation, preparation, experience, memory, decompression. You need to breathe, see the sky, after being buried in the exhibits" one flight below. An auditorium, a gift shop, a media studio and support area, archaeological study and conservation rooms, a library, offices, and a balcony-level café are other customary amenities in museums, found in this one as well.

While not visually referential to Pequot architectural tradition, about which little is known, the museum design is made specifically for its clients, who live as part of the mainstream society, yet want to emphasize their land, their history, their specific culture, and their traditions of hospitality. Because Pequots established the museum program and have final decision-making power, the museum may be seen as Pequot, however recognizable it may be as a work of late-twentieth-century architecture.

White-sponsored museums devoted wholly to Native civilizations have varied in form from the Late Renaissance Revival palace of the Museum of the American Indian in New York City to modest former Indian boarding-school buildings around the country, as at the Sherman Museum in California. As part of the New Deal, the federal government, through the Indian Arts & Crafts Board, sponsored museums in Browning, Montana; Rapid City, South Dakota; and Anadarko, Oklahoma, to display Indian cultures and to provide sales outlets for modern craft work by Native Americans. Only rarely did white-sponsored museum buildings reflect indigenous architecture, the polygonal Wheelwright Museum in Santa Fe (4) by William P. Henderson being one prominent exception; another was the pueblo-like Taylor Museum (1936) of the Colorado Fine Arts Center by John Gaw Meem. The state of California sponsored another polygonal structure reminiscent of indigenous architecture at the Chaw'Se Indian Grinding Rocks State Park using elderly Indian advisers (50).

In 1992, the Iroquois Indian Museum at Howes Cave, New York, opened (43); its functional and economical modified longhouse form was designed by C. Treat Arnold of Banwell White Arnold Hemberger & Partners, working with a museum board that included three Iroquois. It demonstrates that museums not sponsored by tribes can look as "Indian" (or more so) as those that are: Its dimensions (40 by 156 by 20 feet) double those of historical longhouses; the curved roof reflects the bent-sapling structure; the skylight is a modern variant on the smokehole; the entrance is at a rounded end, as it was in the longhouse; the exterior bands and texture are meant to recall the scale of the traditional elm-bark surface; the mezzanine is the modern replacement for the upper tier of living space in a longhouse; and the visitor flow through the museum is counter-clockwise, reflecting Iroquois tradition.

The five-story Museum of Native American Cultures, formerly the Pacific Northwest Center in Spokane, has the form of a truncated twenty-four-sided tipi made of pre-stressed concrete. It rises about 55 feet in the air, and is 76 feet in diameter at its base. The plan seemed useful for directing circulation, with visitors descending from the top level to see displays of various Native cultures on each floor; besides, some tribes in the areas used tipis as well as longhouses. Father Wilfred Schoenberg, S.J., and Euro-Americans Jerry Pelletier and Richard Lewis promoted this museum, aided by loans of artifacts owned by Gonzaga University and a gift of land from the local railway company. Despite this help, the museum, initiated in 1966, could be completed only in 1974 after money was given in connection with the World's Fair held in Spokane.[38]

Today, however, most museums wholly devoted to Native American culture are conceived and built by tribes, individually or in collaboration with other compatible Native groups. When they turn to outside consultants, the clients direct their activity. The Alabama–Coushatta decided as early as 1963 "to get into cultural exhibition" and built a round shingled wooden museum to hold tribal members' collections. The Texas State Indian Commission assisted by administering the facility and paying for an architect to expand it around 1970, when new storage space was needed. The facility was then enlarged to include a gift shop, a "living Indian village" with craft demonstrations and dances, and an educational center. Architect Barry Moore toured comparable facilities with Roland Poncho*, the tribal cultural program manager, and with the council chairman, then a Euro-American. Moore "would have welcomed design direction, but...didn't get any, so [he] did some research in the Smithsonian Institution concerning the racial origins and archaeology and the artifacts. [He] created an architectural vocabulary and a palette of colors based on pottery and crafts. It turned out colorful and woodland; they lived in the woods....It was artificial, but [he] had looked it up....[His firm] got design awards for this."[39]

The village entrance is reached along a line of rectilinear wooden portals. Beyond it are the dodecagonal log council house (34), with a skylight over the central fire and benches in four tiers; an amphitheater in which evocations of dwellings are seen behind the seats and allusions to a ritual dance floor and sacred building on a mound are evident; a hotel decorated with clan banners and ornaments, including the double-headed woodpecker motif; and buildings housing turtles, alligators, and snakes, each identified by a stylized motif based on carved shellwork.

Changes from old norms are also caused by the special nature of most tribally sponsored museums. The range in architectural design extends from original and symbolic forms to updated traditional structures, representing varied desires and possibilities. Some museums are unobtrusive local vernacular buildings, while others reflect the sentiments of one participant in a symposium on Indian museums held in 1974: "We want to be unique. We don't want the typical white man's thing that they can see in New York," nor did they want "a contemporary cement and steel longhouse."[40]

Tribally sponsored museums often do not focus only on art (sometimes thought of as craft work), nor do they concentrate solely on ethnography and history. Instead, they combine museum types. The Makah called their museum a Cultural Research Center (36) to underline the fact that its main goal is not to be an exhibition space for tourists. Frequently the focus of displays—as at Lac du Flambeau in Wisconsin (80), at Warm Springs in Oregon (40–42), and at the Yakima Nation Museum in Washington (39)—is on a central diorama or reconstructed traditional building, often with mannequins showing aspects of daily life. Display cases nearby present especially fine examples of tribal arts such as beading and quillwork, so that aesthetic achievements are integrated spatially and visually with ethnographic presentations. This method of display is based on that of natural history museums, but the differences include the greater emphasis in Native American museums on aesthetic achievement of high quality, and the likelihood that the central diorama will not be separated from the public by glass.

It is also common in tribal museums, as in ethnographic ones, to show old photographs of the reservation and its inhabitants in order to connect past and present. Small museums place historic photographs near artifacts depicted in them, integrating the images with the other displays. Plaques and portraits identify current tribal officials. Recent examples of fine artistry are often shown close to older ones, to demonstrate the continuity and adaptability of traditional practices. Rarely does one find a label that seems to apologize for changes made to older art forms, although such labels used to be common in other museums and in books. Awareness is developing that change is not necessarily bad, that new times require new evaluative criteria, and that even tourist arts reflect ingenuity and adaptability as well as intelligence in understanding a market,[41] as do the commercial arts of couturiers and designers of art glass. The great Giambattista Piranesi was, after all, printmaker for eighteenth-century tourists in Rome.

A good many tribal museums are not professionally directed and lack sophisticated design strategies. Handsome display materials of the kind seen in metropolitan museums might be unwelcome, even if they were affordable. Most tribal museums aim at the Native population primarily, even if most visitors are outsiders, so that a familiar interior may represent a conscious choice, not just necessity. In addition, elegance usually requires selectivity, and the aim in tribally sponsored museums may be inclusivity. Where museum interiors are particularly handsome, the directors may hope to suggest to tribal members and outsiders that the local population is as advanced (by Anglo standards) as any other.

The Suquamish Museum (37) and the Indian Pueblo Cultural Center (67) achieve an unobtrusive blend of pleasant modern design, comfort, familiarity, and information. This is the ambition of the Agua Caliente Band of Cahuilla Indians in Palm Springs, California. They have as yet no building plan, but they do have an idea—a wish to foster knowledge of their own culture, "for without this, we will lose everything," and to promote awareness of their people among other local groups. They cannot duplicate their traditional impermanent architecture, nor will they demand particular shapes. They have adopted the city's building codes. But their museum, envisioned as having 25,000 square feet, and a small amphitheater near it, must blend with the environment and must house and explain objects, leaving room for demonstrations and participatory events. Elders will teach crafts and the Cahuilla language. Hunter Johnson of American Development Consultants has recently drawn an initial site plan, but additional work will depend on obtaining authorization from the band and outside funding.[42]

Many Native American museums have interior arrangements that seem independent of the surrounding architectural shell. This may be due to the sponsors' inexperience in supervising architectural projects or to the architects' lack of sensitivity. It is more likely to reflect the slow process of design caused by pauses in funding, by changes of tribal administration and direction, by unforeseen problems, or by simple lack of concern about coordination of inside and out. The exterior may be designed to give an instantaneous message to passersby and to make a strong statement about the culture and tradition to visitors, tribal or not; the interior may be intended for slower contemplation, or may have required economizing if the shell's cost rose unexpectedly high (39–42, 67, 84–87, 95–96, 119–120, 142–147).

Two dramatic buildings by the Hopi artist and architect Dennis Numkena* incorporate his favored solid geo-

147. Camp Verde Visitor Center, Montezuma Castle National Monument, Camp Verde, Arizona. Dennis Numkena*, 1971; opened 1981.

metric shapes and towers that connect earth and sky, as ladders do in a kiva.[43] Both were intended to draw tourists, and that may explain the unusual and striking forms used. At Pyramid Lake, Nevada, the conical form might evoke a tipi along with the kiva ladder, if it were not for the massive and stable surfacing of artistically chosen local stones that fix what might be called a curved pyramid permanently on the reservation land (119, 120). Tribal officials decline to explain why the Pyramid Lake building stands incomplete and vandalized.

The Camp Verde Visitor Center (147) was a joint venture of the National Park Service and the Yavapai Apache, intended as a tribal cultural facility but now temporarily operated by supervisors of the Montezuma Castle National Monument. The building owes its existence to intense lobbying by the tribe and to Senator Barry Goldwater's posi-

tive response. It was intended to provide construction jobs for the Yavapai and then to be a continuing base of economic activity. Softly tinted angular prisms nestle at the base of two towers, like refined boulders tumbled from an ancient structure. The building "stresses earthbound geometrical symbolism of buildings" rather than a specific historic style, which the Yavapai never had. The walls lean inward at 7.5 and 10 degrees, suggesting the battered walls of pueblos without any attempt to imitate buildings of non-Yavapai cultures. One tower has a ladderlike succession of rectangles within it, while the other houses the office of the director of this facility (because the Park Service considered it wasteful to have an unoccupied five-story tower space).[44]

Tribes that hope for tourists but do not go to great lengths to attract them, or tribes that have never succeeded in raising enough money for more dramatic designs, employ more modest but perhaps equally meaningful strategies to make their museums and cultural centers appropriate; examples include those for the Seneca, Bad River Band, and Salt River Pima–Maricopa. To attract visitors, they rely on putting up highway signs, advertising in local newspapers, and developing cordial relations with local chambers of commerce and tourism authorities. Their continuing success will depend on increasing curatorial knowledge and developing expertise in financial management, administration, and marketing among members of both staff and boards of directors; there must also develop a new tradition of volunteer activity.[45]

* * *

It is too early to tell whether the imaginative and unusual buildings emphasized here will become standards by which "true" Native American museums are defined in the architectural press and history books. Distinctive—and often large—buildings tend to be the ones to define a culture, but that kind of definition may prove to be irrelevant to Indian museums, given the multiplicity and fundamental differences among Native American groups.

15

Gambling Halls

Bingo: The New Buffalo
Casinos: The Indians' Revenge

Surprisingly enough, those bumper sticker phrases are all about Native American legal status and self-determination. Most of what proponents call "gaming" establishments on Indian reservations are inaugurated with statements about the benefits that casino profits will bring to tribal members—jobs for heads of families, training for young people, improved nutrition for children and the elderly, and other life-sustaining activities. The casino offers today's means to traditional ends, if we imagine a student machinist or croupier trainee as an apprentice buffalo-hunter. And since most of the gambling is done by Anglos, at least monetary revenge is exacted from descendants of the Indians' old enemies.

The history of Indian-owned gambling establishments is a brief one. Native peoples played traditional games of chance with bones, sticks, and other aids, but it was only when the Seminoles in Florida introduced larger-scale gambling attractive to outsiders that anyone paid attention to games of chance on Indian lands. State and local officials tried to regulate or stop them,[1] but in 1980, the decision in *Seminole Tribe* v. *Butterworth* prevented the sheriff of Broward County from acting on behalf of the state to halt gambling on Indian property. Because Florida permitted and regulated bingo elsewhere—that is, playing bingo

in Florida did not violate state policy—Florida had to allow it, free of state control, on Seminole territory. Seven years later, after five years of litigation, *California* v. *Cabazon and Morongo Bands of Mission Indians* came before the United States Supreme Court, which affirmed the ruling in Florida on behalf of a few dozen Native people. The court further held that although PL 83-280 of 1953 automatically delegated civil and criminal jurisdiction over most Indian reservation activities to certain states, including California, states had no authority to regulate gambling on reservations; moreover, under the Indian Civil Rights Act of 1968, states had to conduct special elections to obtain Indian consent to state assumptions of jurisdiction.

Indian-run bingo nights and lotteries then increased. In response to state pressure for some regulation of these activities, in 1988 Congress passed PL 100-497, the Indian Gaming Regulatory Act (IGRA). Its declared purposes included "promoting tribal economic development, self-sufficiency, and strong tribal governments"[2] as well as creating federal regulatory authority. The IGRA created three classes of gambling, with Class I—traditional native games played for low stakes—left entirely in Indian hands. Class II includes bingo, lotto, and pull-tabs; Class III, all other games—those played in casinos, parimutuel bets, those played on video terminals, and lotteries. If any Class III games are permitted in a state, all games in that category may be offered at Indian casinos. That makes it potentially profitable to invest large sums in building casinos. In 1993, between 2 and 3 percent of all legal gambling in the United States was conducted under tribal auspices.[3]

For regulation of Class II and III games, tribes collaborate with the National Indian Gaming Commission, an entity created by Congress to approve tribal ordinances and management contracts. The BIA is also involved, as it places into trust land for gambling purposes, supervises equipment leasing and service contracts, and enters into compacts to govern Class III operations. The compacts set rules about jurisdiction and the application and enforcement of laws in each state where Class III games are permitted on lands owned by federally recognized tribes. In order to open a legal casino, a tribe must negotiate a compact with the state, but by June 1993, tribes had filed lawsuits against sixteen states that procrastinated about negotiations.[4]

There are special reasons for the efflorescence of Class II and III establishments on Indian lands. Poor roads and transportation facilities on remote, barren reservations and problems in recruiting workers make most industries reluctant to establish operations there. Unemployment among Native people is therefore shockingly high, and on most reservations, much of the employment has been tied to government work or to education and health-care programs rather than to a diversified economic base.[5] Trust lands are hard to mortgage for start-up capital. Tribal officials may make it hard to get permits for outsiders to open businesses, especially small ones that do not employ many people immediately.[6] A job must pay more than the usual minimum wage to attract workers who might otherwise receive public assistance along with auxiliary benefits. Then, too, a Native American is no different from any other American who disdains dead-end, repetitive, minimum-wage labor as a perennial underling, on the rare occasions when such work is even available on reservations. Senator John McCain of Arizona put it succinctly: "One of the tragedies is that more acceptable businesses refuse to locate on Indian land. So what do the reservations get? Gaming and waste sites."[7]

Because they have their own traditional games of chance, Native groups, even traditionally oriented ones, understand gambling better than they do certain other activities, according to anthropologist Nancy O. Lurie.[8] Peterson Zah*, chairman of the Navajo Nation, says that "gambling is a part of Navajo culture," and Arapaho architectural designer Dennis Sun Rhodes* agrees.[9] Special prizes and enticements can be seen as giveaways, traditional acts of generosity and status-earning.[10] Gambling draws outsiders to spend money on the reservations, as they normally do not for any reason other than some tourism. Gambling may also be important as a symbol of independence, because the BIA and other government agencies have relatively little to do with it.[11]

Indian gambling establishments provide many jobs that pay more than the minimum wage, and these employers do not discriminate in hiring. Jobs are also generated in building construction, logging, and milling. The Winnebago planned a casino in 1994 to be built by tribal contractors using lumber from the reservation's mill. The Bad River casino, built of logs by local men, is another example of coordinated employment policy.[12] In several tribes, large-scale gambling operations have virtually eliminated unemployment, which had stood at about 45 percent among the Mille Lacs Band of Ojibwe and about 60 percent among the Oneida. At the Fort McDowell Reservation in Arizona, unemployment fell from 30 percent to 5 percent while the casino was in operation.[13] At Leech Lake in Minnesota, 70 percent were jobless in 1989 but fewer than 30 percent in 1994, the gaming operations having trebled in those five years.[14] Several casinos offer flexible schedules that attract some Indians as well as other workers. Hundreds of Anglos in Connecticut, Minnesota, and elsewhere have jobs in Native American–owned casinos;[15] collaboration at work forms a bridge between Native Americans and others that is otherwise often hard to construct.

In a short time, revenue is generated for tribes or individuals to use locally, assisting regional economies. Although most tribes discourage their members from gambling, no doubt some Indians welcome the casinos as exciting places where they may "get rich quick" without doing anything illegal. Widespread Native American opinion is summarized by Fred Dakota*, chairman of the Keweenaw Bay Band in Michigan. "We used to hear gambling was bad," he said, "that we should stick to the tourism business. Well, we've been standing along the side of the highway selling blankets for a long time. It has not helped. Casinos have been a godsend."[16]

As of December 1993, seventy-nine tribes in nineteen states had completed compacts with their states.[17] The prudent tribes put the money in trust, in order to build schools, water tanks, sewer systems, roads, clinics, and daycare and senior centers, or to invest in reservation-based businesses and college scholarships.[18] Some tribes have had to build new bingo halls, while others have made do with existing spaces for Class II gambling, but Class III operations have almost always required new construction, some of it financed by federally guaranteed loans obtained through the BIA. Casinos with the greatest range of activities are arranged by gambling business consultants.

Studies conducted in Michigan and Wisconsin under tribal auspices and in Minnesota by KMPG Peat Marwick suggest that local employment increased, seasonal unemployment and crime decreased, while welfare outlays declined among Native people although they rose statewide. Tax revenues increased because off-reservation facilities for or related to gambling are not tax-exempt. Services rendered to their members by the tribes increased dramatically—the Royal River casino yielding per capita payments, a retrofitted house for disabled occupants, youth programs including job training, services to latchkey children, contributions to the public schools, summer programs for children, sports facilities, and so on.[19] It is no wonder that Rosebud chairman Alex Lunderman* looked forward to gambling: "In 1987...we had 93 percent unemployed. With construction and building a hospital it dropped down to 90 percent. What is going to happen like it done for other tribes, is the casino—even if it's temporary—is going to create employment....It is a band-aid on the sore. It gives us a chance to get to the sore."[20]

Many tribal members are, however, uneasy about relying on gambling for employment and revenue. The fact that most of the casinos are not designed to "look Indian" may reflect the wish to separate the source of the helpful money from other visual manifestations of tribal identity. Some, such as the traditional chiefs of the Grand Council of the Iroquois Confederacy, oppose negotiation of gambling compacts.[21] Richard Hill* even recalled that in 1799 Handsome Lake*, the Seneca prophet, foresaw that gambling would destroy the Iroquois Nation.[22] Senecas on the Cattaraugus Reservation shut down the tribe's filling station to protest the opening of a gambling facility that they feared would breed crime.[23] Some Pine Ridge Lakota oppose gambling on philosophical and economic grounds. Joe Swift Bird* of the reservation's Grey Eagle Society has said, "Alcohol and gambling is not for the Indians." His associates say that they do not gamble with anything because everything is sacred.[24]

Native Americans often defend having to resort to the modern buffalo by pointing out that "not one single bureaucrat came up with a solution to the survival of the Indian people when the budget axes of the 1980s" created serious economic problems.[25] In speaking of plans for a

gambling facility meant to generate investment capital for his tribe, Richard LaFramboise*, chairman of the Turtle Mountain Chippewa in North Dakota, said, "I don't believe that gaming is the only avenue in which a community hopes to obtain funds. But it does give some foundation to our capabilities."[26] Julia A. Davis*, Nez Perce vice chairwoman, pointing out that her people had "no common resource base," asked, "What else can we do?"[27] Commenting on the Cow Creek Umpqua Casino, the tribal chairwoman, Susan Shaffer*, asserted that "we have pulled ourselves up from nothing." Former Arizona Supreme Court judge Frank X. Gordon, mediator in a dispute over gambling on several reservations, was shocked by the Tohono O'odham standard of living and observed that

none of the tribes would favor gambling as its primary resource if other sources of revenue were available. Yet the tribes see the opportunities under the [gambling law] as being the only ones left to them which will provide a jump start to give them the money to provide a higher level of quality education to their young and old so that they can compete in the Anglo economic world, to preserve their cultures, and to fulfill the most basic needs of housing and health care to their people.[28]

Increasing numbers of Native Americans see gambling as a short-term solution and hope to amass enough capital to invest in infrastructure, education, and conventional businesses against the day when wealthier rivals or antagonistic legislators take revenge for the "Indians' revenge." The hope invested in casinos can be seen in a ceremony held at the Heard Museum in Phoenix after eight tribes in Arizona signed gaming compacts with the state on June 24, 1993; participants offered traditional prayers and music for the occasion. The Indian gaming subcommittee of the National Congress of American Indians, formed in 1993, was to be "directed solely by tradition and consensus by elected tribal leadership," so as to encourage contributions from all participants—thus lending some indigenous character to these political deliberations.[29]

Nevertheless, threats to Indian gambling abound. Even Anthony Hope, when chairman of the three-member National Indian Gaming Commission, envisioned a twenty- to twenty-five-year life span for most Indian gambling; competition from other tribes and from expanded Anglo gambling may halt the increase that he saw continuing until about 1997.[30] Gambling operations and racing interests lobby against competitive Indian casinos, especially in nearby states; this is true even though a few large companies in Nevada began consulting businesses to advise tribal gambling enterprises. Donald Trump, casino entrepreneur in Atlantic City, lobbied against federal recognition of the Ramapough Tribe, lest it become entitled to open competitive casinos in New Jersey.[31] Religious groups and others morally opposed to games of chance try to influence legislators to ban gambling, even if it means diminished revenues for local churches. Sometimes tribal members oppose the casinos because they fear gambling addiction and family breakdown, resent payments to the tribe rather than to individuals, or fear risking tribal sovereignty through making compacts that give states new jurisdictional rights.[32] One opponent states that casino operators—whites and people of mixed ancestry—"are using the White 'Indians' as a front to maintain their gaming monopoly." He believes that "the U.S. Government is using the Indian Casinos" to help "support the 1934 I.R.A. [Indian Reorganization Act] Governments established as puppets" by "entrench[ing] their Indians on Aboriginal Indigenous People's land."[33] Oneidas in New York State burned their own bingo hall in 1985, apparently suspecting that gambling revenue was enriching certain politicians and their families. The same suspicion was related to an armed assault by 140 Winnebago in one political group on a tribal bingo hall in 1991, followed by arson and a shootout in early 1992.[34]

Because a mediator allowed five tribes in Arizona to have far more gambling machines than state officials wanted, Governor Fife Symington signed a bill in 1993 prohibiting all forms of gambling, ostensibly for the sake of "protecting our quality of life and balancing that with the needs of the Indians"[35]—needs that appear to have been ignored at other times. Governors and states' attorneys general, acting through their professional associations, have expressed dissatisfaction with the IGRA, which they see as infringing on states' rights by inserting casinos within state borders.[36] Antigambling bills have been introduced in Congress by members supposedly concerned about inroads by organized crime in Indian and other casinos, and Iowa's legislators proposed to allow so much competition that the state's three Indian casinos offered to pay the state $10 million a year to eliminate the threat.[37] Senator Daniel Inouye, considered a friend of the Indians, supported changes to the IGRA that Native Americans saw as infringing on their sovereignty.[38]

Outside observers, including the *Economist*, emphasized financial scandal and murder resulting from corrupt gambling operations, even though Senator Thomas Daschle of South Dakota said that "tribal gaming operations are well managed and handled very professionally," and Inspector General James Richards, in his report to the Department of the Interior in 1992, found that the tribes themselves had discovered most cases of fraud and corruption perpetrated by consultants and suppliers.[39] The tribes had every reason to want to keep maximal revenue, and every incentive to keep gambling clean enough to withstand efforts to end it. The Gaming Commission has not reviewed all management contracts, however, and the Gaming Enforcement Division of the Minnesota Department of Public Safety has only three investigators to check 11,000 video machines at seventeen casinos.[40]

Nevertheless, despite some internal opposition and a good deal of inner discomfort with the idea of prospering through gambling, Native nations continue to use the major economic lever available to them. Occasionally, tribes are even willing to commission buildings for gambling that incorporate aspects of local architectural or ornamental tradition, as if to acknowledge the economic importance of the activities conducted inside.

* * *

The form of an Indian gambling establishment is usually a simple shed with walls. It is convenient to have a porch in front where arriving car passengers may alight under its shelter or wait to be picked up. On the porch or in its pediment may be a logo, while the casino's name is likely to be on a large freestanding sign or on a broad stretch of the building's wall, in either case easily visible from the road. Inside, there are defined areas for various games, for financial transactions, for food consumption, and for toilets and rest facilities. Class II games are normally held in plain rooms filled with tables arranged in monotonous rows, where players spread their bingo cards and look up to the master of ceremonies' platform. Class III games are conducted usually on one floor, although two-story casinos exist.

Most casinos are still little more than sheds with some ornament to break up the bulk of large contained spaces. The buildings may be surrounded by plants or a berm, as at the proposed Eastern Shawnee bingo and community hall (13) and the Tulalip wood-surfaced "entertainment center" at Marysville, Washington, where the tribe approved landscaping rather than additional parking spaces. Wood-post and thin truss construction, silhouettes of trees in the lobby, exhibits of historic artifacts, and tribal colors refer to things important to Tulalip officials.[41] Prairie Knights, the Standing Rock Tribe's facility, has a mural in the main circular room showing "the Hunkpapa and their relationship to the land," including petroglyph records, flowing rivers, buttes, and building tipis; the carpets have Indian motifs.[42] While the nature-referential embellishments may reflect the Native American connection to Mother Earth, few claims are made for the "Indianness" of most casinos.

Fortune Bay Casino in Minnesota, owned by the Bois Forte Band of Ojibwe, has a more restrained design (148). It was completed in 1986 by the Hibbing office of Architectural Resources. It is in fact located at Everette's Bay on Lake Vermilion, but the word "Fortune," taken from a nearby site, seemed better for a bingo and off-track-betting hall.

The approach leads through woods, and the architects created a site plan with a meandering path in order to avoid cutting down more than a few of the local red pines. One member of the design team spoke of maintaining trees "to respect the concern for the preservation of wilderness." Although other team members recall receiving few suggestions from the clients, the firm had previously worked on Native American commissions and had learned about traditional thought. Because they understood the circle as "an organic form that reflects the Indian view of the universe and nature," they made the main hall a quarter circle, conceived the roofline as a curve referring to "round birch bark huts," and incorporated circles as windows, in screens along the side walls, and in a quarter-circle skylight. Connections to nature appear in the wood siding and a Douglas fir ceiling over the main hall that continues outside to the ground, a glass elevator that affords views of the landscape, and the sheathing of the main hall in river-rock textured precast concrete. Earth tones were used in several places, but the general effect of the casino is colorful, with red facade and cornice accents, purple trusses, and blue side panels on the exterior and even mauve exposed ducts indoors. These colors and the designs of chair backs are based on beadwork, a major tribal art form. As with many other recent buildings for Native American clients, this one may be read either as an attractive contemporary structure or as specifically Native architecture embodying whatever Ojibwe ideas could be logically incorporated into the program.[43]

The references to tradition are strong, although not obvious, at the Bad River Ojibwe casino near Odanah, Wisconsin, because the rectilinear log building with a pitched roof is of the same generic form as local vernacular wooden buildings of all types, including others for the tribe. Local tradition, materials, and manpower are emphasized, because, as planner Richard Ackley* put it, the tribe wanted to build something of its own. Tribal youth

148. Fortune Bay Casino, Everette's Bay, Minnesota. Architectural Resources, 1986. (John Peterson Photography [Minnesota])

in training for the construction trades erected two log buildings convertible into a small casino. No one wanted either outside management or outside architects. Ackley considers architects to be either conventional thinkers, able to produce only standard, efficient buildings of no visual distinction, or people interested in glamorous design "who try to rip off the tribes." That is why he employed an interior designer who offered only "visualization of the potential," leaving the Native people to "try to make our own decisions."

The small casino is, then, the product of local decision-making and labor, an authentic expression of the tribal will. It is identifiably Indian more because of that than because of distinctive appearance, for the main visible references to Native American life are designs of buffalo and other traditional images incised at the junction of supports and beams inside the casino. Both the Four Winds Casino, planned in 1993 for the western edge of the

Pine Ridge Reservation, and the Oneida bingo hall near the airport in Green Bay, Wisconsin, are similar to the Bad River building in being wooden, with pitched roofs, rectilinear but with projecting elements to avoid monotony. Four Winds will have large windows in the restaurant as a foil to the enclosed casino. This establishment changed its name to Prairie Wind, so as not to offend traditions regarded as sacred.[44]

In his office at Sand Springs, Oklahoma, Ray Byron Frogge, Jr., drew preliminary designs for bingo halls for the Chickasaw and Eastern Shawnee tribes, cleverly emphasizing the inevitable angles of his shed buildings as though they were willed elements of the design; the buildings evoke the manner of his teachers, Bruce Goff and Mendel Glickman, both formerly associated with Frank Lloyd Wright. To distinguish the Chickasaw facility from large Anglo structures, the architect incorporated local stone at corners and angles of the facade, and introduced glazed oriels in the vestibule. Windows are rare in Anglo casinos, but increasingly common in new Indian ones. For the Eastern Shawnee, Frogge employed patterns and colors favored in their crafts, enlivening a low-cost building (13).

Slightly closer to traditional architecture are plans made in 1994 by Dennis Holloway for Pojoaque Pueblo's casino, to be called Cities of Gold, as if to evoke the myths that tempted the Spanish conquistadors. There is to be a kind of rebuilt pueblo, but with a dome over it. It will extend over 1 acre and cover a circular and a rectangular building. Between the buildings will be a 14-ton soapstone buffalo, designed by George Rivera*, a Pojoaque artist. Around the walls of the principal circular space will be the overlapping planes that one would see in a pueblo. This is a design as persuasive as a film set and, like one, it is a background for entertainment.

A tipi motif appears in renderings published in 1993 of the Dakota 7 Family Entertainment Center, designed by the Sisseton-Wahpeton Dakota Cultural Affairs Committee working with John Kasterowicz of JKA Architects, a firm in Los Angeles experienced in theme-park design. The number 7 was supposedly chosen because it represents the number of council fires (clan groups) among the Sisseton-Wahpeton. The design, now replaced, showed a rectilinear casino concealed from the approach road by immense tipis of permanent materials, raised on high arches over the treetop level of a garden. The tipis were to be painted with designs of buffalo, birds, stripes, and other Native patterns. In this case, the tipis were not building enclosures but signposts to attract passing drivers.[45]

More utilitarian in concept are the Lac Courte Oreilles Band of Lake Superior Chippewa casino in Wisconsin and the Turning Stone Casino for the Oneida of New York, both of which opened in mid-1993. The former was designed as a rectangle so that it could be turned into an office building if gambling failed.[46] The Oneida casino was built before the tribe and state agreed on a compact, so the tribe asked David Smotrich, the architect, to design a building that could be used as a shopping mall if the compact were not made final.[47]

More than practicality went into the Oneida design (112). The tribe settled a court case and won land back for the first time in two centuries, having seen its historic homelands reduced to a mere 32 acres in the recent past. When the Oneida recovered the 200 acres, "they wanted to treat it the right way. From day one, respect for the land was first on their mind." As the casino site had been a farm with exhausted soil, it was seen as a business property. A museum would not be appropriate there because Ray Halbritter*, a tribal leader, believed that a museum belonged at the core of the reservation, near the children who were to be its most important visitors. Smotrich's preliminary master plan therefore included the casino–shopping mall.

After a rigorous environmental audit that was not required of a sovereign nation but that "respected nature,... complied with all the environmental laws and the New York State code, respected the wetlands as much as possible," and used only 35 of the 200 acres, Smotrich designed a low structure with a central glazed and arched corridor, meant to look as though it were growing out of a berm or a local hill. The raised land comes from excavation on the site, and it protects the building from water now channeled into a stream and pond around the casino. Wildflowers and trees dot the site. A restaurant overlooks the pond. Inside are windows and skylights, discomfiting at first to managers unused to them, but pleasing to them now. Because Standing Stone, a historic symbol, was not acceptable as the name of a casino, something close but inoffensive was adopted, and large "stones" designed by an artist named DiGiacomo are set up at the entrance to the property and inside the lobby; the one outdoors turns, propelled by a motor. The interior is open and spacious, light and pleasant, its walls lined with outstanding graphics by Chermayeff Associates showing appropriate motifs such as card suites. The most remarkable expression of concern for Native values here is the absence of alcoholic beverages, as Halbritter and others understand well their dangers for Native people and others. Revenues are not paid per capita, but are directed toward a medical program, housing, scholarships, and community building projects.

Windows and a small museum are the most remarkable features of Foxwoods, the Mashantucket Pequot casino near Ledyard, Connecticut. The tribe, nearly obliterated in 1637, retained its identity and was recognized by the Mashantucket Pequot Indian Land Claims Settlement in October 1983.[48] This enabled the Pequots to add to their land. Finding the local job base insufficient, the Tribal Council decided in 1983 and 1984 to offer high-stakes bingo starting in 1986, and negotiated a compact with the state's reluctant governor. The large Foxwoods Casino opened in late 1991 and is now the most profitable Native-owned casino in the country. By 1993, the Pequots agreed to contribute $100 million annually to improve Connecticut's cities and towns if no non-Indian gambling is allowed in the state.[49]

New England Design of Mansfield, Connecticut, designed windows to allow views outdoors. "The land is everything," said Terry Bell*, director of the tribe's Cultural Resources Department. "If you lose the land, you lose yourself."[50] References to nature include a grotto of artificial stone with a waterfall cascading over the rocks into a pool, plastic leaves replacing capitals at the tops of structural pillars, and stained-glass inserts in ceiling trusses that show the state's native plants. More seriously, the tribe obtained the most environmentally sensitive systems despite their higher cost. Respect for the Pequots' heritage was displayed "when the water line to the casino was discovered to be in the path of ancient tribal encampments.... It was rerouted."[51] Slow Turtle*, a spiritual healer from Cape Cod, blessed the building at its inauguration.

To be sure, Foxwoods looks much like other casinos, and Thomas Hine, architecture critic for the *Philadelphia Inquirer*, understood why that had to be the case, however sincere the intent to make this one different from the hermetic spaces of Nevada and Atlantic City: "Gambling is about alienation... impatient, self-absorbed, out of tune with any sense of natural harmony."[52] It is also about generating money, an abstraction different from the naturally derived goods produced and traded by the Pequots' ancestors.

Nevertheless, the casino contains features that remind visitors of its distinctive owners. A small museum room presents such information on Pequot history as is available. It contains a replica of a wigwam. Geometric ornament here and there alludes to arrowheads and circles. Small rectangular designs evoking wampum belts adorn cornices. When Pequots found a casino motif too close in design to a belt found in a tribal grave, the design was changed to avoid offending the spirits of a long-dead ancestor. Paintings and prints on Indian themes by Native American artists hang on many walls and are for sale. A urethane sculpture of the "Rainmaker" shows a large "brave who shoots a laser arrow into the heavens,"[53] bringing tradition up to date.

At its best, the mixture of Indian elements has to do with more than commerce, although the cocktail waitresses' pink and teal fringed minidresses have only to do with commerce. But while other casinos and their managers "think in terms of quarterly profits and annual results, they [Pequots] really think in terms of the millennium."[54] The casino is meant to finance the taking of additional local land into trust, and to pay for the much larger museum discussed in Chapter 14 that is now being built to the design of Polshek and Partners. Profits will also pay for housing, scholarships, health care, business investments, and community improvements.

Native America's second most profitable casino is the most assertively "Indian" of all casinos built so far. Operated by the Shakopee Mdewakanton Dakota of Prior Lake, Minnesota, Mystic Lake Casino opened in May 1992 (149, 150). Very large for an Indian facility at 135,000 square feet, and with a 240,000-square-foot addition built a year later, it features a circular casino with 1000 slot machines and numerous tables for blackjack, preceding a semicircular bingo hall holding 1100 seats; there are also restaurants, shops, a beauty parlor, and banquet rooms.

The distinctiveness of this casino is not due to its size, but to a set of searchlights. Twelve "high-powered, computer controlled spotlights crown the main circular shape forming the lodgepoles of a Dakota teepee... visible for up to 30 miles, beckoning guests to experience Mystic Lake. At rest, the lights return to form a teepee... reaching for the sky... sheltering the casino" (150).[55]

The architect, Paul Pink of Minneapolis, and the tribal clients included Indian references whenever possible, although they "were trying to be sensitive, to isolate the cultural symbolism from the religious symbolism" because of the inappropriateness of mixing religion and roulette. A brochure issued at the time of the casino's opening connected acceptable symbols and forms to gambling. The casino's logo, for instance, incorporates the tree, which "symbolizes the environmental concerns" of the operating company and all other Indians. "With the addition of the quarter moon, it lends the aura of

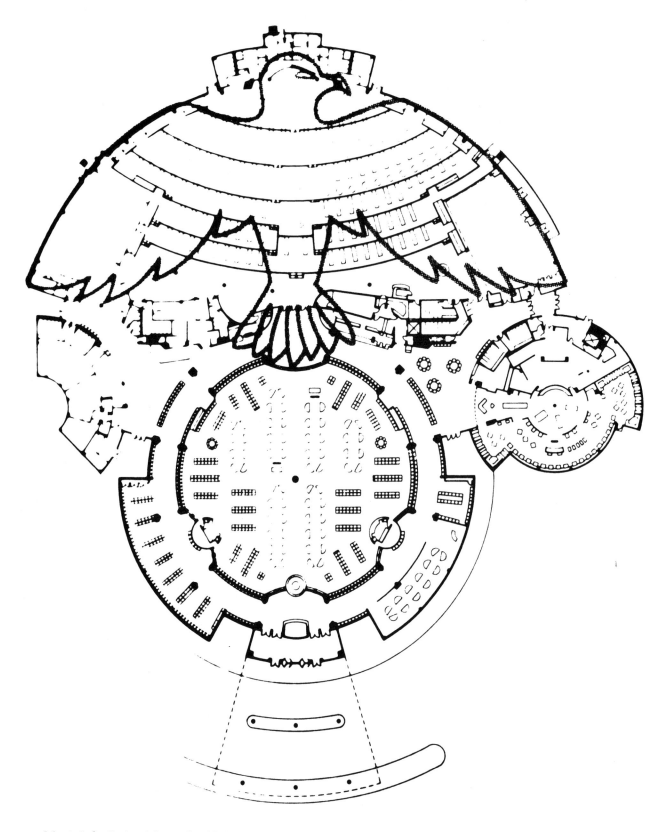

149. Mystic Lake Casino (plan with added symbolic animal), Prior Lake, Minnesota. Paul Pink Architecture, 1992. (Courtesy Leonard Prescott, Little Six)

night, the excitement of evening entertainment," while a diamond, "the gaming industry, a platform from which to launch other economic ventures...is also a vital representation of the repeating pattern of four" sides, seasons, directions, "and even four ages in life." Near the entrance, water, the life-giver, is embodied in a fountain surmounted by Roger Brodin's sculpture *Water Spirit Woman*, because "Mystic Lake Casino is dedicated to Indian women and Mother Earth." She is surrounded by turtles, "traditional symbols of fertility and productivity." The element of fire is evoked by a 22-foot-high "waterfall chandelier" in the main room, where the lights are said to summon everyone to the center of a room ringed by supports, as a fire welcomes Indians to the center of a circle of tipi poles. A sloping floor in the bingo hall makes that

space reach "upward to the sky and downward to the earth, completing the remaining two cardinal points" found earlier in the diamond.

The insistent symbolism pervades the plan, a circle that "invites all to join the unbroken Circle of Life...oriented to the four compass points." When speaking of the genesis of the plan, Paul Pink said that "the casino is really 'form follows function.' The form started out to incorporate the circle and the four compass points and the six cardinal points....This was a very conscious effort to bring the Indian culture into the building." The four compass points also symbolize the four seasons, "so vital in arcadian times," which are represented in nearly life-size murals by Al White*. No matter that Arcady is evoked in a building inconceivable there, and that aboriginal Native life is

150. **Mystic Lake Casino at night.** (© Bob Perzel [Lakeville, Minnesota], 1993)

more likely to have been demanding than arcadian, for as Pink says, the power of suggestion soon took hold and forms began to suggest themselves as they do in a Rohrschach test.

The circular room is "only the third circular casino in the world"; Caesar's Palace in Las Vegas comes to mind, and Pink was in Las Vegas working on some retail stores when he got the invitation to submit ideas to the tribe. The circle is "divided into 12 segments for the 12 moons of the year." Seven of them, visible from the front of the casino, recall the "seven tribes of the Dakota (Sioux) Nation." The color palette of mauve, burgundy, rich purple, and blue is said to be traditional, along with coral and turquoise, which surely are not found in the vicinity. The carpet is described as a natural "moss" green, and in it are feather patterns.

The imaginative explanations do not stop here. Drawings show a turtle and twelve lunar segments superimposed on the casino's circular plan, and a thunderbird, an eagle, a "sinewed" bow, and a sacred white buffalo superimposed on the semicircular bingo hall (149). These forms are all invisible to the patrons, but are part of an insistence on the casino as a means to preserve the integrity of the tribe and its traditions. The architect spent several days reading about aspects of Sioux cultures. "I'll be honest with you," he says. "I didn't design the building to be a buffalo... but mystically, suddenly, forms just came out of the use of the circle and the semicircle. The circle and semicircle were very conscious attempts to incorporate these forms into the building—the drum, the circle. But some of the other symbolism—the thunderbird, the eagle, possibly the turtle—just began to appear."

There was bound to be some dissent among those who saw the results. Neighbors sued the casino because of the disturbing searchlights, which are now lit only at certain times. The application of symbols to any modern building might be questioned by anyone from a traditional elder to a skeptical Anglo critic. Casino officials knew that publicizing the symbolic references might be controversial, but they were not blessing gambling; they simply "wanted to bring out that we are sovereign" and hoped to educate the public about Indian culture while attracting their attention with advertisements connecting eagles and buffalo to good fortune.[56] Tim Giago*, editor of the *Lakota Times*, also pointed out that the sponsors were Indians deciding to use their symbols to promote their own welfare;[57] they were not insensitive white entrepreneurs using stereotypes for sports teams' names.

An aesthetic canon for casinos will probably never be developed, although Robert Venturi and his colleagues have shown us what we can learn from Las Vegas. In Mystic Lake Casino, we have a lavish and cheerful building that seems close to Disney World's EPCOT Center and its rhetoric. There, reductionist versions of traditional foreign village centers are purely commercial activity centers, masked by messages about fraternity in our small world. One might see the Mystic Lake Casino as nothing more than a Native American EPCOT. But while we may feel surfeited by the symbolic icing on an unpalatable cake, justifiable pride can feed the soul. There is pride here in sponsoring something imaginative and attractive, in running a business successfully, in offering jobs to Indians and others, in providing a model for efficient management. The entire casino was erected for less than $100 a square foot, an unusually low cost. The tribal corporation that runs tribal gambling has established a consulting firm to help other tribes learn to run casinos without hiring expensive Euro-American consultants. All of that is important in Indian country.

* * *

The phenomenon of the Indian casino may not last long if too many are built, if competitors build them on Mississippi riverboats and Gulf Coast barges, if business rivals and moralists (sincere or hypocritical) succeed in overwhelming Indian operations, if Congress allows states to forbid or limit Indian casinos, or if enough people have the good sense to stop gambling. But John Cuningham, who has designed successful casinos for the Mille Lacs Band and other clients, describes the metamorphoses of the gambling industry from something small-scale and disreputable through a glamorous stage to its present re-formation as part of family entertainment; he therefore finds the future unpredictable.[58] In the meantime, however, the new buffalo and their architectural trappings demonstrate that even dubious building types may embody serious thoughts about self-determination.

Final Observations

At the start of the movement for cultural regeneration that underlies the architectural creativity presented here, the novelist N. Scott Momaday*, a Kiowa, won the Pulitzer Prize for *House Made of Dawn* (1968). He described the people of a pueblo who have "assumed the names and gestures of their enemies, but have held on to their own, secret souls; and in this there is a resistance and an overcoming, a long out-waiting."[1] In the years since the novel's publication, there has been more than selective resistance; there has been positive action.

Some of the results are incomplete, impure. That is due in part to inexperience with such self-determination as is possible. As cultural renewal is one response to societal rupture, the buildings discussed here have been created under pressure that may cause cracks in the conceptual landscape. If some of the programs seem to overinterpret the architecture, that is probably due to the sponsors' intense desire to establish a firm foundation for an uncertain future. Even the labored interpretations are usually clear enough to impress the users— members of Native American society; many tribal spokesmen claim indifference to the reaction of outsiders, except when the buildings are meant to appeal to tourists.

When Native Americans have forgotten or cannot understand the imagery or spatial messages, or when they express hostility or indifference to their new buildings, we think that the design has failed. Forms that once had meaning seem to have been reduced to ornament. Ralf Weber calls this "socio-romantic drapery, because the forms thus discovered originated in socio-cultural conditions and patterns we no longer share. To create an architecture with a human dimension, there is no choice but to look forward."[2]

Nevertheless, the buildings described here do look forward. No clients or architects have expressed the desire to go back in time in either daily life or architecture. They are happy to introduce electric fixtures into ceremonial buildings and log homes, computers into schools and tribal offices and libraries. They want to build on past forms, processes, and values because those retain meaning, strengthening people today and promising to do so in the future. An athlete must lean back in order to throw a ball farther; this physical drawing back is analogous to partly retrospective design concepts familiar to Native Americans and their architects.

The buildings may be attractive, even those like the Gila River Arts & Crafts Center and the Pine Point

School (88, 89), which convey little meaning to the local or visiting public, or the Nett Lake houses (91), which a tribal official described as handsome but built in the wrong location. There is, of course, justifiable criticism of a number of recent buildings, criticism that may be expressed differently depending upon whether the listeners are tribal members or outsiders. But despite it, Etienne Gaboury found that those who spoke of the architecture by Hodne–Stageberg "felt an affinity to 'their' buildings which many could not explain. Criticisms notwithstanding, there is a momentum to the whole experience that reaches beyond functional preoccupations or architectural details. These projects have become symbolic beacons, rallying points for a people in search of direction, identity, and perhaps most of all, pride."[3]

By referring to the Hopi village of Old Oraibi, perhaps the oldest continuously inhabited place in North America, the Creek poet Joy Harjo* has expressed the importance of this search, one that may include architecture but that goes beyond it to the basis of inspiration:[4]

> 3 A M
> in the albuquerque airport
> trying to find a flight
>   to old oraibi, third mesa
>
> T W A
> is the only desk open
> bright lights outline new york, chicago
> and the attendant doesn't know
> that third mesa
> is a part of the center
>   of the world
>
> and who are we
> just two indians
> at three in the morning
>   trying to find a way back.

APPENDIX

Poeh Center:
A Statement by Pojoaque Pueblo

Written by Nycha Leia Zenderman, administrative assistant, with the approval of George Rivera*, lieutenant governor of the Pueblo, October 21, 1994.

The Tewa-speaking people of Pojoaque Pueblo in northern New Mexico embarked, sixty years ago, on an arduous path of cultural revitalization after centuries of disenfranchisement, migration, and near extinction. This path has led them directly to the development of the Poeh Cultural Center and Museum, as representative of that striving toward cultural revitalization, part of a long process of Pueblo cultural development. In design and construction, this remarkable Cultural Center is based on traditional Anasazi stone and adobe architecture that existed in this region of the country long before the Spanish conquest. *Poeh* means "path" or "road" in Tewa, or the Tewa road as a philosophy to be taken in life. The Poeh Cultural Center and Museum strives to help its people re-establish this path firmly into the future, as the "Poeh" life cycle complex brings to the Pojoaque a lasting reinforcement of all aspects of their heritage.

The Pueblo people are one of the indigenous cultural groups in North America who have survived with clearly unbroken cultural continuity for well over 2,000 years. At the peak of their development, from the tenth through the thirteenth centuries, they built and occupied the massive architectural structures of Chaco Canyon, Mesa Verde,

Casa Grande, and hundreds of villages throughout the southwest. During the devastating drought of the thirteenth century, the Pueblo people began consolidating into the Rio Grande Valley of northern New Mexico, attracted by its reliable water supply and abundant game, and villages of adobe and stone follow the Rio Grande and its tributaries. Pueblo people are known to be "incorporating" people, receiving new ideas and integrating them with their traditional customs. The descendants of these Pueblo groups in present-day New Mexico have maintained a lifestyle intensive in horticulture, elaborate in ceremonial cycles, and highly cohesive in social organization. Pojoaque (*Po suwae geh*) Pueblo is one of six Tewa pueblos in the northern Rio Grande Valley whose inhabitants date back to around A.D. 900. Archaeological studies indicate a large population in the late fifteenth and early sixteenth centuries which eventually divided into the Tewas to the north and the Tanos to the south. A large ruin on the southern slope of the hills of Pojoaque called *Teje Owinge* once marked that division. Not only was Pojoaque the nucleus of Indian settlement in ancient times, but it has continued to be a Tewa center from which its name *Po-suwae-geh*, or drinking water place, derives.

Since its re-establishment in 1934, cultural activities

and awareness within Pojoaque Pueblo have increased and are at the forefront of the Tribe's development. Acting under the advice of their elders, the Pueblo conducted research into their lost cultural heritage, and not only revived the dance cycle, but also re-instated several tribal members in traditional positions of War Chief and War Captains. The Tribal Council is in full support of these revitalization efforts. Additionally, for the last twenty years, social and economic strategies of the Pueblo have focused on developing a long-term land use plan. Land use allocation designated in the 1988 plan allows commercial development and new business expansion along U.S. [highway] 84-285, which traverses the reservation. The Pueblo has attracted commercial businesses to which it leases land and/or buildings, and which have provided the Pueblo with dependable revenue. Like many other tribes nationally, Pojoaque Pueblo also operates a gaming facility called Cities of Gold, which, it is hoped, will bring in much additionally needed revenue.

The design ideas for the Pojoaque Pueblo Poeh Cultural Center and Museum were gained through several envisioning processes that began in 1988 when George Rivera, the Center's first Executive Director, along with other Tewa-speaking people—educators and artists—from the Pueblos of San Juan (Dr. Alfonso Ortiz, Herman Agoyo, Andy Garcia), Santa Clara (Dr. Greg Cajete, Dr. Tessie Naranjo), Nambe (Ernest Mirabal, Richard Montoya) and Pojoaque (George Rivera) recognized the dire importance of creating a center to support the renaissance of Tewa culture. Dr. Susan Guyette, Planner, organized the envisioning process, and the Pueblo participants were visually "walked" through the future Center. They then talked about the design envisioned. Fundamental to that design and infused in its creation, was to be an emphasis on the five senses, the individual's relationship to the natural world. The group came to understand that it was first necessary to think of who the Tewa people are, and then to design the Cultural Center according to that self-definition.

The group provided information on the traditional villages and set the basis for a five-year long-range plan which gave definition to the Poeh Center's purpose. As such, the design features developed only after the group determined the essence of the Poeh Center, its projects and activities; the group had to consider design requirements for a building that would include the feel and mood they were seeking that would appropriately reflect their vision. The size of the rooms, the construction materials, the lighting, and more importantly, the ambiance and the fuction of the

Center, came directly from this group of Tewa Pueblo people. Joining this group of consultants was master builder Joel McHorse from Taos Pueblo, a village that is one of the most traditional villages, architecturally speaking, of this northern New Mexican group of pueblos. Growing up in Taos, with its definite traditional architecture, he was able to master its architectural concepts and style, and put those to use in the original design ideas for the Center.

As stated, the Poeh Cultural Center project has been in progress since 1988 and has, to date, been aided by a three-year development grant from the Administration for Native Americans, various foundation grants, a National Endowment for the Humanities Challenge Grant and New Mexico State Legislative appropriations. Construction began in 1993, and the entire Cultural Center is scheduled to be completed within the next five years. The Poeh Cultural Center and Museum will provide a place where Native Americans of the Northern Pueblos can work together and re-establish contact with their heritage. It will provide an outlet for the more than 800 artists of these Pueblos by creating a place for artists and tribal members to recreate their traditional ties to the Tewa culture and beliefs, and to express these with their art. The Center will include a permanent gallery, rotating exhibition gallery and museum shop for the sale of artists' works, as well as a Tewa Research Center, an outdoor amphitheater, an indoor theater, a story-telling room and hands-on sculpture and pottery studios. Educational facilities will offer an opportunity to involve children and their parents in such activities as dance, song, Tewa-language classes, drum-making, oral history, story-telling, sculpture, costume-making, and pottery-making, among other things. The Northern Pueblo Arts Council, comprised of one member from each of the Eight Northern Pueblos, will be housed in the Center and will help establish inter-tribal cooperation, and advise the Pueblos on priorities as they move toward cultural revitalization.

The Santa Fe architectural firm of McHugh, Lloyd & Tryk was initially commissioned to design a preliminary concept for the Center. During this phase, some of the programming for the project was completed with input by Tribal members from various of the Tewa Pueblos, as discussed. The first master plan concept consisted of groups of structures clustered around two overlapping rectangular plazas. The plan included a round tower and a traditional-looking round underground room with a ladder ascending from an opening in its roof, as well as more contemporary facilities such as an amphitheater, snack shop for serving traditional Tewa foods, a place for cooking demonstrations, an herb garden for traditional medicines, a museum with a round story-telling room, an art gallery, summer studios for artists, a hands-on arts demonstration area, a gift shop, and studios for potters and sculptors. On a separate site, a Cultural Training Center would be housed in a sub-surface circular building inspired by the archaeological reconstruction efforts at Aztec Ruins in northern New Mexico and was to be used like a sun tracker to mark the solstices and equinoxes. Eight monuments, each to be designed by one of the six Tewa-speaking Pueblos, would surround the Training Center at a distance. These two sites would be connected by a path that would be designed in keeping with the natural vegetation.

Joel McHorse reviewed the architectural plans as designed by McHugh, Lloyd & Tryk, and in 1993, decided to approach Taos-based architect Dennis Holloway for his input. In keeping with the intent of the Pueblo's cultural and economic development, the Pueblo decided to start its own architectural firm, Poeh Architecture & Planning, and contracted its own construction company, Pojoaque Pueblo Construction Services Corporation, Inc., which is headed by McHorse, to build the cultural complex. And so in 1993, Dennis Holloway was officially appointed by the Pojoaque Pueblo Tribal Council as Director and Principal Architect of Poeh Architecture & Planning, an internal clearinghouse for all new architecture at the Pueblo. This move allowed the Pueblo to have maximum control over the final design of the Cultural Center, and would ensure the traditional integrity of the complex. The essential components of the Cultural Center, however, remained the same: The functions, the concepts, and the design specifications as developed by McHugh, Lloyd & Tryk were moved and relocated to other settings, but not fundamentally altered. In collaboration with George Rivera and Joel McHorse, Holloway, utilizing state-of-the-art virtual reality computers, prepared a revised design for the Poeh Cultural Center, described by Rivera as being "even closer in design language to the ancient pueblos... in the design of the plaza space, the scale of the buildings, and the complex changes in levels of the rooftops and parapets as suggested by McHorse." The revised plan is directly inspired and informed by the architectural design principles of Pojoaque's ancestors, the Anasazi, and from the surviving architecture of the Northern Pueblos: Taos, Santa Clara, San Juan, San Ildefonso, Nambe, Picuris, and Tesuque. Built on 3.5 acres of tribal land donated by the Pueblo of Pojoaque, construction and development of the Center will continue well toward the end of this decade.

All reference to Spanish-pueblo architecture of the preliminary design was negated in favor of pre-Columbian design idiom. The portals (porches) of the preliminary McHugh, Lloyd & Tryk proposal, which were considered Spanish in origin, were eliminated from the design. Instead, the plan called for more traditional shade (corn-drying) structures, and the buildings were to be constructed in traditional massive adobe to keep people cool in summer and warm in winter. The new plan provided for outdoor plaza and rooftop ovens, as well as the *moo-oos*, or small low rooms that project into the plazas. Holloway relocated the tower of the preliminary proposal, as a focal point in a row of rooms dividing the two plazas; he expanded and further developed the idea of a "Sun Tower" that could track the sun. University of New Mexico Anthropology Professor Alfonso Ortiz, of San Juan Pueblo, who was part of the group that originally met in 1988, is an authority on the Tewa culture and people, and serves as Design Program Advisor to the Poeh Project. He took the collaborating design team on a tour of the astronomical observatory kiva towers of Hovenweep National Monument, an Anasazi ruin with scattered towers near the Utah/Colorado border, 45 miles from the town of Cortez, Colorado. These ancient ruins reaffirmed the inspiration for the Poeh Center "Sun Tower."

The four stories of the tower signify the four worlds of the Tewa. The seemingly random window orientations and locations of each story have in fact deep cultural and cosmological significance. The eight monuments, which had surrounded the orignal Training Center, would now surround the Sun Tower, be viewed through the windows referencing the direction of the pueblo from which the artist who made the monument came. The Training Center, which was in a separate location in the McHugh, Lloyd & Tryk design, was relocated in the revised design to be included as a continuous part of the Cultural Center complex.

Rivera's vision is to build "a pueblo for the present," finding it "crucial to incorporate the design principles of the past, because in those principles, one finds the identity of the people." There were, of course, modifications needed for "making it functional for today and for the future." Reinforced concrete footings and bond beams, hidden from view by high-tech stabilized adobe plasters, would be allowed. Thus Rivera, Holloway, and McHorse found it possible to incorporate new elements within the pueblo architectural idiom. Pueblo architecture, like pueblo culture in general, relied on a strong set of rules, but these rules were never static and could be applied to contemporary requirements of the late twentieth century. With such a rich ancestral architecture, in which all rooms of the pueblo are integrated into a continuous community infrastructure, there was a rich architectural vocabulary with which to work. And these culturally appropriate design efforts are precedent-setting for the pueblos. The intense desire for cultural revitalization that has been the capstone motivating this project will continue to find expression.

Through a revived language of architecture, the Poeh Center is bringing to the Pojoaque people a lasting reinforcement of all aspects of their heritage, which through generations of displacement and migration have almost been lost, and stands as a symbol of a pueblo rebuilt from nearly total extinction to a community of approximately 244 members in a span of sixty years. Not only is this center well past Phase One construction, but it is moving into Phase Two construction and will, without a doubt, be completed as envisioned. And it is certainly a vision—an idea—that has found its time.

NOTES

ABBREVIATIONS

AICRJ   *American Indian Culture and Research Journal*

"Cosmos, Man & Nature"   Wheelwright Museum, "Cosmos, Man and Nature: Native American Perspectives on Architecture" (unedited transcript of conference, October 20–22, 1989)

ICT   *Indian Country Today,* formerly *Lakota Times*

Keepers of the Treasures   P. L. Parker, ed., *Keepers of the Treasures: Protecting Historic Properties and Cultural Traditions on Indian Lands* (Washington, D. C.: Department of the Interior, 1990)

LT   *Lakota Times,* now *Indian Country Today*

NAPr   *Native American Press*

NA20C   M. B. Davis, ed., *Native America in the Twentieth Century: An Encyclopedia* (New York: Garland, 1994)

NEIQ   *Northeast Indian Quarterly*

NYT   *New York Times*

PL   Public Law

Stat.   Statutes at Large

TDSR   *Traditional Dwellings and Settlements Review*

INTRODUCTION

1. A. Ortiz*, quoted in "Commentary," in *Breaking Barriers: Perspectives on the Writing of Indian History*, ed. D. L. Beaulieu (Chicago: Newberry Library, 1978), p. 33.

2. H. L. Gates, Jr., "The Education of Little Tree," *NYT*, November 24, 1991, sec. 7, p. 30.

3. C. H. Krinsky, *Synagogues of Europe: Architecture, History, Meaning* (New York: Architectural History Foundation; Cambridge, Mass.: MIT Press, 1985). [To be reprinted with revisions: New York, Dover, 1996]

CHAPTER 1

1. I am not competent to judge the opinions. For estimates of nearly 2 to about 18 million, see *NA20C*, s.v. "Population," and further references. See the debate in *Ethnohistory* 36, no. 3 (1989), and, most recently, A. J. Jaffe with C. Sperber, *The First Immigrants from Asia: A Population History of the North American Indians* (New York: Plenum, 1992), and J. D. Daniels, "The Indian Population of North America in 1492," *William and Mary Quarterly* 49, no. 2 (1992): 298–320. There is a political aspect to the debate: Euro-American depredations were worse if the aboriginal population was higher. Another contested issue is the possible origin of Amerindians' ancestors in Asia: Some Native Americans call this white man's history, since their own histories say that their people arose from the earth in specific North American locations, emerged from the sea, or emanated from the sky.

2. S. C. Jett and V. A. Spencer, *Navajo Architecture* (Tucson: University of Arizona Press, 1981); Jett, "Cultural Fusion in Native American Architecture: The Navajo Hogan," in *A Cultural Geography of North American Indians*, ed. T. Ross and T. G. Moore (Boulder, Colo.: Westview Press, 1987), pp. 243–56.

3. Not to control all Indian affairs. This control has come from federal assumption of this role. See N. J. Newton, "Federal Powers over Indians: Its Sources, Scope, and Limitations," *University of Pennsylvania Law Review* 132 (1983): 195–225.

4. For laws and treaties, see F. S. Cohen, *Handbook of Federal Indian Law* (Washington, D. C.: Government Printing Office, 1942), and R. Strickland*, ed., *Felix Cohen's Handbook of Federal Indian Law* (Charlottesville, Va.,: Michie, 1982) (with omissions and additions; cited hereafter as Strickland–Cohen). For treaties, see K. Kickingbird* et al., *Indian Treaties* (Washington, D. C.: Institute for the Development of Indian Law, 1980), and R. Costo* and J. H. Costo*, *Indian Treaties: Two Centuries of Dishonor* (San Francisco: Indian Historian Press, 1981). Recent related publications include F. P. Prucha, *The Great Father* (Lincoln: University of Nebraska Press, 1984); C. S. Calloway, ed., *New Directions in American Indian History* (Philadelphia: Temple University Press, 1988); and L.

Rosen, ed., *American Indians and the Law* (New Brunswick, N.J.: Transaction Books, 1978).

5. Family affiliation and community affiliation had sufficed for most Native Americans. The federal government recognizes about 550 of the tribal entities it created, and about 200 more have state recognition or self-definition. For questions about the definition, see, among others, J. Campisi, "The Iroquois and the Euro-American Conception of Tribe," *New York History* 63, no. 2 (1982): 165–82; S. Cornell, *The Return of the Native* (New York: Oxford University Press, 1988); Strickland–Cohen, pp. 3–7, 11–16; and M. Fried, *The Notion of Tribe* (Menlo Park, Calif.: Cummings, 1975). As the term is in common use despite the associated problems, I continue to use it here.

6. The weekly *Native American Press* carries editorials by an Anishinabe (he rejects Ojibwe and Chippewa), Francis Blake* (Wub-e-ke-niew), who expresses these sentiments often. He is not alone in this, but he is among the most often published.

7. I use this phrasing because other areas were open to settlement by acculturated Indians. There has been a great deal of intermarriage between Native Americans and people of other races. People sometimes falsely claim Indian heritage, generally Cherokee; claims of descent from Cherokee princesses are always spurious, as the tribe had none.

8. Trust status has existed since 1837 when Congress ended direct payment to Indian nations for land ceded or sold to the United States. See Cornell, *Return of the Native*, p. 48.

9. 24 Stat. 388–391. See *NA20C*, s.v. "Allotment," and I. Sutton, *Indian Land Tenure* (New York: Clearwater, 1975).

10. W. Washburn, *The Indian in America* (New York: Harper & Row, 1975), p. 242. The Indian Citizenship ("Bryan") Act of 1924 (43 Stat. K 253) made all Indians citizens.

11. 1902: 32 Stat. 888; 1906: 34 Stat. 388.

12. M. T. Smith, "The Wheeler-Howard Act of 1934: The Indian New Deal," *Journal of the West* 10 (1971): 521. R. H. Weil, "The Loss of Lands Inside Indian Reservations," in *Geography of North American Indians*, ed. Ross and Moore, pp. 149–71. Some lands were rendered economically useless to their owners by being fragmented among many heirs. Numerous studies address what is known as the "heirship problem."

13. The classic text about revitalization movements is A. F. C. Wallace, "Revitalization Movements," *American Anthropologist* 58 (1956): 264–81.

14. H. Gans, *The Urban Villagers: Group and Class in the Life of Italian-Americans* (New York: Free Press, 1962).

15. Institute for Government Research, *Problem of Indian Administration* (Baltimore: Johns Hopkins University Press, 1928).

16. 48 Stat. 984–988.

17. Every history of twentieth-century Native America discusses this act (25 U.S.C. 476 [e]), John Collier, and the Indian

New Deal. See D. L. Fixico*, "Twentieth Century Indian Policy," in *Scholars and the Indian Experience*, ed. W. R. Swagerty (Bloomington: Indiana University Press, 1984), pp. 123–62; and, for summaries and essential books, see NA20C, s.v. "Indian Reorganization Act," "Tribal Governments," and "Federal Indian Policy." See also F. J. Stefon, "The Indians' 'Zarathustra': An Investigation into the Philosophical Roots of John Collier's New Deal Educational and Administrative Policies," *Journal of Ethnic Studies* 11, no. 3 (1984): 1–28, 11, no. 4 (1984): 28–46; G. P. Castile and R. L. Bee, eds., *The Politics of American Indian Policy* (Cambridge, Mass.: Schenkman, 1982); Castile and Bee, eds., *State and Reservation* (Tucson: University of Arizona Press, 1992); W. Washburn, "A Fifty-Year Perspective on the Indian Reorganizaiton Act," *American Anthropologist* 86, no. 2 (1984): 279–89; D. L. Parman, *The Navajos and the New Deal* (New Haven, Conn.: Yale University Press, 1976); and L. C. Kelly, *The Assault on Assimilation: John Collier and the Origins of Indian Policy Reform* (Albuquerque: University of New Mexico Press, 1986). For the differences between Collier's proposals and the enacted IRA, see V. Deloria*, Jr. and C. Lytle, *The Nations Within* (New York: Pantheon, 1984).

18. Publications since the review of the literature in Swagerty, ed., *Scholars and the Indian Experience*, include D. Champagne*, "Organizational Change and Conflict: A Case Study of the Bureau of Indian Affairs," *AICRJ* 7, no. 3 (1983): 3–28; S. Novak, "The Real Takeover of the BIA: The Preferential Hiring of Indians," *Journal of Economic History* 50, no. 3 (1990): 639–54; and T. W. Taylor, *The Bureau of Indian Affairs* (Boulder, Colo.: Westview Press, 1984); see also V. Deloria, Jr.*, "The Bureau of Indian Affairs: My Brother's Keeper," *Art in America* 60, no. 4 (1972): 110–15. For accusations of incompetent management, see *NYT*, January 12, 1901, p. 11; *LT*, September 18, 1991, sec. A1, p. 2; and U.S. House of Representatives, Government Operations Subcommittee, *Misplaced Trust* (1992). The Senate Select Committee on Indian Affairs has also reported on serious problems.

19. 48 Stat. 596. Funds support services not otherwise available, such as remedial programs and school lunches. Allocations vary among states and among districts within them.

20. As well as Cohen, *Handbook*, see, for a review of the literature and an excellent bibliography, G. S. Grossman, "Indians and the Law," in *New Directions*, ed. Calloway, pp. 97–126; and C. Wilkinson, *American Indians, Time, and the Law* (New Haven, Conn.: Yale University Press, 1987).

21. J. Collier, "At the Close of Eight Weeks," *Indians at Work*, September 1, 1933, pp. 1–4. The publication's title informed readers that the Native population was exerting itself, not passively receiving federal handouts.

22. W. C. Ryan, Jr., "Community Day Schools for Indians," *Indians at Work*, December 1, 1933, pp. 7–9. As urban students and parents were not expected to make their own desks, this was discriminatory, but because standard state curricula had little meaning for most Indian students the officials probably thought that vocational training, and providing showers, laundries, and modern kitchens, would help at least some reservation residents.

23. "Indian Architecture and the New Indian Day Schools," *Indians at Work*, February 15, 1934, pp. 31–33, illus. on p. 32. This firm executed other projects for western tribes during the 1930s.

24. Sara Loe, letter to the author, August 1, 1991.

25. "Indian Reservation Architecture for the Southwest: Mayers, Murray & Phillip, Architects," *American Architect and Architecture* 150, no. 2658 (1937): 3, 34–40. Forty-seven Indian day schools were built. D. J. Kammer called the BIA Hospital at Crownpoint, New Mexico, (1938) "typical Navajo WPA, rusticated [red sand-] stone variation of the Pueblo revival style" (Tour notes, Vernacular Architecture Forum tour (1991), courtesy Christopher Wilson and Jean-Louis Bourgeois). Navajos were not Pueblo people, which explains his ironic tone. A hogan-like library (1936) is still in use at Tuba City, Arizona.

26. Emory Sekaquaptewa* December 3, 1990. He also discussed training and work given to Hopi masons who built reservation schools and other structures in the later 1930s.

27. "Indian Reservation Architecture," pp. 38, 40; quote on p. 40.

28. C. W. Short and R. Stanley-Brown, *Public Buildings: A Survey of Architecture of Projects Constructed by Federal and Other Governmental Bodies Between the Years 1933 and 1939 with the Assistance of the Public Works Administration* (Washington, D.C.: Government Printing Office, 1939), p. 644. Interior murals are by Gerald Naylor* (1934–1935).

29. Candi Helms, former tribal architectural historian, "The Impact of Federal Indian Policies on the Navajo Nation's Constructed Landscape" (lecture at the annual meeting of the Society of Architectural Historians, April 3, 1992); she kindly sent a copy of her talk and other material.

30. J. Collier, "The First Tribal Capital," *Indians at Work*, August 1, 1934, p. 5. A rare photograph of the interior in use, showing murals of ancient and modern Navajo life is in W. Lindig and H. Teiwes, *Navajo* (Zurich: Bär Verlag, 1991), p. 167.

31. E. Way, in "Cosmos, Man, and Nature," p. 226.

32. M. C. Wheelwright, "The House of Navajo Religion," *El Palacio* 45, no. 24–26 (1938): 116–17. As the culture did not die, some Navajo now feel that their privileged information should not have been given to outsiders and displayed in a white-sponsored museum, but this hindsight was impossible in 1938. See also B. Bernstein and S. B. McGreevy, "Journey Toward Understanding," *Native Peoples* 2, no. 4 (1989): 36–42; and M. L. Grossman, "The Wheelwright Museum," *American Indian Art* 2, no. 3 (1977): 15–16.

33. A. R. Bernstein, *American Indians and World War II*

(Norman: University of Oklahoma Press, 1991); G. Nash, *The American West Transformed: The Impact of the Second World War* (Bloomington: Indiana University Press, 1985). Nash emphasizes breakdown of tribal isolation, political activism among veterans, and ideas about human equality based on the relative egalitarianism of the armed forces.

34. B. H. Hackenberg, "Social Mobility in a Tribal Society: The Case of Papago Indian Veterans," *Human Organization* 31, no. 2 (1972): 201–9.

35. Hank Adams* made this claim and also asserted that the NCAI's lawyers had helped to formulate provisions for termination. See K. R. Philp, *Indian Self-Rule* (Salt Lake City: Howe, 1986), p. 239.

36. 60 Stat. 1049. See I. Sutton, *Irredeemable America* (Albuquerque: University of New Mexico Press, 1985); and L. W. Burt, *Tribalism in Crisis* (Albuquerque: University of New Mexico Press, 1982).

37. 67 Stat. B. 132. There is a great deal of literature about the termination policy, virtually all of it highly critical. Sixty-two tribes were terminated during the 1960s; the result was usually appalling economic distress and steep rises in welfare applications. See, for instance, Philp, *Indian Self-Rule*, pp. 22, 113; and, for Indian accounts, P. Nabokov, *Native American Testimony* (New York: Viking, 1991). See also NA2oC, pp. 221–23, with essential bibliography.

38. S. O'Brien, *American Indian Tribal Governments* (Norman: University of Oklahoma Press, 1989), p. 308, says that there are eleven executive departments with Indian programs, eight federal agencies, and numerous state agencies and departments. In 1994, moves were initiated in Congress to coordinate the agencies.

39. Some tribes preferred state jurisdiction. An important reason why certain Pueblos did not want protection under the Bill of Rights is that they wish to lower barriers between church and state. On the Indian Civil Rights Act of 1986, see Prucha, *Great Father*, vol. 2, p. 1106.

40. See Burt, *Tribalism in Crisis*, esp. pp. 86–93.

41. B. Medicine*, "Native American Resistance to Integration," *Plains Anthropologist* 26, no. 94, pt. 1 (1981): 277–86, esp. 280–82, and comments about the intertribal nature of the Sun Dance.

42. R. David Edmunds, authority on the Potawatomie, Mesquakie (Sac & Fox), and others, quoted in Philp, *Indian Self-Rule*, p. 113.

43. See N. O. Lurie, "The Voice of the American Indian: Report on the American Indian Chicago Conference," *Current Anthropology* 2 (1961): 478–500; J. Ablon, "The American Indian Chicago Conference," in *Currents in Anthropology: Essays in Honor of Sol Tax*, ed. R. Hinshaw (The Hague: Mouton, 1974),

pp. 445–56; and R. A. Rubinstein, "A Conversation with Sol Tax," *Current Anthropology* 32, no. 2 (1991): 175–83, esp. 178–79. Reports vary about the number of attendees and who they were.

44. Nabokov, *Native American Testimony*, p. 358; all general histories discuss the youth council. See also H. W. Hertzberg, *The Search for an American Indian Identity* (Syracuse, N.Y.:Syracuse University Press, 1971); J. Nagel, "The Political Mobilization of American Indians," *Social Science Journal* 19, no. 3 (1982): 37–45; and L. M. Hauptman, "The Voice of Eastern Indians: The American Indian Chicago Conference of 1961 and the Movement for Federal Recognition," *American Philological Society, Proceedings* 132 (1988): 316–29. For the postmodern aspects of this revival, see P. Rabinow, "Representations are Social Facts: Modernity and Post-Modernity in Anthropology," in *Writing Culture: The Poetics and Politics of Ethnography*, ed. J. Clifford and G. Marcus (Berkeley: University of California Press, 1986), pp. 234–61, esp. pp. 247, 252.

45. W. A. Brophy and S. D. Aberle, *The Indian: America's Unfinished Business. Report of the Commission on the Rights, Liberties, and Responsibilities of the American Indian* (Norman: University of Oklahoma Press, 1966). For the period, see D. L. Fixico*, *State and Reservation: Federal Indian Policy, 1945–60* (Albuquerque: University of New Mexico Press, 1986).

46. PL 88–452 (78 Stat. 508).

47. See pp. 180–81. By 1965, six demonstration schools were being funded by foundations: Rough Rock (Arizona), Ramah (New Mexico), Rocky Boy (Montana), Rama (Iowa), Blackwater (Arizona), and Menominee (Wisconsin).

48. H. F. Dobyns, "Therapeutic Experience of Responsible Democracy," in *The American Indian Today*, ed. S. Levine and N. O. Lurie (Baltimore: Penguin, 1970), p. 272. On tribalism, see references in R. Thornton, "Contemporary American Indians," in *Scholars and the Indian Experience*, ed. Swagerty, p. 171. See also R. L. Barsh, "Contemporary Marxist Theory and Native American Reality," *American Indian Quarterly* 12, no. 3 (1988): 187–212, esp. 204–7.

49. For instance, F. C. Miller, "Involvement in an Urban University," in *The American Indian in Urban Society*, ed. J. O. Waddell and O. M. Watson (Boston: Little, Brown, 1971), pp. 312–39, esp. p. 337; G. P. Horse Capture*, "Survival of Culture," *Museum News* 70, no. 1 (1991): 50; J. McManus, "The Angry American Indian: Starting Down the Protest Trail," *Time*, February 9, 1970, pp. 14–20; the cover title, "Tonto Is Dead," refers to the death of stereotypes rather than of the Native American population.

50. H. Doc. 91-363, *Congressional Record* 116, p. 17, rec. 23131, in *The American Indian: A Rising Ethnic Force*, ed. H. L. Marx, Jr. (New York: Wilson, 1973), p. 74–78.

51. T. McGuire, "Federal Indian Policy: A Framework for Evaluation," *Human Organization* 49, no. 3 (1990): 206–16.

52. PL 93-638 (88 Stat. 2203); Strickland–Cohen, p. 662. On the limitations of this law, see G. P. Castile, "Indian Sign: Hegemony and Symbolism in Federal Indian Policy," in *State and Reservation*, ed. Castile and Bee, pp. 173, 182–83; W. Washburn, "Indian Policy Since the 1880s," in *The Aggressions of Civilization: Federal Indian Policy Since the 1880s*, ed. S. Cadwalader and V. Deloria, Jr.* (Philadelphia: Temple University Press, 1984), pp. 46–57; R. L. Barsh and K. Diaz-Knauf, "The Structure of Federal Aid for Indian Programs in the Decade of Prosperity, 1970–1980," *American Indian Quarterly* 8, no. 1 (1984): 1–19; T. Biolsi, "'Indian Self-Government' as a Technique of Domination," *American Indian Quarterly* 15, no. 1 (1991): 23–28; and M. P. Gross, "Indian Self-Determination and Tribal Sovereignty: An Analysis of Recent Federal Indian Policy," *Texas Law Review* 56 (1978): 1195–1244.

53. P. Boyer, "The Legacy of Columbus," *Tribal College* 3, no. 2 (1991): 5; see, however, W. Willard, "Self-Governance for Native Americans: The Case of the Pascua Yaqui Tribe," pp. 3–13; F. J. Lyden and E. G. Miller, "Designing a Tribal Organization for Self-Government," pp. 15–35; W. Churchill, "American Indian Self-Governance: Fact, Fantasy, and Prospects for the Future," pp. 37–53; and R. L. Barsh, "Indian Policy at the Beginning of the 1990s: The Trivialization of Struggle," pp. 55–69, all in *American Indian Policy*, ed. L. S. Legters and F. J. Lyden (Westport, Conn.: Greenwood Press, 1993), pp. 3–69.

54. *ICT*, March 2, 1994, pp. B1–2.

55. B. Came, "In Search of Pride," *Maclean's*, July 3, 1989, p. 41. For exceedingly high costs within tribes of administering scholarships to Native American students, see *ICT*, July 27, 1994, pp. A1–2.

56. Legters and Lyden, eds., *American Indian Policy*.

57. PL 95-471 (92 Stat. 1325); Strickland–Cohen, p. 195.

58. PL 95-341 (92 Stat. 469); Strickland–Cohen, p. 662.

59. See in NA2oC, s.v. "American Indian Religious Freedom Act," with recent bibliography.

60. Abbott Sekaquaptewa*, in *Indian Voices: The Native American Today* (San Francisco: Indian Historian Press, 1974), p. 55. The Indian concern with nature is not an impractical intention to preserve everything all the time. Native peoples exhausted soil and game supplies and moved on. More than just the useful animals died at buffalo jumps. Economics has forced some tribal councils to accept toxic waste dumps. These facts do not vitiate a spiritual connection to nature.

61. For alterations to Chief Seattle's speech by Ted Perry in 1982, which are widely taken as Seattle's words, see *NYT*, April 21, 1992, pp. A1, A7.

62. This is taken from opening remarks by John A. Shapard, former head of the Bureau of Acknowledgment and Research, BIA, at the Second Mashantucket Pequot History Conference, October 23, 1993.

63. Early participants included the Makah, Port Gamble, Sac & Fox, and Leech Lake Band of Chippewa. All have culturally suitable buildings. For legal hurdles, see J. Gendar, "Sovereignty," *News from Native California* 7, no. 1 (1992–1993): 25–27; A. Slagle*, Esq., currently writes a legal news and analysis article in each issue of this journal.

64. For Watkins, see *LT*, December 8, 1991, p. B8.

65. PL 101-601. See NA2oC, s.v. "Repatriation," with essential bibliography. See also A. Tabah, *Native American Collections and Repatriation*, ed. S. Dubberly (Washington, D.C.: American Association of Museums, 1993); V. Deloria, Jr.*, "A Simple Question of Humanity: The Moral Dimensions of the Reburial Issue," *NARF Legal Review* 14, no. 4 (1989): 1–12; and G. Smith, "Keepers of the Past," *Audubon*, May 1993, pp. 88–99. I thank Katherine Poole April for several other references. An enormous periodical literature exists already, mainly in tribal publications.

66. *LT*, May 13, 1992, p. A5.

67. P. Stuart, "Financing Self-Determination: Federal and Indian Expenditures, 1975–1988," *AICRJ* 14, no. 2 (1990): 1–18. PL 93-638 provides no protection against budget cuts, as he points out.

68. That certain sites associated with Jesus acquired sanctity as a result of pagan, not Judeo-Christian influence, has not impressed the Vatican, which participates with the University of Arizona in a project to erect an observatory atop Mount Graham, sacred to the San Carlos Apaches. See J. E. Taylor, *Christians and the Holy Places* (Oxford: Clarendon Press, 1993), passim. For recent developments on Mount Graham, see *NYT*, August 28, 1991, sec. 1, p. 20.

69. *LT*, December 11, 1991, p. B4.

70. Elgin Bad Wound*, fund-raising letter for Oglala Lakota College (n.d.).

71. Ibid.

72. For Pine Ridge, see Senator Paul Simon, quoted in *LT*, February 26, 1992, p. A2. Dale Looks Twice*, program director of tribal radio station KILI, puts the rate at 82 to 85 percent. C. Hamilton, "For the Oglala Nation, Unity Comes with Differences," *Native Peoples* 1, no. 3 (1991): 14; *NYT*, September 20, 1992, sec. 1, pp. 1, 32, gives 93 percent and the 63.1 percent poverty figure.

73. Cheyenne River: R. Spector, "Tribes Eye Job Incentives," *Rapid City News*, August 11, 1991, p. B2. For all tribes: A. Serwer, "American Indians Discover Money Is Power," *Fortune*, April 19, 1993, pp. 136–42, who says that nearly one-third of Indians have incomes below the poverty line (p. 138). Unemployment at Picuris Pueblo in 1991 was 38 percent: "Reservation Required,"

New York, April 8, 1991, p. 32. Rosebud: *LT*, February 26, 1992, p. B2, using 1990 census figures.

74. Among thousands of studies, the following indicate their range in the last two decades: A. Sorkin, "The Economic Basis of Indian Life," in *The American Indian Today*, ed. J. M. Yinger and G. E. Simpson (Philadelphia: American Academy of Political and Social Science, 1978), pp. 1–12; V. Deloria, Jr.*, "Native Americans: The American Indian Today," *Annals of the American Academy of Political and Social Sciences* 454 (1981): 139–49; S. J. Kunitz, "Underdevelopment and Social Services on the Navajo Reservation," *Human Organization* 36, no. 4 (1977): 398–405; Sinte Gleska University, "A Whole Approach to Indian Education" (Document for White House Conference on Indian Education, January 21–24, 1992); *LT*, December 18, 1991, p. A5; *NA2oC*, s.v. "Alcohol Abuse," with bibliography; R. Bachman, *Death and Violence on the Reservation* (Westport, Conn.: Greenwood Press, 1992); a dissertation being completed at University of Colorado by Charles Cambridge* on AIDS and Native Americans; T. O'Nell, "Psychiatric Investigations and American Indians and Alaska Natives: A Critical Review," *Culture, Medicine, and Psychiatry* 13, no. 1 (1989): 51–87; K. Swisher* and D. Deyhle*, "Styles of Learning and Learning of Styles: Educational Conflicts for American Indian/Alaska Native Youth," *Journal of Multilingual and Multicultural Development* 8, no. 4 (1987): 345–60; J. Kleinfeld and P. Nelson, "Adapting Instruction to Native Americans' Learning Styles," *Journal of Cross-Cultural Psychology* 22, no. 2 (1991): 273–82; T. D. Graves, "Urban Indian Personality and the 'Culture of Poverty,'" *American Ethnologist* 1, no. 1 (1974): 65–86.

75. For a succinct overview, see "Reaganomics on the Reservation," *Economist*, April 9, 1983, p. 26. For a longer view, see Barsh and Diaz-Knauf, "Structure of Federal Aid." The Supreme Court's decision in *Robert Hagen, Petitioner* v. *Utah* (1994), which "handed over 75 percent of Northern Ute tribal lands to state control" (*ICT*, March 2, 1994, pp. A1, A2), is a stunning reversal of general policy since the 1970s. See *United States Law Week*, February 22, 1994, pp. 4118–41, Justices Blackmun and Souter dissenting. For threats to tribal status in California, see A. Slagle*, "Groundhog Day," *News from Native California* 8, no. 1 (1994): 57–59.

76. Bad Wound, fund-raising letter for Oglala Lakota College.

CHAPTER 2

1. T. J. Morgan, quoted in A. Chapman, "Introduction," *Literature of the American Indians: Views and Interpretations*, ed. A. Chapman (New York: New American Library, 1975), p. 16.

2. E. L. Whitung, "Education and Communication," *Tawow* 2, no. 2 (1971) reports on children's egalitarian rather than hierarchical training.

3. Bernard Fontana, December 3, 1990.

4. V. Deloria, Jr.*, quoted in Nabokov, *Native American Testimony* (New York: Viking, 1991), p. 382.

5. C. Plimpton, "Cultural Reidentification Expressed through Vernacular Architecture," *TDSR* 4, no. 1 (1992): 31.

6. E. Saïd, "Criticism, Self-Criticism," *Lingua Franca* 2, no. 3 (1992): 41, 43.

7. B. G. Miller, "After the F.A.P.: Tribal Reorganization After Federal Recognition," *Journal of Ethnic Studies* 17, no. 2 (1989): 89–100. See later in the text for L. Joe's* borrowing of the Lummi smokehouse ritual, and for the Mashantucket Pequot powwow staged to learn how to perform Native American activities.

8. A. F. C. Wallace, "Revitalization Movements," *American Anthropologist* 58, no. 2 (1956): 264–81.

9. A. Hultkrantz, *The Religions of the American Indian* (Berkeley: University of California Press, 1967) and later publications by this author; S. Gill, *Native American Religions: An Introduction* (Belmont, Calif.: Wadsworth, 1982).

10. L. M. Silko*, *Ceremony* (New York: Viking, 1977), p. 132.

11. Voluntary affiliation, which may include racism, may account for separate white and Indian churches of the same Protestant denomination seen in the same town; this is unlikely to occur in Roman Catholicism, with its parishes based on geography.

12. W. Stolzman, *The Pipe and Christ: A Christian–Sioux Dialogue* (Chamberlain, S.D.: Tipi Press, 1986); Patrick J. Twohy, *Finding a Way Home: Indian and Catholic Spiritual Paths of the Plateau Tribes* (Spokane, Wash.: University Press of Spokane, 1983). Surrounded-by-Enemy* and Marvin Kastning introduced me to these books.

13. F. J. Newcomb, "How the Navajo Adopt Rites," *El Palacio* 46, no. 2 (1939): 25–27.

14. Builder: Custom Log Homes, Stevensville, Montana; contractor: Walter McBride, Gallup; architect: Edward Preston, Gallup.

15. Artists: Robert Draper*, Teddy Draper, Jr.*, Justin Tso*. A statue of the Madonna is by Navajo sculptor Nelson Yazzie*.

16. Thanks are due to Father Blane Grein, OFM, and Deacon Robert Kloepping. See also D. von Hagel, "The People of God in Chinle," *Friarworks* 28, no. 7 (1991): 1–3.

17. Father D. von Hagel, OFM, "Diamond Jubilee Celebration," *Padres Trail* 36, no. 3 (1973–1974): 7. I owe this reference to Father Martan Rademaker, OFM.

18. Other hogan-shaped churches are St. Jerome's, in a rehabilitation center for alcoholics, Chichiltah, New Mexico; Salt Mill, Arizona; Crownpoint, New Mexico, where a spiritual healer blessed the site, and where healingway images have

replaced the Stations of the Cross and the altar is made from stones from sacred mountains; Pinon, Arizona (1984), by Father Blane Grein and two other Franciscans, building a wooden church inside metal facing. St. Isabel Mission, Lukachukai, Arizona, has a miniature hogan as the tabernacle designed by Father Martan Rademaker; it stands in front of a mural by Navajo artist Juan Nakai* that shows corn, the Navajo symbol of life and growth, flanking a carved crucifix. See von Hagel, "Diamond Jubilee Celebration," 14. St. Christopher's Episcopal Mission, Bluff, Utah, is also hogan-shaped; I owe this information to the Reverend Davis Given.

19. Other churches with Indian decoration or forms evoking Native architecture are San Francisco de Assisi (1976), Nambe Pueblo, by Allen McNown, illustrated in F. David, *Contemporary Third World Architecture* (Brooklyn, N.Y.: Pratt Institute, 1983), p. 97; Roman Catholic church, Ethete Road, Wind River, Wyoming; Baptist church, Briggs, Oklahoma; Our Lady of Guadalupe, Zuni Reservation (K. Seowtewa*, "Adding a Breath to Zuni Life," *Native Peoples* 5, no. 2 [1992]: 10–16); St. Agnes Roman Catholic church, Manderson, South Dakota; St. Labre Roman Catholic church, South Dakota; Pascua Yaqui reservation; Sandia Pueblo, where the Eagle Dance is performed on January 6, although the priest absents himself (I thank Henry Walt for this information); Bloomfield Avenue Lutheran Church, Minneapolis (the vault, like that of a longhouse, was described by R. Hernandez*).

20. L. Fowler, *Shared Symbols, Contested Meanings* (Ithaca, N.Y.: Cornell University Press, 1987), p. 123.

21. V. Black Cloud*, "Children Need Spirituality in Teaching," *LT*, February 11, 1992, p. A6.

22. Lorraine Canoe*, at a panel at the American Indian Community House, June 9, 1991.

23. For parallels elsewhere, see D. E. Whisnant, *All that Is Native and Fine: The Politics of Culture in an American Region* (Chapel Hill: University of North Carolina Press, 1983), p. 6. I thank Christopher Wilson for this reference.

24. "Learning to Walk the Lakota Way," *LT*, July 22, 1992, p. B5.

25. Known also as Tom Porter, he is quoted in *Akwesasne Freedom School* [fund-raising brochure] (c. 1990). See also D. R. Parks, "The Importance of Language Study for the Writing of Plains Indian History," in *New Directions in American Indian History*, ed. C. S. Calloway (Philadelphia: Temple University Press, 1984), pp. 153–97; J. W. Bennett, ed., *The New Ethnicity: Perspectives from Ethnology* (St. Paul, Minn.: West, 1975); and R. A. White, "Value Themes of the Native American Tribalistic Movement Among the South Dakota Sioux," *Current Anthropology* 15, no. 3 (1974): 284–89, 299–302.

26. O. Zepeda*, quoted in F. Barringer, "Faded but Vibrant Indian Languages Struggle to Keep Their Voices Alive," *NYT*, January 8, 1991, p. A14.

27. Quoted in M. Ambler, "Arapaho Elders Launch Effort to Save Language," *ICT*, March 16, 1994, p. B4. For brown-skinned white people, see P. Locke*, *NAPr*, November 6, 1992, p. 2, and a similar quote in Ambler, "Arapaho Elders." For California's fifty languages and dialects, see L. Hinton and Y. Montijo*, "In Our Own Words," *News from Native California* 7, no. 4 (1993–1994): 4–9. The Oneida, exceptionally, promoted language revival from 1938 to 1941 as well as after 1972. See F. Lounsbury, "Recollections of the Works Progress Administration's Oneida Language and Folklore Project 1938–41," and "Recollections of the Oneida Language Revival, 1972–1985," in *The Oneida Indian Experience: Two Perspectives*, ed. J. Campisi and L. Hauptman (Syracuse, N.Y.: Syracuse University Press, 1988), pp. 131–34, 139–44. Among the languages now being revived in other regions are Makah, Lushootseed, Hualapai, Tohono O'odham, Gros Ventre, Assiniboine, Lakota, Kickapoo, Choctaw, Cree, Chippewa, Wyandotte, Osage, Michif, Ute, and Mohawk.

28. T. Giago and W. Mesteth, quoted in *Star Tribune* (Twin Cities), May 11, 1994, p. 10E. For boundaries and the definition of ethnicity, see G. Devereux and E. M. Loeb, "Antagonistic Acculturation," *American Sociological Review* 7 (1943): 133–47; E. Spicer, ed., *Perspectives in American Indian Culture Change* (Chicago: University of Chicago Press, 1961); F. Barth, *Ethnic Groups and Boundaries* (Boston: Little, Brown, 1969), especially the introduction; C. Geertz, "From the Native's Point of View: On the Nature of Anthropological Understanding," *Bulletin of the American Academy of Arts and Sciences* 28, no. 1 (1974); 26–45; G. Devereux, "Ethnic Identity: Its Logical Foundations and Its Disruptions," in *Ethnic Identity: Culture Continuities and Change*, ed. C. DeVos and L. Romanucci-Ross (Palo Alto, Calif.: Mayfield, 1975), esp. pp. 42–70; and W. Sollors, *Beyond Ethnicity: Consent and Descent in American Culture* (New York: Oxford University Press, 1986), and *The Invention of Ethnicity* (New York: Oxford University Press, 1989).

29. B. Anderson, *Imagined Communities: Reflections on the Origin and Spread of Nationalism*, 2d ed. (New York: Verso, 1991), stresses print and a common language as leading to the idea of a nation. Both are now available to Native American nations.

30. Rosebud Reservation's contract school in South Dakota reduced the dropout rate, estimated at 56 percent in 1992; S. Red Owl*, tribal education director, address at New York University, April 11, 1992.

31. Quoted in "30,000 Indians Celebrate Their Culture," *NYT*, April 23, 1990, p. A16. See also D. Whitehorse*, *Pow Wow: The Contemporary Pan-Indian Celebration* (San Diego, Calif.: San Diego State University, 1988).

32. Quoted in B. Bibby, "Still Going: Bill Franklin and the Revival of Miwuk Traditions," *News from Native California* 7, no. 3 (1993): 34.

33. B. Medicine*, "Native American Resistance to Integration," *Plains Anthropologist* 26, no. 94, pt. 1 (1981): 283.

34. C. Dailey, "Major Influence in the Development of Twentieth-Century Native American Art," in *Sharing a Heritage: American Indian Arts*, ed. C. Heth and M. Swarm (Los Angeles: UCLA, 1984), pp. 39–47, esp p. 44.

35. *NYT*, August 25, 1991, sec. 5, p. 6.

36. *LT*, February 12, 1992, p. B8.

37. S. Knapp, "A Nez Perce Journey," *Native Peoples* 6, no. 2 (1993): 64.

38. M. St. Pierre*, "The Status of Contemporary Lakota Tribal Arts," in *Sharing a Heriage*, ed. Heth and Swarm, pp. 13–23; W. S. Jilek, "The Renaissance of Shamanic Dance in Indian Populations of North America," *Diogenes*, no 158 (1992): 87–100; C. Ellis, "Truly Dancing Their Own Way: Modern Revival and Diffusion of the Gourd Dance," *American Indian Quarterly* 14, no. 1 (1990): 19–33.

39. C. R. Jasper, "Change in Ojibwa (Chippewa) Dress, 1820–1890," *AICRJ* 12, no. 4 (1988): 17–37.

40. A. Tate, review of *Native American Dance*, ed. C. Heth, *Native Peoples* 6, no. 3 (1993): 66.

41. John Mohawk*, at symposium at Learning Alliance, Columbia University Law School, April 20, 1991.

42. Advertisement for Toh-Atin Gallery, Durango, Colorado, *Native Peoples* 6, no. 3 (1993): 58.

43. George H. J. Abrams* supplied information about the origin of dreamcatchers.

44. For V. Colombe*, see *ICT*, February 2, 1994, p. B1. For craft types that have declined and risen in popularity since around 1970, see *ICT*, March 9, 1995.

45. On hardships, see K. Walking Stick*, "Indian Law," *Artforum*, November 1991, pp. 20–21, and R. Shiff, "The Necessity for Jimmie Durham's Jokes," *Art Journal* 51, no 3 (1992): 74–75.

46. On the jingle dress, and Oklahoman inspiration, see *LT* [powwow supplement] March 25, 1991. On the Yakima, see *Yakima Nation Souvenir Edition* (n.d.), p. 108. C. Heth, "Update on Indian Music, Contemporary Trends," in *Sharing a Heritage*, ed. Heth and Swarm, esp. p. 95. On the New Deal, see R. F. Schrader, *The Indian Arts and Crafts Board: An Aspect of New Deal Indian Policy* (Albuquerque: University of New Mexico Press, 1983). The Northwest Coast potlatch, widely regarded as quintessentially Native, has recently been analyzed as an anthropological construct that became the basis of indigenous development. See M. Mauzé, "Boas, les Kwagul, et les potlatch: Éléments pour une réévaluation," *L'Homme* 26, no. 4 (1986): 21–63.

47. J. Clifford, *The Predicament of Culture: Twentieth Century Ethnography, Literature, and Art* (Cambridge, Mass.: Harvard University Press, 1988), p. 10.

48. A. Ortiz*, "San Juan Pueblo," in *Handbook of North American Indians: The Southwest*, ed. A. Ortiz (Washington, D.C.: Smithsonian Institution Press, 1979), p. 294.

49. N. H. H. Graburn, ed., *Ethnic and Tourist Arts* (Berkeley: University of California Press, 1976), pp. 4–5.

50. J. H. Bushnell, "From American Indian to Indian American: The Changing Identity of the Hupa," *American Anthropologist* 70, no. 6 (1968): 1108.

51. K. Maly, comp., *A Guide to Kule Loklo* (Point Reyes National Seashore Association, n.d.), p. 3, referring to Coast Miwuk and Pomo.

52. R. Gault*, "Swinomish Smokehouse," *Native Peoples* 7, no. 3 (1994): 36.

53. R. H. Thompson, "Looking to the Future," *Museum News* 70, no. 1 (1991): 36–40; M. Fischer, "Ethnicity and the Post-Modern Arts of Memory," in *Writing Culture: The Poetics and Politics of Ethnography*, ed. J. Clifford and G. Marcus (Berkeley: University of California Press, 1986), pp. 194–233; R. Coe, *Lost and Found Traditions* (Seattle: University of Washington Press, 1986); J. Linnekin and R. Handler, "Tradition, Genuine or Spurious?" *Journal of American Folklore*, July–September, 1984, pp. 273–90; Graburn, *Ethnic and Tourist Arts*; Fowler, *Shared Symbols*, esp. pp. 141–95, 226–35, for differing interpretations of similar rituals by two tribes on a single reservation.

54. For modern Asian Indian art, see later for comment by V. Desai; for comments about Mexican-American art, see T. Ybarra-Frausto, "The Chicano Movement/The Movement of Chicano Art," in *Exhibiting Cultures*, ed. I. Karp and S. D. Lavine (Washington, D.C.: Smithsonian Institution Press, 1991), pp. 135, 141.

55. For the work at Pojoaque Pueblo, see the Appendix for an account of the history, concept, and design. I thank Nycha Leia Zenderman, assistant to the lieutenant governor of the Pueblo, George Rivera, who prepared the document in October 1994, and to Lieutenant Governor Rivera for approving it and having it sent to me with permission to reprint it in its entirety. Their discussion addresses various matters pertinent to this book. I thank Wayne Lloyd and Dennis Holloway, former architects for Pojoaque, for helpful information.

56. On Acoma, see Christopher Wilson, tour notes for Society of Architectural Historians, 1993, and *New Mexico Vacation Guide* (1993), pp. 37–38.

57. "Fort McDowell/Beeline Highway Development Guidelines," (April 1993), esp. sec. 2, p. 1, secs. 4–6. I thank Don Ryden for sending various documents and speaking to me about this.

58. E. Hobsbawm and T. Ranger, eds., *The Invention of Tradition* (Cambridge: Cambridge University Press, 1983).

59. *LCT*, April 17, 1991, p. 3C.

60. Pura Fe*, quoted in R. Martin*, "Urban Indian Artists," *NEIQ* 7, no. 4 (1990): 57; M. Hodgson*, quoted in *LT*, July 8, 1992, p. A2; P. Butler*, in *Keepers of the Treasures*, p. 10. M. Vera*, "The Creation of Language, a Yowlumni Story," *News from Native California* 7, no. 3 (1993): 19–20. R. G. Runs After*, in *ICT* August 3, 1994, p. A4; on P. White, see *NAPr* January 8, 1993, p. 1.

61. *ICT*, May 28, 1994, p. C3.

62. N. Stremmel, "The Politics of Illness," *American Indian Community House Bulletin* 9, no. 14 (1993): 12, 21; 8 (Spring–Summer 1992): 15, printed the Youth Agenda. On Sinte Gleska, see *LT*, May 20, 1992, p. B4. J. L. Flyinghorse*, in *LT*, July 22, 1992, p. B3. On Lame Deer, see *LT*, August 17, 1991, p. A3. Thousands of such statements have been made. For a balanced view, see also *NA20C*, s.v. "Alcohol Abuse."

63. J. Weibel-Orlando, "Hooked on Healing: Anthropologists, Alcohol, and Intervention," *Human Organization* 48, no. 2 (1989): 148–55. The most effective methods and types of programs are discussed on p. 153.

64. *LT*, April 15, 1992, p. A2.

65. "Declaration of the International Indigenous Aids Network," *American Indian Community House Bulletin* 9, no. 14 (1993): 18.

66. *NYT*, February 17, 1994, p. C8.

67. M. Ambler, "Making Room for Tradition," *Tribal College* 5, no. 3 (1994): 17.

68. G. Harden, "Hogans in Hospitals," *Tribal College* 5, no. 3 (1994): 21.

69. John Breuninger, January 31, 1994.

70. I thank G. C. Pearl for a helpful interview and photographs.

71. *LT*, January 28, 1992, p. C5.

72. Quoted in Gault, "Swinomish Smokehouse," p. 36.

73. J. Brant*, "Tribute to Iroquois Beadworkers," *NEIQ* 7, no 4 (1990): 74.

74. I thank Guidance Center director Jim Hahn for this information and much other help. The building was first erected in 1920, enlarged in 1936, and remodeled in its present form around 1986 by architect David Smith.

75. Velma Yazzie*, director, kindly supplied this information. Begay & Begay* copyrighted the design in 1982. The builders were Kealy Construction. The penalty of a mural was also exacted from Dean Narcho*, a Tohono O'odham muralist, at the Tucson Indian Center in 1991.

76. Quoted in Bibby, "Still Going," p. 36.

77. I thank Ray James, architect in Ada, for helpful information.

78. Robert Webb and Winton Smith of Arctic Slope Consulting Group explained this project. Architect Robert Montoya* is project manager for the BIA. For more about these buildings, see Chapter 8.

79. Quoted in *LT*, September 14, 1991, p. A2.

80. Quoted in J. Barreiro, "Architectural Design: An American Indian Process. An Interview with Dennis Sun Rhodes," *NEIQ* 7, no. 2 (1990): 27. I thank Arlene Hirschfelder for this reference.

CHAPTER 3

1. J. Sklansky, "Rock, Reservation, and Prison: The Native American Occupation of Alcatraz," *AICRJ* 13, no. 2 (1989): 29–68.

2. See H. L. Gates, Jr., "'Authenticity', or the Lesson of Little Tree," *NYT Book Review*, November 24, 1991, pp. 1, 26, 30. On the authenticity of so-called primitive societies, see C. Lévi-Strauss, *Structural Anthropology* (New York: Basic Books, 1963), pp. 367–68.

3. J. Abu-Lughod, "Disappearing Dichotomies: First World-Third World," *TDSR* 3, no. 2 (1992): 11. Authors who have addressed the dynamism of Indian cultures include D. McNickle*, "Americans Called Indians," in *North American Indians in Historical Perspective*, ed. E. B. Leacock and N. O. Lurie (New York: Random House, 1971), pp. 29–63; E. H. Spicer, ed., *Perspectives in American Indian Culture Change* (Chicago: University of Chicago Press, 1961); W. E. Washburn, ed., *The Indian and the White Man* (Garden City, N.Y.: Doubleday, 1964); F. P. Prucha, "American Indian Policy in the Twentieth Century," *Western Historical Quarterly*, 15 (1984): 5–18.

4. See G. Horse Capture*, "Some Observations on Establishing Tribal Museums," *History News* 36, no. 1 (1981): 1. M. Warburton explains what Navajos take from Anglos and what is essential to them in building in "Culture Change and the Navajo Hogan" (Ph.D. diss., Washington State University, 1985).

5. On this issue, see G. Toffin, "Ecology and Anthropology of Traditional Dwellings," *TDSR* 5, no. 2 (1994): 9–20.

6. I thank James Laban*, Kurt Dongoske*, and Jim Hahn for their advice; Selena Hill* and David Sloan* for their help.

7. E. Norris, study prepared for Santo Domingo Pueblo (n.p., n.d.). L. A. Olsen of Billings, Montana, architect of Pine Ridge High School (1994), and CTA Architects, also of Billings, who designed the Crow and Northern Cheyenne IHS Hospital (1995) and the Northern Cheyenne tribal administration building in Lame Deer, Montana (1995), used Indian-inspired design—that is, plan features and ornament to recall local and pan-Indian elements. See *ICT*, January 26, 1995, p. B1; April 6, 1995, p. A7; April 13, 1995, p. A3.

8. I note Peter Whiteley's objection to the term "acculturation," which he feels diminishes the role of the respondent. See

his *Deliberate Acts: Changing Hopi Culture Through the Oraibi Split*, Tucson: University of Arizona Press, 1988, p. 288. The approach taken in my book is actor-oriented whenever that approach corresponds to the apparent reality of the situation.

9. J. Clifford, *The Predicament of Culture: Twentieth Century Ethnography, Literature, and Art* (Cambridge, Mass.: Harvard University Press, 1988), p. 95.

10. K. Frampton, "Towards a Critical Regionalism: Six Points for an Architecture of Resistance," in *The Anti-Aesthetic: Essays on Postmodern Culture*, ed. H. Foster (Port Townsend, Wash.: Bay Press, 1983), pp. 16–30; he later expanded the six to "Ten Points on an Architecture of Regionalism," *CENTER: A Journal for Architecture in America* 3, (1987): 20–27. See, however, T. Schumacher, "Regional Intentions and Contemporary Architecture: A Critique," *CENTER* 3 (1987): 50–57, esp. 55. A. Rapoport observed a neo-Québecois style around 1980 in *The Meaning of the Built Environment* (Beverly Hills, Calif.: Sage, 1982), p. 76; it is probably connected to nationalist politics, as some Native American architecture is. Edward Rojas and his associates developed a new "vernacular" for Chiloe that residents began to accept as theirs, see C. Morales, "Edward Rojas," *Mimar*, no 42 (1992): 70–75. In New York City, William Davis is trying to develop Afrocentric architecture based on disparate models throughout the African continent. For North Africa, see N. M. Albasani, "Toward the Rebirth of Contemporary Regionalism: Reconciling Culture and Technology," *TDSR* 4, no. 1 (1992): 47, and K. Hadjri, "Vernacular Housing Forms in North Algeria," *TDSR* 5, no. 1 (1993): 65–74, with the aim of reforming foreign-introduced practices and components. For New Zealand, see C. A. Bird, "The Invention of Urban Form in Post-Colonial Aotearoa," *TDSR* 4, no. 1 (1992): 40–41. For curved roofs on contemporary official Chinese buildings, see "Provided They Have Curly Tops," *Economist*, July 16, 1994, p. 80.

11. On adopting past forms for creating a new identity, see G. M. Tartakov, "Art and Identity: The Rise of a New Buddhist Imagery," *Art Journal* 49, no. 4 (1990): 409–17, esp. 412–14, on architecture.

12. *NYT*, September 26, 1993, sec. 2, p. 44.

13. M. St. Pierre*, "The Status of Contemporary Lakota Tribal Arts," in *Sharing a Heritage: American Indian Arts*, ed. C. Heth and M. Swarm (Los Angeles, 1984), p. 18.

14. S. R. Dixon, "The Essential Spirit," *NEIQ* 7, no. 4 (1990): 11.

15. F. Johnson, "Stylistic Change in Classroom Native Music," *Journal of Ethnic Studies* 9, no. 2 (1981): 39–42.

16. S. Begay*, in "Cosmos, Man & Nature," pp. 27–28.

17. Dixon, "Essential Spirit," p. 9.

18. R. Houle, "Search for Identity," *Tawow* 2, no. 2 (1971): 3.

19. E. McGaa*, *Mother Earth Spirituality: Native American Paths to Healing Ourselves and Our World* (San Francisco: Harper & Row, 1990).

20. M. L. Wax, review of *Mother Earth Spirituality*, by E. McGaa, *Ethnohistory* 38, no. 4 (1991): 458–59. Marlies Yearby, founder of Movin' Spirits Dance Theater in New York, in approving of friends' invented wedding ritual, observed, "That's very important to who we are as African-Americans, because we constantly have to remake and invent our culture" (*NYT*, June 12, 1994, sec. 9, p. 13). This might be said of all people, but it has special poignancy for minorities, whether African- or Native American.

21. T. H. Lewis, "The Changing Place of the Oglala Medicine Man," *Plains Anthropologist* 25, no. 89 (1980): 265.

22. E. J. Dickson-Gilmore, "Finding the Ways of the Ancestors: Cultural Change and the Invention of Tradition in the Development of Separate Legal Systems, " *Canadian Journal of Criminology* 34, nos. 3-4 (1992): 489–302.

23. R. A. Warrior*, "A Marginal Voice," *Native Peoples* 1, no. 3 (1991): 30.

24. P. Apodaca*, "Permanent Sand-Painting as an Art Form," in *Sharing a Heritage*, ed. Heth and Swarm, pp. 159–63.

25. I thank Margaret Houston for this information.

26. N. Scott Momaday, *The Names: A Memoir* (New York: Harper & Row, n.d.), p. 25. For artists who have sought their Indian identity, see also N. H. H. Graburn, "Ethnic Arts of the Fourth World: The View from Canada," in *Imagery and Creativity: Ethnoaesthetics and Art Worlds in the Americas*, ed. D. S. Whitten and N. E. Whitten (Tucson: University of Arizona Press, 1993), p. 192.

27. V. Dominguez, "The Marketing of Heritage," *American Ethnologist* 13, no. 3 (1986): 546–55.

28. H. T. Hoover and J. Cash, *To Be an Indian: An Oral History* (New York: Holt, Rinehart, 1971), p. 191.

29. Smithsonian advertisement for the book, mailed May 1993.

30. M. Ames, "How Anthropologists Fabricate the Cultures They Study," in *Museums, the Public, and Anthropology: A Study in the Anthropology of Anthropology* (Vancouver: University of British Columbia Press, 1986), pp. 48–49.

31. On ethnological collecting as the invention of heritage, see Dominguez, "Marketing of Heritage," p. 550.

CHAPTER 4

1. Quoted in O. Grabar, "Why History: The Meanings and Uses of Tradition," *TDSR* 4, no. 2 (1993): 19.

2. American Indian Council of Architects and Engineers, *Our Home: A Design Guide for Indian Housing* (Washington, D.C.: National Endowment for the Arts, n.d. [ca. 1994]), esp. pp. 24–34.

3. David Sloan* points out that he and his colleagues come from towns rather than from remote parts of the reservation.

4. [Society of Architectural Historians] *Newsletter* 37, no. 1 (1993): 1–2.

CHAPTER 5

1. For information, I thank Barbara and Sherman Sass, Anne-Marie Fleming, Lucinda Yandell*, Surrounded-by-Enemy*, and Daves Rossell. For the Paiute building, see P. Russell-Roberts, "A Tribe Goes Home," *Native Nevadan*, April 1986, pp. 3–4, 26.

2. I thank Douglas Whitney and Michael Czarnecki of this firm; the latter was architect in charge of the project.

3. *LT*, April 17, 1991, p. C3. The headline is suggestive: "Art Is Powerful Medicine at New Rosebud Hospital."

4. "Visiting the Nations: Turtle Mountain Band of Chippewa," *ICT*, May 12, 1993 [supplement], p. 10.

5. I thank Tony Davis* for this information.

6. I thank Dale Sickles of A&E for this information.

7. A. Deer*, in "Cosmos, Man, & Nature," pp. 104–5.

8. The description that follows, some of it questionable according to George H. J. Abrams*, and quotes, except as noted, come from Carson Waterman*. I thank Michelle Dean Stock* and Judith Greene*, present museum director, for information. Waterman also designed the part of a longhouse displayed inside; it was constructed inauthentically because of the minimal budget, space, and materials available. Waterman and Barnwell collaborated also on the Seneca Library next door to the museum, where Waterman's designs of horizontal bands are made of cast iron to last for the life of the building. Martha I. Symes* designed clan and other symbols for an ornamental frieze inside. The Seneca added to the EDA funds for construction.

9. See E. Tooker, "The United States Constitution and the Iroquois League," *Ethnohistory* 35, no. 4 (1988): 305–6.

10. For alternative interpretations of wampum images, see S. Fadden, "Beaded History," *NEIQ*, Fall 1987, pp. 17–20.

11. *NYT*, December 2, 1991, p.B1. Other articles may be found in the *NYT Index* for 1990–1992.

12. See *Salamanca Press* concerning events of May 14 and 25, 1992, and of January 2, 1993. Thanks to Judith Greene*, museum director, for the references.

CHAPTER 6

1. Navajo National Division of Community Development, Design, and Engineering Services, and Department of Energy, *Navahomes: A Dinelogical Study of Navajo Dwelling in Balance with the Land* (Window Rock, Ariz.: Navajo Nation, 1992).

2. I thank Rayna Green* for introducing me to Anna Mitchell.

3. I thank Norman Suazo* for this information.

4. I thank Dorothy Dandy* and Sylvena Mayer* for information.

5. I thank Thomas Hodne for information on this and other projects. A plaque in the vestibule gives the date as 1975; other sources say 1978. Hodne was director of architecture; Gerald S. Johnson, coordinator architect; Dennis Sun Rhodes*, cultural architect. R&S Construction Co., Glenn C. Barber, construction manager; Merle Bunge and Harold Haux, project superintendents. Craig Smith, EDA regional director. Bill Roberts, Lakota Public Works Program director. See E. Gaboury, "Amerindian Identity, Architects: The Hodne–Stageberg Partners," *Architectural Review* 168, no. 1002 (1980): 79–86.

6. I thank Bruce Knutson for information and images. See *NAPr*, September 24, 1993, p. 3.

7. C. Townsend-Gault, "Ritualizing Ritual's Rituals," *Art Journal* 51, no. 3 (1992): 57. For information, I thank Leanne Doxtater* and Sara Loe.

8. *NAPr*, September 17, 1993, p. 1; H. Landecker, "Designing for American Indians," *Architecture* 82, no. 12 (1993): 98.

9. For information, I thank Patty Cornelius* and Sara Loe. The BIA owns the school, but the tribe operates and maintains it. Architects: Partners of Architectural Concern; mechanical engineer: George Mesgoda; electrical engineer: John A. Skurla & Associates; structural engineer: Hurst and Henrichs; general contractor: Leech Lake Reservation Construction.

10. Factors in his firm's selection were experience in museum design and some work for Laguna Pueblo with the Hopi–Laguna architect David Riley*. The latter consulted on the original conceptual sketches, which relate the Navajo Museum to its setting and define circulation patterns. I thank Dave Dekker and D. Riley for this information.

11. Draft of publication for "An American Indian Cultural Heritage Conference" (University of Oregon at Eugene, May 9–10, 1986), p. 1. For additional comments on museums that reflect tribal perspectives, see "Cosmos, Man and Nature," esp. pp. 186–190.

12. Information thanks to Dave Dekker, Loren Miller*, and Robert Roessel. See R. A Barrenche, "Dine Museum Center," *Architecture* 82, no. 12 (1993): 35. For earlier expressions of the museum's philosophy, see J. C. Wright, "Proposal for a New Library Facility," May 17, 1982; R. P. Hartman and D. E. Doyel,

"Preserving a Native People's Heritage: The Navajo Tribal Museum," *Kiva* 47, no. 4 (1982): 239–55; and Hartman, "The Navajo Tribal Museum: Bridging the Past and the Present," *American Indian Art Magazine* 9, no. 1 (1983): 30–35, 81. For Riley*'s vision of walls as canyons, see *ICT* [Navajo Nation supplement], April 1995, p. 28. One Navajo-owned participating construction company is Arviso–Oakland. This article also names Del Dixon of DCSW as a major participant.

13. G. Ball and L. A. Platteter, "New Plains Indian Museum," *American Indian Art Magazine* 4, no. 3 (1979): 48.

14. Quotes thanks to George Horse Capture*. Architects were Malone Iverson & Associates, now Malone & Belton, Sheridan, Wyoming.

15. A. Lee* [Mohawk student], quoted in N. Vearil, "Under the Eagle's Watch," *Native Peoples* 6, no. 3 (1993): 48.

16. I thank Peter T. Flynn and Sandy Cook* of the American Indian Program; Ronald LaFrance*, director of the program; and Barbara L. Michaels and William L. Krinsky for Cornell publications. See *The Web*, December 1989, p. 4; Summer 1991, p. 1; *Cornell*, Summer 1991, p. 12; Winter 1992, p. 16; and "Treating Students Like Family Is Key to American Indian Program," *Agriculture and Life Sciences News*, Spring 1991. See also S. Fadden, "Beaded History," *NEIQ* 4, no. 3 (1987): 17–20; R. W. Venables, R. LaFrance*, and S. Fadden, "Symbols of Akwe:kon" (typescript, September 3, 1991); "Program to Study American Indians Opens a House," *NYT*, September 8, 1991, sec. 1, p. 51; and C. Shea, "Does Student Housing Encourage Racial Separation on Campus?" *Chronicle of Higher Education*, July 14, 1993, pp. A26–27. A good number of Akwe:kon residents are not Native American, and 83 percent of Cornell's Indian undergraduates live elsewhere. See letter from Cornell officials, *NYT*, April 15, 1995, p. 18.

CHAPTER 7

1. For the Wichita and Washat, see P. Nabokov and R. Easton, *Native American Architecture* (New York: Oxford University Press, 1989), pp. 149, 186.

2. For particularly helpful material on pueblos, see R. N. Swentzell*, "An Architectural History of Santa Clara Pueblo" (M. Arch. thesis, University of New Mexico, 1976); Nabokov and Easton, *Native American Architecture*; D. G. Saile, "Architecture in the Pueblo World: A Study of the Architectural Contexts of Pueblo Culture in the Late Nineteenth Century" (Ph.D. diss. University of Newcastle-upon-Tyne, 1981); *Expedition: The University [of Pennsylvania] Museum Magazine of Archeology and Anthropology* 35, no. 1 (1993); A. Rapoport, "Pueblo and Hogan," in *Shelter and Society*, ed. P. Oliver (London: Barrie & Jenkins, 1969), pp. 66–73; A. Ortiz*, ed., *New Perspectives on the Pueblos* (Albuquerque: University of New Mexico Press, 1972), esp. F.

Eggan, "Summary," pp. 288–305; and Wo Peen* house, probably early 1950s, in O. LaFarge, *A Pictorial History of the American Indian* (New York: Crown, 1956), p. 250. For many aspects of pueblos, see N. C. Markovich, W. F. E. Preiser, and F. G. Sturm, eds., *Pueblo Style and Regional Architecture* (New York: Van Nostrand Reinhold, 1990).

3. G. Horse Capture*, in "Cosmos, Man & Nature," pp. 36, 40–41, 43.

4. I thank his sister, Antoinette*, for showing it to me in the company of Joseph Cushman, planner.

5. Marley Porter to author, February 13, 1992.

6. Nabokov and Easton, *Native American Architecture*, p. 339.

7. L. New*, foreword and acknowledgments to *Painted Tipis by Contemporary Plains Indian Artists* (Anadarko, Okla.: Indian Arts & Crafts Cooperative, 1973).

8. *NYT*, May 21, 1994, sec. 14, p. 8.

9. For example, Wigwam [really tipis] Village Motel (1937), Cave Creek, Kentucky, built and patented by Frank Redford; a sister village in Horse Cave; Wigwam Motel, West Foothill Boulevard (Route 66), Rialto, California; Grants, New Mexico; Nambe, New Mexico; one in a recreational-vehicle park 18 miles south of Gardnerville, Nevada, on Highway 395; Palm Springs, California; see also the Tee Pee Barbecue (ca. 1930), Long Beach, California. I thank Carol Betts and Alison K. Hoagland for several examples. See also F. Scholder, "Indian Kitsch," *American Indian Art Magazine* 4, no. 2 (Spring 1979): 64–69, esp. 68.

10. B. Parkman, "Dedicating Sumeg," *News from Native California* 5, no. 2 (1991): 6–7.

11. Victoria Young and Leon Satkowski helped me obtain photographs of this.

12. *LT*, August 15, 1992.

13. S. Begay*, in "Cosmos, Man & Nature," pp. 28, 32.

14. Nabokov and Easton, *Native American Architecture*, p. 336.

15. I thank Theodore Evans* for this information.

16. Begay, in "Cosmos, Man & Nature," p. 29; Evans.

17. R. Shanks and L. W. Shanks, *North American Indian Travel Guide* (Petaluma, Calif.: Costano Books, 1989), p. 75.

18. For the buildings mentioned and others, see D. Eargle, *The Earth Is Our Mother: A Guide to the Indians of California*, 3rd ed. (San Francisco: Trees Company Press, 1990); see also Shanks and Shanks, *Travel Guide*. Peter Nabokov is preparing a publication about roundhouses.

19. *Mimo-Bimadiziwin* [newsletter], Winter 1993, p. 22; Fall 1994, pp. 6–8.

20. I thank Rosemary Ellison* for this information.

21. Saile, "Architecture in the Pueblo World," p. 174.

22. B. Bibby, "Still Going: Bill Franklin and the Revival of

Miwuk Traditions," *News from Native California* 7, no. 3 (1993): 21–36; see allso B. Ortiz, "Big Time Special Times: Chaw'se and the Amador Tribal Council," *News from Native California* 4, no. 4 (1990): 20–23.

23. Chief Irving Powless*, lecture at New York Public Library, November 4, 1992.

24. *The Confederated Tribes of the Warm Springs Reservation. Annual Report* (1985), p. 6.

25. For much of this information, I am indebted to Stuart Jones*, in the tribal planning office.

26. I thank Norma Joseph* and Marvin Kastning.

27. Information from Andres Fernando* and Joseph Cushman. See B. Smith, "Return of the Great Canoes," *Native Peoples* 6, no. 2 (1993): 10–20, and D. Neel, "The Rebirth of the Northwest Coast Canoe," *Native Peoples* 7, no. 2 (1994): 10–18.

28. M. Antone, "Museum Project Update," *Au-Authm Action News*, April–May 1987, p. 1. For additional information, I thank Jack Gauman, Doreen Duncan*, and R. Gwinn Vivian. Ann Hedlund, an anthropologist at Arizona State University, was consultant to the museum; Jack Gauman was construction supervisor.

29. L. Fowler, *Shared Symbols, Contested Meanings* (Ithaca, N.Y.: Cornell University Press, 1987), p. 166.

30. I thank Robbin Obomsawin and Charles Garriott in addition to those named.

31. Thanks to R. Ackley, J. Blanchard, and Bob Powless* for information about these buildings.

32. Parkman, "Dedicating Sumeg," pp. 4–8.

33. For information, I am grateful to Michelle Dean Stock* and Adele Levine of Molinaro/Rubin. George H. J. Abrams* informs me that as of early 1995, plans were suspended, perhaps abandoned.

34. In addition to those named in this chapter, reconstructed villages and buildings are listed in Shanks and Shanks, *Travel Guide*, and are seen in California at Anderson Marsh State Park, Yosemite National Park, and Kule Loklo, and are planned for East Bay Regional Park District. The Ute Mountain tribe hopes to reproduce a prehistoric cliff dwelling in Colorado. The New York State Museum contains a reconstructed longhouse. Indian City USA in Oklahoma, and Ohio Frontier Land near Columbus are Anglo-owned rebuilt villages. I thank Phyllis Myers for the East Bay reference; Alfonso Ortiz* for the Ute Mountain information.

35. An illustration is in *Chickasaw Times*, May 1991, p. 6.

CHAPTER 8

1. Illustration in *Chickasaw Nation Annual Report to the People* (n.d.), [p. 20]. I thank Glenda Galvan* for this reference.

2. Mechanical engineer: Ben Notkin; landscape architect: Jones* & Jones; builder: Del Buzzi Construction.

3. H. F. Hughes, "A History of the Development of the Makah Cultural and Research Center, Neah Bay, Washington" (master's thesis, University of Washington, 1978), p. 2.

4. Ibid., p. 28.

5. G. Arnold*, in "Cosmos, Man & Nature," p. 86; see also pp. 85–88, 93, 182–83.

6. *Keepers of the Treasures*, p. 26–27.

7. See also R. Hayward*, J. Campisi, and W. Starna, Report to Mashantucket Pequots concerning tribal museums (June 23–July 1, 1984); A. M. Renker and G. W. Arnold*, "Exploring the Role of Education in Cultural Resource Management: The Makah Cultural and Research Center Example," *Human Organization* 47, no. 4 (1988); 302–7; K. Keister, "In the Native Tongue," *Historic Preservation*, July 1992, pp. 36–41, 77–79; G. I. Quimby and J. D. Nason, "New Staff for a New Museum," *Museum News*, May–June 1977, pp. 50–52; and *Seattle Times* [pictorial section], August 19, 1975, pp. 8–11.

8. Milton Hunt was the contract architect for Lower Elwha, although someone else did the design. I thank Carol Brown* for information. Joseph Cushman kindly took me to see Squaxin Island. I thank Molly Aalbue for information on a proposed library-museum.

9. Planning document, p. 6, courtesy of C. Jackson.

10. C. T. Caldwell, "Suquamish Tribal Cultural Center and Suquamish Museum Development and History," (master's thesis, University of Washington, 1987). I thank Mary Alice Morley for first calling the building to my attention.

11. For information, thanks are due to Nick Zaferatos, director, and Stuart Jones* of the planning department.

12. I thank Brycene Neaman*, museum director; A. Robert Williams; the library staff; and Meredith Clausen, who interviewed Pietro Belluschi for me. For symbols of local identity, see S. O'Brien, *American Indian Tribal Governments* (Norman: University of Oklahoma Press, 1989), p. 190; *Keepers of the Treasures*, p. 63; *Yakima Herald-Republic*, June 3, 1980, pp. 1A–8A; and *Yakima Nation Cultural Center Souvenir Edition*, June 4, 1980.

13. Information on materials comes from Duane King; quotes are from Christopher Boothby, project architect.

14. In addition to the designers, I thank Michael Hammond, director; Lisa Watt*; Jarold Ramsay; and Duane King. See *Twanat: A Quarterly Publication of the Museum at Warm Springs*, esp. 1, no. 1 (1994); M. L. Bierman, "Tribal Tribute," *Architecture* 82, no. 12 (1993): 70–77; J. Krakauer, "AD Travels: The Museum at Warm Springs," *Architectural Digest* 50, no. 10 (1993): 94–100; M. Leccese, "Cultural Collaborations," *Landscape Architecture* 83, no. 1 (1993): 50–52; O. Patt, Jr.*, "The Museum at Warm

Springs: The Story of Three Tribes," *American Indian Art Magazine* 19, no. 2 (1994): 42–49; Patt, "The Museum at Warm Springs: A Timeless Heritage," *Oregon Heritage* 1, no. 2 (1994): 18–21; Patt, "Warm Springs: People of the Community Create Their Own Museum," *Native Peoples* 8, no. 2 (1995): 50–56; B. Rasmussen, "A Building of the Land," *Native Peoples* 8, no. 2 (1995): 22; and J. Nason, "Community and Continuity: The Museum at Warm Springs," *American Anthropologist* 96, no. 2 (1994): 492–94. For earlier projects, see Smithsonian Institution Museum Resource Center, projects by Reddick, Waldron, Benner (Portland), Pacific Economica (Salem), Waldron Huston Barber (Bend); *Spilyay Tymoo (Warm Springs News) Coyote News*, October 7, 1983, p. 7; October 21, 1988, p. 3; *Twanat: The Museum at Warm Springs* [presentation booklet by Stastny–Burke] (n.d.). The museum won the fiscal year 1994 HUD award for Cultural Design—Tribal Facility.

15. Marcellene Norton* and her sister, Vera Houston*, provided information about the house.

16. Ramona Charles* supplied this information. The longhouse, another WPA project, dates from 1936 to 1939. A kitchen was added in 1977.

17. For information and opinions, I thank John Tippeconnic III* and Robert Roessel. Dave Bell discussed maintenance problems. See D. Dedera, "To Walk in Two Worlds," *The Lamp* 74, no. 4 (1992): 12–17. I thank Linda Gerstein for this reference. See also most issues of *Tribal College*; W. J. Stein, *Tribally Controlled Colleges. Making Good Medicine* (New York: Peter Lang, 1992); N. T. Oppelt, "The Tribally Controlled Colleges in the 1980s: Higher Education's Best Kept Secret," *AICRJ* 8, no. 4 (1984): 27–45; M. Ambler, "The Nation's First Tribal College," *Native Peoples* 4, no. 2 (1991): 22–23; S. Schonbach, "What the Redman Needs," *Catholic World*, November 1971, pp. 66–70; and J. C. Wright, "Proposal for a New Library Facility," Window Rock, Arizona, May 17, 1982.

18. Information and photographs from Charles Cambridge*, Dennis Holloway, Thomas Noel, and Peter Caughey. See H. G. Bradley, "Solar Hogans: Houses of the Future?" *Native Peoples* 3, no. 3 (1990): 44–50; T. Jones, "Culturally Relevant Campus Housing Adds a Technological Twist to a Navajo Tradition," *Los Angeles Times*, February 26, 1990; *LT*, October 11, 1988, p. A6; C. Hodge, "Hogans Go Solar for Power," *Arizona Republic*, December 19, 1988; J. Berman, "CU's Solar Hogans," *Boulder Fall Magazine*, 1989, p. 7; and P. Caughey, "Home Again," *Summit Magazine*, Fall 1989, pp. 2, 4.

19. My thanks to David Sloan* and his associates, and to Candi Helms.

20. This information from Marley Porter, former Navajo tribal architect.

21. T. Evans*, quoted in *ICT*, December 22, 1993, p. B8.

22. Robert Webb and Winton L. Smith at Arctic Slope Consulting Group, architects. I thank David Griffin for other information.

23. Information from Rita Nunes, chief of docent program. See also B. Bibby, "Still Going: Bill Franklin and the Revival of Miwuk Traditions," *News from Native California* 7, no. 3 (1993): 21–36, esp. 34–35. The name Miwuk is also spelled Miwok.

24. Landscape architect and civil engineer: EDAW; structural engineer: GKT Consulting Engineers.

25. Neil Stoughton supplied helpful information.

26. Sara Loe, letter to the author, August 1, 1991.

27. I thank the architect for a site visit, and also Louis Biederstedt, construction supervisor for Capital City Construction.

28. I am indebted to Matthew Uses-the-Knife* for information.

29. I thank John Cuningham, Robert Zakaras, and members of the Cuningham Hamilton Quiter staff for helpful information, comments, and images. See also *The Woodlands Voice: A Publication of the Mille Lacs Band of Ojibwe Indians*, Fall 1993, p. 5; H. Landecker, "Designing for American Indians," *Architecture* 82, no. 12 (1993): 100–101.

30. For Erskine, see S. Cantacuzino, *Modern Houses of the World* (London: Dutton Vista, 1964), pp. 94–97.

31. O'Brien, *American Indian Tribal Governments*, p. 242. I owe thanks to Andrew Gokee*, Sara Loe, and Verna DeLeon*, Menominee public-relations director.

32. I thank Edward Larrabee Barnes for conversation, a photograph, and a copy of *Edward Larrabee Barnes Museum Designs* [exhibition catalogue] (Katonah, N.Y.: Katonah Gallery, 1987), pp. 16–17.

33. D. G. Saile, "Architecture in the Pueblo World: A Study of the Architectural Context of Pueblo Culture in the Late Nineteenth Century" (Ph.D. diss., University of Newcastle-upon-Tyne, 1981), p. 175.

34. For information and opinions, I thank Emory Sekaquaptewa*, the late Abbott Sekaquaptewa*, R. Gwinn Vivian, Bennie Gonzales, James Swearingen, and Jim Hahn. See "Hopi Cultural Center Dedicated to Traditions of the Past," *Journal of American Indian Education* 11, no. 1 (1971): 32, and F. Kabotie*, *Fred Kabotie: Hopi Indian Artist* (Flagstaff, Ariz.: Northland Press, 1977), pp. 77–95.

35. R. N. Swentzell*, "Santa Clara Pueblo: A Changing Community," in "The Architectural and Cultural Landscape of North Central New Mexico: Field Guide for 12th Annual Vernacular Architectural Forum, Sante Fe, May 15–18, 1991," ed. B. C. Pratt and C. Wilson [typescript], pp. 13–21; I thank Jean-Louis

Bourgeois and Chris Wilson for this, and John Garrigan and Winton Smith for other help. See also R. N. Swentzell*, "Conflicting Landscape Values: The Santa Clara Pueblo and Day School," *Places* 7, no. 1 (1990): 18–27.

36. Saile, "Architecture in the Pueblo World," p. 175.

37. Robert Montoya and Val Cordova offered helpful information.

38. Apart from Dennis Holloway, George Rivera*, and Alfonso Ortiz*, I must thank Nycha Leia Zenderman, Adele Levine, and Wayne Lloyd and Wendy Cox, who supplied the McHugh Lloyd Tryk planning document. See also M. F. Lambert, "Pojoaque Pueblo," in *Handbook of North American Indians: Southwest*, ed. A. Ortiz* (Washington, D.C.: Smithsonian Institution, 1978–), pp. 324–29.

39. Quoted in N. Zollinger, "Heritage of the Pueblos," *Travel and Leisure* 14, no. 12 (1984): E27.

40. Typescript statement prepared by the sponsors.

41. Zollinger, "Heritage of the Pueblos," p. E24.

42. Information from Andy Acoya*.

43. University of New Mexico Design Planning and Assistance Center, "Santo Domingo Pueblo: Development Projects," December 1, 1981. I thank Edward Norris for this report.

44. Architect Ron Hernandez* and Patrick Cudmore kindly supplied information.

45. Carlyle Sorensen of Johnson, Sheldon & Sorensen, and James R. Grover of Hickey Thorstensen Grover; Bill Rudnicki, tribal planner. Victoria Young and Leon Satkowski provided help and information of various kinds. For Mystic Lake, see pp. 228–30.

46. Quoted in *LT*, August 14, 1991, pp. A1–2. I thank Aaron Swan*; the late Lyle LaFramboise*, architect; and Surrounded-by-Enemy*. See M. Lawson, *Dammed Indians: The Pick-Sloan Plan and the Missouri River Sioux, 1944–1980* (Norman: University of Oklahoma Press, 1982), pp. 188–89.

47. For information, I thank Carl Ponca* and Neal McCaleb*.

48. In the same state, the Kullihoma alcohol-rehabilitation clinic (1976) and Tishomingo Health Clinic (1979), both by James-Childers of Ada, are built into berms. Although they look like mounds and seem to wed culture to curing, the first was built as a conference center and its sides and back recall the work of Frank Lloyd Wright and perhaps Bruce Goff. In both, the berms were designed for energy conservation, not cultural reference. Architect Ray James provided this information.

49. Barbara Sass offered this observation and the reference to *American Desert* 1, no. 2 (1993): 28.

50. For information, I am indebted to Jan Vasser*; for the use of her picture, Bette Hubbard.

CHAPTER 9

1. Knutson Construction Company was the builder.

2. For an instructive visit, I am grateful to Wayne Trottier, Jr.*. Thanks are due also to Glenn Walking Eagle* and to all three architects. On Lakota youth and military enrollment, see C. Hamilton, "For the Oglala Nation, Unity Comes with Differences," *Native Nations* 1, no. 3 (1991): 13–16, esp. 14–15.

3. Information from Michelle Dean-Stock* and Adele Levine. The existing museum is to be renovated as a visitor center, or perhaps for archives. For a supratribal circular exhibition space, see L. Williamson*, "As We Tell Our Stories," *NEIQ* 7, no. 4 (1990): 17–25.

4. *LT*, August 19, 1992, p. C1. On communications, see G. Himebaugh, "The Image Never Fades: A Survey of Tribal College Presidents on Media Stereotyping," *Tribal College* 6, no. 1 (1994): 32–36.

5. Thanks to Tom Sindelaar of the firm. See also *ICT*, January 28, 1992, p. B6.

6. Alex White Plume*, August 14, 1991.

7. For opinions, I thank Wynema Morse* and Mark Hoistad.

8. For information, I thank Verdaine Farmilant*, Patricia Morning*, and Fritz Dreger.

9. An earlier proposal for a Sioux Indian Cultural Center there was prepared around 1975 by Pacheco & Graham of Albuquerque for the Indian Arts & Crafts Board. The Department of the Interior Library has plans for buildings and an amphitheater.

10. Thanks to Larry Garcia* for information and a tour, and to Dina Thomas*, librarian, for the date, which has been given elsewhere as 1976. The participation of a Native American architect, whose name was given as Hanna Hannaniwa, has been mentioned. The closest name known to me is that of Gilbert Honanie*. He prepared a master plan for the tribe around 1978 and designed an octagonal health center that he says was not related to Tohono O'odham cultural concerns.

11. For information, I am indebted to Charles Boyd*, King, and Martin Hagerstrand.

12. My debt to Clifford Jackson, source of the quotes, is clear. I thank also Debbie Lematta at his firm; Mac Silverhorn*; Grant Jones; and Chester Sprague, who reported on water condensation in the walls. See G. D. Monthan, "Daybreak Star Center," *American Indian Art Magazine* 3, no. 3 (1978): 28–35; M. Graves and A. de los Angeles, eds., *United Indians of All Tribes Foundation: A Ten Year History, March 8, 1970–March 8, 1980*; "Master Plan. National Indian Cultural and Educational Center" (C. Jackson and D. Lematta kindly supplied these publications); tape of session, "Grassroots Native American Tribal Museums" chaired by Carla Roberts* at College Art Association Annual Meeting, February 5, 1993.

13. James P. Burke kindly sent a copy of the master plan. The architects included Tommy Yazzie*, director of engineering for the Navajo Nation; Marley Porter, tribal architect; and Virgil Gatewood*, designer.

14. Raymond Thompson informed me of this, and directed me to others who might have known about the symbols but did not. Agnese Nelms Haury, R. Gwinn Vivian, and Alan Ferg kindly suggested explanations and asked others on my behalf. Jill Copeland, librarian at Rio Grande, tried in vain to find local newspaper articles that explained the form. Neither Pat McDermott of the architectural firm nor John Long*, director of the center, was able to help.

15. Information from Raymond Thompson.

16. Information from Raymond Thompson. See also *ICT* [Gila River Indian Community supplement], Summer 1993; and K. Walenga, "Gila River Arts & Craft Center," *Pinal Ways*, Autumn 1992, pp. 4–5, courtesy of Jill Copeland.

17. Diane Lehse*, school principal.

18. Leonard Smith*, school custodian.

19. Sara Loe, letter to author, August 1, 1991.

20. Ibid.

21. Information from Thomas Hodne.

22. Dennis Sun Rhodes*, in "Cosmos, Man, and Nature," p. 142.

23. E. Gaboury, "Amerindian Indentity, Architects: The Hodne–Stageberg Partners," *Architectural Review* 168, no. 1002 (1980): 86.

24. Jim Noonan, business manager, made available the school's mission statement, and allotted time for an interview.

25. L. M., "Bringing Native Spirit Home," *Architecture Minnesota* 11, no. 3 (1985): 48.

26. My informant requested anonymity. Another housing official would not discuss designs regarded as flawed.

27. Quoted in J. Barreiro, "Architectural Design: An American Indian Process. An Interview with Dennis Sun Rhodes," *NEIQ* 7, no. 2 (1990): 26.

28. Structural engineer: Bakke, Kopp, Ballou * McFarlin; electrical engineer: Ericksen/Ellison & Associates; civil engineer: Warren White, P. E. In 1973 to 1975, Marcel Breuer designed an unbuilt high school for Pine Ridge. The solid trapezoid with a glazed sloping wall facing a stand of trees looked more pueblo-like than Lakota but was probably not meant to be Indian at all. It was characteristic of his style at the time, as his biographer, Isabelle Hyman, points out, and may have been intended for energy conservation.

29. G. Johnson, "Completion of Little Wound School Fulfills Dream," *Rapid City Journal*, May 26, 1982.

30. Thomas Hodne discussed candidly all his buildings. For information on this one, I also thank H. John Haas. See also

Gaboury, "Amerindian Identity," and T. David, *Contemporary Third World Architecture* (Brooklyn, N.Y.: Pratt Institute, 1983), pp. 80–81.

31. Sun Rhodes, in "Cosmos, Man & Nature," p. 146.

32. For information, I thank Thomas Hodne, Dennis Sun Rhodes*, Arthur Zimiga*, Alex White Plume*, and Surrounded-by-Enemy*. See Barreiro, "Architectural Design," p. 26; the college's fund-raising mailings; *ICT*, February 25, 1993, on background to changes in tribal chairmen; *Buffalo Evening News*, May 7, 1977, p. C7; *Architecture Minnesota* 6, no. 6 (1980): 36; Gaboury, "Amerindian Identity"; David, *Third World Architecture*, pp. 82–83; and *Chronicle of Higher Education*, April 6, 1988, pp. A15, 16. Structural engineer: Bakke, Kopp, Ballou & McFarlin; mechanical engineer: Sheesley Plumbing and Heating; electrical engineer: Branch Electrical; general contractor: Henry Hackett & Son.

33. Gaboury, "Amerindian Identity," p. 82.

34. Sun Rhodes, in "Cosmos, Man & Nature," p. 239.

35. Ibid.

36. Sun Rhodes, quoted in *Buffalo Evening News*, May 7, 1977, p. C7.

37. Sun Rhodes, in "Cosmos, Man & Nature," p. 145.

38. The Mohegan of Connecticut proposed to have people enter their tribal casino through the mouth of a wolf, their symbol.

39. *NYT*, June 13, 1993.

40. For information, I thank Thomas Hodne, Dennis Sun Rhodes*, Fred Laubaugh* (director), Elwood Green* (curator), and Henry Gobin*. See *Buffalo Evening News*, May 7, 1977, p. C7, and March 5, 1978, pp. 8, 10, 11; J. Wake and R. Hill*, "The Native American Center for the Living Arts in Niagara Falls," *American Indian Art Magazine* Summer 1980, pp. 22–26; W. Hayward*, J. Campisi, and W. Starna, Report to Mashantucket Pequots (June 23–July 1, 1984); W. Trimm, "The Turtle for the Living Arts," *Conservationist* 36, no. 3 (1981): 22–26; *Niagara Gazette*, March 27, 1977; and "Special Report: The Third National Indian Cultural Conference," *Tawow* 3, no. 1 (1972): 1–5. Structural engineers: Bakke, Kopp, Ballou & McFarlin; mechanical engineers: Jacus Assocs.; construction: Scrufari–Siegfried Joint Venture.

41. I am most grateful to Richard Thern for information and for making possible a vist to the school, which was completed in 1994. Ronald Hill* and Ben Cannon* were also kind enough to spend time discussing the school, and especially the importance of its cultural and educational mission.

42. Richard deLappe was probably the designer. Tom Martinson informed me about this project.

43. I thank Chairman Alfreda Mitre* and Dennis Sun Rhodes*. See also P. Russell-Roberts, "A Tribe Goes Home," *Native Nevadan*, April, 1986, pp. 3, 4, 26.

44. Both partners supplied information, but the quotes are from Sun Rhodes*.

45. For information and tours, I thank Thomas Hodne, Don Vermeland, Phyllis Gotzh*, Gail Thomas, Ron Gittings, and Mary Ellen Sigmond. In Hodne's firm, Vermeland is the design coordinator, and Roger Kipp the project director. For Damberg, Scott, Peck & Booker, John Damberg is architect of record, John Scott is project administrator, and Greg Granholm is project architect. Contractor: Adolfson and Peterson; landscape architect: Herb Baldwin; civil engineer: Sathre-Berquist; mechanical and electrical engineer: Gausman & Moore. See also *ICT*, February 11, 1993, p. A3; *Saint Paul Pioneer Press*, October 13, 1992, p. 8B; M. Johnson, "Fond du Lac College Builds a New Campus," *Tribal College* 3, no. 1 (1991): 10–11; and H. Landecker, "Designing for American Indians: Fond du Lac Community College," *Architecture* 82, no. 12 (1993): 94–95.

46. Thanks to the architect and to the rangers at the site.

47. Helen Scheirbeck*, David Francis, and Margaret Houston earned my sincere thanks. See also "Visitors Center, Indian Cultural Center," *Architecture* 80, no. 2 (1991): 36.

48. I thank Anselmo Valencia*, Kathy Ann Valencia, and Don Ryden for information and a copy of the development concepts. See W. Willard, "Self-Governance for Native Americans: The Case of the Pascua Yaqui Tribe," in *American Indian Policy*, ed. L. S. Legters and F. J. Lyman (Westport, Conn.: Greenwood Press, 1993), pp. 3–13.

CHAPTER 10

1. I thank Anna Sofaer for these references, among others: A. Sofaer, V. Zinser, and R. M. Sinclair, "A Unique Solar Marking Construct," *Science* 206 (1979): 283–91; A. Sofaer, R. M. Sinclair, and L. Doggett, "Lunar Markings on Fajada Butte," in *Archaeoastronomy in the New World: American Primitive Astronomy*, ed. A. F. Aveni (Cambridge: Cambridge University Press, 1982), pp. 169–81; A. Sofaer and R. M. Sinclair, "Astronomical Markings at Three Sites on Fajada Butte," in *Astronomy and Ceremony in the Prehistoric Southwest*, ed. J. Carlson and W. J. Judge (Albuquerque: Maxwell Museum of Anthropology, 1987), pp. 43–70; S. Curral, "Mapping the Sun Dagger," in *Technical Papers 1987 ASPRS-ACSM Annual Convention* (1987), vol. 2, pp. 1–7. In "Architecture at Chaco Canyon: Spirituality and Siting," A. L. Marshall presented practical reasons for siting of the canyon's major architectural complexes without denying that solar markers were created (Paper delivered at the annual meeting of the Society of Architectural Historians, April 29, 1994.

2. For information about the school and plans, I thank Al Qöyawayma*, James Stewart Polshek, Paolo Soleri, Edmund Gonzales*, Anna Sofaer, and James Swearingen. D. Cardinal*, "Institute of American Indian Arts and Alaska Native Culture and Arts Development Campus Master Plan Final Report" (June 1993); Campbell Okuma Perkins, "Institute of American Indian Arts and Alaska Native Culture and Arts Development Campus Master Plan" (June 1993).

3. Cheryl Crazy Bull*, vice president of the university, and Gregory Adams kindly offered information about this project.

4. For varied perspectives, see C. Martin, "The American Indian as Miscast Ecologist," *History Teacher* 14, no. 2 (1981): 243–52; C. Martin, *Keepers of the Game: Indian–Animal Relationships and the Fur Trade* (Athens: University of Georgia Press, 1981); B. W. Powell, "Were These America's First Ecologists?" *Journal of the West* 23, no. 6 (1987): 17–25; J. B. Callicott, "American Indian Land Wisdom? Sorting Out the Issues," *Journal of Forest History* 33, no. 1 (1989): 35–42; J. Weatherford, *Native Roots: How the Indians Enriched America* (New York: Crown, 1991); E. McGaa*, *Mother Earth Spirituality* (San Francisco, Harper & Row, 1990); and P. Schneider, "Other People's Trash," *Audubon*, July 1991, pp. 108–19. On votes preceding the Mescalero Apache agreement to store spent nuclear fuel rods, see *NYT*, February 1, 1995; April 23, 1995, sec. 1, p. 6, illustrates a rendering of a storage facility decorated with patterns meant to look Indian.

5. Happy Camp: structural engineer: Savikko; electrical engineer: Marquess & Associates; contractor: Eger Construction. I thank Gary Stevens* and Leaf Hillman for information.

6. For information, I thank Robert Cain, architect; Susan Key; and Duane King. Planner for tribal council: Robert Blankenship*; construction manager: Ken Blankenship*; contractor: Collins & Hobbs. See D. H. King, "History of the Museum of the Cherokee Indian," *Journal of Cherokee Studies* 1, no. 1 (1976): 60–64.

7. Information from Charles Boyd* and Martin A. Hagerstrand. The initial design for the Cherokee Museum was created as Boyd's master of architecture thesis at the University of Colorado.

8. Information from Martin Hagerstrand.

9. Johnny Arlee* made a sign with the tribal emblem. The arbor was erected by the Kicking Horse Job Corps Center trainees, all Native American. The dome design is by Marie Torosian*. Agnes Kemille's* geometric bead design for a purse has been adapted by artist Jaune Quick-to-See Smith* for a tile flooring in the rotunda, not yet in place. War veterans will be honored in displays and by an honor roll done in beadwork. A memorial will record reservation family names that have died out. Subcontractor: Salish–Kootenai Building Trades. I thank Paul Bishop and Shelly McClure for helpful information. See also *ICT*, September 8, 1994, pp. C1, 2.

10. Emory Sekaquaptewa* said that in 1939, the point was less to have the building look Indian than to make work for Native quarrymen and masons; he spoke of the Hopi, but his remarks are equally true for the Zuni. He and Joseph Laban* confirm the desire to relate Hopi High School to the landscape. Robert Kallstrom, architect, said that there was more cultural relevance and a greater attempt to blend the building into nature in an original scheme proposed when the budget was larger. I thank James Rowland for candid comments on Zuni Middle School. See also T. J. Ferguson, B. Mills, and C. Seciwa*, "Contemporary Zuni Architecture and Society," in *Pueblo Style and Regional Architecture: The Mystique of New Mexico*, ed. W. F. Markovich, E. Preiser, F. G. Sturm (New York: Van Nostrand Reinhold, 1990), pp. 116–17, who describe the Zuni as modernizers who prefer convenience in architecture to older but less convenient buildings.

11. I thank Gregory Hicks and David Kines, architects, for information.

12. Information kindly supplied by J. Ostler and J. Brawley.

13. Wyatt*/Rhodes, Architects and Don W. Ryden AIA/Architects, "Fort McDowell Yavapai Indian Tribe Development Guidelines" (1994); "Fort McDowell/Beeline Highway Development Guidelines" (April 1993). I thank Don Ryden for the documents and for helpful conversations.

14. Quotes from information sheets distributed by Friends of Satwiwa.

15. William McDonough, architect, conversation with author, April 1993.

16. M. Wagner, "Native Americans," *Interiors* 153, no. 3 (1993): 65.

17. Information from William McDonough, John Amatruda of his office, and Stephen L. Gomes, executive director of the Global Infrastructure Foundation.

18. Designer: John Abrams; construction manager: Gino Mazzoferro. See *Vineyard Gazette*, February 11, 1992; January 29, 1993, p. 10. I am grateful to John Ex Rodgers for these articles.

19. Donald Stastny provided information; I also thank Lynn Parker of his office for photographs.

CHAPTER 11

1. "Honor Award: Minneapolis Regional Native American Center," *Architecture Minnesota* 1, no. 4 (1975): 22.

2. S. Stephens, "Of Nature and Modernity," *Progressive Architecture* 56, no. 10 (1975): 66.

3. See "Native American Center," *Space Design*, no. 151 (1977): 60–62; W. Lawrence, "The Minneapolis Indian Center: Who Does It Serve?" *NAPr*, February 25, 1993, pp. 1, 6; and "George Morrison, Artist," *Skyway News* (Minneapolis), September 1, 1992, p. 33. I am grateful for help from Thomas Hodne; Dennis Sun Rhodes*, associate architect; Surrounded-by-Enemy*; Joe Potter*; Sara Loe; and Mary Ellen Sigmond. Landscape architect: Herb Baldwin; mechanical engineer: Erickson Ellison Associates; structural engineer: Meyer Borgman & Johnson; general contractor: Acton Construction.

4. A. O. Dean, "Alternative Approach," *Historic Preservation* 45, no. 3 (1993): 15.

5. D. Sun Rhodes*, "My Home: A Communal American Indian Home," *Native Peoples* 6, no. 3 (1993): 40–43, esp. 43.

6. D. Saile, in "Cosmos, Man & Nature," pp. 159, 222.

7. I thank Don Jiran, Jane Booher*, and Phyllis Howard* for speaking with me.

8. I thank Dennis Numkena* and Carolyn*, tribal secretary, for information. For background about the inception of a cultural center, see M. C. Knack and O. C. Stewart, *As Long as the Rivers Shall Run: An Ethnohistory of Pyramid Lake Reservation* (Berkeley: University of California Press, 1984). No one explains why the building was never finished.

9. Many issues discussed as racial seem also to be issues of class. In this case, when discussing two Euro-American architects, the speaker made his class affiliations explicit.

10. Quotes from Andres Fernando*, interview with author.

CHAPTER 12

1. Quoted in H. Landecker, "Designing for American Indians," *Architecture* 82, no. 12 (1993): 93.

2. Ibid.

3. All quotes from D. Kristine Woolsey. See H. de Varine, ed., *Museum* [special issue on eco-museums] 37, no. 4 (1985).

4. In addition to Kristine Woolsey, I thank Chester Sprague, an early consultant, and Nancy Fuller for several helpful meetings. See N. Fuller, "The Museum as a Vehicle for Community Empowerment: The Ak-Chin Indian Community Ecomuseum Project," in *Museums and Communities: The Politics of Public Culture*, ed. I. Karp, C. Kreamer, and S. D. Lavine (Washington, D.C.: Smithsonian Institution Press, 1992), pp. 327–65; R. White, *Tribal Assets: The Rebirth of Native America* (New York: Holt, 1990), chap. 4; text accompanying Woolsey's drawings at Felissimo Gallery, New York; and Charles Carlyle*, a museum committee member, quoted in *LT*, December 4, 1991, p. A6.

5. I thank Brian Burke and Christopher Boothby for their help. See M. L. Bierman, "Tribal Tribute," *Architecture* 82, no. 12 (1993): 70–77.

6. W. J. Ames, *User Participation and Requirements in Planning Navajo School Facilities in New Mexico* (Albuquerque: University of New Mexico School of Architecture, 1978), pp. 44–45, 54.

7. *LT*, November 13, 1991, p. A3.

8. Charles Bluewolf*, Steve Chrisjohn*, Dave Colit*, Berkly Dickerman*, Terry Halsey*, Clint Hill*, Raymond Robert*, Larry Thomas*, and Dave Winder*. For information, I thank Robbin Obomsawin and Craig Noordmans.

9. Quoted in "Nay Ah Shing Lower and Upper Schools," *Architecture* 82, no. 12 (1993): 93.

10. Information from Thomas Hodne and Milo Thompson. See also Landecker, "Designing for American Indians," p. 93.

11. Landecker, "Designing for American Indians," p. 96.

12. R. G. Brittain and M. J. Myhrman, "Toward a Responsive Tohono O'odham Dwelling," *Arid Lands Newsletter*, Spring–Summer 1989, pp. 20–23. I thank Richard Brittain for this article and for a helpful interview.

13. Chester Sprague and John Steffian, "A Self-Help Housing Process for American Indians and Alaska Natives" (1970).

14. From July 18 to 25, 1994, 1575 Habitat for Humanity volunteers built thirty houses at the Cheyenne River Reservation, South Dakota; to conform to Lakota preference, the houses were more widely spaced than usual HFH houses are, they included basements that can accommodate extended-family members, and there is a central common ground, used in part for children's play. See *ICT*, July 27, 1994, p. A6, and *Habitat World* 11, no. 5 (1994): 7–10.

15. D. A. Dunlap, "Educational Processes of Rough Rock Community High School: Program for Community and School" (Chinle, Rough Rock Community High School, January 1972), p. 47.

16. Chester Sprague and Robert A. Roessel, former principal and superintendent, kindly offered information. See T. R. Reno, "A Demonstration in Navajo Education," *Journal of American Indian Education* 6, no. 3 (1967): 1–5; R. A. Roessel, "The Right to Be Wrong and the Right to Be Right," *Journal of American Indian Education* 7, no. 2 (1968): 1–6; Roessel, "An Overview of the Rough Rock Demonstration School," *Journal of American Indian Education* 7, no. 3, (1968): 2–41; *School Review* 79, no. 1 (1970), for articles debating this project; G. P. Castile, "The Community School at Rough Rock," (master's thesis, University of Arizona, 1967); S. Billson and H. Blatchford, Sr.*, "Navajo Evaluators Look at Rough Rock Demonstration School" (Chinle, R.R.D.S., September 1971); "Native Control of Education: The Real Thing," N*avajo Times*, January 21, 1971; "Navajo School: A Study in Community Control," *Architectural Forum* 137, no. 2 (1972): 54–57; R. F. Tonigan, "Evaluation of Rough Rock Demonstration School" (Rough Rock, 1976); and J. Collier, Jr., "Survival at Rough Rock: A Historical Overview of Rough Rock Demonstration School," *Anthropology and Education Quarterly* 19, no. 3 (1988): esp. 262–69.

17. Marley Porter, letter to author, February 13, 1992.

18. In addition to Sanford Hirshen, I thank Quinn Meyers and Gabriel Harrison in his firm, Gloria Emerson*, and Loren Miller*. See H. C. Dennis, *The American Indian, 1492–1972*, 2d ed. (Dobbs Ferry, N.Y.: Oceana, 1977), p. 79; S. B. Woodbridge, "School Designed Both with and for a Navajo Community," *Journal of the American Institute of Architects* 69, no. 14 (1980): 40–45; Ames, *User Participation*; and *First Nations Financial Report 1986–87*, p. 17.

19. *Albany Times-Union*, August 21, 1991, p. B1.

20. J. Post, D. Benedict*, J. Ransom*, George Rosenvold, and Barbara MacLean contributed information and various kinds of help. For the quote from Porter, see the school's fund-raising brochure. For tribal politics, see *NYT*, April 30, 1990, p. B2. Engineer: Ryan & Biggs of Troy, New York.

CHAPTER 13

1. I omit urban housing from this discussion because it is no different from that available to other people of the same income level. For background, see D. Stea, "Indian Reservation Housing: Progress Since the 'Stanton Report'?" *AICRJ* 6, no. 3 (1982):1–14; F. Harjo*, *Indian Housing in the 1990s: Still Waiting* (Washington, D.C.: National American Indian Housing Council, 1991); and National Commission on American Indian, Alaska Native, and Native Hawaiian Housing, *Building the Future: A Blueprint for Change* (Washington, D.C.: U. S. Government Superintendent of Documents, 1992). Census reports and annual reports from HUD offer important statistics. See also G. Esber, "Indian Housing for Indians," *Kiva* 37, no 3 (1972): 141–47; *HUD Challenge* [news bulletin]; S. M. Low and E. Chambers, ed., *Housing, Culture and Design: A Comparative Perspective* (Philadelphia: University of Pennsylvania Press, 1989), esp. K. McDowell, "Housing and Culture for Native Groups in Canada," pp. 43–55; A. Rapoport, "Identity and Environment: A Cross-Cultural Perspective," in *Housing and Identity: Cross-Cultural Perspectives*, ed. J. S. Duncan (New York: Holmes & Meier, 1982), pp. 6–35; S. Kent, ed., *Domestic Architecture and the Use of Space: An Interdisciplinary Cross-Cultural Study* (Cambridge: Cambridge University Press, 1990). I thank Sidney Landau for the gift of this book.

2. *ICT*, January 21, 1993, p. A2, reporting on hearings of the Senate Select Committee on Indian Affairs, January 12, 1993.

3. H. Cisneros, speech at Pine Ridge, South Dakota, July 21, 1994, quoted in *ICT*, July 27, 1994, p. B1. For his concerns about the fiscal year 1996 budget for Indian housing and community services, see *ICT*, March 9, 1995, p. A2.

4. For farmers, see National Commission, *Building the Future*, pp. 38–43, from which one will perceive the impediments

to lenders; see esp. p. 39, for Section 708 of the National Affordable Housing Act of 1990. For Federal Housing Act, Section 248, see National Commission, *Building the Future*, p. 38, and ICT [special edition, business ventures], May 25, 1994, p. 13, reprinted from *ABA Banking Journal*, May 1994. To assist potential users, HUD published a brochure describing Section 248 help: *Home Ownership for Indians* (1989).

5. This was created under the Housing and Community Development Act of 1987. Information on the lack of building comes from the Department of Housing and Urban Development, *Annual Report*, fiscal years 1988–1990. The report does not explain why the program insured no loans for so long.

6. As of 1988, 15 of a total of 21,204 Indian veterans living on trust lands held Veterans' Administration home loans, which were funded under a program for the disabled; they were not VA-guaranteed loans. For the Housing Loan Guarantee Program, see letters by Representative D. Bereuter, ICT, January 12, 1995, p. A4, and R. T. Parry, ICT, February 16, 1995, p. B5.

7. ICT, February 12, 1992, p. A7; June 17, 1992, p. A4; Joseph G. Schiff, Assistant Secretary for Public and Indian Housing, testimony before the Commission on American Indian, Alaska Native, and Hawaiian Housing, November 21, 1991, praising the potential of this program (pp. 11–14), apparently overoptimistically. President Clinton's proposed 1996 budget eliminated HOME in favor of higher funding for the Affordable Housing Program. See ICT, February 16, 1995, p. A2.

8. Federal Home Loan Bank of Seattle, "Bringing Private Resources to Native Lands" (1993). On assistance given to 549 units in 1995, see also ICT, February 16, 1995, p. C5.

9. For a summary of many of the pertinent laws and financing mechanisms, see National Commission, *Building the Future*, pp. 25–50.

10. Department of Housing and Urban Development, *Annual Report*, for each of the six years noted.

11. Dominic Nessi, conversation with the author at HUD, July 22, 1992.

12. ICT, March 31, 1992, p. A6.

13. *HUD Challenge* 5, no. 2 (1974): 6.

14. Robert Gauthier*, chairman of the National Commission on American Indian, Alaska Native, and Native Hawaiian Housing, testimony before the Senate Select Committee on Indian Affairs, January 12, 1993. See also Harjo, *Indian Housing*.

15. On Cheyenne River, see M. Lawson, *Dammed Indians: The Pick–Sloan Plan and the Missouri River Sioux, 1944–1980* (Norman: University of Oklahoma Press, 1982), p. 175. On 35 percent, see ICT, June 17, 1992, p. A4.

16. Navajo National Division of Community Development, Design, and Engineering Services and Department of Energy, *Navahomes: A Dinelogical Study of Navajo Dwelling in Balance with the Land* (Window Rock, Ariz.: Navajo Nation, 1992), sec. 1. This and other Navajo sources estimate that 30,000 houses are needed and 10,000 should be replaced. For Oklahoma, see Harjo, *Indian Housing*, p. 1.

17. On 30 percent rule, and on trailers: information from Jack Valliant*, Mescalero Apache housing management assistant, February 3, 1994; on no help: Theodore Evans*, Chinle district manager, Navajo reservation; on contractors: Hemsley Martin Lee*, architect; on roads: Joseph Cushman, planner for the Nisqually, and Robert Joe*, Swinomish chairman. See also R. L. Bee, "Self-Help at Fort Yuma: A Critique," *Human Organization* 29, no 3 (1970): 151–61.

18. Information from architect Mark Wirtanen, in Minnesota, who is quoted; Larry Sanchez* in Washington; Linda Howard* in Nevada; Aaron Swan*, architect in South Dakota; Theodore Jojola* in New Mexico; and Theodore Evans* in Arizona. Theodore Jojola* of the University of New Mexico spoke about housing problems. See "Cosmos, Man, and Nature," pp. 117–18. The others not identified as architects are tribal officials. See also National Commission, *Building the Future*, esp. pp. 55–59.

19. T. Rayala, "Housing for the Chippewa Band of Great Lakes American Indians on the Lac du Flambeau Reservation in Northern Wisconsin" (master's thesis, University of Wisconsin-Milwaukee, 1991), p. 22. I thank Dominic Nessi for this reference.

20. Information from Sharon Bailey*, Redding Rancheria housing official in California.

21. See "The Navajos Trade Hogans for Air-Conditioning," *Business Week*, October 23, 1971, pp. 100, 104.

22. For these and other problems, see Harjo, *Indian Housing*. I have benefited greatly from conversations with Dominic Nessi, director of the Office of Indian Housing, at HUD.

23. ICT, June 17, 1992, p. A4.

24. For Senator McCain, see ICT, March 30, 1994, p. A1. For Secretary Cisneros, see ICT, July 27, 1994, p. B1; February 23, 1994, p. A7.

25. Thanks to James T. Arnot, executive director, Southern Ute Indian Housing Authority.

26. On Fort Washakie, see *Casper Star Tribune*, December 30, 1966, cited in G. E. Vlastos, "Indian and non-Indian Interaction" (B. Arch. thesis, Arizona State University, 1970), p. 272. On Lower Brule, see S. Steiner, *The New Indians* (New York: Dell, 1968), pp. 136–37. Information on Shoshones and ramadas for cooking came from Bernard Fontana, interview with author; on non-Anglo sleeping arrangements for the Hopi: Emory Sekaquaptewa*, December 12, 1990; on the Arapaho, see D. Sun Rhodes*, "My Home: A Communal American Indian Home,"

Native Peoples 6, no. 3 (1993): 42. On HUD: Frank Gregor*, Office of Indian Programs, HUD, Phoenix. On the bathroom, see T. J. Jojola*, "Memoirs of an American Indian House: A Descriptive Essay on U.S. Federally Subsidized Housing and Its Impact on the Native American Cultures of the Northern Cheyenne and Sandia Pueblos" (Ph.D. diss., University of New Mexico, 1973), p. 88.

27. J. B. Gillette, "On Her Own Terms," *Historic Preservation* 44, no. 6 (1992): 26–33, 84, 86; Swentzell spoke in a similar vein at the annual meeting of the Society of Architectural Historians, April 3, 1992. For Mishongnovi, see J. D. Loftin, *Religion and Hopi Life in the Twentieth Century* (Bloomington: Indiana University Press, 1991), p. 109. Residents of Hotevilla reject even running water and electricity. See Loftin, *Religion and Hopi Life*, pp. 98–99; information from Jim Hahn.

28. Quoted in R. White, *Tribal Assets: The Rebirth of Native America* (New York: Holt, 1990), p. 121.

29. D. G. Saile, "Architecture in the Pueblo World: A Study of the Architectural Contexts of Pueblo Culture in the Late Nineteenth Century" (Ph.D. diss., University of Newcastle-upon-Tyne, 1981), p. 176. See also J. S. Chisholm, "Social and Economic Change Among the Navajo: Residence Patterns and the Pickup Truck," *Journal of Anthropological Research* 37, no. 2 (1981): 148–57.

30. Information from Winton Smith, architect, January 27, 1994.

31. Dennis Numkena* says that this happened at the housing he designed for the Paiutes.

32. Information from Alex White Plume*.

33. Ron Hernandez* supplied this information.

34. For this information, I thank Jean-Louis Bourgeois, Theodore Jojola*, Christopher Wilson, Bernie Teba*, Herman Agoyo*, and Peter Pino*. See S. Foster, "Adobe Is Adorable but Today's Pueblos Can't Build with It," *Wall Street Journal*, February 4, 1980.

35. A. Gabor, "From Teepee to Solar-Heated Mobile Homes," *Architectural Record* 169, no. 15 (1981): 36. I thank Dale Zinn for additional information. The report may be at the New Mexico Department of Energy Conservation, Division of Energy and Minerals.

36. Information from Marley Porter. On Navajo housing, see Navajo Nation, *Navahomes*, sec. 4–6; on Matts Myhrman's work, see *NYT*, December 12, 1991, pp. B1, B5. See also R. L. Welsch, "Baled Hay," in *Shelter* (New York: Random House, 1973), p. 70. I thank Robert Easton for this publication.

37. Marley Porter, letter to author, September 5, 1993. I thank Porter also for photographs of the building under construction.

38. Information on Yerington from Linda Howard*; information on Pine Ridge from C. Cambridge*, in "Cosmos, Man, & Nature," p. 154; on need for training: Jim Hahn at Hopi Reservation; on energy repair problems: Frank Gregor* and Dominic Nessi.

39. American Indian Council of Architects and Engineers, *Our Home: A Design Guide for Indian Housing* (Washington, D.C.: National Endowment for the Arts–Design Arts Program, 1994), p. 13.

40. Edward Norris, "Santo Domingo Pueblo: Development Projects, December 1, 1981." I thank Edward Norris for this and for a helpful interview.

41. R. McDonald, "Proud Homes," *Bremerton Sun*, September 3, 1993, courtesy of Miles Yanick, architect.

42. A. Ortiz*, ed., *New Perspectives on the Pueblos* (Albuquerque: University of New Mexico Press, 1972), p. 157.

43. D. G. Saile, "Making a House in the Pueblo World," *Architectural Association Quarterly* 9, nos. 2–3 (1977): 77.

44. Information from George H. J. Abrams*. See also R. John, *Social Integration of an Elderly Native American Population* (New York: Garland, 1995), courtesy of G. H. J. Abrams*.

45. Information from Theodore Evans*, July 21, 1991. For aspects of Navajo housing, see M.-A. Tremblay, J. Collier, Jr., and T. T. Sasaki, "Navaho Housing in Transition," *America Indígena* 14, no. 3 (1954): 187–219, and E. K. Sadalla, P. Z. Snyder, and D. Stea, "House Form and Culture Revisited," in *The Behavioral Basis of Design*, ed. P. Suedfeld and J. A. Russell (Stroudsburg, Pa.: Dowden Hutchinson & Ross, 1977), bk. 2, pp. 279–84.

46. Advice from Andres Fernando*, Upper Skagit Reservation, July 3, 1992.

47. Upper Skagit, 1984; Stillaquamish and Sauk–Suiattle, 1985.

48. On the Navajo, see Sadalla, Snyder, and Stea, "House Form and Culture Revisited."

49. Navajo Nation, *Navahomes*, sec. 6. For the connection between wood-burning stoves and illness, see K. Morris, "Wood-Burning Stoves and Lower Respiratory Tract Infection in American Indian Children," *American Journal of Diseases of Children* 144, (1990): 105–08.

50. J. D. Balcomb, *Energy Efficiency Guide for Indian Housing* (Boulder, Colo.: National Renewable Energy Laboratory, 1993), and illustration of an example at Nambe Pueblo facing the acknowledgments page. This helpful publication offers clear explanations, suggestions, procedures, and figures.

51. R. G. Brittain and M. J. Myhrman, "Toward a Responsive Tohono O'odham Dwelling," *Arid Lands Newsletter*, Spring–Summer, 1989, pp. 20–23. For aspects of historic open space planning, see N. A. Rothschild, "Incorporating the Out-

doors as Living Space: Ethnoarchaeology at Zuni Pueblo, New Mexico," *Expedition* 33, no. 1 (1991): 24–32.

52. Jojola,"Memoirs of an American Indian House," p. 141.

53. For information, I thank Thomas Hodne, Ron Hernandez*, and Dennis Sun Rhodes*. See also "Bringing Native Spirit Home," *Architecture Minnesota* 11, no. 3 (1985): 48–51.

54. I thank the architect for information and images. See "Honor Award: Tribal Leaders Issued a Challenge. Eaglewing Is the Answer," *Sunset*, October 1991, pp. 98–99.

55. Andres Fernando*, Upper Skagit planner, July 3, 1992; James Gudger of Architectural Resources Collaborative, July 9, 1992; Joseph Cushman, Nisqually planner, July 3, 1992; Jay Watson, Stillaguamish planner, April 27, 1992.

56. For information, I thank Selena Hill*; Joseph Laban*, Hopi housing authority director; Jim Hahn at the Hopi Reservation; and David Sloan*.

57. Ramona Bennett*, conversation with author, May 1, 1992. I thank John Meyer for referring me.

58. Navajo Nation, *Navahomes*, sec. 8.

59. Rayala, "Housing for the Chippewa," esp. pp. 32–43.

60. For information, I thank Celene Elm* and Leanne Doxtater*.

61. I thank Patty Clark* and Lisa McCarson* at White Earth.

62. *NAPr*, July 2, 1993, p. 1.

63. All quotes from Celine Larkin, on several occasions. She points out that when the client is also the builder, the architect cannot intervene with the builder to protect the client—for example, to make sure that all those on the payroll have actually done work. See also *Vineyard Gazette*, 1989–1995, esp. July 30, 1993, among frequent articles, for which I thank John Ex Rodgers, and *Boston Globe*, July 24, 1994, pp. 65–66. Two of the three-bedroom houses are barrier-free. For helpful discussions, I also thank Laurie J. White, executive director of the Aquinnah Wampanoag Tribal Housing Authority, and Daniel Tenney.

64. Sun Rhodes*, "My Home," pp. 40–43.

65. J. Barreiro, "Architectural Design: An American Indian Process. An Interview with Dennis Sun Rhodes," *NEIQ* 7, no. 2 (1990): 24–29, for which I thank Arlene Hirschfelder; "Bringing Native Spirit Home"; Sun Rhodes*, "My Home."

CHAPTER 14

1. See *NA2oC*, s.v. "Tribal Museums." A suggestion that the marginalized cultures are seen as lower on the evolutionary scale is made by A. E. Coombes, "Museums and the Formation of National and Cultural Identities," *Oxford Art Journal* 11, no. 2 (1988): 57–68.

2. See M. Ames, "How Anthropologists Fabricate the Culture They Study," in *Museums, the Public, and Anthropology* (Vancouver: University of British Columbia Press, 1986); Ames, "Free Indians from the Ethnological Fate: The Emergence of the Indian Point of View in Exhibitions of Indians," *Muse* 5, no. 2 (1987): 14–18; J. D. Nason, "Museums and American Indians: An Enquiry into Relationships," *Western Museums Quarterly* 8, no. 1 (1971): 13–17; J. D. Nason, K. R. Hopkins, and B. Medicine, "Finders Keepers?" *Museum News* 51, no. 7, (1973): 20–26; J. A. Hanson, "The Reappearing Vanishing American," *Museum News* 59, no. 2 (1980): 44–51.

3. Quoted in L. Biddle, "Keeping Tradition Alive," *Museum News* 55, no. 5 (1977): 37.

4. For the Maori, see I. Karp and S. D. Lavine, eds., *Exhibiting Cultures: The Poetics and Policies of Museum Display* (Washington, D.C.: Smithsonian Institution Press, 1991), p. 2. See also J. Clifford, *The Predicament of Culture: Twentieth Century Ethnography, Literature, and Art* (Cambridge, Mass.: Harvard University Press, 1988), p. 189. For the Southwest, see R. H. Thompson, "Looking to the Future," *Museum News* 70, no. 1 (1991): 36–40, and R. G. Vivian and M. Norcini, "Help for the Asking," *Museum News* 70, no. 1 (1991): 53. On Milwaukee, see *NAPr*, September 10, 1993, p. 1. On the Field Museum, see *Museum News* 70, no. 1 (1991): 46–48.

5. An exception is the National Museum of the American Indian, which was established by PL 101-85 in 1989, but will be built mainly with public funds as a branch of the Smithsonian Institution. Architects bidding for work had to be Native American or partners with Amerindian-controlled firms. For the division on the Mall, Douglas Cardinal*, a Canadian of part-Blackfeet (Métis) ancestry, will be the principal design architect, working with Geddes Brecher Qualls Cunningham. For the Suitland, Maryland, Study and Storage Center, a consortium of small Native American firms is collaborating with Polshek & Partners. Another exception is the Mashantucket Pequot cultural center.

6. See Coombes, "Museums"; and Karp and Levine, eds., *Exhibiting Cultures*, esp. pp. 2, 6, 14.

7. L. C. Corrin, ed., *Mining the Museum: An Installation by Fred Wilson* (New York: New Press, 1994). The *Economist*, however, reported that critics found an underrepresentation of Indian cruelty and of African participation in the slave trade in new museum exhibits: "Is history, they ask, for white men to be a search for historical truth and for everybody else a search for role models?" ("Politically Correct Museums," January 16, 1993, pp. 85–86). For display principles, see M. Baxandall, "Exhibition Intention: Some Preconditions of the Visual Display of Culturally Purposeful Objects," pp. 33–41; M. Yamaguchi, "The Poetics of Exhibition in Japanese Culture," pp. 57–67; S.D. Lavine,

"Museum Practices," pp. 151–58; and P. T. Houlihan, "The Poetic Image and Native American Art," pp. 205–11, all in *Exhibiting Cultures*, ed. Karp and Lavine. See also A. Gopnik, "Out of Africa," *New Yorker*, March 22, 1993, pp. 97–10, esp. p. 97; D. S. Whitten and N. E. Whitten, eds., *Imagery and Creativity: Ethnoaesthetics and Art Worlds in the Americas* (Tucson: University of Arizona Press, 1993), esp. introduction, pp. 3–44. The Rochester, New York, Museum of Science and Industry is still unusual in presenting parallel Seneca and Euro-American experiences and artifacts in its exhibition "At the Western Door." The first exhibits at the National Museum of the American Indian branch in New York City emphasized indigenous perspectives.

8. Clarinda Begay* and William Day, speakers at the session "Grassroots Native American Tribal Museums" at the annual meeting of the College Art Association of America, February 5, 1993.

9. Christopher Wilson suggested this. At the Makah facility, the display methods may have been proposed by Ann Renker, then a (non-Indian) reservation resident, rather than by Richard Metler and Phillip Norton, architects with the Fred Bassetti architectural firm. Greig Arnold*, a Makah on the museum staff (and Renker's husband), may also have been influential.

10. Bette Mele* pointed out that opinions about what to show would vary among tribes. See Mele, participant in conference session: "Museums and the American Indian," in *Indian Voices: The Native American Today* (San Francisco: Indian Historian Press, 1974), p. 203.

11. On keeping locations secret, see *Keepers of the Treasures*, pp. 70–71.

12. Anonymous participant in conference, in *Indian Voices*, p. 306.

13. D. Garfield, "Ceci n'est pas une pipe," *Museum News* 72, no. 1 (1993): 12–13.

14. L. Davis, "Indian and Non-Indian Museums. What's the Difference?" *News from Native California* 4, no. 1 (1989): 8–9.

15. As this book deals with recent tendencies, I shall not discuss the exceptional cases of the Cherokee museum collection of 1828, or the Osage Museum (1930), paid for by revenue from leased oil wells.

16. Day, at annual meeting of College Art Association.

17. G. E. Burchard, quoted in N. O. Lurie, "Museumland Revisited," *Human Organization* 40 (Summer 1981): 180–87. See also I. Karp and S. F. Cairns, "Museums Must Take on New Roles in This Multi-cultural Society," *Chronicle of Higher Education*, April 14, 1993, pp. B3, B6.

18. J. Nason, "Community and Continuity: The Museum at Warm Springs," *American Anthropologist* 96, no. 2 (1994); George

Horse Capture*, "Some Observations on Establishing Tribal Museums" [technical leaflet 134], *History News* 36, no. 1 (1981), suggested eight steps for establishing an Indian-sponsored museum.

19. On financing museums and potential income, see George H. J. Abrams*, at Native American Museums Program National Workshop, Southwest Museum, Los Angeles, June 22, 1983, pp. 45–49 (transcript at Program Office, Smithsonian Institution, Arts & Industries Building).

20. Information from Vic Runnels* and Patrick Cudmore. Also *ICT*, May 19, 1993, pp. B1–2, February 23, 1994, p. B5; *LT* [visions section], June 1, 1992, p. 3.

21. Thompson, "Looking into the Future," p. 39.

22. Abrams, Museums Program Workshop.

23. Information from Bob Smith*, former director, and Nancy Fuller. R. Hayward*, J. Campisi, and W. Starna, Report to Mashantucket Pequots. On deficiencies, see Mary Lee Lemieux, letter (Oneida file, Smithsonian Institution Office of Museums Program). For a comprehensive view, see also, in the same file, S. Fabritius, "Das Oneida Nation Museum: Eine stammeseigene Institution auf einer indianischen Reservation in Wisconsin, USA" (thesis, Johann-Wolfgang Goethe University, Frankfurt am Main, 1988).

24. On the Onondaga, see "The Indian Wampum Controversy," *Indian Historian* 3, no. 2 (1970): 4–17. On the Colville, see *ICT*, March 9, 1995, p. A11.

25. Clifford, *Predicament of Culture*, p. 247.

26. There have been hundreds of repatriation stories in periodicals: for example, *Museum News* 70, no. 1 (1991): 41–53; V. Deloria*, Jr., "A Simple Question of Humanity: The Moral Dimensions of the Reburial Issue," *NARF Legal Review* 14, no. 4 (1989): 1–12; G. H. J. Abrams*, "The Case for Wampum: Repatriation from the Museum of the American Indian to the Six Nations Confederacy, Brantford, Ontario, Canada," in *Museums and the Making of "Ourselves,"* ed. F. E. S. Kaplan (New York: St. Martin's Press, 1994): pp. 251–84; W. Echo-Hawk*, "Museum Rights vs. Indian Rights: Guidelines for Assessing Competing Legal Interests in Native Cultural Resources," *Review of Law and Social Change* 14 (1986): 437–53; and "Native American Repatriation: History, Requirements, and Outlook," *Western Museums Conference Newsletter*, Winter 1990/1991, pp. 1–6. I thank Kathleen Poole April for copies of the last two. For a model of conflict resolution between scholars and tribes, see A. Klesert and M. Andrews, "The Treatment of Human Remains on Navajo Lands," *American Antiquity* 53, no. 2 (1988): 310–20. See also H. M. Price III, *Disputing the Dead: U.S. Law on Aboriginal Remains and Grave Goods* (Columbia: University of Missouri Press, 1991).

27. *LT*, September 4, 1991, pp. A6–8.

28. Nason, Hopkins, and Medicine, "Finders Keepers?" pp. 24–26.

29. Pemina YellowBird*, who dismissed "white man" concerns for the objects' stability, in *ICT*, September 22, 1993, p. A7.

30. *NYT*, August 13, 1990, pp. A1, 12.

31. Mark Hoistad kindly sent two typewritten accounts of the project. See summary description and simplified plan in *Daily Nebraskan*, February 25, 1992, pp. 1, 6; *Architectural Record* 180, no. 11 (1992): 25.

32. I thank M. Hoistad, D. Hastings, and D. King. See *In the Spirit of Sequoyah* (Vonore, Tenn.: Friends of Sequoyah, [ca. 1987]); *NYT*, August 2, 1987, sec 5, p. 21.

33. PL 98-134; 25 U.S.C.A. 1751–1760.

34. Museum Mission Statement Workshop, November 4, 1988. For information on the Pequot Museum, I thank all the architects named in the text. For the museum interior, see M. Wagner, "Pequot Initiative," *Interiors* 152, no. 10 (1993): 86–88.

35. Material about the student projects comes from T. Atkin and C. H. Krinsky, "Cultural Identity in Modern Native American Architecture: A Case Study," *Journal of Architectural Education* 49, no. 4 (1996): 237–47.

36. K. Frampton, "Towards a Critical Regionalism: Six Points for an Architecture of Resistance," in *The Anti-Aesthetic: Essays on Postmodern Culture*, ed. H. Foster (Port Townsend, Wash.: Bay Press, 1983), pp. 16–30; C. Norberg-Schulz, *Genius Loci: Towards a Phenomenology of Architecture* (New York: Rizzoli, 1980).

37. Polshek and Partners' text beside drawings exhibited at the Second Mashantucket Pequot History Conference, Mystic, Connecticut, October 21–23, 1993.

38. Information courtesy of Henry Swoboda, architect. The museum is now closed for lack of operating funds.

39. Conversations with Roland Poncho* and Barry Moore, now of the Mathes Group, Houston, who is the source of the quotes.

40. *Indian Voices*, p. 195; Henry Gobin*, conversation with the author, October 11, 1994.

41. Especially important in this connection are N. H. H. Graburn, ed., *Ethnic and Tourist Arts* (Berkeley: University of California Press, 1976), and Graburn, "Ethnic Arts of the Fourth World: The View from Canada," in *Imagery and Creativity: Ethnoaesthetics and Art Worlds in the Americas*, ed., D. S. Whitten and N. E. Whitten (Tucson: University of Arizona Press, 1993), pp. 171–204.

42. Conversations with Ray Patencio* of the tribe, and Hunter Johnson.

43. See "Mozart Among the Hopi," *Art News* 81, no. 4 (1982): 14, and E. M. Beall, "Anasazi Renaissance," *Arizona Living* 13, no. 10 (1982): 47–49.

44. "The Two Worlds of Dennis Numkena," *Indian Arizona*, p. 14 (undated clipping in Heard Museum artists' files), for which I thank M. N. Klimiades, librarian. Information on Parks Department comes from interviews with the supervisor and with Dennis Numkena*.

45. Thompson, "Looking to the Future," p. 38, expands on these observations.

CHAPTER 15

1. Traditional stick games were made legal again in Washington State only when the state and several tribes negotiated gambling contracts around 1990. See *Explore Indian Country*, September 1992, p. 1.

2. Page 1 of the twenty-three-page act, quoted in *ICT* [Winner's Circle supplement], November 5, 1992, p. 7.

3. *ICT*, August 4, 1993, p. A7.

4. *ICT*, May 26, 1993, p. A2. For remedies against procrastination, see *ICT* [Winner's Circle supplement], November 5, 1992, p. 7; for one of several tribal lawsuits, see *ICT*, July 28, 1993, p. A7. States can, of course, continue to procrastinate, denying that they are refusing de facto.

5. S. O'Brien, *American Indian Tribal Governments* (Norman: University of Oklahoma Press, 1989), p. 228.

6. "Burgers or Blackjack?" *Economist*, March 12, 1994, p. 35.

7. Quoted in *NYT*, May 17, 1992, sec. 1, p. 18.

8. N. O. Lurie, "Money, Semantics, and Indian Leadership," *American Indian Quarterly* 10, no. 1 (1986): 47–63.

9. P. Zah*, quoted in G. Judson, "Some Indians See Gamble in Future with Casinos," *NYT*, May 15, 1994, sec. 4, p. 5; D. Sun Rhodes*, interview with the author, May 16, 1994.

10. *Saint Paul Pioneer Press*, May 14, 1994, p. D1.

11. I thank Tom Martinson for this observation.

12. For the Winnebago, see *ICT*, December 22, 1993, p. C4. Bad River site visit and information from Richard Ackley*, planner.

13. Mille Lacs: conversation with Don Wedll; *LT*, February 12, 1992, p. A1, gives the figure of 50 percent; see also *NYT*, January 31, 1993, sec. 1, p. 42; *ICT*, June 2, 1993, A2, gives 45 percent in 1991, 0 percent in 1993. Oneida: *Milwaukee Sentinel*, March 25, 1992, series on Indian gambling. Fort McDowell: *NYT*, May 11, 1992, sec. 1, p. 18.

14. Election advertisement for Jim Michaud* of this band in *Circle* (Minneapolis) May 1994, p. 8.

15. *NAPr*, February 12, 1993, p. 2.

16. Quoted in *NAPr*, July 30, 1993, p. 2.

17. *ICT*, December 15, 1993, p. A2.

18. Tribes that have distributed revenues on a per capita basis are considered by officials of investment-oriented tribes as both being improvident and asking for trouble; for instance, are payments to be made only to those tribal members who reside within the confines of the reservation? For the problems of the Flandreau Santee Sioux, see *LT*, January 8, 1992, pp. A1–2, and for inequities in distribution and judicial remedies for aggrieved Lower Sioux, see *NAPr*, March 19, 1993, p. 1, and April 9, 1993, p. 4. For benefits at Mille Lacs, see *ICT*, March 30, 1995, p. A4; for Mashantucket Pequots, see R. R. Cooper, "Placing Bets, Catching Dreams," *American Way* 28, no. 4 (1995): 64–71, 100–103.

19. For studies and tax payments: *ICT* [Winner's Circle supplement], 1993, p. 22; *ICT*, January 19, 1994, pp. A1–2; *NAPr*, June 18, 1992, p. 2; *LT*, [special issue], November 13, 1991, pp. 2, 4. I cannot assess the studies' objectivity or methods.

20. *ICT*, February 11, 1993, p. A2.

21. *NAPr*, May 28, 1993, p. 2; *ICT*, November 17, 1993, p. A6. The situation on the St. Regis Mohawk Reservation, where three major groups dispute the issue of casino gambling, is especially complicated.

22. *NYT*, May 15, 1994, sec. 4, p. 5.

23. *ICT*, July 28, 1993, p. A7.

24. *NYT*, June 1, 1993, p. A12; see also *NYT*, May 15, 1994, sec. 4, p. 5.

25. *LT*, November 29, 1991, p. A4.

26. Quoted in *LT*, August 5, 1992, p. A3.

27. Quoted in *NYT*, June 1, 1993, p. A12.

28. Quoted in *ICT*, February 18, 1993, pp. A1–2.

29. *ICT*, May 4, 1994, p. C1.

30. Quoted in *ICT* [Winner's Circle supplement], November 5, 1992, p. 7.

31. *NYT*, July 27, 1993, p. B6.

32. *ICT* [Winner's Circle supplement], November 5, 1992, p. 2.

33. F. Blake, Jr. (Wub-e-ke-niew)*, quoted in *NAPr*, January 8 and October 8, 1993, p. 5.

34. Oneida: *NYT*, March 11, 1993, p. B9; Winnebago: *Navajo Nation Today*, July 24–30, 1991, p. 10. For arson and shootout, see *ICT* [Winner's Circle supplement], 1993, p. 16. Corruption, usually petty by big city standards, has often been exposed, sometimes by hostile political rivals. It has been investigated by the FBI on occasion. For examples, see *NAPr*, February 26, 1993, p. 6; April 30, 1993, p. 2; May 21, 1993, p. 4; May 28, 1993, pp. 1, 2; June 4, 1993, p. 2; August 20, 1993, p. 1; and *NYT*, January 31, 1992, sec. 1, p. 42.

35. Quoted in *NYT*, May 7, 1993, sec. 1, p. 25.

36. *ICT*, December 15, 1993, p. A1.

37. *ICT*, March 30, 1994, p. A3.

38. *ICT*, July 27, 1994, p. A1.

39. *Economist*, March 21–27, 1992, p. 28; T. Daschle, quoted in *ICT*, October 17, 1992, p. B3; J. Richards, cited in *NAPr*, January 15, 1993, p. 2. For federal officials' refutations of "rife" criminality, see also *LT*, March 25, 1992, pp. A1–2; *NAPr*, October 8, 1993, p. 4; for Arizona official's agreement with them, see *ICT*, May 26, 1993, p. A3.

40. W. J. Lawrence, editorial, *NAPr*, July 2, 1993, p. 4.

41. The officials include Henry Gobin*, planner, and Wayne Williams, casino manager. I thank them for a site visit.

42. *ICT*, December 22, 1993, p. C1. The building style, however, is modified Dutch colonial.

43. I thank Mark Wirtanen and Mark Speer of Architectural Resources for information, and Ronald L. M. Ramsay for the reference to E. K., "Bingo!" *Architecture Minnesota* 17, no. 3 (1990): 44–45. A casino manager, later replaced, held an interest in the company from which the facility leased slot machines; that represents the type of corruption known, but by no means everywhere, in Indian casinos.

44. *ICT*, March 2, 1994, p. A1.

45. I thank Gary Johnson, director of planning and development, for information beyond that given in *Sota Iya Yapi*, July 22, 1993, p. 1.

46. Statement of Al Trepania*, the band's vice chairman, in *NAPr*, September 3, 1993, p. 2.

47. Information about the casino, and all quotes, are from David Smotrich, whom I also thank for an extensive site visit and introductions to Ray Halbritter* and Raymond Obomsawin*. See also *NYT*, July 18, 1993, sec. 1, p. 27; *LT*, January 14, 1992, p. A8; and *Syracuse Herald-Journal*, August 11, 1993, pp. A1, 5.

48. PL 98-134. See *NYT*, October 20, 1983, p. B2, and N. A. Silberman, "Pequot Country," *Archaeology* 44, no. 4 (1991): 34–39.

49. *NYT*, January 14, 1993, p. B1. The agreement was made with the governor, but was not ratified in the state legislature. The Mohegans now hope to open a second casino.

50. Quoted in *NYT*, January 21, 1991, p. B1. Plans as of 1994 include a theme park, golf course, and day-care center to provide family-oriented entertainment and to accommodate children of desirable employees. The Pequots now collaborate with local chambers of commerce. See *ICT*, May 4, 1994, p. C5. For other consequences, see *NYT*, May 22, 1994, sec. 1, pp. 1, 32.

51. *NYT*, January 21, 1991, p. B1.

52. *Philadelphia Inquirer*, April 26, 1992, p. C1. Paula Spilner thoughtfully sent this reference.

53. *NYT*, May 15, 1994, sec. 4, p. 5.

54. Alfred J. Luciani, former chief executive, explaining his resignation, in *NYT*, October 21, 1992, p. B8.

55. Quotes not attributed to the architect are taken from *Mystic Lake, Souvenir Edition*, commemorating the opening in 1992. Leonard Prescott*, former president of Little Six, the casino operator, kindly sent this publication.

56. Leonard Prescott, quoted in *Mystic Lake, Souvenir Edition*.

57. *Mystic Lake, Souvenir Edition*.

58. John Cuningham, interview with the author, May 17, 1994.

FINAL OBSERVATIONS

1. N. S. Momaday, *House Made of Dawn* (New York: Harper & Row, 1968), p. 58.

2. R. Weber, "The Myth of Meaningful Forms: Comparing the Forms of Indigenous and Classical Architecture," *TDSR* 2, no. 2 (1991): 71.

3. E. Gaboury, "Amerindian Indentity, Architects: The Hodne–Stageberg Partners," *Architectural Review* 168, no. 1002 (1980): 86.

4. Quoted by kind permission of the poet.

SELECTED BIBLIOGRAPHY

REFERENCE WORKS

Davis, M. B., ed. *Native America in the Twentieth Century: An Encyclopedia*. New York: Garland, 1994.

Eargle, D. H., Jr. *The Earth Is Our Mother: A Guide to the Indians of California, Their Locales and Historic Sites*. 3d ed. San Francisco: Trees Company Press, 1990.

Haas, M. L. *Indians of North America: Methods and Sources for Library Research*. Hamden, Conn.: Library Professional Publications, 1983.

Heard Museum, Phoenix, Arizona. Library files on Native American artists and architects.

Hirschfelder, A. B. *Guide to Research on North American Indians*. Chicago: American Library Association, 1983.

Hoover, H. T., and K. P. Zimmerman. *The Sioux and Other Native Cultures of the Dakotas: An Annotated Bibliography*. Westport, Conn.: Greenwood Press, 1993.

Klein, B. T., ed. *Reference Encyclopedia of the American Indian*. 5th ed. New York: Todd, 1990.

Laird, D. W. *Hopi Bibliography*. Tucson: University of Arizona Press, 1977.

Lobb, M. D., and T. D. Watts. *Native American Youth and Alcohol: An Annotated Bibliography*. Westport, Conn: Greenwood Press, 1990.

Ruby, R. H., and J. Brown. *A Guide to the Indian Tribes of the Pacific Northwest*. Rev. ed. Norman: University of Oklahoma Press, 1992.

Salzmann, Z. *The Arapaho Indians: A Research Guide and Bibliography*. Westport, Conn: Greenwood Press, 1988.

Shanks, R., and L. W. Shanks. *North American Indian Travel Guide*. Petaluma, Calif.: Costano Books, 1989.

Smithsonian Institution, Office of Museum Studies. Files on Native American museums.

Sturtevant, W. C., ed. *Handbook of North American Indians*. Washington, D.C.: Smithsonian Institution Press, 1978–.

Sutton, I. *Indian Land Tenure: Bibliographical Essays and a Guide to the Literature*. New York: Clearwater, 1975.

Swagerty, W. R., ed. *Scholars and the Indian Experience: Critical Reviews of Recent Writing in the Social Sciences*. Bloomington: Indiana University Press, 1984.

Thornton, R., G. D. Sandefur, and H. G. Grasmick, eds. *The Urbanization of American Indians: A Critical Bibliography*. Bloomington: Indiana University Press, for the D'Arcy McNickle Center, Newberry Library, 1982.

Washburn, W. E., ed. *The American Indian and the United States: A Documentary History*. New York: Random House, 1973.

ART AND ARCHITECTURE

American Indian Council of Architects and Engineers. *Our Home: A Design Guide for Indian Housing*. Washington, D.C.: National Endowment for the Arts, Design Arts Program, 1994.

Ames, W. J. *User Participation and Requirements in Planning Navajo School Facilities in New Mexico.* Albuquerque: University of New Mexico School of Architecture, 1978.

Balcomb, J. D. *Energy-Efficiency Design Guide for Indian Housing.* Golden, Colo.: National Renewable Energy Laboratory, 1993.

Ball, G., and L. A. Platetter. "New Plains Indian Museum." *American Indian Art Magazine* 4, no. 3 (1979): 48–55.

Barreiro, J. "Architectural Design, an American Indian Process: An Interview with Dennis Sun Rhodes." *NEIQ* 7, no. 2 (1990): 24–29.

Biddle, L. "Keeping Tradition Alive." *Museum News* 55, no. 5 (1977): 35–42.

Blair, B. "Indian Rights: Native Americans versus American Museums—A Battle for Artifacts." *American Indian Law Review* 7, no. 1 (1979): 125–54.

Bradley, H. G. "Solar Hogans: Houses of the Future?" *Native Peoples* 3, no. 3 (1990): 44–50.

"Bringing Native Spirit Home." *Architecture Minnesota* 11, no. 3 (1985): 48–51. [On Hodne–Stageberg Partners and Dennis Sun Rhodes]

Brittain, R. G., and M. J. Myhrman. "Toward a Responsive Tohono O'odham Dwelling." *Arid Lands Newsletter,* Spring–Summer 1989, pp. 20–23.

BRW, Ryden Architects. "Yuma Crossing Master Plan, Fort Yuma Quechan Tribal Council: Master Plan and Draft Implementation Program." January 25, 1990.

Caldwell, C. T. "Suquamish Tribal Cultural Center and Suquamish Museum Development." Master's thesis, University of Washington-Seattle, 1987.

Coe, R. *Lost and Found Traditions: Native American Art, 1965–1985.* Seattle: University of Washington Press, 1986.

Cook, J. "A Jury's Dilemma: The Native American Preparatory School Design Competition." *Competitions* 2, no. 3 (1992): 20–33.

Cuningham Architects. "Community Projects: Indian–Mille Lacs Band, Mille Lacs, East Lake, Lake Lena." Cuningham Hamilton Quiter, P. A., Minneapolis, August 12, 1992.

David, T. *Contemporary Third World Architecture: Search for Identity.* Brooklyn, N.Y.: Pratt Institute, 1983.

Davis, L. "Indian and Non-Indian Museums: What's the Difference?" and "Locating the Live Museum." *News from Native California* 4, no. 1 (1989): 4–9.

De Varine, H., ed. *Museum* 37, no. 4 (1985). [On ecomuseums]

Doxtator, D. "The Idea of the Indian and the Development of Iroquoian Museums." *Museum Quarterly* 14, no. 2 (1985): 20–26.

Duncan, J. S., ed. *Housing and Identity: Cross-Cultural Perspectives.* New York: Holmes & Meier, 1982.

Esber, G. S., Jr. "Indian Housing for Indians." *Kiva* 37, no. 3 (1972): 141–47.

———. "Indians, Architects, and Anthropologists: A Study of Proxemic Behavior in a Western Apache Society." *Man–Environment Systems* 2, no. 2 (1972): 101–4.

Feest, C. "Contemporary Native American Visual Arts and Identity." *Revue française d'études américaines* 13, no. 38 (1988): 338–41.

Gaboury, E. "Amerindian Identity, Architects: The Hodne–Stageberg Partners." *Architectural Review* 168, no. 1002 (1980): 79–86.

Gillette, J. B. "On Her Own Terms." *Historic Preservation* 44, no. 6 (1992): 26–33, 84, 86. [On Rina Swentzell]

Graburn, N. H. H., ed. *Ethnic and Tourist Arts: Cultural Expressions from the Fourth World.* Berkeley: University of California Press, 1976.

Hardeen, G. "Hogans in Hospitals." *Tribal College: Journal of American Indian Higher Education* 5, no. 3 (1994): 20–24.

Harjo, F. *Indian Housing in the 1990s: Still Waiting.* Washington D.C.: National American Indian Housing Council, 1991.

Helms, C., and R. Johnson. "The Neo-Hooghan Building: An Attempt in a Modern World to Maintain Navajo Traditions Through Architecture." Typescript, 1993.

Heth, C., and M. Swarm, eds. *Sharing a Heritage: American Indian Arts.* Los Angeles: UCLA, 1984.

Hoistad, M. A. "Omaha Interpretative Center: An Act of Faith," and "Omaha Interpretative Center: An Affirmation of Culture." Omaha Interpretive Center, Lincoln, Neb. [ca. 1993]. Typescript.

Horse Capture, G. "Some Observations on Establishing Tribal Museums" [technical leaflet 134]. *History News* 36, no. 1 (1981).

History of Native American Housing. Wasington, D.C.: Department of Housing and Urban Development, 1990. Video.

Hughes, H. F. "A History of the Development of the Makah Cultural and Research Center, Neah Bay, Washington." Master's thesis, University of Washington, 1978.

Jett, S. C., and V. A. Spencer. *Navajo Architecture: Forms, History, Distribution.* Tucson: University of Arizona Press, 1981.

Jojola, T. J. "Memoirs of an American Indian House: A Descriptive Essay on U.S. Federally Subsidized Housing and Its Impact on the Native American Cultures of the Northern Cheyenne and Sandia Pueblos." Ph.D. diss., University of New Mexico, 1973.

Kaplan, F. E. S., ed. *Museums and the Making of "Ourselves": The Role of Objects in National Identity.* Leicester: Leicester University Press, 1994.

Karp, I., C. Kreamer, and S. D. Lavine, eds. *Museums and Communities: The Politics of Public Culture.* Washington D.C.: Smithsonian Institution Press, 1992.

Karp, I., and S. D. Lavine, eds. *Exhibiting Cultures: The Poetics and Politics of Museum Display.* Washington, D.C.: Smithsonian Institution Press, 1991.

Kent, S. "Hogans, Sacred Circles, and Symbols—The Navajo

Use of Space." In *Navajo Religion and Culture: Selected Views*, edited by D. Brugge and C. Frisbie, pp. 128–37. Santa Fe: Museum of New Mexico Press, 1982.

King, J. C. H. "Tradition in Native American Art." In *The Arts of the North American Indian*, edited by E. L. Wade, pp. 65–92. New York: Hudson Hills, 1986.

Landecker, H. "Designing for American Indians." *Architecture* 82, no. 12 (1993): 93–101.

Lawrence, D. L., and S. M. Low. "Spatial Form and Built Environment." *Annual Review of Anthropology* 19 (1990): 453–505.

Leccese, M. "Cultural Collaborations." *Landscape Architecture* 83, no. 1 (1993): 50–52. [On Warm Springs Museum]

Markovich, N. C., W. F. E. Preiser, and F. G. Sturm, eds. *Pueblo Style and Regional Architecture: The Mystique of New Mexico*. New York: Van Nostrand Reinhold, 1990.

Martin, A. "The Butterfly Effect: A Conversation with Rina Swentzell." *El Palacio* 95, no. 1 (1989): 24–29.

Massachusetts Institute of Technology, Department of Architecture. "Basic Architectural Scheme: New High School. Rough Rock Demonstration School." September 1971.

McAllester, D. P. *Hogans: Navajo Houses and House Songs*. Middletown, Conn.: Wesleyan University Press, 1980.

Molinaro/Rubin Associates. "A Report to the Seneca Nation of Indians: The Seneca Nation Cultural Center Project." August 1991.

Monthan, G., and D. Monthan. "Daybreak Star Center." *American Indian Art Magazine* 3, no. 3 (1978): 28–35.

Mooney, R. *Anglo-American Environments and the American Indian Nations of the Great Plains*. Working Papers Series no. 94, Berkeley, Calif: International Association for the Study of Traditional Environments, 1994.

"Mozart Among the Hopi." *Art News* 81, no. 4 (1982): 14. [On Dennis Numkena]

Muse 6, no. 3 (1988). [On museums and the first nations in Canada]

Nabokov, P., "The Roundhouse: Giving Life to the Community." *News from Native California* 3, no. 1 (1989): 4–9.

Nabokov, P. and R. Easton. *Native American Architecture*. New York: Oxford University Press, 1989.

Naranjo, T., and R. N. Swentzell. "Healing Spaces in the Tewa Pueblo World." *American Indian Culture and Research Journal* 13, nos. 3–4 (1989): 257–65.

Nason, J. "Community and Continuity: The Museum at Warm Springs." *American Anthropologist* 96, no. 2 (1994): 492–94.

National Commission on American Indian, Alaska Native, and Native Hawaiian Housing. *Building the Future: A Blueprint for Change*. Washington, D.C.: Government Printing Office, 1992.

"Native American Center" [Minneapolis]. *SD Space Design*, April 1977, pp. 60–62.

Navajo Nation, Division of Community Development, Design, and Engineering Services and Department of Energy.

Navahomes: A Dinelogical Study of Navajo Dwelling in Balance with the Land. Window Rock, Ariz.: Navajo Nation, 1992.

"Navajo School: An Exercise in Community Control" [Rough Rock]. *Architectural Forum* 137, no. 2 (1972): 54–57.

Norris, E. B. "Santo Domingo Pueblo: Development Projects." University of New Mexico Design Planning and Assistance Center, Albuquerque, December 1, 1981.

"Numkena: Architect of Dreams." *Arizona Living*, February 1, 1981, pp. 6–7.

Oliver, P., ed. *Shelter and Society*. London: Barrie and Jenkins, 1969.

Oneida Indian Nation of New York. *Cultural Center: Past, Present, Future*. Oneida Territory: Oneida Indian Nation, 1993.

Parker, P. L., ed. *Keepers of the Treasures: Protecting Historic Properties and Cultural Traditions on Indian Lands*. Washington, D.C.: Department of the Interior, 1990.

Perlman, B. H. "Spirits and Dreams." *Arizona Arts and Travel*, March–April 1983, pp. 14–18. [On Dennis Numkena]

"Phoenix Indian School Park: Task Force Report." Phoenix, Municipal Offices, January 1993.

Rapoport, A. "Culture and Built Form: A Reconsideration." In *Architecture in Cultural Change: Essays in Built Form and Culture Research*, edited by D. G. Saile, pp. 157–75. Lawrence: University of Kansas School of Architecture, 1986.

———. "Development, Culture Change, and Supportive Design." *Habitat International* 7, nos. 5–6 (1983): 249–68.

———. *House Form and Culture*. Englewood Cliffs, N.J.: Prentice-Hall, 1969.

———. *The Meaning of the Built Environment: A Non-Verbal Communication Approach*. Beverly Hills, Calif.: Sage, 1982.

Rayala, T. "Housing for the Chippewa Band of Great Lakes American Indians on the Lac du Flambeau Reservation in Northern Wisconsin." M. Arch. thesis, University of Wisconsin-Milwaukee, 1991.

Ross, T., and T. G. Moore, eds. *A Cultural Geography of North American Indians*. Boulder, Colo: Westview Press, 1987.

Saile, D. G. "Architecture in the Pueblo World: A Study of the Architectural Contexts of Pueblo Culture in the Late Nineteenth Century." Ph.D. diss., University of Newcastle-upon-Tyne, 1981.

———. "Making a House in the Pueblo Indian World." *Architectural Association Quarterly* 9, nos. 2–3 (1977): 72–81.

Schumacher, T. "Regional Intentions and Contemporary Architecture: A Critique." *CENTER: A Journal for Architecture in America* 3 (1987): 50–57.

Stea, D. "Indian Reservation Housing: Progress Since the 'Stanton Report'?" *American Indian Culture and Research Journal* 6, no. 3 (1982): 1–14.

Stephens, S. "Of Nature and Modernity." *Progressive Architecture* 56, no. 10 (1975): 66–69. [On Hodne–Stageberg Partners]

Suedfeld, P., and J. A. Russell, eds. *The Behavioral Basis of Design*. Book 2. Stroudsburg, Pa.: Dowden, Hutchinson & Ross, 1977.

Sun Rhodes, D. "My Home: A Communal American Indian Home." *Native Peoples* 6, no. 3 (1993): 40–43.

Swentzell, R. N. "An Architectural History of Santa Clara Pueblo." M. Arch. thesis, University of New Mexico, 1976.

———. "Bupingeh: The Pueblo Plaza." *El Palacio* 94, no. 2 (1988): 14–19.

———. "A Comparison of Basic Incompatibilities Between European/American Philosophies and the Traditional Pueblo World View and Value System." Ph.D. diss., University of New Mexico, 1982.

———. "Conflicting Landscape Values: The Santa Clara Pueblo and Day School." *Places* 7, no. 1 (1990): 18–27.

———. "Remembering Tewa Pueblo Houses and Space." *Native Peoples* 3, no. 2 (1990): 6–12.

———. "An Understated Sacredness." *MASS: Journal of the School of Architecture and Planning, University of New Mexico* 3 (Fall 1985): 24–25.

Swinomish Land Use Advisory Board. "The Draft Swinomish Comprehensive Plan." September 1990.

Tremblay, M. A., J. Collier, Jr., and T. T. Sasaki. "Navaho Housing in Transition." *America Indigena* 14, no. 3 (1954): 187–219.

University of Washington Student Design Studio. "Swinomish Waterfront Plan." June 1991.

U.S. Congress. Senate. Select Committee on Indian Affairs. *Report on Indian Housing*. Washington, D.C.: Government Printing Office, 1979.

U.S. Department of Housing and Urban Development. *Home Ownership for Indians*. Washington, D.C.: Government Printing Office, 1991.

Vearil, N. "Under the Eagle's Watch." *Native Peoples* 6, no. 3 (1993): 48–51 [On Akwe:kon dormitory, Cornell University]

Wade, E. L., and C. Haralson, eds. *The Arts of the North American Indian: Native Traditions in Evolution*. New York: Hudson Hills, 1986.

Warburton, M. "Culture Change and the Navajo Hogan." Ph.D. diss., Washington State University, 1985.

West, P. "The Miami Indian Tourist Attractions: A History and Analysis of a Transitional Mikasuki Seminole Environment." *Florida Anthropologist* 34 (1981): 200–224.

Wheelwright Museum. "Cosmos, Man, and Nature: Native American Perspectives on Architecture." Unedited transcript of conference, October 20–22, 1989.

Whitten, D. S., and N. E. Whitten, eds. *Imagery and Creativity: Ethnoaesthetics and Art Worlds in the Americas*. Tucson: University of Arizona Press, 1993.

Woodbridge, S. B. "School Designed Both with and for a Navajo Community." *Journal of the American Institute of Architects* 69, no. 14 (1980): 40–45.

Wyatt/Rhodes Architects, Don W. Ryden, AIA/Architects. "Fort McDowell/Beeline Highway Development Guidelines." April 1993.

Yelverton/Architect P.A., and Edward D. Stone & Associates. "North Carolina Indian Cultural Center: A Master Plan." November 1, 1988.

SOCIAL AND CULTURAL LIFE

Ablon, J. "Relocated Indians in the San Francisco Bay Area: Social Interaction and Indian Identity." *Human Organization* 23, no. 4 (1964–1965): 296–304.

Bachman, R. *Death and Violence on the Reservation: Homicide, Family Violence, and Suicide in American Indian Populations*. Westport, Conn.: Greenwood Press, 1992.

Bahr, H. R., B. A. Chadwick, and R. C. Day, eds. *Native Americans Today: Sociological Perspectives*. New York: Harper & Row, 1972.

Bennett, J. W., ed. *The New Ethnicity: Perspectives from Ethnology*. St. Paul, Minn.: West, 1975.

Buenker, J. D., and L. A. Ratner, eds. *Multiculturalism in the United States: A Comparative Guide to Acculturation and Ethnicity*. Westport, Conn.: Greenwood Press, 1992.

Bushnell, J. H. "Hupa Reaction to the Trinity River Floods: Post-Hoc Recourse to Aboriginal Belief." *Anthropological Quarterly Journal* 42, no. 4 (1969): 316–24.

Carter, G., and B. Mouser, eds. *Identity and Awareness in the Minority Experience*. Lacrosse: University of Wisconsin Institute for Minority Studies, 1975.

Castile, G. P. "Federal Indian Policy and the Sustained Enclave: An Anthropological Perspective." *Human Organization* 33, no. 3 (1974): 219–28.

Castile, G. P., and G. Kushner, eds. *Persistent Peoples: Cultural Enclaves in Perspective*. Tucson: University of Arizona Press, 1981.

Chadwick, B. A., and J. A. Stauss. "The Assimilation of American Indians into Urban Society: The Seattle Case." *Human Organization* 34, no. 4 (1975): 359–69.

Champagne, D. *American Indian Societies: Strategies and Conditions for Political and Cultural Survival*. Report no. 32. Cambridge, Mass.: Cultural Survival, 1989.

Chisholm, J. S. "Social and Economic Change Among the Navajo: Residence Patterns and the Pickup Truck." *Journal of Anthropological Research* 37, no. 2 (1981): 148–57.

Clifford, J., and G. Marcus, eds. *Writing Culture: The Poetics and Politics of Ethnography*. Berkeley: University of California Press, 1986.

Clifton, J. A., ed. *Being and Becoming Indian: Biographical Studies of North American Frontiers*. Chicago: Dorsey, 1989.

———. *The Invented Indian: Cultural Fictions and Government Policies*. New Brunswick, N.J.: Transaction Books, 1990.

Cornell, S. "American Indians, American Dreams, and the Meaning of Success." *AICRJ* 11, no. 4, (1987): 59–70.

——. *The Return of the Native: American Indian Political Resurgence*. New York: Oxford University Press, 1988.

Feraca, S. E. *Why Don't They Give Them Guns? The Great American Indian Myth*. Lanham, Md.: University Press of America, 1990.

Fowler, L. *Shared Symbols, Contested Meanings: Gros Ventre Culture and History, 1778–1984*. Ithaca, N.Y.: Cornell University Press, 1987.

Funke, K. A. "Educational Assistance and Employment Preference: Who Is An Indian?" *American Indian Law Review* 4, no. 1 (1976): 1–45.

Gates, H. L., Jr. "'Authenticity,' or the Lesson of Little Tree." *NYT Book Review*, November 24, 1991, pp. 1, 26–30.

Gellner, E. *Nations and Nationalism*. Ithaca, N.Y.: Cornell University Press, 1983.

Gill, S. *Mother Earth: An American Story*. Chicago: University of Chicago Press, 1987.

Goodenough, W. H. *Culture, Language, and Society*. 2d ed. Menlo Park, Calif.: Benjamin-Cummings, 1981.

Graves, T. D. "Urban Indian Personality and the 'Culture of Poverty.'" *American Ethnologist* 1, no. 1 (1974): 65–86.

Hagan, W. T. "Tribalism Rejuvenated: The Native American Since the Era of Termination." *Western Historical Quarterly* 12, no. 1 (1981): 5–16.

Handler, R., and J. Linnekin. "Tradition: Genuine or Spurious?" *Journal of American Folklore* 97, no. 385 (1984): 273–90.

Hauptman, L. M. *The Iroquois Struggle for Survival: World War II to Red Power*. Syracuse, N.Y.: Syracuse University Press, 1986.

Hertzberg, H. W. *The Search for an American Indian Identity: Modern Pan-Indian Movements*. Syracuse, N.Y.: Syracuse University Press, 1971.

Hobsbawm, E., and T. Ranger, eds. *The Invention of Tradition*. Cambridge: Cambridge University Press, 1983.

Indian Voices: The Native American Today. San Francisco: Indian Historian Press, 1974.

Jackson, J. "Is There a Way to Talk About Making Culture Without Making Enemies?" *Dialectical Anthropology* 14 (1989): 127–43.

Joe, J. R., ed. *American Indian Policy and Cultural Values: Conflict and Accommodation*. Los Angeles: UCLA, 1986

Leacock, E. B., and N. O. Lurie, eds. *North American Indians in Historical Perspective*. New York: Random House, 1971.

Levine, S., and N. O. Lurie, eds. *The American Indian Today*. Baltimore: Penguin, 1970.

Lewis, J. R. "Shamans and Prophets: Continuities and Discontinuities in Native American Religions." *American Indian Quarterly* 12, no. 3 (1988): 221–28.

Marx, H. L., Jr., ed. *The American Indian: A Rising Ethnic Force*. New York: Wilson, 1973.

Medicine, B. "Native American Resistance to Integration: Contemporary Confrontations and Religious Revitalization." *Plains Anthropologist* 16, no. 94, pt. 1 (1981): 277–86.

McFee, M. "The 150% Man, a Product of Blackfeet Acculturation." *American Anthropologist* 70 (1968): 1096–1107.

Nabokov, P., ed. *Native American Testimony: A Chronicle of Indian–White Relations from Prophecy to the Present, 1492–1992*. New York: Viking, 1991.

Neils, E. *Reservation to City: Indian Migration and Federal Relocation*. Chicago: University of Chicago Press, 1971.

Nowicka, E. "Intertribal Solidarity Among North American Indians: A Socio-Historical Study." *Polish Sociological Bulletin*, nos. 3–4 (1981): 75–84.

Olivas, M. A. "The Tribally-Controlled College Assistance Act of 1978: The Failure of Federal Indian Higher Education Policy." *American Indian Law Review* 9, no. 2, (1981): 219–51.

Olson, J. S., and R. Wilson, eds. *Native Americans in the Twentieth Century*. Provo, Utah: Brigham Young University Press, 1984.

Oppelt, N. T. "The Tribally Controlled Colleges in the 1980s: Education's Best Kept Secret." *American Indian Culture and Research Journal* 8, no. 4 (1984): 27–45.

Ortiz, A. *The Tewa World: Space, Time, Being and Becoming in a Pueblo*. Chicago: University of Chicago Press, 1969.

——, ed. *New Perspectives on the Pueblos*. Albuquerque: University of New Mexico Press, 1972.

Rostkowski, J. *Le Renouveau indien aux États-Unis*. Paris: l'Harmattan, 1986.

Schulte-Tenckhoff, I. "L'Indianité aujourd'hui: Nostalgie ou utopie concrète? À propos de Joëlle Rostkowski, *Le Renouveau indien aux États-Unis*." *Bulletin annuel du Musée d'Ethnographie de la Ville de Genève* 28 (1985): 97–109.

Smith, A. D. *The Ethnic Revival*. New York: Cambridge University Press, 1981.

Sollors, W., ed. *The Invention of Ethnicity*. New York: Oxford University Press, 1989.

Sorkin, A. *The Urban American Indian*. Lexington, Mass.: Heath, 1978.

Spicer, E. H. *Perspectives in American Indian Culture Change*. Chicago: University of Chicago Press, 1961.

Spindler, G. D., and L. S. Spindler. *Native North American Cultures: Four Cases*. New York: Holt, Rinehart and Winston, 1977.

Stanley, S. "American Indian Power and Powerlessness." In *The Anthropology of Power: Ethnographic Studies from Asia, Oceania, and the New World*, edited by R. D. Fogelson and R. N. Adams, pp. 237–42. New York: Academic Press, 1977.

Steiner, S. *The New Indians*. New York: Dell, 1968.

Strickland, R. "The Idea of the Environment and the Ideal of the Indian." *Journal of American Indian Education* 10, no. 1 (1970): 8–15.

Stuart, P. "Financing Self-Determination: Federal Indian Expenditures, 1975–1988." *American Indian Culture and Research Journal* 14, no. 2 (1990): 1–18.

Trafzer, C., ed. *American Indian Identity: Today's Changing Perspectives*. Sacramento, Calif.: Sierra Oaks, 1986.

Waddell, J. O., and O. M. Watson, eds. *The American Indian in Urban Life*. Boston: Little, Brown, 1971.

Walker, D. E., Jr., ed. *The Emergent Native Americans: A Reader in Culture Contact*. Boston: Little, Brown, 1972.

Wallace, A. F. C. "Revitalization Movements." *American Anthropologist* 58, no. 2 (1956): 264–81.

Washburn, W. E. "The Writing of American Indian History: A Status Report." In *The American Indian: Essays from the Pacific Historical Review*, edited by N. Hundley, Jr., pp. 1–26. Santa Barbara, Calif.: Clio Books, 1974.

Wax, M. L. *Indian Americans: Unity and Diversity*. Englewood Cliffs, N.J.: Prentice-Hall, 1971.

Weaver, T., ed. *Indians of Arizona: A Contemporary Perspective*. Tucson: University of Arizona Press, 1974.

Whiteley, P. *Deliberate Acts: Changing Hopi Culture Through the Oraibi Split*. Tucson: University of Arizona Press, 1988.

LAW AND POLITICS

"American Indian Environmental History." *Environmental Review* 9, no. 2 (1985). [special issue]

The American Indian Experience, a Profile: 1524 to the Present. Arlington Heights, Ill.: Forum Press, 1988.

American Indian Policy Review Commission. *New Directions in Federal Indian Policy: A Review*. Los Angeles: UCLA, 1979.

———. *Final Report* and *Appendixes to the Final Report*. Washington, D.C.: Government Printing Office, 1977.

Anderson, B. R. O'G. *Imagined Communities: Reflections on the Origin and Spread of Nationalism*. 2d ed.. London: Verso, 1991.

Barsh, R. L. "Contemporary Marxist Theory and Native American Reality." *American Indian Quarterly* 12, no. 3 (1988): 187–212.

Barsh, R. L., and K. Diaz-Knauf. "The Structure of Federal Aid for Indian Programs in the Decade of Prosperity, 1970–1980." *American Indian Quarterly* 8, no. 1 (1984): 1–35.

Barth, F. *Ethnic Groups and Boundaries: The Social Organization of Culture Differences*. London: George Allan, 1969.

Beaulieu, D. L., ed. *Breaking Barriers: Perspectives on the Writing of Indian History*. Chicago: Newberry Library, 1978.

Bee, R. L. *The Politics of American Indian Policy*. Cambridge, Mass.: Schenkman, 1982.

Berkhofer, R. F., Jr. "The Political Context of a New American Indian History." In *The American Indian: Essays from the Pacific Historical Review*, edited by N. Hundley, Jr., pp. 101–26. Santa Barbara, Calif.: Clio Books, 1974.

Bernstein, A. R. *American Indians and World War II: Toward a New Era in Indian Affairs*. Norman: University of Oklahoma Press, 1991.

Burt, L. W. *Tribalism in Crisis: Federal Indian Policy, 1953–1961*. Albuquerque: University of New Mexico Press, 1982.

Cadwalader, S., and V. Deloria, Jr., eds. *The Aggressions of Civilization: Federal Indian Policy Since the 1880s*. Philadelphia: Temple University Press, 1984.

Calloway, C., ed. *New Directions in American Indian History*. Norman: University of Oklahoma Press, 1988.

Castile, G. P., and R. L. Bee, eds. *State and Reservation: New Perspectives on Federal Indian Policy*. Tucson: University of Arizona Press, 1992.

Cohen, F. *Handbook of Federal Indian Law*. Washington, D.C.: Government Printing Office, 1942.

"Contemporary Native Americans." *Daedalus* 110, no. 2 (1981). [special issue]

Deloria, V., Jr. *American Indian Policy in the Twentieth Century*. Norman: University of Oklahoma Press, 1985.

———, ed. "American Indians: Policy, Paradigms, and Prognosis: A Symposium." *Social Science Journal* 19, no. 3 (1982).

Deloria, V., Jr., and C. Lytle. *The Nations Within: The Past and Future of American Indian Sovereignty*. New York: Pantheon, 1984.

Erikson, K. T., and C. Vecsey, eds. *American Indian Environments: Ecological Issues in Native American History*. Syracuse, N.Y.: Syracuse University Press, 1980.

Executive Office of the President. *Budget of the United States Government and Appendices: Fiscal Year 1993*. Washington, D.C.: Office of Management and Budget, 1993. (Also *Historical Tables*, 1989)

Fixico, D. L. *State and Reservation: Federal Indian Policy, 1945–1960*. Albuquerque: University of New Mexico Press, 1986.

Forbes, J. D. *Native Americans and Nixon: Presidential Politics and Minority Self-Determination*. Los Angeles: UCLA, 1981.

Grobsmith, E. S., and B. R. Ritter. "The Ponca Tribe of Nebraska: The Process of Restoration of a Federally Terminated Tribe." *Human Organization* 51, no. 1 (1992): 1–16.

Institute of the American West. *Indian Self Rule: Fifty Years Under the Indian Reorganization Act*. Sun Valley, Idaho: Institute of the American West, 1983.

Kvasnicka, R. M., and H. J. Viola, eds. *The Commissioners of Indian Affairs, 1824–1977*. Lincoln: University of Nebraska Press, 1979.

Legters, L. H., and F. J. Lyden, eds. *American Indian Policy: Self-Governance and Economic Development*. Westport, Conn.: Greenwood Press, 1993.

Novak, S. J. "The Real Takeover of the BIA: The Preferential Hiring of Indians." *Journal of Economic History* 50, no. 3 (1990): 639–54.

O'Brien, S. *American Indian Tribal Governments*. Norman: University of Oklahoma Press, 1989.

Parman, D. *The Navajos and the New Deal*. New Haven: Yale University Press, 1976.

Paschal, R. "The Imprimatur of Recognition: American Indian Tribes and the Federal Acknowledgment Process." *Washington Law Review* 66, no. 1 (1991), 209–28.

Peroff, N. *Menominee Drums: Tribal Termination and Restoration, 1954–1974*. Norman: University of Oklahoma Press, 1982.

Philp, K., ed. *Indian Self-Rule: First-Hand Accounts of*

Indian–White Relations from Roosevelt to Reagan. Salt Lake City: Howe, 1986.

Pommersheim, F. *Braid of Feathers: American Indian Law and Contemporary Tribal Life.* Berkeley: University of California Press, 1995.

Prucha, F. P. *American Indian Treaties: The History of a Political Anomaly.* Berkeley: University of California Press, 1995.

——. *Documents of United States Indian Policy.* Lincoln: University of Nebraska Press, 1990.

——. *The Great Father: The United States Government and the American Indians.* Lincoln: University of Nebraska Press, 1984.

——. *The Indians in American Society from the Revolutionary War to the Present.* Berkeley: University of California Press, 1985.

Rosen, L., ed. *American Indians and the Law.* New Brunswick, N.J.: Transaction Books, 1978.

Strickland, R., ed. *Felix Cohen's Handbook of Federal Indian Law.* Charlottesville, Va.: Michie, 1982.

Sutton, I., ed. *Irredeemable America: The Indians' Estate and Land Claims.* Albuquerque: University of New Mexico Press, 1987.

Washburn, W. E. "A Fifty-Year Perspective on the Indian Reorganization Act." *American Anthropologist* 86, no. 2 (1984): 279–89.

——. *Red Man's Land, White Man's Law: A Study of the Past and Present Status of the American Indian.* New York: Scribner's, 1971.

White, R. *Tribal Assets: The Rebirth of Native America.* New York: Holt, 1990.

Wilkinson, C. F. *American Indians, Time, and the Law: Native Societies in a Modern Constitutional Democracy.* New Haven: Yale University Press, 1987.

Yinger, J. M., and G. E. Simpson, eds. *American Indians and American Life.* Philadelphia: American Academy of Political and Social Science, 1975.

——. *The American Indian Today.* Philadelphia: American Academy of Political and Social Science, 1978.

INDEX

Names of Native nations refer to all or part of a person's ancestry, not necessarily to official tribal enrollment. References to the profession of architect refer to diploma training, not necessarily to active practice or registration. Numbers in italics refer to pages on which illustrations appear.

financing for, 189–90
Hopi, 42, 42–43, 43, 191, 192, 193, 194, 198
Klallam, 199
Navajo, 93, 93–95, 94, 191, 194, 196, 198, 199, 199, 202, 203, 256n.16, 257n.45
Ojibwe, 134–35, 135, 142, 179, 199, 200
Omaha, 192–93, 196, 200
Oneida, 192–93, 200
Paiute, 142, 194, 257n.31
Pascua Yaqui, 193
Pima–Maricopa, 197, 197–98, 198
Plains peoples, 166–67, 167, 198, 202–3
Pueblo, 194, 196, 202, 203, 203
rejected, 180, 192, 195
Santee Sioux (Wahpekute, Mdewakanton), 196
Seneca, 194
Southern Ute, 192, 193
statistics on, 190
Swinomish, 200
Tohono O'odham, 179, 196
Upper Skagit, 169–70
Wampanoag, 196, 200, 201, 202
Housing and Community Development Act, 189, 256n.5
Housing Loan Guarantee Program, 256n.6
Howard, David (architect), 155–56
Howard, James, 47
Hubbard, Bette, 116–17
HUD. See Department of Housing and Urban Development
HUD Reform Act, 190
Huerta, J. Lawrence (Pascua Yaqui), 80
Hunt, James, 145
Hunt, Milton (architect), 249n.8
Hupa. See Hoopa

Indian Arts & Crafts Board, 217
Indian Arts and Crafts Board Act, 31. See also Arts and crafts
Indian Civil Rights Act, 221, 240n.39
Indian Claims Commission Act, 19
Indian Country Today (newspaper), 29
Indian Gaming Regulatory Act (IGRA), 22, 221–22, 224
Indian Health Service (IHS), 10, 33, 75, 191, 192
Indian Housing Act, 192
Indian Pueblo Cultural Center, 109–10, 110
Indian Reorganization (Wheeler-Howard) Act, 15
Indian Self-Determination and Economic Assistance Act, 21, 44, 181
Indians at Work, 16, 18
Ingram, Lee J. (architect), 210
Inouye, Daniel, 224
Institute of American Indian Arts, 149
Inupiat, 95
Iroquois, 58–59, 68, 73, 139–40, 223
Iroquois Indian Museum, 89, 89–90, 205, 217

Jackson, Clifford (architect), 130
Jackson, Dana (Ojibwe), 77

James, Ray (architect), 81, 251n.48
Jemez Pueblo elementary school, 106, 107
Jiran, Don (architect), 167
JKA Architects, 226
Joe, Jimmy (Upper Skagit), 38
Joe, Lawrence "Okie" (Upper Skagit), 37–38
Johnson, Gerald (architect), 70, 133, 136, 162
Johnson, Hunter (planner), 166, 218
Johnson, Sheldon & Sorensen (architects), 112
Johnson-O'Malley Act, 16, 70, 133, 136
Johnston, Brian (architect), 211, 213
Johnston, Thomas R., 45
Jojola, Theodore (Isleta Pueblo) (architect), 53, 256n.18
Jones, Darryl T. (landscape architect), 68
Jones, Johnpaul (Cherokee–Choctaw) (landscape architect), 53, 129–30, 149, 249n.2
Jones & Jones. See Jones, Johnpaul
Joseph, J. Lawrence (Sauk–Suiattle), 75
Joseph, Norma (Sauk–Suiattle), 75

Kabotie, Fred (Hopi), 104–5
Kallstrom, Robert (architect), 35, 254n.10
Karuk Indian Community, government building, 149
Kasprisin, Ron (architect), 200
Kasterowicz, John (architect), 226
Kastning, Marvin, 75
Keeline Pizzi Young (architects), 167
Kennedy, John F., 20
Kicking Woman, Molly (Blackfeet), 70
Kiley, Daniel U. (landscape architect), 215
Kills Straight, Birgil (Lakota), 136
King, Duane, 128, 210
Kiowa Nation Culture Museum, 57
Kipp, Roger (architect), 134, 253n.45
Kisto, Ed (Tohono O'odham), 179
Kiva, 69, 73, 105–6, 168, 219
as model, 235
Klah, Hastiin (Navajo), 18–19
Knife River Indian Villages Historic Site, 99, 145, 145
Knutson, Bruce (architect), 62, 91
Kommers, Peter (architect), 123–24
Kootenai, 151
Kramer, Peter (architect), 175
Kullihoma Treatment Center, 38, 80

Laban, Joseph (Hopi), 148, 192
Lac Courte Oreilles Reservation, casino on, 226
Lac du Flambeau Chippewa Museum and Cultural Center, 124, 124–25, 125, 218
Lac du Flambeau Reservation, 162
LaFramboise, Richard (Ojibwe), 223
Laguna Pueblo, 56, 73, 106
Lakota, 13, 14, 21, 29, 45, 77, 125–26, 149, 155–57, 166, 179, 241n.72, 246n.13
museum (proposed), 207
Lakota Times, 33

schools, 30, 39, 124, 136, 136–37, 243n.30, 245n.7, 252n.28
Lander Valley Medical Center, 34
Lane, Vernon (Lummi), 74
Language instruction, 10, 16, 29, 30, 82, 138, 144, 184, 207, 218, 243nn.26, 27
Lara, Walt (Yurok), 78
Larkin/Tenney (architects), 196, 200–202, 258n.63
Las Vegas Paiute, administration building, 54
Leader Charge, Paul (Lakota), 179
Lee, Hemsley Martin (Navajo) (architect), 53, 91
Leech Lake Reservation, 222
Chief Bug-O-Nay-Ge-Shig School, 64, 65
Lehse, Diane (?Ojbiwe), 134
Lewis, Carl (architect), 52
Lewis, Hayes (Zuni), 152
Lewis, Richard, 217
Lewis, T. H., 45
Little Turtle, Jimmy (Mohawk), 183
Lloyd, Wayne (architect), 108, 244n.55
Lodge, 37, 37–38, 38, 62, 69, 70, 85, 98–99, 119, 132, 133, 145, 147, 197
Loe, Sara (Ojibwe) (architect), 132
Long, John (?Pima), 131
Longhouse, 47, 62–63, 68, 73, 73–76, 74, 75, 81, 83, 122, 184–85, 108, 250n.16
Lower Brule Reservation, 192
Lower Elwha, 73, 83, 249n.8
Lower Sioux Reservation, community building, 63
Lumbee, 12, 79
Lummi, 38
Lunderman, Alex (Lakota), 224
Lurie, Nancy Oestreich, 222
Lyons, Oren (Onondaga), 45

MacDonald, Peter (Navajo), 94
Mahoney, James (architectural consultant), 146
Makah, 81–83, 130, 206, 241n.63, 249n.7
Cultural Research Center, 47, 74, 81–83, 83, 206, 209, 218, 259n.9
Malone Iversen & Associates (architect), 248n.14
Mandan, 119, 133
Mariah Log Homes, 75
Maricopa, 131–33
Marinakos, Plato (architect), 212–13, 215
Marionito, Fred (Navajo) (architect), 53
Marmon, Lee (Laguna Pueblo), 56
Martell, Leo (Ojibwe) (architect), 53
Martin, Dennis (architect), 56
Martin, Harrison (Navajo) (architect), 52, 53
Maryland Historical Society, 205
Mashantucket Pequots. See Pequots, Mashantucket
Mattson, Wes (architect), 71
Mayer-Reed, Carol (landscape architect), 86, 88